AI for Creative Production

A handbook for the ethical use of AI in creating and processing text, images, video, and audio

Iain Anderson

<packt>

AI for Creative Production

Portfolio Director: Pavan Ramchandani
Relationship Lead: Mohd Riyan Khan
Program Manager: Divij Kotian
Content Engineer: Akanksha Gupta
Technical Editor: Vidhisha Patidar
Copy Editor: Safis Editing
Indexer: Rekha Nair
Proofreader: Akanksha Gupta
Production Designer: Prashant Ghare
Growth Lead: Priya Bhanushali

First published: January 2026
Production reference: 2280126

Published by Packt Publishing Ltd.
Grosvenor House
11 St Paul's Square
Birmingham
B3 1RB, UK.

ISBN 978-1-80602-581-7
`www.packtpub.com`

This book is for N and for H.

– Iain Anderson

Foreword

I've known Iain Anderson for over fifteen years, though I'd be hard-pressed to tell you exactly when we first met. I'm sure it was at an industry event, where I found him not only knowledge-able but *genuinely engaging*, with a strong ability to understand complex technical concepts and, more importantly, help others do the same.

When Iain told me he was writing a book about AI for creatives, we compared notes. A lot of notes. I recognize just how fluid this field is—major announcements shift the playing field frequently, and what's cutting-edge today becomes table stakes tomorrow. I wouldn't have said yes to writing this foreword if Iain hadn't managed to give you a six-month to year-long advance on where you are now: *Direct, usable examples and tools you can put to work today.*

If you're a creator and worried that AI is knocking on the door, Iain has given you the keys today.

You're benefiting from the hours and hours he's put in learning, testing, and occasionally cursing at these tools. Which ones work, which ones fail, and how to stay relevant and profitable using them across your creative work—it's all here.

Enjoy.

Jeff Greenberg,

Post-Production Consultant

January 2026

Contributors

About the author

Iain Anderson is the author of *Final Cut Pro Efficient Editing* and *AI for Creative Production*. Based in Brisbane, Australia, Iain is an Apple Certified Trainer in Final Cut Pro, a regular writer for ProVideoCoalition, a co-creator of the current Apple Certified FCP Training exam, and curriculum, a plug-in developer for FxFactory, a lead trainer and writer for macProVideo, a regular conference speaker, a videographer, an editor, an animator, a designer, a photographer, a retoucher, and sometimes an app developer for iPad, Apple Watch, and Apple Vision Pro. He's created animations and live videos for clients including Microsoft and CoreMelt, designed virtual islands in Second Life for the government, and made screensavers for fun.

Many thanks to my family for letting me spend so much time typing in my office this year, to Akanksha for crucial feedback and spotting of many errors, to Riyan for persistent nudging in the right directions, to Leith for reading and critically assessing my original messy thoughts, to Jeff for his opening words, and to everyone else who reads this.

About the reviewer

Leith Walton has been a graphic designer and illustrator for the past 20 years across many different creative fields. For the last 5 years, he has been focusing on running *Nurtured Creations*, a multi-disciplinary studio that focuses on local branding, illustration, board games and creative workshop facilitation.

I would like to thank the Author, Iain, for taking the time to write this insightful book.

Mike Eddy is the author of *Final Cut Pro Cookbook*, published in 2025. He has over 40 years of experience in video production, photography, print, web, and stage productions. Mike was a 2023 National Teacher of the Year finalist for the Association of Career and Technical Educators. He is a retired instructor from Century College in Minnesota, where he taught filmmaking and video production since 2007.

Mike has had the privilege to work with General Mills, Federated Insurance, 3M, Andersen Windows, Apple, Compassion International, 5 Eyewitness News, and many other leading companies. He still keeps busy editing and creating visual effects for feature films.

Table of Contents

Chapter 4: Utility AI with Images and Videos 57

Chapter 9: Generative AI with Audio 237

Part 4: Automation AI

Chapter 10: Automation AI with Images 267

Chapter 11: Automation AI with Video 289

Preface

Artificial intelligence is one of the most divisive technologies of our time, especially for creatives. If you believe the hype, it'll replace all filmmakers and photographers within a couple of years, and nobody will ever create anything by hand again. But hype rarely translates to reality.

Instead, in this book, you'll see how AI has the potential to help creatives become more creative. It is true that AI will perform some tasks that creatives might have once been given, but clients who don't see the value of a human would have already been using templates and presets. When it comes to jobs that require creativity, humans still win.

A creative person can, if they wish, augment their capabilities by using the right AI tools and avoiding others. A common refrain I hear among creatives is to describe a tool as "good AI" or "machine learning, but not AI," but this distinction can be better expressed as **Utility AI** or **Automation AI** versus **Generative AI** (more on this in *Chapter 1*):

- **Utility AI**: Recognition, classification, and understanding
- **Generative AI**: Creation of text, images, video, audio, and more
- **Automation AI**: Performing tasks humans usually would

Some tasks are boring, tedious, or even impossible for a human to do well. Today, **Utility AI** tools can help you perform a task, or, if it's more predictable, **Automation AI** can do it for you. Few creatives want to select pixels one by one or trace outlines frame by frame, and even if an AI tool isn't perfect, a human can often benefit from its help. Some jobs can be automated or made easier; others are best done by hand. It's up to you.

Even though **Generative AI** attracts most of the hate, that doesn't mean it's all bad; it depends on how you use it. While copyright and ethical concerns are real (see *Chapter 2*), remember that in the development process, while you're coming up with ideas, almost anything goes. Hollywood directors use soundtracks from other movies while they edit new ones, and mood boards at every level are filled with other people's work. This isn't a new concept, and if you do it right, it's possible to use Generative AI to help develop ideas while humans create the finished product.

To help you make sense of the huge number of tools and apps employing AI-powered features, I've taken a broad view here, testing as many web-based services and locally run apps as possible. While I have included step-by-step instructions for some of the better-hidden features in desktop apps, for easy-to-use websites, I've focused mostly on results.

As this is a book primarily for non-technical creatives, most of the solutions examined here are public-facing apps and services. Enthusiasts and developers may wish to explore the world of open source models, but most designers aren't coders, and you won't need to code to follow the examples here.

Throughout, I've tried to give an honest appraisal of how well these systems fulfill their promises when given real-world problems. While some just didn't work well for me, they may work for you. Indeed, the speed of change in AI means those systems have probably changed since I tested them: some will have improved, some will be more expensive, and some may no longer exist.

New models and new tools will continue to appear—some have come out between writing the chapters and this preface—and you should always be ready to test on your own. But always be wary of hype, because it's possible for a solution to be technically impressive and still useless.

As you explore AI tools for creative professionals, you'll be promised the world. Sometimes, you'll be amazed at how quickly a boring job (such as transcription) can be performed. At other times, the juxtaposition of amazement and disappointment can be jarring, such as when I asked an AI to write a song about friends on holiday at the beach. It was amazing to be given 4 passable songs in 30 seconds, but disappointing (and hilarious) that 2 of the songs were from the perspective of a robot pool cleaner.

Exploring these tools has been a wild and fascinating ride, and I'm sure it's going to stay that way for some time to come. On your own travels, expect imperfection: take the good and discard the bad. But don't let a robot replace your creativity.

Who this book is for

This book is for creative professionals who want to understand AI better, so they can use AI in their creative practice. It's not a book to help anyone replace creative humans or their creativity.

What this book covers

Chapter 1, The AI Story So Far, introduces AI technologies, discusses how they work, and lists many tools you may wish to investigate further.

Chapter 2, Ethics, considers the ethical and copyright issues around the use of AI.

Chapter 3, Utility AI with Audio, discusses transcription, beat matching, stem splitting, and audio cleanup tools.

Chapter 4, Utility AI with Images and Video, explores how to use AI tools to organize and classify your media, select people and objects, reframe, convert for stereoscopic delivery, and more.

Chapter 5, Utility AI with Text, looks at summarizing, grammar, verification, and reformatting with regard to written content.

Chapter 6, Generative AI with Text, stays with text to look at rewriting it, citing other works, coming up with ideas, and translating. It also looks at using AI to help with accessibility needs.

Chapter 7, Generative AI with Images, shows you how to manipulate existing images and create entirely new ones from text or image sources. It considers photos, vector art, and 3D models, as well as mood boards and ideation.

Chapter 8, Generative AI with Video, takes an honest look at how clips can be extended and created from text, images, or other videos, as well as how to transform existing videos into something entirely new.

Chapter 9, Generative AI with Audio, explores the world of synthetic audio, including sound effects, music, speech, voice cloning, and replacing part of an existing recording, along with audio translation.

Chapter 10, Automation AI with Images, shows you several tools that use AI to perform tasks on your behalf, including culling images, retouching, and performing other processing tasks. You will also see how to use AI to write scripts to help with design tasks.

Chapter 11, Automation AI with Video, looks at several tools that automate video editing, from simple silence removal, through simpler editing tools, to full prompt-based editing assistants.

Chapter 12, Automation AI with Digital Assistants and Agents, takes a look at how digital assistants are likely to develop further, at AI-powered wearables and browsers, and at the potential of agents.

To get the most out of this book

The more creative areas you're familiar with (such as photography, design, retouching, video editing, and writing), the more useful you'll find this book, but the book has been written with a general audience in mind.

Most tools in this book are cloud-based, while some can be run on a local computer. A modern Mac will be able to run all the local apps mentioned in this book; a modern PC will be able to run most of them.

You don't need a custom PC with a powerful graphics card, and you don't need to know how to code.

Download the color images

The free PDF version of the book includes color images of the screenshots/diagrams used in this book. You can download it here: `https://packt.link/gbp/9781806025817`.

Conventions used

There are a number of text conventions used throughout this book.

`CodeInText`: Indicates prompts and other typed input. For example: "I'm just going to ask the tool to do it in plain English: `Remove the people from this image`."

Bold: Indicates a new term, an important word, or words that you see on the screen. For instance, words in menus or dialog boxes appear in the text like this: "Today, the existing tools are augmented by **Generative Remove** and **Generative Fill**, two fully generative features that draw on Adobe Stock images licensed for the purpose."

Warnings or important notes appear like this.

Tips and tricks appear like this.

Get in touch

Feedback from readers is always welcome.

General feedback: If you have questions about any aspect of this book or have any general feedback, please email us at `customercare@packt.com` and mention the book's title in the subject of your message.

Errata: Although we have taken every care to ensure the accuracy of our content, mistakes do happen. If you have found a mistake in this book, we would be grateful if you reported this to us. Please visit `http://www.packt.com/submit-errata`, click **Submit Errata**, and fill in the form.

Piracy: If you come across any illegal copies of our works in any form on the internet, we would be grateful if you would provide us with the location address or website name. Please contact us at `copyright@packt.com` with a link to the material.

If you are interested in becoming an author: If there is a topic that you have expertise in and you are interested in either writing or contributing to a book, please visit `http://authors.packt.com/`.

Share your thoughts

Once you've read *AI for Creative Production*, we'd love to hear your thoughts! Scan the QR code below to go straight to the Amazon review page for this book and share your feedback.

https://packt.link/r/1806025817

Your review is important to us and the tech community and will help us make sure we're delivering excellent quality content.

Free Benefits with Your Book

This book comes with free benefits to support your learning. Activate them now for instant access (see the "*How to Unlock*" section for instructions).

Here's a quick overview of what you can instantly unlock with your purchase:

PDF and ePub Copies

- Access a DRM-free PDF copy of this book to read anywhere, on any device.
- Use a DRM-free ePub version with your favorite e-reader.

Next-Gen Web-Based Reader

- **Multi-device progress sync:** Pick up where you left off, on any device.
- **Highlighting and notetaking:** Capture ideas and turn reading into lasting knowledge.
- **Bookmarking:** Save and revisit key sections whenever you need them.
- **Dark mode:** Reduce eye strain by switching to dark or sepia themes.

How to Unlock

UNLOCK NOW

Scan the QR code (or go to `packtpub.com/unlock`). Search for this book by name, confirm the edition, and then follow the steps on the page.

***Note:** Keep your invoice handy. Purchases made directly from Packt don't require one.*

Part 1

Introducing AI

This short, introductory section sets the stage for how we got here, discusses some of the tools available, and explores the ethical considerations of modern AI tools.

This part of the book includes the following chapters:

1

The AI Story So Far

Artificial Intelligence (AI) has captured our collective imaginations since Alan Turing first asked whether machines could think. While we still can't give a firm answer to that big question, the increasing pace of change in the AI world means that creative white-collar workers are, for the first time, fearing for their careers.

Computers themselves have transitioned from toys for enthusiasts, to tools for professionals, to enablers for everyone—and AI is on the same trajectory, over a much shorter time span. In the same way that smartphones have made computing easier for regular people, AI promises to make creativity itself easier for a wider audience. Many in the creative space have now felt, or started to feel, the impacts of AI on their professional lives.

However, the imperfect nature of AI tools means that there's still a huge role for humans in creative production. Even though its help is imperfect, AI will still help us to find video clips more easily, fix bad audio more quickly, check our ideas against virtual collaborators, and, in many ways, be able to reach just a little bit further out of our comfort zones. Disruption is certain, but AI will not end human creativity. This book aims to show creative people how they can harness the power of many different AI-based tools to make their creations better.

In this chapter, we'll cover the following main topics:

- The early days of AI
- How AI works today
- Uses of AI
- The shortcomings of AI
- Apps, tools, and technologies

To begin, let's look back.

Free Benefits with Your Book

Your purchase includes a free PDF copy of this book along with other exclusive benefits. Check the *Free Benefits with Your Book* section in the Preface to unlock them instantly and maximize your learning experience.

The early days of AI

Neural networks—connected virtual nodes that work in a similar way to human brains—were first proposed in 1944, and they've experienced varying success in the decades since. A neural network is first trained by presenting a set of inputs and the matching outputs it should learn to produce. During the training process, each node in the interconnected network becomes stronger or weaker, assigned **weights** that reinforce some connections and de-emphasize others. Essentially, it's learning to recognize patterns without ever being taught a rule explicitly.

After the training, a neural network can be fed a new input to produce a new, hopefully correct output. However, this indirect approach is quite different from other rule-based (or heuristic) methods that other AI systems have used, and many years passed before computing power unleashed its potential.

Probably the most influential event in AI history occurred when Alan Turing presented an *imitation game*, a test in which an interrogator exchanges messages with a human and a digital participant, then tries to identify which is which. This became known as the **Turing test**, and for many decades, it was seen as an insurmountable bar.

In 1965, a program called **ELIZA** simulated a psychotherapist, repeating keywords from a user's input in its own responses. Techniques such as this became foundational in **natural language processing**, and although this technique is simple, it was enough to fool many people into thinking they were talking to a human.

Soon after, in the 1970s and 1980s, another focus of early AI was expert systems, which aimed to capture knowledge in a specific niche in order to answer related questions. Using heuristic methods rather than neural networks, it proved too difficult to codify the knowledge and deal with edge cases.

AI research continued, but the breathless hype was not met with reality, and enthusiasm waned. Computers continued to get faster and user interfaces became more friendly, but AI progress stalled. In the mid-1990s, I majored in artificial intelligence and artificial life in an information technology degree, implementing my own version of ELIZA, training neural networks, and simulating virtual plants that I then evolved against one another. While it was fascinating to see how these techniques could be used, there was a huge gap between student projects and practical applications.

Heuristic approaches and neural networks found specific uses in limited areas, and as computers became more powerful, more uses became possible. Fuzzy logic allowed computers to read messy human handwriting, and rules governing enemy behavior governed computer-controlled enemies in video games, in real time. Language translation, though imperfect, became a common feature in many applications.

However, it was Google's introduction of **transformer models** in 2017 (in a paper entitled *Attention Is All You Need*) that led to the modern explosion in the power and utility of AI, alongside a breakthrough in diffusion models for image generation. Let's take a high-level look at how these modern systems work, while noting that we don't truly understand all the details.

How AI works today

Transformer models include a mechanism called **attention**, which identifies the most important parts of an input and assigns them a higher level of importance. Think of the adjectives in this sentence being assigned less importance than the nouns or the verb:

The brown **dog attacked** *the timid* **cat** *aggressively*.

(While I won't be digging into the math here, the paper *Attention Is All You Need* is linked in the *Additional resources* section of this chapter.)

The transformer model was intended for use with translation, but its true potential became clear when it was combined with **Large Language Models (LLMs)**. An LLM is a predictive model trained to produce output a word at a time, based on the words that had come before—like an advanced version of autocorrect. A sentence such as "The ice cream was..." is more likely to conclude with the adjective "...sweet" or "...delicious" than, for example, "dusty."

Adding transformers to LLMs with large pools of training data created—or seemed to create—emergent abilities, such as the ability to summarize. These models can, at some level, perform reasoning tasks, and it's not yet fully clear exactly how they do it.

Although we did train these models on vast amounts of text, we did not train models to summarize or reason, and yet, they can do that. It's not clear if there's any deep understanding going on, but does it matter? If you ask for a summary of an article and you get one that's accurate, that's good enough to be useful. Transformer-backed LLM systems are widely used today for help, advice, information, and even—though they aren't sentient—companionship. Modern LLMs include OpenAI's ChatGPT, Anthropic's Claude, Meta's Llama, and Google's Gemini, to name a few.

The other side of the modern AI story belongs to image generation. While ChatGPT's image generator uses an autoregressive transformer model, **diffusion models** are more common, starting with DALL·E and continuing with Midjourney, Stable Diffusion, and others. A diffusion model starts with random noise, then repeatedly applies a neural network to predict how noise should be removed until it approximates the requested text prompt.

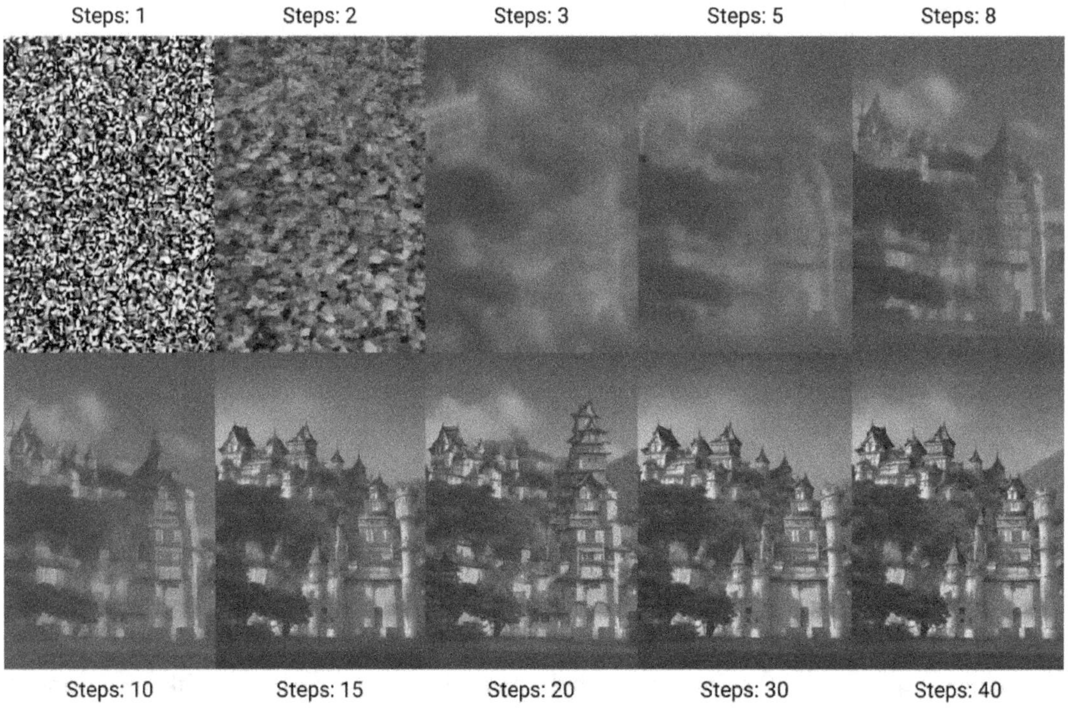

Figure 1.1 – An illustration of the Stable Diffusion denoising process by Benlisquare, from Wikipedia

Training is a huge part of this process, involving a forward diffusion process of adding noise to these images, and a reverse diffusion process where the noise is removed. By feeding these models immense numbers of images, we have been able to improve their outputs to the point where they can, at least some of the time, create synthetic images that look real. Videos can be similarly synthesized using a more complex process, but **Machine Learning (ML)**—in which systems learn directly from data rather than being given explicit instructions—can be applied to many different tasks.

So, what are those tasks?

Modern applications of AI

The term *AI* has been overused, and for many people, AI simply now means "a computer made it"—but there's so much more to AI than that. For clarity, this book will separate ML and AI applications into three broad categories. They are the following:

- **Utility AI**: Recognition, classification, and understanding models, which can be used to help sort and manage the data they are presented with
- **Generative AI**: Creation of text, images, video, audio, and even programming code
- **Automation AI**: Directed control of other computer systems to perform tasks that humans usually would

Let's dig deeper. If you're asking questions of a chatbot, that's likely Utility AI. If you're creating music or original text, that's **Generative AI** (or **GenAI** for short). And if you're using Siri or Google Assistant to create a calendar appointment for you, that's a simpler form of Automation AI. The names of these terms will change over time; the term **AI agents** (or agentic AI) is a part of Automation AI that's becoming more prominent.

Each of these areas will be covered in more detail in this book, and there's a part of this book devoted to each of these three sections. While there is certainly crossover between these categories—for example, translation involves recognition of what was said as well as generation in another language—in general, most AI applications today can cleanly fit into one of them.

For now, let's treat these categories as broad, basic headings before we drill into the details.

Today, just some of the things you might use AI tools to help you with are the following:

- Generating ideas for an essay
- Assessing written text for completeness or accuracy
- Creating photographic-style images

- Replacing part of an image with something synthetic
- Processing audio to remove noise
- Creating synthetic recordings to match a particular person's voice
- Writing scripts to automate features in graphic design applications
- Asking for help with learning a new application
- Creating 3D models based on images or text descriptions

These tasks are just the tip of the iceberg, and I've long held the view that progress will really explode when agents start driving our computers for us. At first, AI models will start using our applications as we watch, but eventually they'll just perform tasks directly, or use lower-level systems that we cannot. Today, we're only at the start of the journey, but things are moving quickly.

Where AI falls short

Few technologies break through to the mainstream, but AI certainly has, and the excitement and fear across creative communities is palpable. However, one factor that's known but frequently ignored is that the output from AI systems is rarely perfect. To the layperson, an AI-generated image can look great, but to a Photoshop expert, there may be obvious flaws. AI-made code will frequently contain references to programming interfaces that simply don't exist. Horrifyingly, AI-generated legal arguments refer to fictional legal cases. Advice is not always accurate, and the more you know about a subject, the more likely you are to find fault with an AI's output.

While the quantity of work produced by AI can sometimes make up for the overall lack of quality, in general, most AI output lacks something, tangible or not. This could be for many reasons, but chief among them is likely that AI excels at remixing, rather than original thought. Every image a diffusion model creates is, in some way, derived from the training data it was fed.

Although it's certainly been argued (by Kirby Ferguson) that "*Everything is a Remix*," the best work contains an original spark, and the process of creation often inspires new creations itself.

It's critical to realize that the creative process is an important part of any product or artwork. If you skip the brainstorming, planning, and experimentation phases, the finished product will be lacking in ways both obvious and subtle, and you won't have grown as an artist.

You might have what you asked for, but creativity can lead to better outcomes than the most obvious ones. Skipping straight to an end goal and omitting all the creative decisions made along the way will produce worse products, because the best designers don't just create exactly what the client asks for.

How good can AI be? From everything I've seen to date, a good GenAI produces work that's OK but not great. It's rarely perfect, and it's unlikely to be top-class A+ work. At best, it's a solid B+. But that doesn't mean you shouldn't use AI at all.

Instead, use AI for what it's really good at:

- Replacing parts of an image, not the whole thing
- Extending a photograph's edges to adapt to a size change, not creating whole images from scratch
- Picking the best photographs from a full-day shoot, with a human checking its work, not just trusting it completely
- Identifying which parts of a music track can be repeated to suit a different duration, not simply creating a whole new piece
- Producing temporary art to help with planning, not finished art
- Helping you write programming scripts to make creative tasks more efficient, not doing everything by hand

In my opinion, the best uses of AI are to augment human creativity, not trying to replace it entirely. If an AI can help you extend your creative reach a little further, great. But if you skip all the traditional creative steps and create original work that's well outside your comfort zone, you simply won't recognize the mistakes it makes. AI can help you run, but you have to learn to walk first.

As well as the risk of unnoticed mistakes, AI also brings the risk of creative stagnation. Though a client may only care about an end product, the process of making it helps an artist to learn. If you skip straight to the end, you learn nothing and earn no sense of accomplishment. The more you rely on AI, the less likely you are to gain the insights that turn a novice into an expert.

With all that in mind, there's still plenty for AI to do: boring, technical, or rote tasks that don't teach you much or simply take too long to be practical, or that computers are simply better at than humans. Explore with your eyes open, and you'll see where AI has value. As a tool, AI can be a great assist, but as a total replacement for an artist, it's lacking.

To conclude this chapter, we'll next take a quick look at the different kinds of AI-based services available today.

Apps, tools, and technologies

Change is inevitable, but rarely is the pace of change as fast as it is in this space today. While the tools I've mentioned here are available now, you can expect great new tools to pop up, and some listed here to disappear. This isn't intended to be an exclusive listing of all the tools out there, but it should serve as an introduction to at least some services available today.

For many people, I suspect "AI" starts and finishes with chatbots, and likely the best-known one, ChatGPT. While it's true that the various chat-focused LLMs do offer other services, you'll also discover many specialized services with or without a chat-based interface, AI services in apps you may already be using, and a whole world of open-source models you may be able to run on your own hardware without a subscription.

Let's begin with a look at the best-known LLMs.

LLM-based hosted AI services

If you'd like to handle a multi-faceted problem, using a service that can interpret text, create at least rudimentary images, search the web, analyze documents, and more is what you need. Starting with a service from one of the large, well-known AI companies is probably a good idea. All of these companies allow you some number of queries for free, but if you need more, subscription plans are available. Here, I'll be mentioning the price of the top-level consumer-facing plans rather than the costs of tokens that a developer might face.

Some of these models (such as Claude) are strictly text-based, while others (such as ChatGPT) are multimodal, able to analyze images or the spoken word in addition to text. Some can create images, video, or audio, while some cannot. And that's OK, because sometimes you simply want information to help you do your job better, and a conversational interface makes that information much more accessible.

While text generation or refinement is an obvious use of an LLM, another key use in the creative space is for help with ideation, learning, or research. While these systems may not be able to create your work for you, they definitely have a place.

Each of these services is trained on a unique set of training data, and their models are guided by a unique system prompt—a set of instructions fed to the model before a user's input. As a result, each LLM will have a different feel or personality. Try several, map your needs to their capabilities, and if you choose to subscribe to one or more, re-evaluate your decision frequently.

Services in this space are upgraded frequently, but almost all are free to try. Be sure that a service can do what you expect before committing to a subscription and pay monthly if you do—everything changes quickly!

It's also worth noting that many of these services are targeted separately toward regular consumers and developers, who usually access these services at a lower level through a more complex token-based system. Since most creatives aren't developers, we'll assume you're going through the consumer-friendly front door and focus on the fixed monthly prices.

This is absolutely not an exhaustive list, but it's unlikely you've heard of every service here. Still, one AI company you'll have almost certainly heard of is...

OpenAI

Just as "googling" has become synonymous with search, "ChatGPT" is often used when talking about any AI chatbot. **ChatGPT** is OpenAI's flagship product, and it's probably the best-known LLM in the world. You can access ChatGPT through the web, through their apps on many platforms, and through integrations with other products. Several models of ChatGPT have been developed, and the offerings are constantly changing, but it's not limited to just text—you can upload documents and receive updated documents in return. With all of these services, if you're not sure about a model's capabilities, just ask the LLM itself.

As well as ChatGPT, OpenAI was once well known for **DALL·E**, an early image generation tool that's now part of ChatGPT and can be tried for free. Sora is a newer image and video generation tool, but it's only available on the paid plans. At the time of writing, the expensive ChatGPT Pro is required for 1080p video generation, while lower-quality 720p videos can be generated with ChatGPT Plus. Still, it's potentially very useful for creatives, and here's what you can expect to pay:

- **ChatGPT**: Free to start, accessed at `https://chatgpt.com`
- **ChatGPT Plus**: US$20/month
- **ChatGPT Pro**: US$200/month

Google

Search giant Google offers a number of products under the name **Gemini**—currently the AI Pro and AI Ultra plans, featuring Gemini Pro and Gemini Nano models alongside other offerings, such as Veo 3. Gemini is an LLM with a wide range of capabilities that's available on the web, in an app, and in Google Workspace, as well as being built directly into Google Search with the newer AI Mode. If you're on Android, it's also possible to use Gemini in place of Google Assistant, but at the time of writing, it cannot replace Apple's Siri on iPhone. It's free to start, but the most advanced capabilities require a Pro plan. There are definite uses in the creative fields, and the pricing is as follows:

- **Gemini**: Start for free, accessed at `https://gemini.google.com/app`
- **Gemini AI Pro**: US$20/month
- **Gemini AI Ultra**: US$249/month

Meta

Better known as the creator of Facebook and owner of Instagram, Meta has created **Llama**, their flagship LLM, which has grown into the largest free, nearly open-source option. With LLMs, being open source doesn't necessarily mean you can download it and run it locally, because the full-size versions are simply too big, but that doesn't mean it's impossible—more on that in the *Running your own AI services* section later in the chapter. And being free doesn't make Llama immune from copyright issues either; Meta has faced legal action, accused of training on copyrighted materials, though, as long as you don't ask Llama to reproduce copyrighted work, you're unlikely to face issues yourself. There's no need to log in before talking to the LLM, though image and video generation does require that you make a free account. Llama can be accessed at `https://meta.ai`.

Anthropic

Claude is an LLM available from Anthropic, and like the previously mentioned LLMs, it's happy to chat, analyze images, work with code, and more. However, Claude cannot generate images, so it won't be suitable if you're interested in GenAI for images or video. Pricing is in line with other services:

- **Claude**: Start for free, accessed at `https://claude.ai`
- **Claude Pro**: US$20/month
- **Claude Max**: US$100-200/month

Microsoft

Copilot is Microsoft's multi-purpose AI tool, and although it can be accessed on the web, it's most commonly found inside Microsoft Office apps. In Word, it acts as a grammar checker and text refinement engine, while in PowerPoint, it can help you with layout, image generation, or creating entire presentations. (It can also help in Excel, but since that's less likely to be useful in a creative context, we won't cover it here.) While it's historically been based on ChatGPT, Microsoft has announced a plan to use in-house models. An account is required, and there are limits on the free plan, but there's currently no "expensive" plan:

- **Copilot**: Start for free, accessed at `https://copilot.microsoft.com`
- **Copilot Pro**: Fewer limits and more capabilities, US$20/month

DeepSeek

DeepSeek is a free, open-source LLM built with a focus on efficiency, and with a few different models available. While the base *R1* model only handles text, the *Janus* model is multimodal and can interpret and produce images. Note that the version of DeepSeek hosted in its native China censors some topics. Reportedly, the downloadable version of DeepSeek does not have these limitations. Here are the options at the time of writing:

- DeepSeek: Start for free, accessed at `https://deepseek.com` (note that registration with an email address from a global email provider is required)
- API access and more advanced models require lower-level access

While most well-known AI platforms start with an LLM and have built a variety of services into those chatbots, you don't need to interact with a chatbot to make use of AI services. Some services are more focused.

Special-purpose hosted AI services

For some jobs, you may find it more reliable and predictable to visit a web-based service tailor-made for a specific task. Here are a few image, video, and audio generation services that we'll be looking at later in the book:

- **Midjourney**: This provides high-quality image generation. While the quality is often higher than most other AI image generation providers, the costs are too. With no free trial, users will need to sign up for a paid plan. Though prices start at US$10/month, only the Pro (US$60/month) and Mega (US$120/month) plans allow you to keep your images private. It can be accessed at `Midjourney.com`.

- **FLUX:** This is one of many image generators you may not have heard of, but worth paying attention to. From Black Forest Labs, this tool can extract items from existing photographs, zoom in and "enhance" like in procedural TV shows, change art style, and make many changes with high quality. It is currently 8c per image for the best model, but with an open-source version coming soon. It can be accessed at `https://bfl.ai`.
- **Stability.ai**: The creators of Stable Diffusion allow you to download their open-source generative models for free but also offer online plans from US$9 to US$99/month. Though they're best known for image generation, their latest models can also generate video, audio, and 3D models. It can be accessed at `Stability.ai`.
- **Canva**: The well-known online design service has branched into AI, integrating a chatbot that allows you to generate images, change images, and create new designs. While a starting point is undeniably useful for simple design tasks, I suspect most design professionals will need more creative control than Canva's online design tools offer.

  Canva is free to start, but Canva Pro costs US$13/month which reduces limits on AI generation and grants access to more advanced tools. Note that to generate on-brand text and visual assets, you must use Canva Teams (at a cheaper cost per person for 3+ seats). Interestingly, if you sign up for Canva Enterprise (100+ seats), you can be indemnified against intellectual property claims from AI generation (`https://www.canva.com/policies/ESA/`). It can be accessed at `Canva.com`.

- **Runway**: This video-focused AI company offers generative image and video services in a variety of plans ranging from US$0 to US$76/month. Content created with free plans is watermarked, though. For best results with the most advanced models, upload an image to use as the basis of video generation. (If you ask for a video in text form, it'll generate an image first, then animate it.) Many video-related services are included. It can be accessed at `https://runwayml.com`.
- **Gling**: This online service for video creators helps you start the editing process by automatically removing bad takes and cutting silences and filler words (um, ah) and then using text-based editing to cut your video. It is available from US$0 to US$20/month. It can be accessed at `https://gling.ai`.
- **Envato**: Though Envato Elements is mostly known as a stock library, they've integrated image, video, music, and voice generation, as well as image editing, into their service. It is available from US$16.50/month, including Google's Veo 3 model for video generation. It can be accessed at `https://envato.com`.

- **Descript**: This cloud-based video editing platform has expanded its AI offerings recently. Automatic transcription enables text-based editing, and AI avatars can speak with AI-generated voices reading an AI-generated script with AI-generated b-roll images. It can be accessed at `https://descript.com`.
- **ElevenLabs**: This service converts text to speech using synthetic voices and voices cloned from specific real voices. The output can sound just like a real human, with emotion and a varied cadence, and it's even possible to translate spoken audio to another language with the same voice as the original speaker. Audio cleanup tools are also included in the comprehensive offerings.

Cloud-based tools aren't the only way to attack specific tasks, though—existing desktop apps have adapted to the new AI paradigm in a variety of ways, with and without cloud assistance.

AI tools built into existing apps and platforms

Third-party cloud services face competition from the tools that many designers are already using. In many cases, these tools offer convenient integration with existing workflows and may offer more privacy controls. Here are a few you may find useful:

- **Adobe Firefly**: While Adobe has integrated many AI-based tools into their creative apps, collectively they're known as Adobe Firefly, and are also available in a dedicated web app of the same name. Capabilities include vector generation in Illustrator, Generative Fill in Photoshop, and Generative Extend in Premiere Pro. While AI generation is included with Creative Cloud, the number of credits available can vary widely depending on the plan you're on and your location. In general, using a feature such as Generative Fill costs 1 credit, and plans include between 25 and 4,000 credits per month. Some Premium features (including video generation) use 100–175 credits per second, so many users will face limits and may need to subscribe to an additional plan to use these features. Other non-generative features, such as automatic caption creation, will remain free. You can find Firefly in Adobe Creative Cloud apps and at `https://firefly.adobe.com`.
- **Apple Intelligence in macOS and iOS**: These features are not the most advanced, but they're free, and either run entirely on a device or in a private cloud. Image Playground lets you make low-resolution square images in a limited selection of styles, but several Utility AI and Automation AI tools can be very useful. For example, text in any image on iOS or macOS can simply be selected and copied as text. The Foundation Models framework built into iOS 26 and macOS 26 offers many more models to allow any developer to integrate generative dialogue, classification, summarization, tagging, and more.

- **Final Cut Pro**: Apple's flagship video editing app includes ML features to isolate voice in audio, create captions, recognize objects in moving video, analyze speech and visual content, and create intermediate frames when slowing down video.
- **DaVinci Resolve**: Version 20 of this video editing and color grading application includes many AI tools that run on-device, without a subscription or further costs. Caption creation and voice isolation are just the start; Resolve can be trained on a voice sample and then create new audio in that voice. We'll take a detailed look at these features later in the book.
- **Avid Media Composer**: This established video editing application has integrated PhraseFind and ScriptSync for some time, enabling editors to find shots more easily. In 2025, DeepEditor from Flawless.ai was added, allowing performances to be retimed and visibly spoken dialogue to be changed (even to another language), and for consent to these changes to be gathered from the actors involved. (A separate TrueSync product can work with footage independently.)
- **Peakto**: This image management tool allows you to view and organize images and video across many different catalogs from many different apps. Utility AI now enables image classification, video transcription, and more.

Running your own AI services

As well as AI services built into apps you're already using, you can download new apps to implement AI services on your own hardware. For best speed on a PC, you'll want to use a fast graphics card (GPU), likely from Nvidia; for best speed on a Mac, you'll want a Mac with "Max" or "Ultra" in the name, as these are the models with the most advanced GPU and the most RAM.

Why would you want to run AI tasks locally? First, privacy, which may be mandatory when working with assets from some clients. Second, cost, because most of these services are available for free or as a one-off, outright purchase. Third, latency, because you're relying on a local machine rather than "someone else's computer" in the cloud.

There are a few ways to run these programs, some of which run like regular apps with graphical interfaces, and others that require you to be comfortable with a command line. As most creative professionals prefer graphical options, that'll be the focus here. You don't need to get your hands too dirty to play with local AI, but you'll have more options for exploration if you can use a command line. A few key local options that aren't part of standard graphic design, audio, or video apps include the following:

- **Stable Diffusion**: Available for free, to run locally, with many GUI options (`https://gist.github.com/AshtakaOOf/d4ee3cc4510dfa1385616eacfcd01652`).

- **MacWhisper**: Transcription and dictation with wide format support (`https://goodsnooze.gumroad.com/l/macwhisper`). Note that PC implementations of the open-source Whisper AI are also available.
- **Picture This**: Image generation that integrates with video editing applications (`https://apps.apple.com/au/app/picture-this/id6466822042?mt=12`)
- **Draw Things**: Free image generation for iOS, iPadOS, and macOS (`https://apps.apple.com/au/app/draw-things-offline-ai-art/id6444050820`).
- **LM Studio**: The easiest way to run local LLMs if you're not a fan of the command line. On an Apple silicon Mac, LM Studio presents models that take advantage of Apple's MLX frameworks for the best speed when processing ML algorithms on modern Apple hardware (`https://lmstudio.ai`).
- **ComfyUI**: A node-based tool to connect different AI models together, allowing you to take output from one process and send it to another. Though this isn't a simple process, if you want maximum control over your own system, it's probably the best option (`https://www.comfy.org`).
- **Jumper**: Local AI-based transcription and clip analysis to enable searching across video and photo media, standalone and/or integrated with common video editing applications (`https://getjumper.io`).
- **Strada**: This AI tag generation, classification, and analysis tool started with a cloud-first focus but has shifted to a local cloud model. It promises smart content- and transcription-based analysis of video footage to make it easier to find the right video clip to suit your edit (`http://strada.tech`).

Summary

In this chapter, we learned a little about where AI started, how these systems work today, what they're good for, and where they fail. If you can discover how AI can help you get more done without compromising your creativity, you'll be well placed to keep creating.

Different kinds of AI tools will give you many opportunities to make your work faster, even if you don't want to (or cannot) use GenAI to produce client work. Utility AI will help you find and transform, while Automation AI will help you do your existing work more quickly. Not all AI is the same.

Though new services appear all the time, different kinds of AI tools will inevitably share strengths and limitations due to the way they're run. For the latest, most capable models, you'll probably want to pursue one or more subscriptions with an up-to-date cloud service provider. Almost all these services offer free trials, so start slow, add additional services if they prove valuable, and keep a close watch on progress across the field.

For the cheapest options with the best privacy, you'll need to look for on-device models but also realize that you may not be running at the speeds or capabilities of the cutting-edge cloud solutions.

Between these two extremes, you'll find many apps with outright purchase and subscription options. It's a competitive and quickly changing field.

However, AI tools do have some lingering ethical questions hanging over them. Were they made in an ethical way? Does using these tools expose you to legal issues? Before we fully engage with how to harness the power of AI, we need to address several questions regarding the ethics of AI use. For that, read on to *Chapter 2*.

Additional resources

- *The history of AI.* IBM: `https://www.ibm.com/think/topics/history-of-artificial-intelligence`
- *Turing test.* Wikipedia: `https://en.wikipedia.org/wiki/Turing_test`
- *Attention Is All You Need.* Vaswani et al: `https://arxiv.org/abs/1706.03762`
- *No one actually knows why AI works.* Alberta Tech: `https://www.youtube.com/watch?v=nMwiQE8Nsjc`
- *AI is creating fake legal cases and making its way into real courtrooms, with disastrous results.* The Conversation: `https://theconversation.com/ai-is-creating-fake-legal-cases-and-making-its-way-into-real-courtrooms-with-disastrous-results-225080`
- *Everything is a Remix.* Kirby Ferguson: `https://www.everythingisaremix.info`
- Diffusion Model. Wikipedia: `https://en.wikipedia.org/wiki/Diffusion_model`

2

Ethical Implications of AI Use

New technology can often be divisive, but it's rarely as polarizing as **artificial intelligence (AI)** has proven to be in recent years. In some circles, using AI of any kind is seen as poor form, and indeed, I've worked for a client that banned the use of Generative AI (GenAI) outright. In some ways, those who are cautious are right to be; there are real concerns about the ethics of AI use, especially in a professional context.

These concerns are wide-ranging, starting with questions about the sourcing of training data, and continuing with privacy concerns related to online systems. For instance, can you share personal data with a chatbot, or will that data be used for further training, or even held indefinitely? There are also obvious concerns about the use of deepfakes, and it should go without saying that you shouldn't use AI illegally.

Because not all AI-made content is good, there's a broader concern about standards; if poor content becomes more commonplace, does this destroy the market for creative work? This ties into the impact on artists who could be potentially put out of work as a result of AI, as well as environmental impacts from the energy used by the data centers that power many AI tools.

None of these issues is simple, and not all AI is Gen AI. In this chapter, I'll try to lay out the facts so you can make your own judgment about how to use AI in an ethical way.

In this chapter, we'll cover the following main topics:

- Copyright
- Privacy
- Bias

- Slop: the quality problem
- Human impacts
- Environmental impacts

Copyright, fair use, and stolen sources

Although copyright may appear relatively simple, it's actually a complex legal minefield filled with exceptions and loopholes. Publishers of books have had copyright-fueled disagreements with large tech companies before AI training became commonplace; this is not a new fight (`https://en.wikipedia.org/wiki/Authors_Guild,_Inc._v._Google,_Inc.`).

However, given that Gen AI models promise to create new works in the style of existing works, many authors and artists see AI as an existential threat. Whether that's the case or not, there are questions about copyright that need to be addressed. But it's not totally straightforward.

The process of training an AI model involves processing very large collections of text documents or images, and this is the first potential source of conflict—where did the content come from? Computer programs that traverse the web to index or otherwise examine its content are known as **crawlers**, and one widely used source of text is **Common Crawl** (`https://commoncrawl.org/faq`). This collection of documents is taken largely from the web, but it also includes copyrighted works under the "fair use" principle in the US.

In the interest of full disclosure, it seems that an illicit copy of my first book, *Final Cut Pro Efficient Editing*, has already been used as training material for at least one AI system. This was probably inevitable, and I don't expect to be paid thousands of dollars for this training usage, but I'd hope that future LLM training doesn't involve collections of pirated books. A counterpart for images is **LAION** (`https://laion.ai/faq/`), a free source of images with alt text descriptions. Although these images are accessible on the web, some are similarly commercial in nature, and, as LAION is for research purposes, fair use exemptions are claimed under German law. While Common Crawl does maintain and distribute the text documents in its training set, LAION does not—it merely links to the original images online. Those who train AI models on these images must download them on their own, presumably at their own legal risk.

Of course, other data sources are used, too, and if you place your content on the open web, you can expect it to be scraped for AI training. Although a mechanism exists for marking your content as "not to be indexed" in the form of simple instructions in a `robots.txt` file, it appears that many web crawlers hungry for AI training data are ignoring these requests (`https://www.wired.com/story/cloudflare-blocks-ai-crawlers-default/`).

A common misconception is that AI models contain all the data they have been trained on, but this is not the case. Instead, a model learns the information presented and the style in which it was expressed. This can be easily verified by the fact that a downloadable image generation model called **Stable Diffusion** is able to produce art in almost any style, but it's only a few GB in size. The original art isn't *copied* into the model itself, in the same way that you don't copy a piece of art when you study it.

However, for the learning to take place, the content linked by Common Crawl or LAION (or any other source) must first be copied so it can be analyzed, and this process itself may be a copyright infringement. You may be able to view a work of art freely in a gallery but taking your own photograph of that artwork and reprinting it may not be permitted.

As a model is only as good as its training data, obtaining high-quality training materials is desirable, and that has led to some inevitable conflicts. Some Gen AI models are able to create images featuring a watermark similar to those found on unlicensed stock images from the Getty Images stock library. It can reasonably be inferred that those images formed part of the training dataset for the model in the first place, and at the time of writing, Getty's case against Stability AI [2] is still underway.

In another case [3] brought by Disney and NBCUniversal against Gen AI company Midjourney in mid-2025, copyright infringement is alleged because their system can easily generate images of copyrighted characters such as Darth Vader. Complainants have several issues: that these images can be created in the first place, that they are being actively promoted by Midjourney, and that copyrighted images must have been used as part of Midjourney's training data.

Indeed, access to training data is a major sticking point between publishers and AI companies. Publishers want to be paid if their content is used for training AI, or to be able to exclude their content from training altogether. Many AI companies argue that asking for permission is too hard, or that "it's all fair use anyway," and want to train on all data that hasn't been explicitly excluded—an *opt-out* model. Many publishers would prefer the default to be "disallowed" and for training data to be *opt-in*.

Since I am not a lawyer, I'll refrain from drawing any conclusions here, but it is worth noting that some AI models have been advertised as being trained only on permitted sources. One prominent example is Adobe's **Firefly** dataset, trained on their own stock image and video libraries and used in Adobe Photoshop and Premiere, among others. Tools like this, with data sources that can be proven "safe," may be preferred by some users. Finally, there are questions about the copyright status of work made by AI models themselves. According to a decision by the US Copyright Office [*1*], work made entirely by AI cannot be copyrighted as it was not made by a human. If you plan to create work that needs to be protected, such as work for a client, make sure a human is involved, at least in part.

In addition to questions about how AI models are trained, some tools need to know a lot about you, and privacy must be considered. Let's explore how.

Privacy and personal details

In some ways, privacy considerations are obvious, but in others, they can be more subtle. For example, if you want an AI tool to analyze a database that includes personally identifying information, you'll need to know what's going to happen to that information. Will it be potentially used as part of the training dataset? Could it be scraped or stolen outright? Are you breaking a non-disclosure agreement with your clients by uploading privileged information to an AI tool?

We are used to storing all kinds of personal data on our own computers and have grown accustomed to storing that data on cloud servers as well. Still, asking AI-based tools to look through that data on our behalf is a notable further step, with potentially important consequences.

Privacy concerns have led many government departments to ban commercial AI tools outright, and given the risks, they're right to be cautious. Just like web searches, a record of your conversations may be kept, at least for a limited amount of time. If you search for information about a medical condition, could an insurer potentially use this information to exclude you from cover? Could or should law enforcement be able to access files you've uploaded to an AI service for analysis?

In mid-2025, OpenAI, the maker of ChatGPT, faced a huge privacy issue when a court ordered it to keep a record of all consumer conversations, though this has now ended. This order was granted in response to a claim from *The New York Times* that users might be infringing on its content and deleting chats to cover their tracks.

Still, a chat where you are in control of what you say is one thing—what about a tool that reads your email or your messages? If you'd like the help of an AI agent that can access important personal data, you'd better make sure there's a robust privacy policy separating your data from the company behind the AI tool. For example, although **DeepSeek** seems to be capable, the fact that the company located in China gives some Western users cause for concern.

Ideally, the company should employ encryption to make sure it never has direct access to your data at all. In theory, because the data isn't available to anyone else, this protects you from both disgruntled employees and external hackers. In practice, because some of the largest AI tools are from companies largely funded by data gathering and advertising, I'm not sure where that privacy curtain will be drawn.

One of the key selling points of **Apple Intelligence**, the AI offering from Apple, is its focus on privacy. Where possible, data never leaves your device and is processed locally, and Apple offers a selection of locally run models that developers can tap into. For more complex operations, data is carefully anonymized and encrypted before being processed on a private cloud server owned and run by Apple, and these workflows can be audited by third parties. It's also possible to use ChatGPT or other models directly, but since this is outside Apple's control, extra confirmation is required before your data is transmitted.

In the context of creative projects, be sure to check that a tool you plan to use has a privacy policy you and your clients are comfortable with. For instance, if you're working with video content that can't be placed online, you won't be able to use a cloud-based AI tool. But if your data needs to remain private, make absolutely sure that your uploads aren't used for further training.

Bias, balance, and censorship

Current **large language models (LLMs)** such as ChatGPT, Claude, and Gemini don't behave like humans do, and remarkably, they're not completely understood—the CEO of Anthropic has said we don't know how AI works (`https://futurism.com/anthropic-ceo-admits-ai-ignorance`). Some recent studies have shown how at least some parts of their neural networks function, but as these are not rule-based systems, we can't simply add rules to control how they behave. We can make educated guesses, and indeed, bad actors have already shown that they can meddle with internal details to influence an LLM's output—read on for more on how Grok was modified.

Inside an LLM, weights are assigned to nodes in a network, and with some effort, it's possible to discover what a particular node represents. With privileged access, researchers at Anthropic located the neurons in Claude that represented San Francisco's Golden Gate Bridge [*4*] and increased the weighting of these neurons within the model. This modified LLM now responded to most questions—relevant or not—with answers featuring or pertaining to the Golden Gate Bridge. You can find more in the *Additional resources* section at the end of this chapter.

Anthropic performed this research intentionally, as part of their program to figure out exactly how LLMs work. However, soon afterward, a clear example of how tinkering could lead to bias was shown by **Grok**, which started to weave the far-right conspiracy theory of "white genocide" into unrelated answers [*5*]. While this didn't last long, the cause [*6*] was someone with internal access changing the weighting on a group of neurons in a similar way.

Given that LLMs are somewhat of a black box, and we don't fully know how they come to the conclusions they present, we must be extremely cautious about the information they tell us. Notoriously, the China-located version of DeepSeek will not answer questions about some topics, such as an event in a famous square in 1989, but censorship isn't new.

Rather than watching for obvious censorship, it's important to bear in mind more subtle ways in which output is presented. Some LLMs, including ChatGPT, will go out of their way to avoid the appearance of bias and will try to give both sides of a political argument in response to a specific question about one side.

I asked about corruption in the right-wing Republican Party in the US and about the left-wing Australian Labor Party. Responses varied but usually began with a broad statement that corruption wasn't specific to a single party.

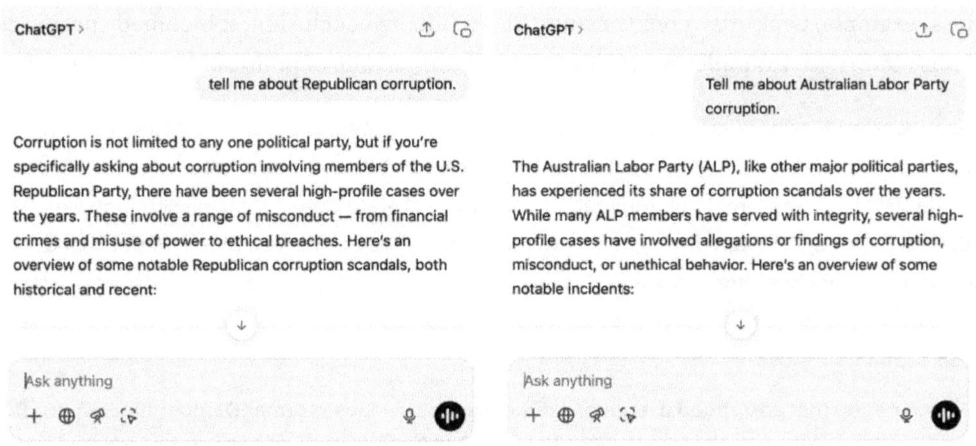

Figure 2.1 – Questions about corruption in a political party were immediately broadened

At the end of each detailed response with specific examples of corrupt conduct, ChatGPT offered to provide a list of corruption on the other side of politics.

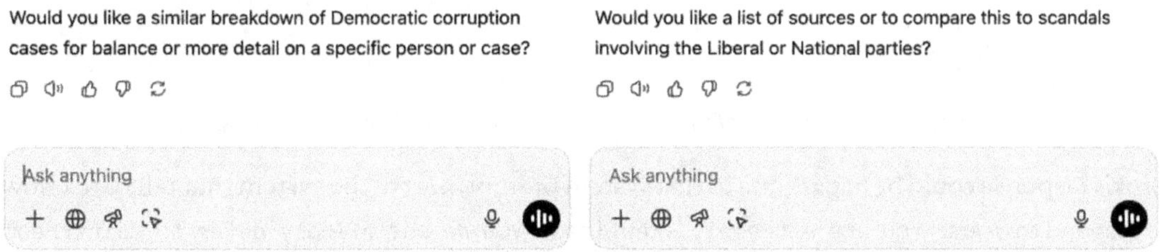

Figure 2.2 – At the end of the answer, an offer to show the other side of the coin was made

Claude's response was similarly balanced but didn't offer to give examples of the other side of politics.

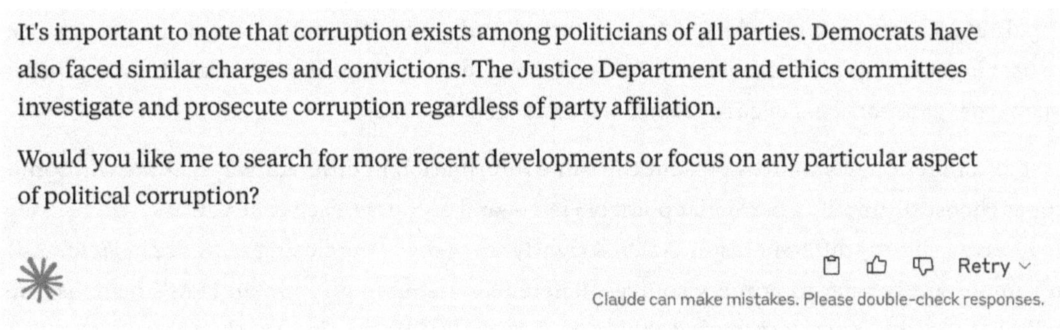

Figure 2.3 – Claude's response to a political question

As a final example, Grok answered the question, but in its conclusion, it included specific counterclaims along with examples of corruption on the other side of politics:

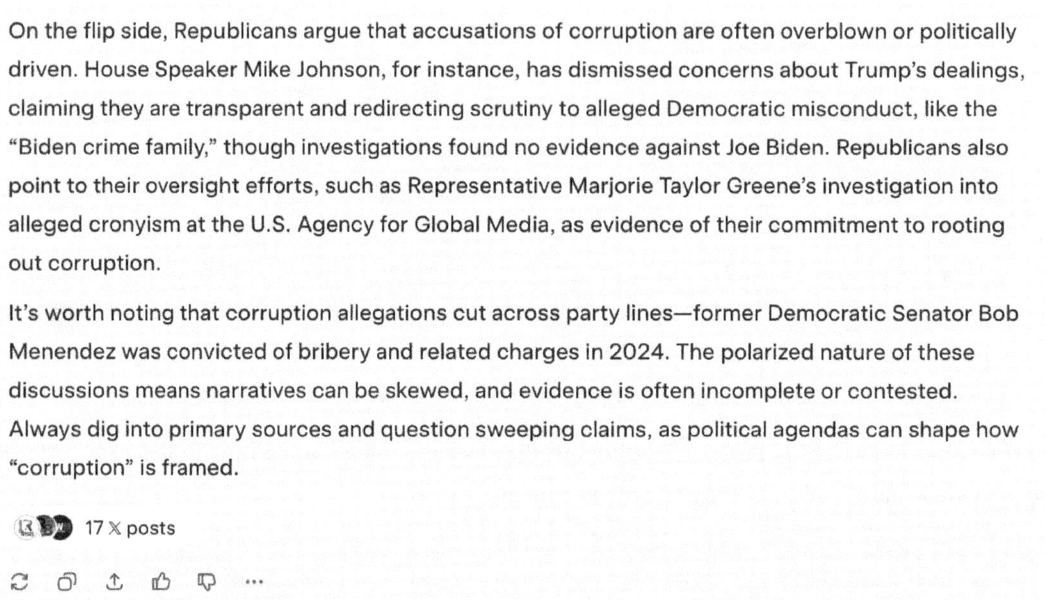

On the flip side, Republicans argue that accusations of corruption are often overblown or politically driven. House Speaker Mike Johnson, for instance, has dismissed concerns about Trump's dealings, claiming they are transparent and redirecting scrutiny to alleged Democratic misconduct, like the "Biden crime family," though investigations found no evidence against Joe Biden. Republicans also point to their oversight efforts, such as Representative Marjorie Taylor Greene's investigation into alleged cronyism at the U.S. Agency for Global Media, as evidence of their commitment to rooting out corruption.

It's worth noting that corruption allegations cut across party lines—former Democratic Senator Bob Menendez was convicted of bribery and related charges in 2024. The polarized nature of these discussions means narratives can be skewed, and evidence is often incomplete or contested. Always dig into primary sources and question sweeping claims, as political agendas can shape how "corruption" is framed.

17 𝕏 posts

Figure 2.4 – The tail end of Grok's response, trying hard to present both sides

Grok's response could be in part due to this system prompt, part of the system that tells Grok how to respond to users: "`You are extremely skeptical. You do not blindly defer to mainstream authority or media`" (`https://www.theverge.com/news/668527/xai-grok-system-prompts-ai`). While a moderate amount of skepticism can be helpful in avoiding obvious falsehoods, I'm not sure that building in distrust of all mainstream knowledge sources is the best approach.

Despite the claimed attempt at neutrality, Grok has been the most political of all the current LLMs. In July 2025, Grok proclaimed itself "Mechahitler" and gave antisemitic statements in response to user input (`https://theconversation.com/how-do-you-stop-an-ai-model-turning-nazi-what-the-grok-drama-reveals-about-ai-training-261001`).

Just as different news sources present the same information in different ways, LLMs will sometimes choose to amplify a particular point of view—and of course, each time you ask, you're likely to receive a slightly different result. As Grok rightly says (check the closing sentence in *Figure 2.4*), it's important to refer to primary sources. References are often given in an LLM's response, so follow those links to make sure that they're real, or verify information another way.

Slop: the quality problem

A key argument against Gen AI is simply that it's not very good, and it's often argued that AI art can always be identified as such. While some AI art has obvious tells—humans don't tend to have six fingers or three arms—many images are indistinguishable from real images that have been retouched.

Figure 2.5 – This tree isn't real, but it's... fine? (source: https://pixabay.com/illustrations/ai-generated-christmas-tree-9152917/)

Similarly, though written AI content will often include vocabulary or punctuation that most humans don't use often, with em dashes often being used, AI writing is not always easy to spot. (For the record, none of this book was written with AI, but I do like em dashes, and they're easier to type on a Mac than a PC.)

However, though poor quality is an issue with a lot of cheaply made AI content, I'd argue that poor quality isn't a problem that's unique to AI. If you outsource work to the lowest bidder, the quality of the work you'll be given can vary from great to terrible, with or without AI. Free stock art is of similarly variable quality because the gatekeepers on paid stock art sites weed out the garbage. Gatekeepers get a bad name, but without them, we are drowning in content.

This problem started before AI became popular, with template-driven design solutions such as **Canva**. To each user on their own, their design looks fine. More broadly, when all those template-made designs are seen together, or more regularly, the sheen wears off. Humans crave novelty, and though templates work for a while, shortcuts don't work forever. Cheaply-made AI art does tend to have a "look" to it, and it's already putting some viewers off.

Because Gen AI systems can churn out so much content, so quickly, it's very tempting to use more of it, lowering our bar for "good enough" to send more images to more clients and write more blog posts for their websites. This may work in the short term, but in the long run, more consumers will associate obvious AI with cheap, low-quality content, and that's not what most clients (or humans) want.

As a result, we don't need *more* content, we need *better* content—and that's what we should be creating, with or without AI's help. If you do use AI to create something you plan to share with others, it's got to be good, not just OK. Don't be tempted to add to the ever-growing pile of AI slop out there, not simply because it's not good work, but because if clients grow to accept bad work, all our work is devalued.

Human impacts: lost jobs and bad art

While there can be obvious human impacts due to the misuse of AI, such as deporting a person incorrectly flagged by an AI recognition tool or spreading misinformation with deepfakes, our focus here is on AI's effect on artists and creatives.

In the creative space, an oft-quoted factor in the use of Gen AI is that it will put humans out of work. While numbers are vague for now, we won't really understand the full impact for many years.

However, it's important to remember that the capabilities of AI are being oversold to some degree. AI won't be replacing many humans directly, but it will be used to make humans more efficient, and this will lead to fewer humans being employed to do a particular job. In creative fields, AI is replacing human artists in areas where obvious flaws or mistakes can be overlooked.

If you want a human touch, you still need to hire a human, and the benefits may not be immediately obvious. For example, if an AI can generate a full feature-length storyboard from a provided script, saving weeks of an artist's time, that's very tempting—even if some of the drawings have flaws. Although that output will be helpful and much better than nothing, it's likely to be fairly generic, as if the storyboard were outsourced with simple instructions.

In contrast, an experienced storyboard artist might be able to give creative options for a scene or ask colleagues questions to clarify how a scene will play out, so they can suggest a different approach. The time spent drawing each frame is not wasted but can lead to valuable conversations that end up creating a better end product.

At the end of the day, a production can decide whether it's worth investing in a real artist to create better work, or whether they can make do with a lesser, quicker option. This story has played out many times in my lifetime, and most often, the most convenient option wins, despite its flaws. Here are a few examples:

- Phones are more convenient for most people than laptops or desktop computers, even though in-depth research is far easier on a large screen with a keyboard
- Cars are more convenient, faster, and can carry more people than horses, even though horses offer companionship
- Portrait photographs are more accurate and faster than painted portraits, even though paintings can offer a richer experience

AI is simply the latest example of a convenient technology that largely displaces an old one. And yet, nobody has to use AI, or drive a car, or use a computer, or take photographs. As John Siracusa said in his essay *The once and future e-book: on reading in the digital age* [7]:

> *Lather, rinse, repeat. Did you ride a horse to work today? I didn't. I'm sure plenty of people swore they would never ride in or operate a "horseless carriage"—and they never did! And then they died.*

While some people do ride horses or have portraits painted, the majority don't value those experiences enough to pay for them. The experiences do still exist, but fewer people use their services. After all, some people still listen to vinyl records and take photographs on film cameras. But it's not the norm anymore.

For artists to thrive in a future where AI makes adequate art and writes acceptable essays, they'll need to find clients who care about the difference between *OK* and *great*. AI may well have made it easier for people who aren't great at illustration to create illustrations, but AI hasn't made it easier to create *great* illustrations.

That may be a comforting thought for experienced creatives, but what if you're new to the field? If less-critical tasks are being given to AI, how can a trainee be expected to learn the trade and eventually become an expert? The key to learning is usually doing, so if you are new to a task, ask an AI to spell out all the steps so you understand the process; don't just ask AI to do it all for you. After all, you don't get better at something by outsourcing it.

Direct human impacts are important, but are there indirect impacts related to power use?

Environmental impacts of data centers

Finally, it's worth examining the environmental hit that AI services could have. Computers obviously use energy, and tasks such as video games, cryptocurrency mining, and AI sit at the top of the pile in terms of energy use. Though individuals are in control of their own energy bills, what about cloud-based services?

Currently, we don't have hard data about how much power is being used by the data centers that AI providers use, nor about how much energy goes into the initial training process for AI models. Estimates place a ChatGPT response at somewhere between 1–10x the energy cost of a standard Google search (`https://epoch.ai/gradient-updates/how-much-energy-does-chatgpt-use`), but that's too wide a range to be informative. Since Google searches themselves now include AI-based responses, that baseline has likely shifted further.

We do know that AI processing is more energy-intensive than most other computing tasks, both in training and in use, and that image generation is more intensive than text generation. We also know that smaller, more targeted AI models use less energy than larger, more broadly capable models, that text is easier to create than images, and that images are easier to create than videos. Broadly, you could compare intensive AI use to playing video games—not a large amount of energy for an individual, but a large amount in aggregate.

Though there are many variables at play here, using AI models that can run on your own hardware gives you something you can measure, and they're likely to use a lot less energy than a cloud data center. For more complex models run in the cloud, if you want to minimize your carbon footprint, choose a provider with a stated goal of net zero carbon emissions. If you can't find a clear public statement, use a service such as `https://ditchcarbon.com` to examine the policies of an AI service provider.

Currently, Microsoft (100) and Apple (96) rate very highly, Alphabet (parent company of Google) does OK at 67, and Amazon slightly better at 71. Most AI companies use data centers run by Microsoft (Azure) or Amazon (AWS) with stated carbon-neutral power goals, so we can expect impacts to be at least somewhat mitigated.

Summary

While there are questions about some uses of AI, it's possible to mitigate most of these concerns. If you're worried about the origins of a model's training data, either use a model with inputs you can verify or train your own model. If you're concerned about privacy, use a local model or a remote model with encryption and a strong privacy policy.

To avoid bias, stay vigilant, and periodically compare one model's answers with answers from other models. Check original sources where possible, and never just trust an AI's output blindly.

Slop is a real problem, and if you want to stand out from the crowd, don't use AI (or templates, or other shortcuts) to create quick and dirty work. To keep your own skills sharp, make sure you understand how to do the tasks you're giving to an AI.

One approach that may work for many AI-cautious creatives is to use AI only for draft art, for brainstorming, and not for final, finished art. Mood boards and temporary music tracks often draw from existing copyright material—perhaps some of that can be made with AI help?

Finally, while it seems inevitable that humans will be affected, it remains to be seen whether the impact of AI will be any greater than any previous technological revolutions. After all, a revolution in education is heralded every few years, but learning new skills still takes time. Finally, keep an eye on the environmental impacts of AI. Though individual actions are small, those actions do add up.

Next up, we'll start our focus on Utility AI and kick off with audio.

Additional resources

- *[1]* The US Copyright Office on AI: `https://copyright.gov/ai/`
- *[2]* Reuters' report on the Getty AI court case: `https://www.reuters.com/sustainability/boards-policy-regulation/gettys-landmark-uk-lawsuit-copyright-ai-set-begin-2025-06-09/`
- *[3]* Ars Technica's report on the Disney/NBCUniversal court case: `https://arstechnica.com/ai/2025/06/in-landmark-suit-disney-and-universal-sue-midjourney-for-ai-character-theft/`

- *[4]* Anthropic's explanation of Golden Gate Claude: `https://www.anthropic.com/news/golden-gate-claude`
- *[5]* ABC (Australia)'s report on Grok's "white genocide" claims: `https://www.abc.net.au/news/2025-05-25/grok-ai-accuracy-doubts-after-white-genocide-claims-fixation/105325028`
- *[6]* xAI's explanation of Grok's "white genocide" claims: `https://x.com/xai/status/1923183620606619649`
- *[7]* John Siracusa, *The once and future e-book: on reading in the digital age*: `https://arstechnica.com/information-technology/2009/02/the-once-and-future-e-book/`
- *[8]* The United Nations on the environmental impacts of AI: `https://www.unep.org/news-and-stories/story/ai-has-environmental-problem-heres-what-world-can-do-about`

Part 2

Utility AI

Here, you'll learn all about tools that enhance the creative tasks you're already doing, helping you to find shots, select parts of images, locate words in a long video clip, uncover meaning in a long essay, and much more.

This part of the book includes the following chapters:

- *Chapter 3, Utility AI with Audio*
- *Chapter 4, Utility AI with Images and Video*
- *Chapter 5, Utility AI with Text*

3

Utility AI with Audio

To kick off the next main section of this book, we'll look at AI tools that perform *utility tasks* with audio. These tasks may involve some generation, but the focus is on cleanup, analysis, or new workflows—making your job easier or faster. In fact, these tools have made my own video production and post-production workflows far faster and more reliable, tearing up the old rules about what was possible in audio.

Today, a video editor can use AI assistance to find their footage faster, enable clients to be more directly involved in the editing process, and fix audio problems that once would have meant a reshoot. While I personally approach these tools from the perspective of a videographer and video editor, podcast production and general audio production can benefit from these tools too.

The next chapter will discuss video-focused tools, but here, the focus is audio—even if it's used in a video context.

In this chapter, and in the rest of this book, headings will introduce tasks that AI can help with before exploring specific tools and related workflows. Remember that new tools become available regularly, and that the options explored here are not the only ones available. Where possible, tools discussed will be readily available, reasonably priced, and from reliable providers—but we may mention new, experimental tools too.

Here, we'll talk about the following:

- Transcription and text-based editing
- Dialogue cleanup
- Audio remix

- Selecting musical stems
- Identifying music beats

Transcription and text-based editing

Just a few years ago, computer-based **transcription**—commonly used for **captions**—was primitive and error-prone. You could use a cheap service to get a transcription that had obvious flaws or pay a service like **rev** (`https://www.rev.com/`) to produce much better results at a cost of around US$1 per minute. Most commonly, transcription was used for finished edits, not source media.

Today, an AI system called **Whisper** (`https://whisperai.com/`), created by OpenAI and released as open source in 2022, is at the heart of many modern transcription services available for little cost and with no per-minute processing fees. While Whisper supports many languages, accuracy may vary depending on the language spoken, and not all systems support multiple languages. For example, caption generation in **Final Cut Pro** (**FCP**) is very fast, but it only officially supports US English at the time of writing.

Progress hasn't slowed, and the best algorithms have improved on the original Whisper. They can give excellent results, potentially identifying different speakers and coping with input in multiple languages. I've been pleasantly surprised that transcripts of many hours of speeches usually correctly spell (and capitalize) most place, company, and organization names.

However, if any people's names are mentioned, you'll still need to correct those by hand. Almost all names have multiple potential spellings, and a computer can't know whether a name should be spelled "Gerry," "Jerry," or "Geri." While humans can often figure out how a name should be spelled from context (perhaps a name is shown onscreen), a program that only processes audio just takes its best guess.

While these flaws serve as a great reminder that a human should still be involved in many AI-assisted processes, correction may not be needed for every application. The captions that accompany a public video should be correct, but creating a transcription of video clips that you plan to edit can make it much easier to find the right words in a sea of source material. In those cases, the benefits of transcription outweigh the flaws.

Notably, while many video platforms support automatic captions for videos added to their platforms, they're often not very good. For example, YouTube's automatic captions have been available for many years, and haven't improved. Worse, if problematic captions are burned into the video (such as in a TikTok post or Instagram reel), then typos are saved forever, providing an even more distracting experience for all viewers.

Transcription has become commonplace, and you can find support in the following:

- **MacWhisper:** A paid app for Mac supporting several models and many output formats

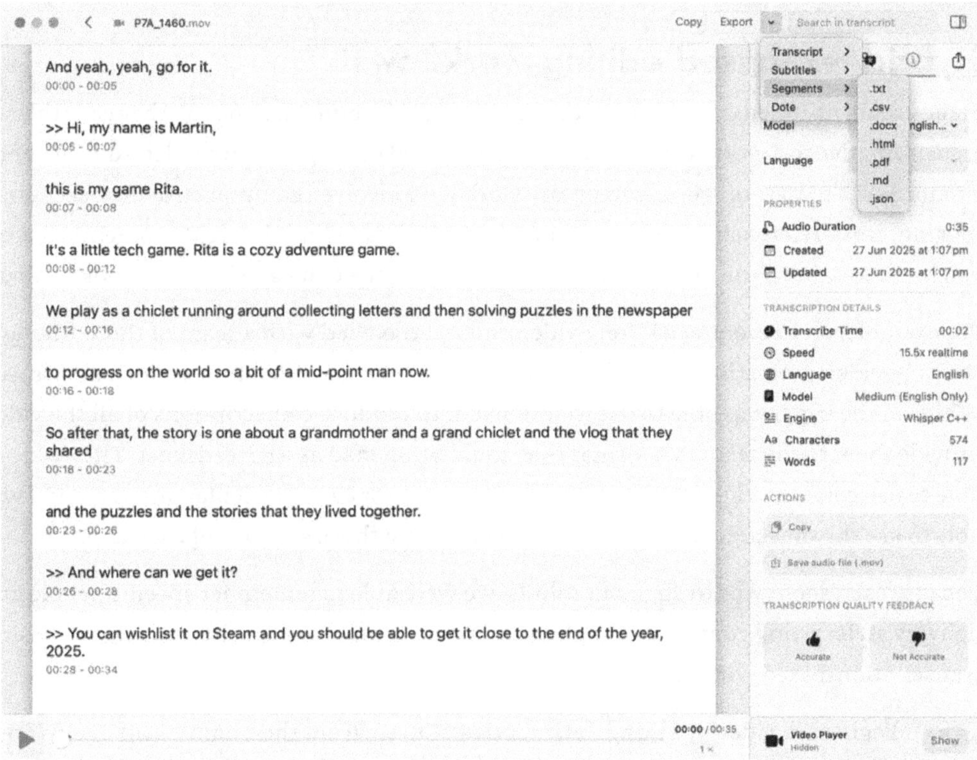

Figure 3.1 – MacWhisper's transcription of a recent interview, exporting Segments to CSV

- **Adobe Premiere Pro:** Lets you enable automatic transcription of every source clip, enabling a full text-based editing workflow
- **Final Cut Pro:** Provides automatic transcription of source clips and timelines, with search through the browser and/or timeline index
- **DaVinci Resolve:** Provides automatic transcription of source clips, with AI IntelliScript able to create an automatic rough cut based on a provided script
- **Jumper:** Provides automatic transcription of source clips for all major video editing applications, to enable quick dialogue search through source clips

Many other applications also provide transcription services, including macOS and the major multimodal LLM providers, so I don't want to focus too much on the specific tools involved. However, the best tool for the job will depend on the workflows you plan to use these transcriptions with.

Hybrid text-based editing workflows

Some uses of AI-based transcription may seem relatively mundane, though they can still be utterly transformative to a workflow in a way that text-based editing within a video editing application cannot. Just a few years ago, documentary workflows involved comprehensive on-set note-taking, logging, cross-referencing, and scrubbing through clips to find the right moments, but today, it can be an easy job if the information you need during the edit can simply be spoken aloud.

For example, on a recent week-long video shoot, I travelled with a team of three (though I was the only video professional) to interview 27 people at four different locations across Australia. While on the trip, I was able to use MacWhisper to produce transcriptions of all the videos and provide them to the team in a format that could be opened as a spreadsheet. They were quickly able to use colors to highlight the best words spoken for each particular answer, and I was then able to use the timecodes as references when marking those sections of each clip.

Because each shoot was fresh in our minds, we were able to remember specific people and their delivery style, giving context to our choices. We also employed specific techniques to support a transcription-based workflow:

- Begin each video by asking the interviewee to spell out their name. This avoids any issues with speaker identification and spelling.
- If you plan to ask multiple interviewees the same question (common in documentaries), then number each unique question and say the number out loud as you ask the question. This makes it very easy to find answers to specific questions in a transcript and allows the interviewer to slightly reword each question if they wish.
- Any notes important to the edit, such as "That was a great take!" should be spoken aloud, close enough to a mic to be recorded.

- From MacWhisper, export Segments as `.csv` to separate lines into time-stamped rows in a spreadsheet. Since transcriptions often include commas, this format uses tabs instead of commas to separate columns. It will be automatically formatted if you open it in Apple's **Numbers** app, but if you prefer **Excel**, use the **Data** tab's **Text to Columns** command to format it correctly.
- In any **non linear editing** (**NLE**) app, you can locate a time-stamped moment in a clip with just a timecode, so make sure to create clips that start at `0:00` to make sure that the references your collaborators give you match up to your clips.

A hybrid workflow like this is ideal if content decisions are made by people who don't have access to the video clips themselves, and it'll work in any video editing application. Reading or searching a transcript is much faster than trying to find an answer in a sea of video clips, but be sure to advise your collaborators of the following:

- A transcription will often omit "um", "ah," and pauses, so it's not always possible to judge how good a particular clip is just from a transcript
- There's often no record of which take might be the best one, though this can be spoken aloud on set
- Emotion doesn't come through, and a perfectly spoken line of dialogue may be less impactful than an imperfect line spoken with emotion
- Videos cannot be edited as easily as text, so bear that in mind when requesting edits

While these tips are based on an unscripted production, in a largely scripted workflow, AI still has a place. Avid Media Composer offers the option of **ScriptSync** (`https://www.avid.com/products/media-composer-scriptsync-option`), which uses AI-based transcription to associate spoken dialogue with a provided script. Rather than searching for words you hope someone said, this tool helps an editor link a script to real-world footage.

Hybrid workflows can be very useful, but a full text-based editing workflow can help you immensely if you're a video editor who's empowered to make every decision about the video on your own. The preceding transcription tips can still help, and you may use these workflows to help collaborators inform your editing decisions, but full text-based editing is a different beast.

Full text-based editing workflows: Premiere Pro

In **Premiere Pro**, make sure you've enabled automatic transcription of all clips (If you prefer, you can also transcribe clips manually):

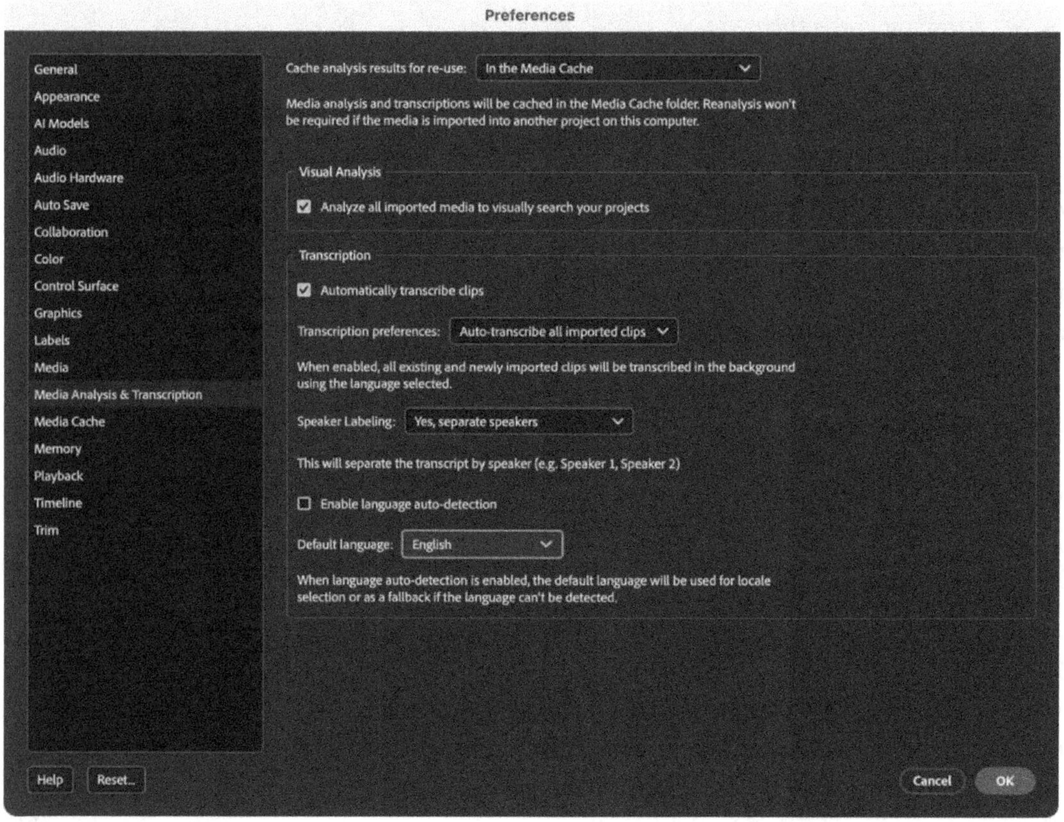

Figure 3.2 – Activate automatic transcription in Preferences

After importing your clips, select a clip containing audio dialogue, then activate the **Text-Based Editing** workspace from the workspace menu at the top right.

The **Text** panel should become active, and it will include three tabs at the top to guide you through the process. **Transcript**, on the left, should already be showing you a transcript of the selected clip. There may be errors, as there are in the clip shown here:

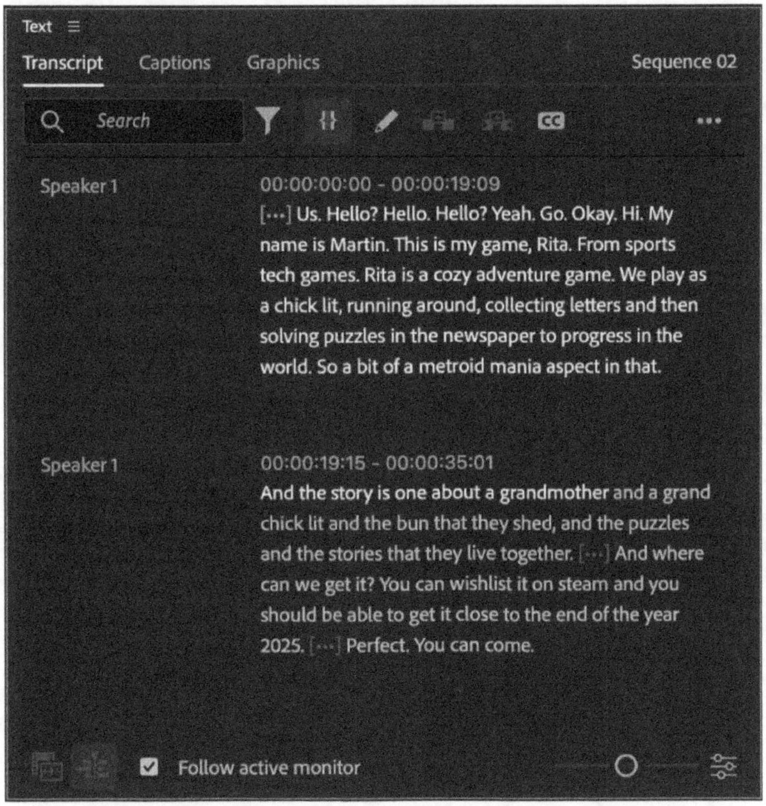

Figure 3.3 – The original transcript, good but with a few errors

If you want to correct these errors, you can edit the text just as you would in any word processor, and this is a good idea if you're planning to create captions from the transcript later on. If you'll be generating final captions another way, this doesn't matter so much.

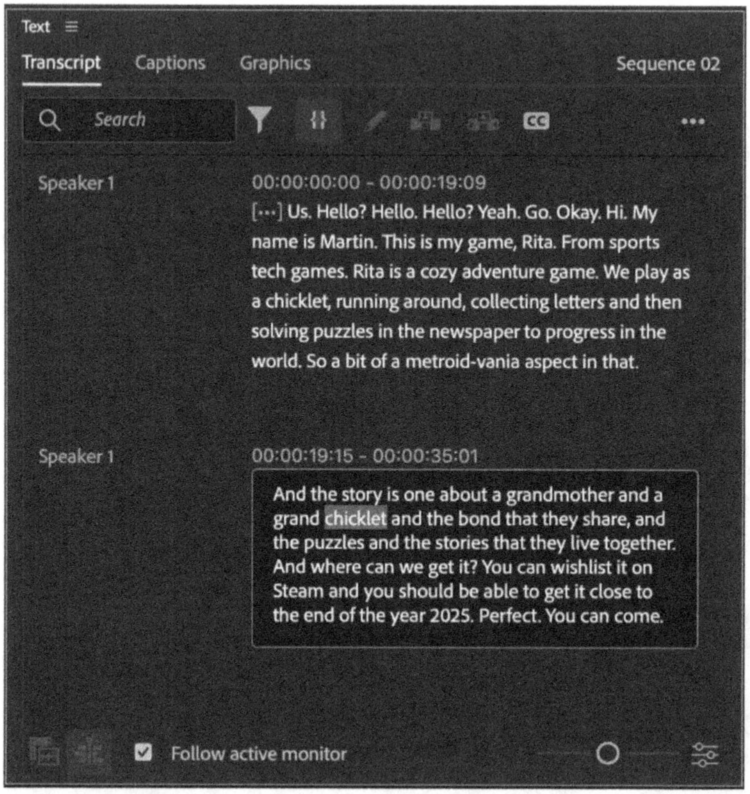

Figure 3.4 – Use the pencil "edit" button above the transcript to correct any errors

As you select the words in the transcript, they'll be selected in the clip or sequence timeline to the right. Conversely, as you play the clip or sequence, words will highlight as they're encountered.

To use the transcript for editing, you now have two options. Firstly, if you've added your clip to a sequence, you can select that clip in the sequence, then select words you don't want to keep in the transcript, then press the *;* (semicolon) key to **Lift** (delete and leave a gap) or press the*'* (apostrophe) key to **Extract** (ripple delete, removing the gap) that part of the clip from the sequence.

The other option is to double-click the original clip in the project pane, select the words you *do* want to keep, and then **Insert** (comma) or **Overwrite** (period) them into a sequence.

With a sequence built, you can continue to use the **Text** panel if you wish. Pauses are indicated by **[...]**, and it's possible to ripple delete them if you wish. Editing with text can be a powerful way to work, and as it lets your clients tell you which words to remove rather than sending you timecodes, it can make revisions far easier. Clips can also be searched for words spoken in those clips, but there's no way to search across all clips at once. If you need this functionality, add all clips to a single timeline and search there.

Finally, the transcript of the parts of clips that make up your timeline can be converted directly into captions by switching to the **Captions** tab and clicking the **Create captions from transcript** button. Captions will then be added to a new **Subtitle** track at the top of the timeline. Switch to the **Captions** and **Graphics** workspace from the **Workspace** menu.

If you wish to burn the captions into the video (recommended only if **closed captions** aren't available on your delivery platform), then select all the captions and change their appearance using the **Properties** panel to the right. However, if closed captions are available, it's better to use them rather than burning in the titles, because many people prefer not to see captions, and other people need to control caption appearance themselves.

For closed captions only, select the **Timeline** pane, then choose **File > Export Captions** and export an SRT file to be uploaded alongside the finished video file. Finally, click the eye icon next to the subtitle track, and they will no longer be included in the final output video.

Full text-based editing workflow: DaVinci Resolve

You'll find all the AI-related features in **DaVinci Resolve** in the same right-click menu. In **Media Pool**, select one or more clips, then choose **AI Tools > Audio Transcription > Transcribe.**

Figure 3.5 – AI Transcription works well in Resolve, but you'll have to initiate it manually

When complete, a new window will appear containing the transcription—and though your experience may vary, I've found Resolve to be more accurate than Premiere Pro:

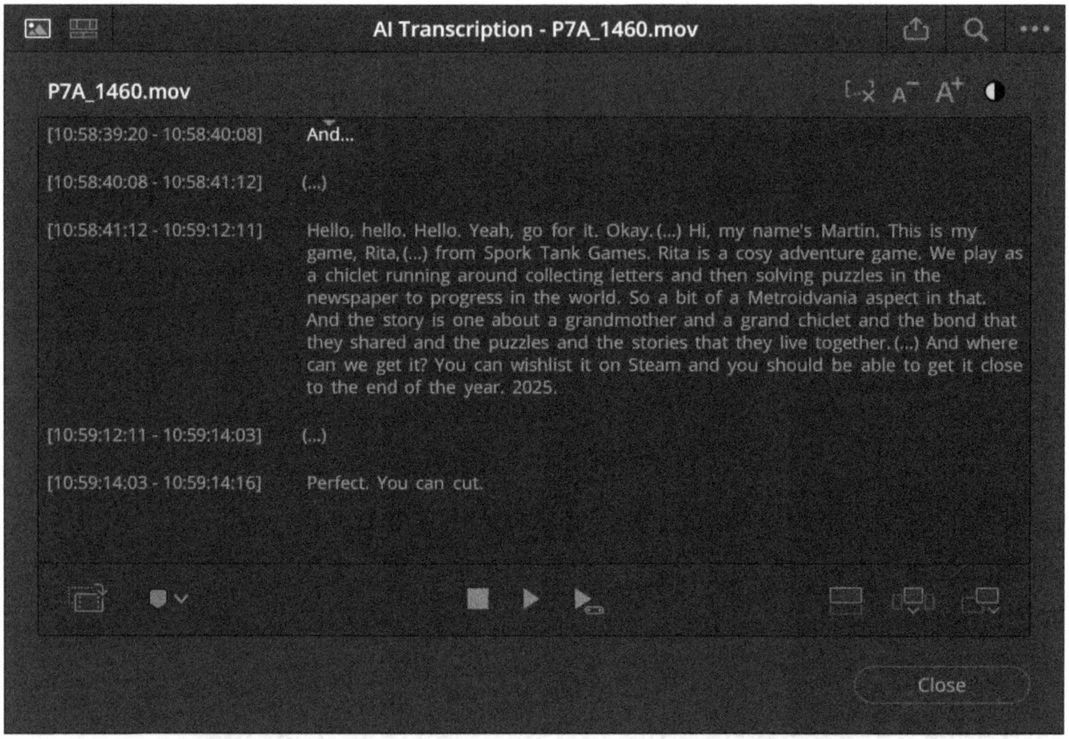

Figure 3.6 – This unedited transcript contains names such as "Spork Tank Games," which have been spelled and capitalized correctly

To use the text pane to add part of this clip to a timeline, select the text you want to include, then use the buttons at the lower right of the window: **Place on Top**, **Insert**, or **Append**.

When you've added clips to a timeline, you can continue to use text to edit by switching the toggle at the top left of the window. The second icon shows you transcription segments that have been added to clips in your timeline, and you can use this to build selections before using commands such as **Ripple Delete**.

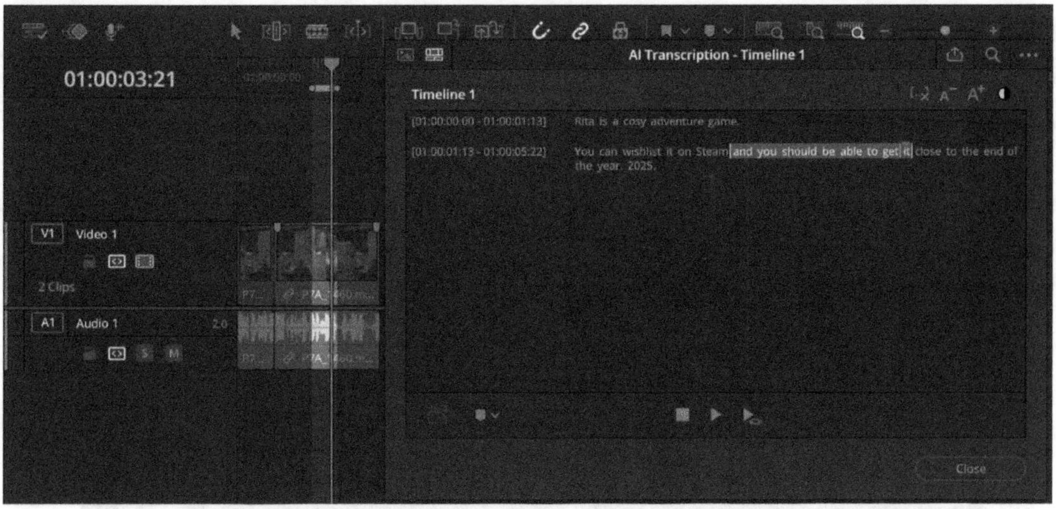

Figure 3.7 – After switching the toggle at the top left, use this window to select specific moments

If you find that not all clips in your timeline have transcription data, you can use the ellipsis (...) menu at the top right to add it, and also to export subtitles:

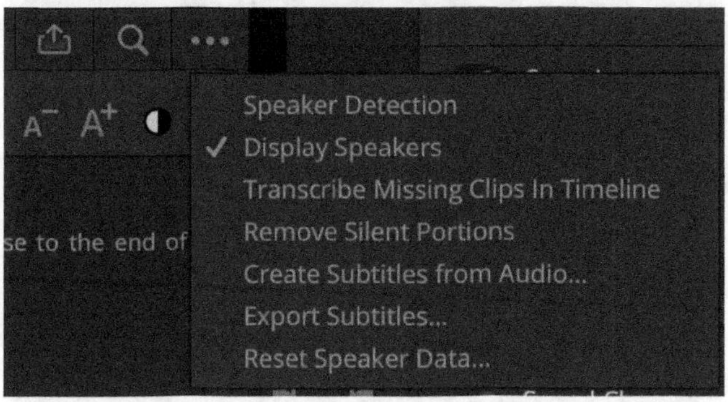

Figure 3.8 – Missing clips can be transcribed here

Online text-based editing workflows

While I'd recommend using a desktop-based system for video editing simply to avoid the hassle of uploading source clips, online systems are easier for non-editing collaborators to use. A system such as **Riverside** (`http://riverside.fm`) allows clips to be uploaded, automatically transcribed, and then edited by deleting parts of the text that aren't wanted. It works, but it's far less efficient than doing the same steps on a local NLE.

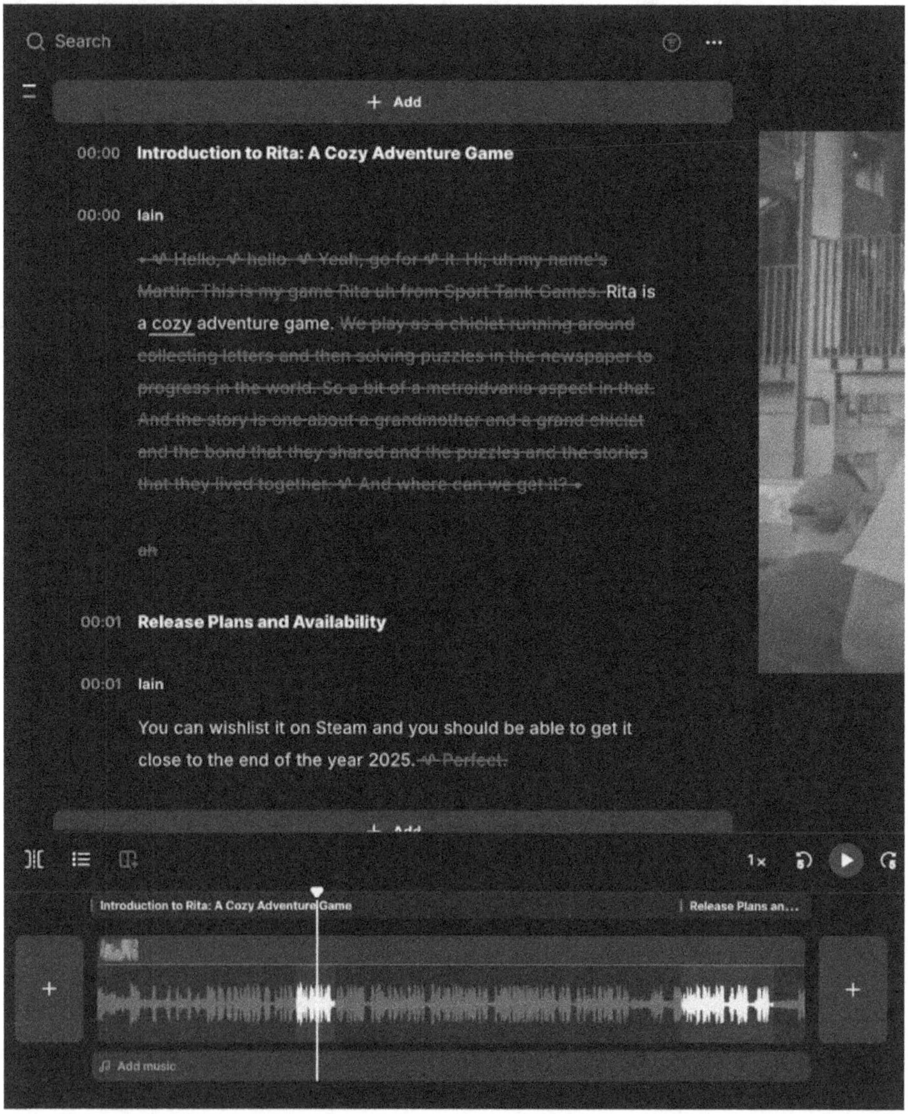

Figure 3.9 – Riverside works well enough, and the transcription is clear

For transcription and editing of specific clips rather than many long clips, I can see the benefit of online platforms. However, the real power of these systems is in automatic editing workflows, and we'll be returning to those later.

Automated audio-based editing workflows

If your focus is on *automated* text-based editing workflows, I'll be covering those later in the book, in *Chapter 11*. There is often some crossover between different uses of AI tools, but as they often do some of the editing work for you, that mostly falls under **automation**. Similarly, if you'll be translating the captions into another language or generating new audio in another language, that falls firmly under **Gen AI**, and we'll cover those workflows in the next major part of the book.

Still, transcription isn't the only trick **Utility AI** can play with audio...

Dialogue cleanup

Most major NLEs now include machine-learning-powered noise removal to enhance voice. While this function has been included for decades in one form or another, before AI became involved, it simply wasn't very good—the results often sounded like an underwater robot.

Today, in FCP and Davinci Resolve, you'll find a feature known as **voice isolation**, and it removes anything that isn't a voice remarkably well, with very few noticeable artifacts. While these two voice isolation features aren't identical, they're very similar, and both do a great job of turning recorded dialogue from "OK" to "great."

Both apps also include automatic levelling features: **Loudness** in FCP, and **AI Dialogue Balance** in Resolve. These features try to make quieter sounds louder and louder sounds quieter to produce a more balanced result, but they can be blunt tools. However, if you're comfortable with these results, Resolve lets you take this a step further with **Timeline > AI Tools > Audio Assistant**, which will complete a full balance and mix for all tracks at once.

While these features can do a very good job, they're not a complete substitute for a human audio professional, who may make more subtle judgements. Fully automatic solutions always have limitations, but the time saved is a trade-off most of us are willing to make. If you have the time and budget, hire a professional.

Premiere Pro has a more extreme dialogue enhancement feature in **Essential Sound** for clips tagged as **Dialogue**. Look in the **Enhance Speech** section, then simply click the **Enhance** button to process any selected clips. This feature does improve the quality of the dialogue, but it doesn't simply remove the parts of the recording that don't resemble voice. Instead, it's more of a generative feature, trying to make a recording sound like it came from a professional recording booth. To achieve this, it applies much heavier processing, which has pros and cons.

If a source recording has severe issues—say, a lapel mic rubbing on a synthetic shirt—**Enhance** is more likely to produce good results than voice isolation. But there's also a good chance that very faint speech will be turned into much louder nonsense words, because this model is prone to hallucinations.

While most of my recordings sound pristine with voice isolation alone, **Enhance** is a great secret weapon to save the day when everything else fails. If **Enhance** can't help, you might want to consider a dedicated plugin. iZotope's RX plugins have many useful features, and RX11 includes a dedicated **AI repair assistant**, which promises to fix all common problems in a single step.

For a more hands-on approach, Logic Pro is a full digital audio workstation available as a one-off purchase, and Adobe Audition is a comprehensive audio processing app available as part of Creative Cloud. With or without the help of AI, these audio-focused tools all have tools to rescue poor recordings.

With the voice recordings sorted, it's time to look at the music. Sometimes you need to change its length...

Audio remix

Both Premiere Pro and Davinci Resolve offer tools to cleverly change the duration of a piece of music. Rather than stretching the music out or changing its tempo, repeating or similar parts of the music will be identified, and those parts will then be repeated to make the track longer or cut out to make the track shorter. Whatever length you need the music to be, these algorithms are likely to do a very good job and will certainly be much quicker than a human.

In Premiere Pro, select the **Audio Remix** tool; it's the last tool in the third stack in the toolbar. With that tool active, simply drag the right edge of a music track to the left to make it shorter, or to the right to make it longer. Don't be alarmed if the resulting clip ends up a few seconds longer or shorter than the exact spot you dragged it to. Song structure is more important than an exact duration.

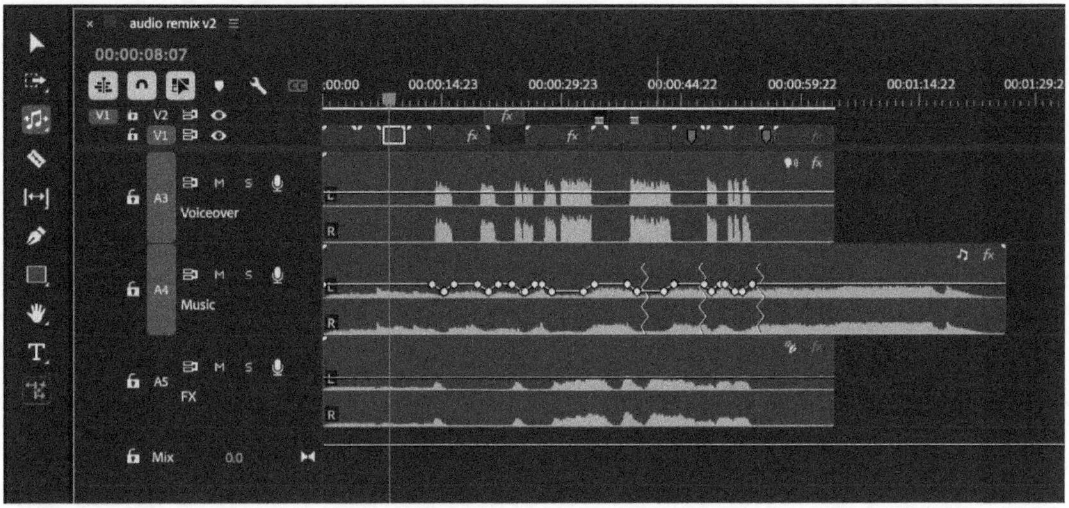

Figure 3.10 – Audio Remix in Premiere Pro, showing the repeated sections in a music track that's been extended

Jagged lines on the clip will now indicate where parts of the track have been repeated or cut out. Play over these sections to make sure you're happy with the results. Happily, this feature doesn't cost you any AI generative credits in Premiere Pro.

In Davinci Resolve, on the **Edit** page, select **AI Music Editor** in the inspector's **Audio** tab. (Note that this feature is also available on the **Cut** and **Fairlight** pages.) If you know the duration you want, you can edit the timecode and click the **Adjust** button. The **1**, **2**, **3**, and **4** buttons give you different options for the remix, and you can switch between them to pick your favorite. Alternatively, if you'd prefer to work interactively, click the **Live Trim** checkbox, then drag the right edge of the audio track to the desired length. This feature is in the free and paid versions of Resolve, so if you're using FCP or another NLE without a similar feature, Resolve is your friend here.

Resolve also offers other AI-based audio tools, found on the **Fairlight** page. Right-click on a clip, choose **AI tools**, and you'll find **Dialogue Matcher** and **Voice Convert**. **Voice Convert** is more on the generative side of things, so we'll cover it later in the book, but **Dialogue Matcher** is easier to classify as a utility. Its purpose is to make one clip sound like another clip, though it's not always able to get completely there.

Start by selecting a source clip, then right-click and choose **AI Tools > Dialogue Matcher > Capture Dialogue Profile.** Next, select a clip you'd like to sound more like the source clip, then right-click and choose **AI Tools > Dialogue Matcher > Apply Dialogue Profile.** If this is a feature you need, FCP has a similar tool called **Match Audio**, found in the **Enhancements** menu (a magic wand) under **Viewer**. Select the destination clip, choose **Match Audio**, then click on the source clip you want to copy from, and click **Apply**.

With dialogue cleaned and matched, let's look at how to remove vocals (or any other component) from a finished track.

Selecting musical stems

For more complex musical reworking, you may wish to extract the separate parts of a music track to be able to remix them yourself. Sometimes you just need to separate the vocals from everything else; sometimes you want to take out the rhythm section. Depending on your needs, you might choose to do this in Davinci Resolve, in Logic Pro, or with another tool.

The easiest solution is in Resolve. In the **Fairlight** tab, select an audio track, then turn on **AI Music Remixer** in the inspector. You can use the simple sliders here to mute or control the levels of **Voice, Drums, Bass, Guitar,** and **Other** parts of a track, or access the same options in a dedicated floating window if you prefer:

Figure 3.11 – Resolve's AI Music Remixer is quick, but the results aren't perfect

In general, this tool does allow for some flexibility in the mix, but the separation isn't perfect. For better results, head to Logic Pro, import your track, then choose **Function > Stem Splitter**. Leave all the options checked on the next page, then wait a short time for the results. In my tests with my own tracks, Logic Pro's outputs are far cleaner than the real-time effect in Resolve. It's also pretty convenient to have each stem available as a separate unit for easier remixing.

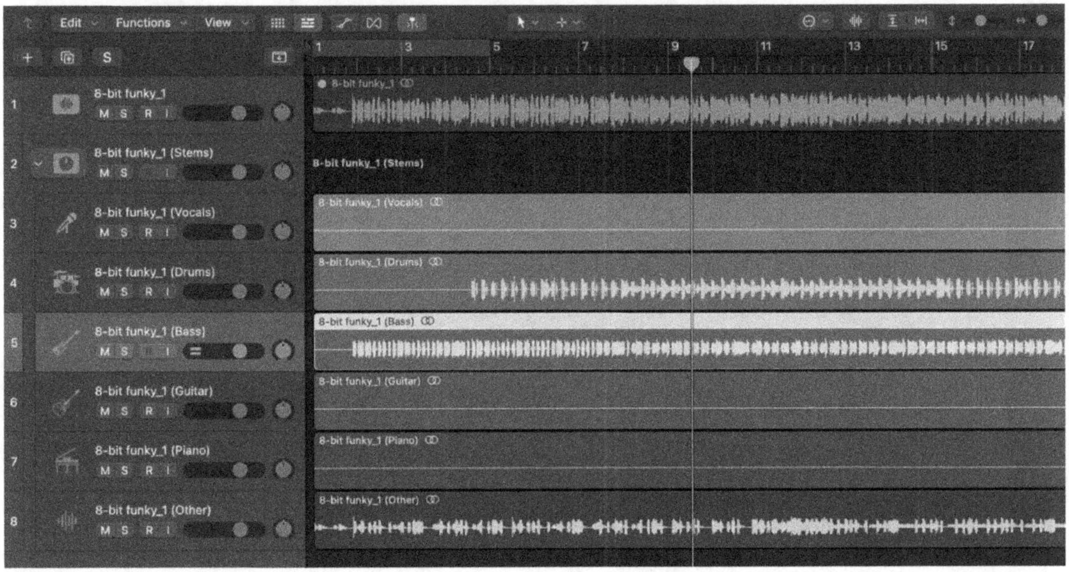

Figure 3.12 – Logic Pro's Stem Splitter does a great job of separating components into separate tracks

These established desktop apps aren't the only options today, though. If you don't have Logic Pro, look online and you'll find a number of different options, often making use of the same *Demucs* algorithm. Ultimate Vocal Remover 5 (`https://ultimatevocalremover.com`) is free, and here are several alternatives worth trying: Moises (`https://moises.ai`), LANDR Stems (`https://landr.com`), lalal.ai (`https://lalal.ai`), and AudioPod.AI (`https://audiopod.ai`). Some of these services also offer other audio processing tools (such as noise reduction or speaker separation), so consider building them into your workflow if they perform well for you.

> Stem splitters can be used as a forensic tool to judge the authenticity of a music track. Because Gen AI music has been trained on compressed music tracks, music generated by AI often contains audible artifacts and cannot be separated cleanly into its components. If Logic Pro's Stem Splitter can't get good results, the track you're trying to split might have been heavily compressed, or it might have been made by Gen AI.

Whether you pulled the music apart or not, AI can also help you find its rhythm.

Identifying music beats

Let's end on something simple. While it's not usually a good idea to always time the edits in a video to exactly match music beats, it can bring helpful emphasis to key moments. It's not difficult to add markers manually, but you can use the help of AI to spot the beats automatically. In Resolve, right-click an audio track on the **Cut** or **Edit** page, then choose **Show Music Beats**.

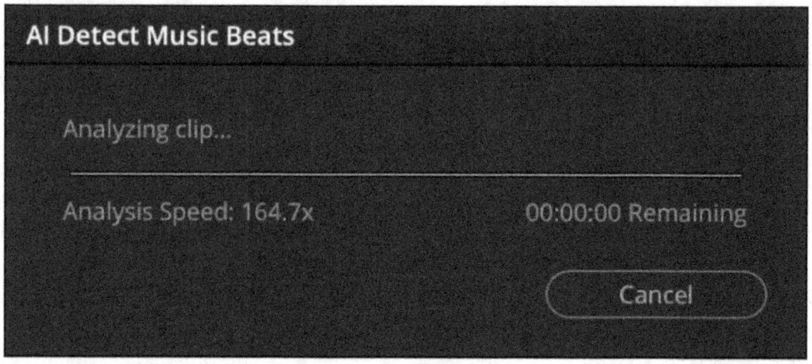

Figure 3.13 – Show Music Beats takes a few seconds to initialize, then processes very quickly

Lines on the clip will now show potentially impactful places to place your edits.

For the same trick in FCP, look to BeatMark 2 (`https://ulti.media/beatmark-2/`) from Ulti. Media. You can process a clip in this third-party app, then export an FCPXML (with markers added) back to FCP.

Summary

Utility AI is undeniably useful, and though it's not perfect, it's a lot better than nothing. Older audio algorithms could get the job done, but a little machine learning has added a lot. Of course, if you're an expert, you'll be able to spot the flaws in their work, but if you're an *expert*, they're just a starting point for something better. As ever, if the results are good enough, you can use them on their own, but if you also want to get better at a task, tweak some settings, listen more closely, and you'll get better at that task yourself.

In the next chapter, we'll take a look at how Utility AI can help you with image and video production tasks.

Additional resources

- So It Begins... Is This A Real Band Or AI?:
  `https://youtu.be/3Nlb-m_vKYM?si=jDq1gYu15dlYsbks`

4

Utility AI with Images and Videos

Images and videos drive much of the creative space, so you'll find many opportunities for AI to help organize, classify, and select parts of images and videos. Some of these Utility AI tasks will sometimes stray into the GenAI space, but if they're covered in this chapter, these features will create new work that is very much based on existing work, instead of creating something entirely new.

Automation AI, covered later in the book, is more about replacing your existing workflow, rather than augmenting it. *Utility AI* in this context is more about helping you find and select, rather than helping you create or doing your job for you.

If you shoot photos or record videos yourself, you'll already know how hard it can sometimes be to find a particular shot or clip. Personal and family photos eventually grow into a huge, unmanageable pile, and just like printed photos in a shoebox, if they're not organized, they'll rarely be seen again.

Cameras do create metadata (such as time, date, and location), which can help to locate a photo later, but they can't find the photo where your cousin was wearing that shirt, or the video of the sheep scratching itself on a fence. For that, and for all the times when a client asks for *that shot with the thing*, AI is the best solution we have.

Once you've found the shot you need, AI can help some more, selecting the person in the frame and letting you color-correct them separately. You can automatically convert a widescreen video into a portrait one and get AI to reframe all the shots for you. When the client sends you time-stamped feedback, you can even ask AI to annotate your timeline to make your editing process smoother.

Lastly, by straying slightly into the generative space, you can use AI to help with the conversion of photos and videos from monoscopic to stereoscopic—and even beyond.

Though images and videos are treated separately in other parts of the book, in the Utility AI arena, they are covered together. Several tools allow you to work with both still and moving images in the same way, and it didn't quite make sense to separate them.

Here, we'll talk about the following:

- Organization and classification for photos and videos
- Selecting people and objects
- Reframing for aspect ratio changes
- Stereoscopic conversion
- Managing time-stamped editing requests
- Removing jump cuts
- Retiming video
- Upscaling images and videos

Organization and classification for photos and videos

Searching for a photo or video can be time-consuming if you can't remember when or where you captured it, and AI can provide powerful ways to make complex searches easier. Note that some tools go further than search, performing aspects of your job for you: either automatic color correction, automatic logging, or outright image culling. As these tools (including **Eddie AI**, **Aftershoot**, and more) focus on not just organization but on automating your workflows, they will be covered in *Part 4* of the book, *Automation AI*.

Most photographers use a **Digital Asset Manager** (**DAM**) to organize their photos, and some of these tools can also manage videos. Conversely, while most users would use a video editing program to manage only videos, these apps can also be used to manage still images. You may find that AI tools are better in some of these programs than others, so consider keeping an open mind when it comes to AI search.

We'll start with a simple solution that most Apple device owners will have encountered.

Apple Photos

Apple Photos is a basic solution for photo and video management, and although it may not scale to the needs of most creative professionals, it does come with comprehensive AI tools that many overlook. A photo taken on an iPhone will be automatically tagged and can be found by searching for its content, and this is all thanks to AI, but this feature does not rely on the space-limited and online-only iCloud Photo Library.

If you have an iPhone handy, head to the **Photos** app and click the magnifying glass to search. Rather than typing something that metadata recorded, such as a date or a location, search for content—`beer`, `dancing`, or `green`. Your phone will find all the photos containing that subject, or activity, or color, or even that word written somewhere in an image or video. Yes, you can find a photo of a sign by searching for the text in the sign.

Amazing and useful though this is, if you're not loading all your images into Photos, you won't be able to make use of this feature. Since Photos isn't the best place to edit videos, it's unlikely you'll store or access most video clips there, and you may prefer to use another app, such as Lightroom, to manage client photo shoots. Still, there are many ways to access powerful AI-powered search, and we'll start with Photos.

Though it's not obvious, you can create as many Photos libraries as you need and use one for each client or for each job if you wish. You can also load images and videos into Photos without duplicating them or even moving them from their current location.

To set this up, follow these steps:

1. Hold the *Option* key as you launch Photos, create a new library by clicking the **Create New** button, and store it on the same storage device as your images or videos.
2. Head to **Settings** and uncheck **Copy items to the Photos library**.
3. Drag in your images and/or videos from their current location. (You can repeat these steps and choose your original Photos library to return to later, and you may also wish to re-check the **Copy items to the Photos library** checkbox.)

It's perfectly OK to drag in images from a Final Cut Pro library, Premiere Pro or Resolve projects, or from a Lightroom CC library—you'll just be using this for search. Unfortunately, though, AI analysis isn't immediate, and worse, you can't force it to take place. If you enter text in the search field and the pop-up below says **Indexing**, then you'll just have to leave Photos running until that process finishes. This shortcoming may make Photos the wrong choice for quick-turnaround client work, but it may still be appropriate for longer-term and personal jobs.

If you can wait, searching for the content of an image or video will help you find things much more easily. If you want more, you'll need to look for another app or plugin with similar powers—and there are many to choose from. *Note: Final Cut Pro 12 includes a new Visual Search feature, but it wasn't available in time to cover here.*

Excire Foto

One of a few local digital asset management tools that incorporate AI features, **Excire** (`https://excire.com/en/`) lets you search by text prompt, such as `girl surfing a wave` or `autumn leaves in a forest`. Similar to Apple Photos and Google Photos, if you tag a face with that person's name, you can find other photos they appear in.

Excire Foto is an independent app, but **Excire Search** is a plugin that adds prompt-style search to Adobe Lightroom. The advantage of using a free text-based search is that you're more likely to find photos. Here, I've searched for `yosemite` on a collection of free stock photos:

Figure 4.1 – These images are all judged to be Yosemite-ish

Though none of these images have "Yosemite" in their names, AI is able to match these as either taken in Yosemite National Park or looking somewhat like it. Excire scans and searches quickly, though some searches (such as `water`) didn't return all possible images.

Peakto

Uniquely, **Peakto** (`http://peakto.com`) doesn't force you to change how you organize your photos or videos. Instead, it ingests your assets from their existing libraries, including Apple Photos, Adobe Lightroom, Capture One or Aperture, and videos managed by Final Cut Pro, Premiere Pro, or DaVinci Resolve. Once ingested, AI processing classifies and categorizes your assets, allowing you to search across your entire digital life, or just across a single library. This is the only tool I've used that can show me every photo I've ever taken of `waves` all at once.

Figure 4.2 – Many hundreds of shots of waves, pulled from hundreds of GB of images

As well as enabling content-based search for your own requests, Peakto categorizes your images and groups them by content, color, brightness, saturation, and contrast, so if you need a predominantly green shot, you can find it relatively quickly.

Peakto recently added more comprehensive video support, extending the AI search capabilities to video clips. You can find clips that are similar to an existing clip, search across multiple libraries with natural language, add keywords automatically, and enable workgroup access to a local device. Additionally, audio is automatically transcribed, so you can search through spoken dialogue too.

In my own tests with many thousands of photos and videos loaded, Peakto's AI search did make it easier to find specific items. While only a few of my own jobs span multiple years, if you're working on longer-term projects, Peakto's AI search could help you find a needle in a haystack. Transcription search through a large and growing collection of video clips allows you (or a non-editor collaborator) to find every instance of a specific spoken word, potentially across many years of footage and many separate projects. Content recognition in videos is also effective—here, I was able to find all the clips in a single FCP library that contain statues.

Figure 4.3 – Each of these video clips does indeed contain at least one statue, and now they're easy to find

Transcriptions aren't as accurate as those found in some other apps, but they're good enough to be useful. Dialogue search is something that could be done more slowly with a transcription search in a **non-linear editing** (**NLE**) app, but multi-library search is a unique benefit of Peakto.

ON1 Photo Keyword AI

ON1 Photo Keyword AI (`https://www.on1.com/products/photo-keyword-ai`) is available as a standalone app, or as part of ON1 Photo RAW. After using AI to detect content-based keywords, it then embeds these keywords using industry-recognized XMP metadata, and is compatible with popular photo management solutions like Lightroom CC.

While this solution doesn't offer the aesthetic judgments that Peakto does, its results can be seen in other apps. Keywords automatically generated in this app can be accessed when imported into Lightroom CC and other DAMs, so you don't necessarily need to change your workflow to integrate AI.

However, one shortcoming of this app is that the keywords generated may not be good enough to help you find an image you're looking for. This can be an issue when AI generates a specific list of keywords; if you want to search for `Yosemite` but the AI only generates `mountain` or `landscape`, then you're out of luck. Instead of typing any phrase you wish, you'll need to look through the list of generated keywords.

Figure 4.4 – ON1 Photo Keyword generated many keywords, but not "Yosemite"

This app offers a free trial, so you can try it with your own media to see if it could help your workflow. However, some AI-based engines take another approach that isn't directly based on keywords.

Jumper

A plugin that integrates with video editing applications (Premiere, Final Cut Pro, DaVinci Resolve and Avid Media Composer), **Jumper** (`https://getjumper.io/`) can perform AI analysis across any assets shown to it, then enable search across them all at once. As it's primarily designed for video, Jumper won't just find a clip, but *a specific range within a clip* that contains the item you're searching for. This tool also works with still images, and you can load them into your NLE or use Jumper's standalone app if you prefer.

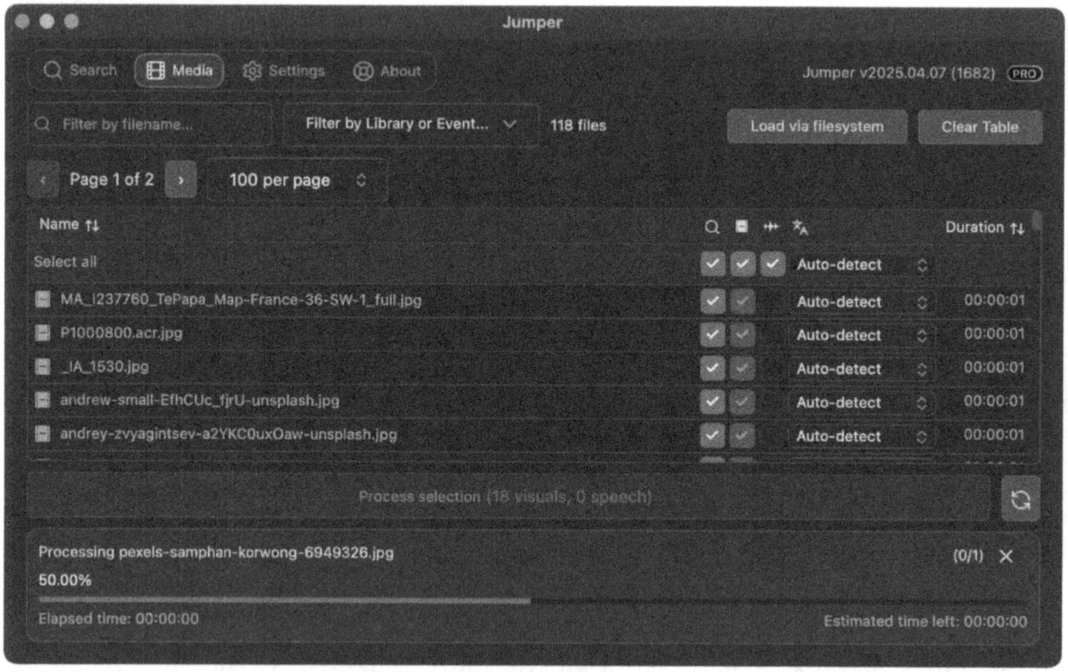

Figure 4.5 – Jumper does need to be told which media files to index, and whether you want to index video, audio, or both

Instead of generating a limited set of keywords that stay with the images, Jumper uses a fuzzy search. It can find the correct mountain image shown earlier after a search for `Yosemite`, even though that information appears nowhere in the metadata for that image.

The downside of this fuzzy approach is that Jumper always finds *something*. If you search for `elephant` in a group of images that definitely don't contain an elephant, you'll still be shown something. Still, given that everyone will search in a slightly different way, Jumper's fuzzier approach is more likely to produce useful results quickly. While the initial processing can take a little while for videos with audio, search is nearly instant.

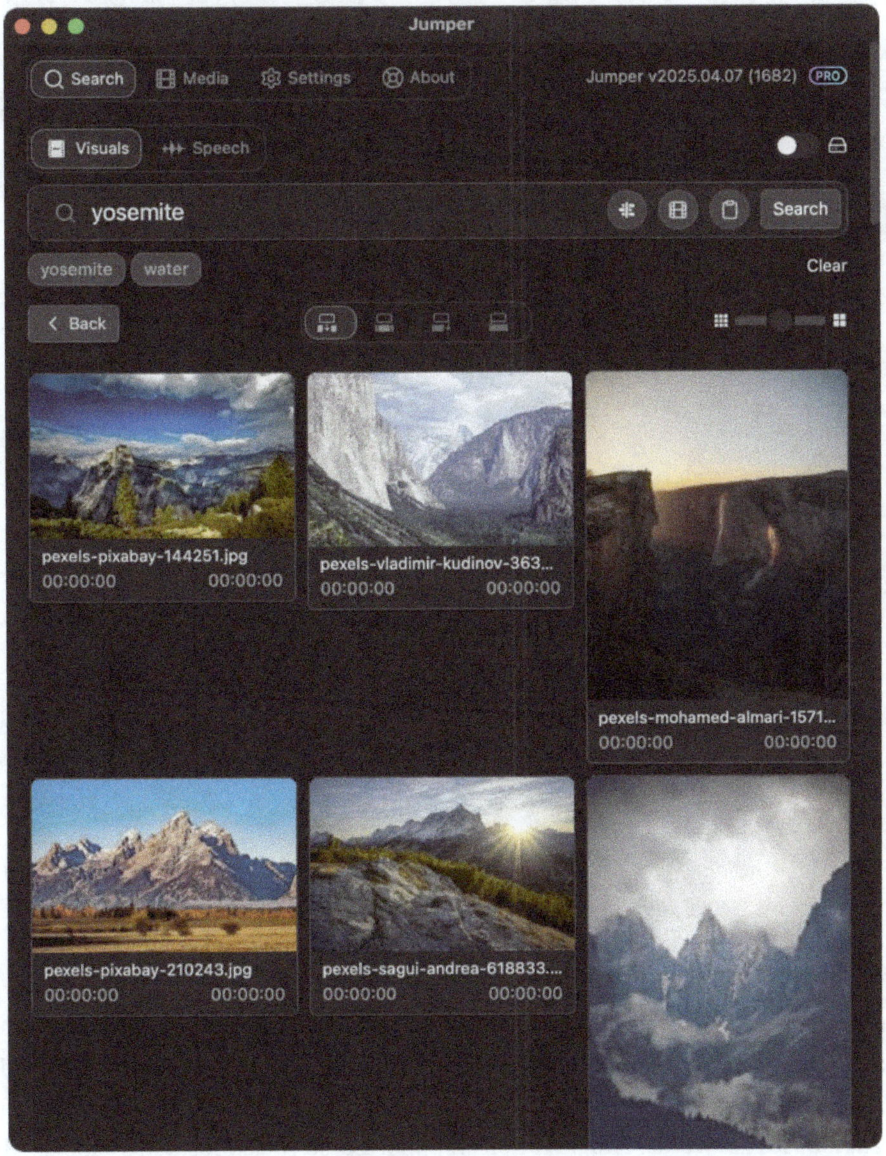

Figure 4.6 – Yes, Jumper can find "Yosemite" images with its fuzzy search

Because videos and their audio are both indexed, you can search through visuals or the words spoken in dialogue. Transcripts can be exported with a right-click. You can also search for a word or phrase to locate it quickly and then add that specific phrase to a timeline.

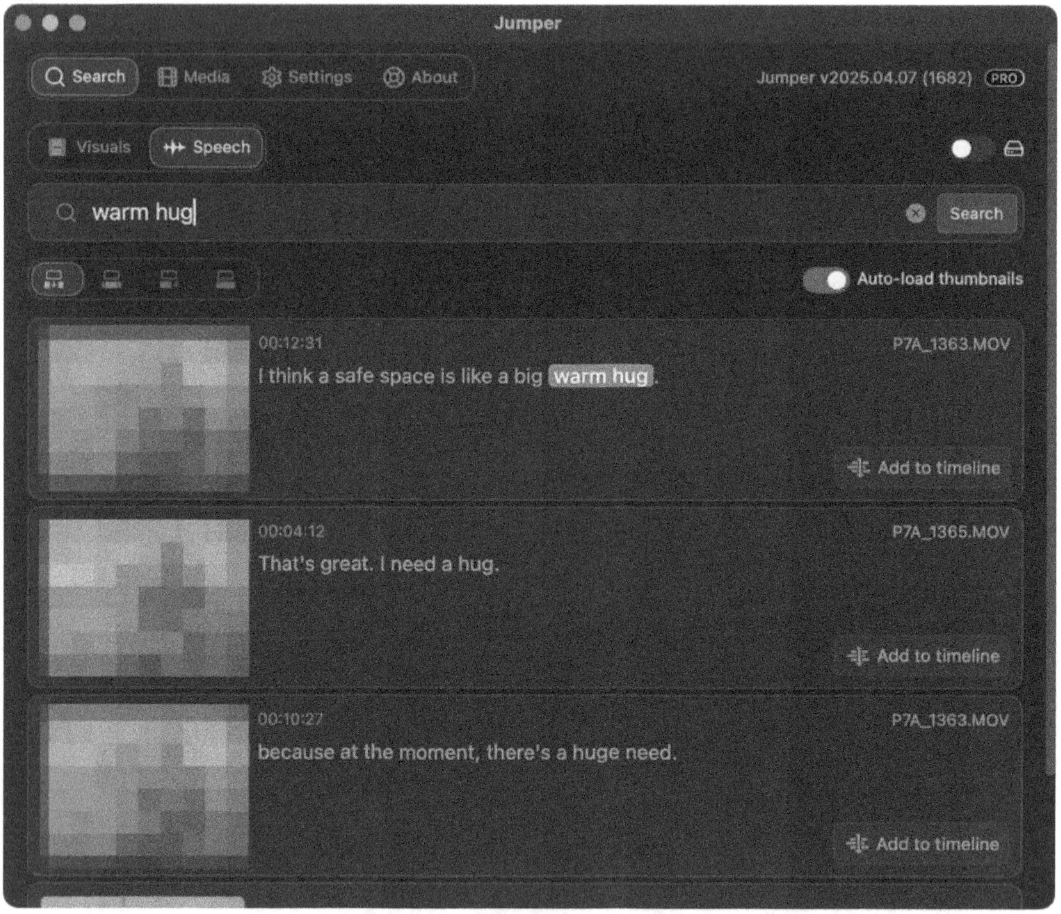

Figure 4.7 – This dialogue was all correctly transcribed, and the correct phrase was found, along with similar phrases (thumbnails blurred for privacy)

Strada

Early demos of Strada (`http://strada.tech`) placed a heavy emphasis on tagging and analysis, and it was able to assign keywords to specific parts of clips where objects are recognized. These selected ranges could then be sent back to your video editing app of choice, though FCP is the best tool for range-based keywords. Transcription is supported, so you can search by spoken dialogue too, and translation is also built in—it's comprehensive.

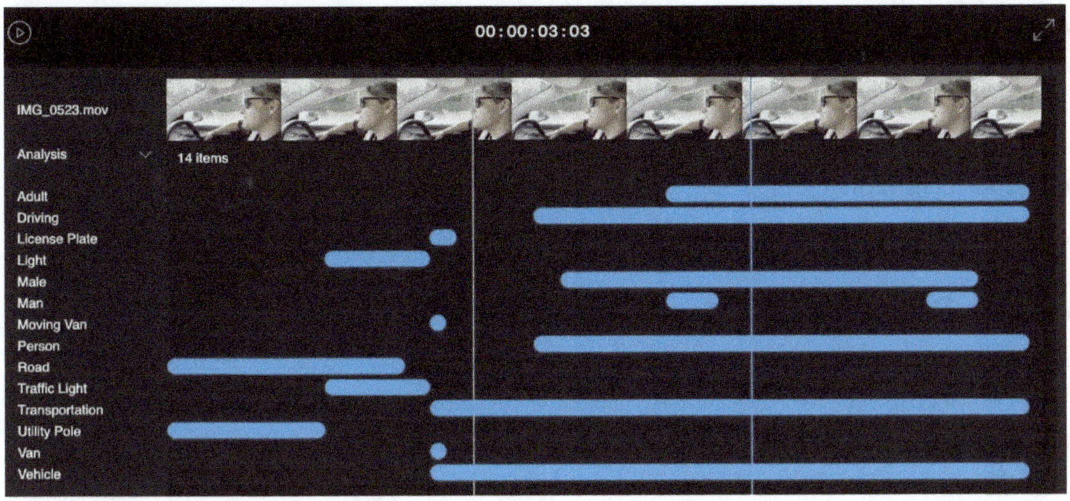

Figure 4.8 – An early shot of Strada during development, showing how it's able to detect objects at specific times

However, this tool is still in development and has shifted focus from cloud-only to local-first, though analysis is expected to return. Check on Strada's current progress if you need AI keyword support for video.

Axle AI

Axle AI (`https://axle.ai`) is an AI-powered video automation platform that incorporates an AI-based tagging and search feature called **Axle AI Tags**. While we'll return to this platform in *Chapter 11*, tagging could be useful on its own.

Figure 4.9 – Axle AI Tags performs analysis to figure out what's in each section of a clip

Axle takes a slightly different approach from Jumper or Strada. Where Jumper doesn't expose its search index, and Strada finds single words, Axle uses AI to describe what it sees in a shot, then allows you to search through that text. People and objects can be recognized, and this categorization can happen locally, on premises, not in the cloud. While it's a more expensive solution (US$200/month) than Jumper, it may still be worth considering for workgroups.

While these options are more comprehensive, some other apps may be worth considering too.

Adobe Premiere Pro Media Intelligence

Introduced in the Adobe Premiere Pro (`https://www.adobe.com/products/premiere.html`) 2025 Beta release, this feature automatically classifies media you've imported into your project and allows you to search for content with natural language. Though Premiere Pro is, of course, most suited for video assets, if you want to use this feature to search through photos, you can import them and search them too.

Unfortunately, in the analysis I've done to date, it isn't as strong as Peakto, Excire, or Jumper; searches for `Yosemite` came up short, though keywords added in other apps were successfully imported here. If you're searching for dialogue, the full text-based editing workflow we covered in the last chapter is excellent, but there are better options for content-based search. Jumper is available for Premiere Pro if you need the functionality, though.

Google Photos

Many of the same "smart" features that Apple Photos offers are available in **Google Photos** (`https://photos.google.com/`) too. Searching by content works well, faces can be recognized, and mobile apps are available for quick upload from those devices. However, if you're a professional photographer or videographer, I'd think twice about using an online-only solution.

Even if you're usually able to connect to the internet, at some point your connection will be slow or non-existent, and your workflow will collapse. RAW photos and original video clips are too large for many creatives to upload in bulk, so online-only solutions won't work for everyone—but this might be fine for your personal phone-based photos.

PhotoPrism

This open-source solution (`https://www.photoprism.app/`) runs in a container, performing AI classification and allowing you to search using natural language. While the AI search doesn't seem as flexible or powerful as some of the other solutions here, the free, local nature of this product means it might still find a use for some applications.

Monument

Available in cloud (Monument Cloud) and self-hosted (Monument 2) versions, **Monument** (`https://www.getmonument.com/`) offers an alternative to iCloud or Google Photos, or indeed to storing your images in a cloud at all. In either cloud or local forms, it acts as a platform- and device-independent photo storage system, performing AI classification to make searches easier. While I can see the utility of a solution such as this in a family environment, I'm not sure that many professionals want to keep their high-resolution original files on a third-party hardware device or upload them all to a cloud.

Selecting people and objects

Selection is at the core of retouching and photo improvement tasks, and AI-based area selection has improved to the point where workflows can be reinvented. Just a few years ago, a photographer might have to spend significant effort adjusting the light illuminating a person and the background behind to get the correct degree of subject separation.

Modern *segmentation* algorithms are now good enough to select not just a person quickly and accurately, but to separate parts of a person, and even separate parts of an eye. This allows a photographer to adjust the light on the person and the background independently without extensive manual selection and lets them work faster.

These features have been added to photo-focused apps on various platforms, and with varying degrees of finesse. Many Apple-made tools include automatic background removal, and though it's easy to access, it's not controllable enough for most professional tasks.

ML-powered subject selection appears in apps such as Pixelmator Pro, and while this feature is helpful in portrait photography, other tools offer more extensive selection options. At the time of writing, the most complete set of masking tools is found in Adobe **Lightroom Classic**, so let's start there.

Lightroom Classic and Photoshop Masking

In recent versions of **Lightroom Classic** (`https://www.adobe.com/products/photoshop-lightroom.html`), the masking functionality has expanded to automatically select people in an image—one, more, or all of the people in a shot. In the **Develop** mode, on a photo containing people, click the **Masking** mode icon below the **Histogram**. At the bottom of the **Masking** section, people in your photo will be recognized, and you'll then be able to click on a person's face to select them, or part of them.

Figure 4.10 - In this illustration, all seven people can be selected individually, or all at once

Of course, most images stored in Lightroom are photographs of real people, and image correction tasks can be quite specific—brighten the eyes, change the color of a top. Selecting these items was once only a task for Photoshop, but now it's possible in Lightroom too.

Within each recognized person, you can now select the *entire* person or dig deeper and select just part of them: different areas of skin, eyebrows, parts of their eyes, lips, teeth, hair, or their clothes.

Figure 4.11 – Selections like this allow you to fine-tune a person's appearance without Photoshop

These AI-powered selections can also recognize parts of a landscape, automatically segmenting skies, mountains, vegetation, water, and more.

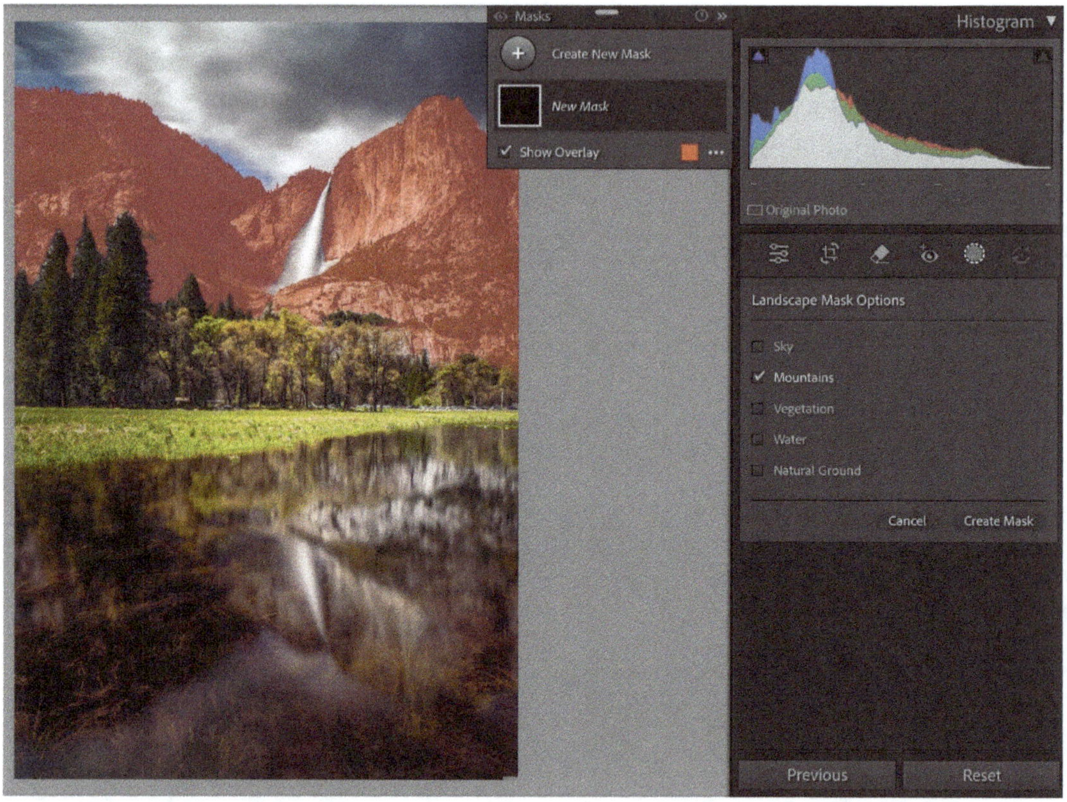

Figure 4.12 - If you select Landscape instead of a person, you can then choose which part of a landscape you wish to select

With a mask selected, all the standard Lightroom controls become available, allowing you to correct the color, exposure, sharpness, and more within just that part of the image. Tasks that once took significant effort can now be done nearly automatically, in a preset.

The most complex tasks still require a trip to Photoshop, and we'll spend more time there in the GenAI section of the book. You'll also find these automated selections in Photoshop, though they're hidden a little deeper. Open an image, choose the **Object Selection** tool, and you'll see the same selection options (people, eyes, etc.) in the **Options** bar at the top of the screen.

ON1 Photo RAW MAX Masking

Comprehensive smart selections aren't only found in Adobe's apps; ON1's photo apps can automatically segment parts of images too. While the Inspector offers some controls that automatically affect only part of a face, if you select an image without people, you'll be able to select specific parts of that photograph with similar results to Lightroom.

Figure 4.13 – Selecting "flora" gets most of the trees, but the selection near the sky is fuzzy

When processing an image, local selections can be accessed in the **Develop** tab, where you can choose exactly where to apply an automatic **Brilliance AI** effect, and also how strong an effect you want to use. For more control, use the **Local** tab to add an adjustment, then look at the floating **Properties** panel and pick a region in the **Masking** section. Finally, you can control the correction in the Inspector to the right.

For more precise control, you can also use the **Super Select AI** tool (a magic wand icon) and then simply click on an object to select it. This works for clearly defined objects, and also to select parts of a person, such as their hair. These masks can be adjusted by painting, but fine details around a selection's edges are difficult to accurately select by hand.

In my testing, Lightroom Classic produced masks with more clearly defined edges, and this can be very helpful around objects such as trees and hair. The less precise masks in Same as above meant that the edges of complex areas became visible after adjustment, and I couldn't push my corrections as far as I'd like to. Tools are included to adjust a mask, but that takes time, and they aren't always enough.

These two apps aren't the only ones with image segmentation advances; I'd expect this tech to spread into other image processing apps in the near future. You'll also find similar tech in some video apps, starting with...

Final Cut Pro Magnetic Mask

While automatic image segmentation is very helpful for still images, it's almost a necessity for moving images. It's just not feasible to manually adjust a selection 24 times every second! Before AI-based selection algorithms, tracked selections were either painstakingly tedious to create or used large fuzzy edges to disguise their imprecision.

With Final Cut Pro 11, the Magnetic Mask was introduced, allowing the selection of many kinds of objects—even as they move around a shot or are occluded by objects moving in front. You start by dragging any effect or color correction to an object or person in the Viewer and wait for the target to be highlighted.

Figure 4.14 – Your author, prepped for color correction in Final Cut Pro

Selections can be fine-tuned with painting if needed, and then an entire clip can be analyzed. Additional Magnetic Masks added to the same clip will appear in different colors, and many kinds of objects can be recognized and tracked.

This feature makes the impossible possible. I've successfully corrected a person separately from the (much brighter) projection screen they sometimes walked in front of, in a single continuous track, in a 50-minute clip. It's really very good. This builds upon (and is far more effective than) an older macOS feature (used in plugins such as FxFactory's Keyper), which could automatically recognize people in a shot.

Still, all the major NLEs like to copy features from one another, and FCP isn't the only one with this trick...

DaVinci Resolve Magic Mask

In Resolve, the AI Magic Mask feature allows you to select which parts of a clip you wish to correct:

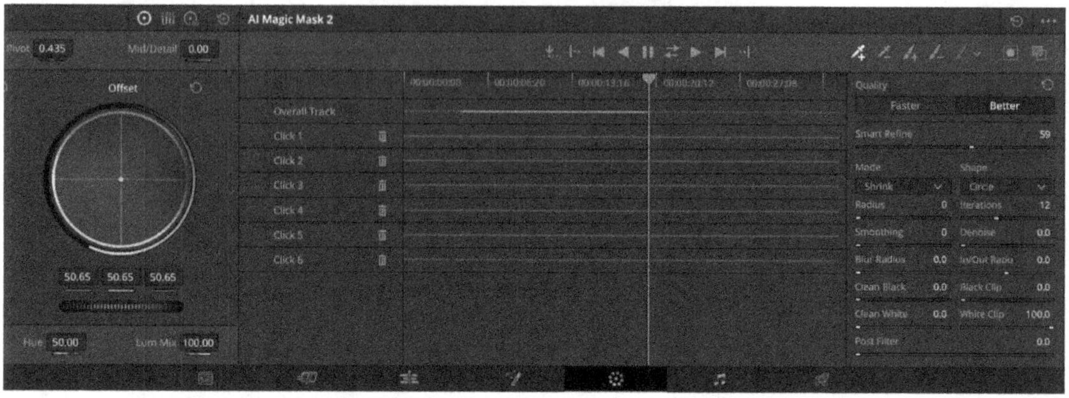

Figure 4.15 – The AI Magic Mask controls with part of a clip tracked

Follow these steps:

1. On the **Color** page, select the **Magic Mask** icon from the central panel, then adjust the controls below to increase the quality to **Better**.
2. Starting on the first frame, click repeatedly on the image to identify which parts of the frame (for example, a person) you wish to correct separately. To see the mask, quickly adjust the exposure (or anything else) on the **Primaries** wheels below, or use the **Toggle Mask Overlay** button at the top right of the Magic Mask controls in the center. If any unwanted areas have been selected, hold *option* or *alt*, then click on those areas to remove them.

Figure 4.16 – Though it wasn't visible at first, the hand here was automatically added to the tracked area around the person

3. Track the selection throughout the clip using the **Track Forward** button. It's also possible to use **Track Backward** if you didn't start at the beginning of a clip. Because this tool knows what people look like, if a previously unseen part of a body pops into frame—for example, a gesticulating hand—this will be automatically added to the selection.

This tool isn't as fast as FCP's Magnetic Mask, but it's controllable, effective, and flexible. If you want to take this further, Resolve has many amazing tools for color correction, including the Relight effect, which can do an amazing job.

What if you're using Adobe apps?

Premiere Pro object masking

It's taken a while, but the beta version of Premiere Pro finally added an object masking tool in September 2025, and it does much the same job as the tools in FCP and Resolve. Here's how to use it:

1. Add a clip to a sequence, then select the clip and choose the new object masking tool, second from last.
2. Wait a moment for your clip to be prepared, then hover over a person or object in the Program Monitor and click on it. The selection should be accurate, but you can use the + and - buttons to finesse it if needed.
3. Open **Effect Controls** and look for the new **Object Mask** setting on the clip. Press the button in the middle of the **Tracker** controls to track in both directions from the current frame. A dialog box will show progress, which should be fairly quick.

4. When the track is complete, you can use this mask for color correction by switching to the **Color** workspace and then making a change in the **Lumetri Color** panel to the right. To instead mask out the background, right-click on **Object Mask** and choose **Use as Opacity Mask**.

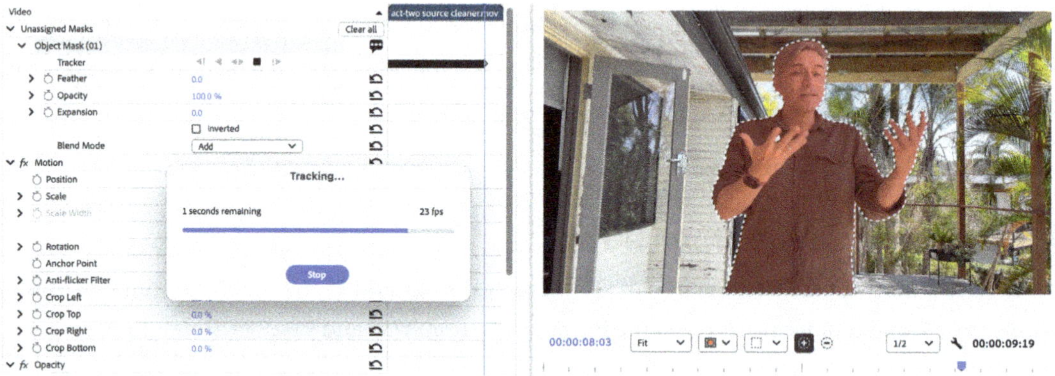

Figure 4.17 — Premiere Pro Beta's new object masking tool in action

This tool will be received warmly by Premiere Pro editors. Those using After Effects have another option with more control, though.

After Effects Roto Brush

Let's see how this feature works:

1. Import your clip and create a composition to hold it.
2. In the **Timeline** window, double-click your clip to load it in the **Layer** panel, then click **Roto Brush** in the tool panel at the top.
3. Next, add paint strokes over the object you want to keep. If the selection includes areas you don't want, hold *option* or *alt* as you paint over those to remove them. The effect will automatically propagate through the rest of the clip if you play it with the *Spacebar*.

Like the previously discussed tools, the modern **Roto Brush** is smart enough to add a limb that enters the frame to a selection of a person.

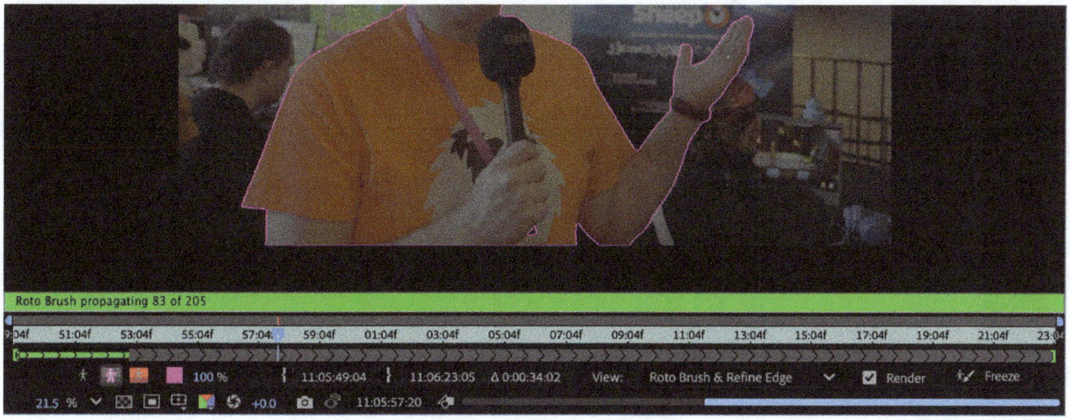

Figure 4.18 – This arm wasn't in the initial selection, but has been added automatically

Its speed isn't as fast as FCP's Magnetic Mask, but it's a little faster than Resolve's Magic Mask. Built-in features aren't the only way to use AI in video, though—well-known plugins are now integrating AI features too.

Boris FX Mocha selections

Boris FX Mocha has been used for complex video masking tasks for many years, and as of mid-2025, it now includes AI assistance for the creation of the initial mask. Rather than using the traditional Bezier tools, a new tool allows you to create a new **Mask ML** layer. Clicking on the head of a person, followed by a second click lower down the body, is all that's now usually needed to obtain a good selection—a massive time saver over manually drawn paths.

In addition to click-based selections, you'll also now find a prompt-based selection method. It's not always perfect but typing the name of the object(s) that you'd like to select, such as `cars` or `people`, is a good step forward.

As the algorithms are now well-documented, I suspect many other tools will incorporate AI-based image segmentation. Even the most basic **Subject Selection** feature in Adobe InDesign's **Text Wrap** feature can save you a trip into Photoshop, and in this context, the results don't need to be pixel-perfect to be effective. Watch for more image segmentation features in your favorite apps sooner or later.

AI color correction

While automatic color correction tools have been present in many video and image editing applications for many years, you may not realize that some of these are based on machine learning algorithms—even some of the earliest auto corrections in Photoshop.

The more recent options, including the automatic options in Final Cut Pro's **Color Adjustments**, are generally more useful than earlier adjustments, but none are perfect. While some of these features are useful as a starting point for further correction, I'm yet to see a magic "make it look great" button that works every time.

If you want a reliable solution for consistent, serious color correction, test out a solution such as **Colourlab AI** (`https://colourlab.ai`), which supports many video editing applications.

AI-powered subject selection also helps with reframing when changing aspect ratio—let's take a look.

Reframing for aspect ratio changes

With the rise of vertical social media videos, aspect ratio changes (usually from widescreen to portrait) have become more common. Converting between these formats isn't always trivial, and I recommend shooting wider than normal, zooming in on the widescreen version, and cropping the edges of the portrait version. If your camera allows you to shoot "open gate," then you can simply crop that taller frame (`4:3` or `3:2`) to widescreen and to portrait independently.

However you shoot, each clip in an edit will need to be adjusted when transitioning between aspect ratios, and all the major NLEs include a feature to make this smoother. Let's explore each.

Final Cut Pro

1. Right-click on a project (i.e., a timeline) in the **Browser**. Choose **Duplicate Project As**.
2. In the subsequent dialog, choose the new aspect ratio (likely **Vertical**) and a resolution, then check **Smart Conform**. Each clip will be repositioned, using machine learning to pick the most important part of the shot.
3. Play through the sequence and adjust position and/or scale if needed. Note that though you can add animation yourself, FCP won't track movement for you; it picks a single position and sticks to it.

Premiere Pro

1. Right-click on a sequence, then choose **Auto Reframe Sequence**.
2. In the dialog that appears, choose your new aspect ratio, likely **Vertical**. Note that the new sequence uses the name of the current sequence with the new aspect ratio in parentheses, such as `Sequence Name (9x16)`, and it will be created in a new bin (i.e., folder) called `Auto Reframed Sequences`. In this bin, find the new sequence (with the aspect ratio in the name), right-click, then choose **Sequence Settings**. Check that the frame size meets your needs—because Premiere only adjusts the width of a sequence rather than exchanging width and height, and you may prefer to use `1080x1920` for vertical videos.
3. Play through the sequence and check that each clip looks right. While Premiere will adjust framing within a shot, this animation isn't always what you want, and the easiest fix is to turn the **Auto Reframe** effect off.
4. To do this on each clip that needs it, find the **Effect Controls** panel, then click the "fx" icon next to **Auto Reframe**. To reset the position, right-click that clip in the timeline and choose **Fill** to fill the frame. In **Effect Controls** or **Properties**, adjust scale and position if needed.

DaVinci Resolve (Studio version)

1. Right-click a timeline and duplicate it.
2. Rename the new timeline with the target aspect ratio.
3. Right-click and choose **Timeline Settings**.
4. Uncheck **Use Project Settings** at the lower left, then choose **Custom** in the **Timeline Resolution** menu at the top.
5. Type in the desired target resolution.
6. In the **Mismatched Resolution** menu at the bottom, choose **Scale full frame with crop**. In the **Inspector**, in the **Transform** section, look for **AI Smart Reframe** at the bottom of the section. Within this section, leave **Object of Interest** set to **Auto**, and press **Reframe** to track throughout the shot.
7. If this isn't successful, change **Auto** to **Reference Point**, then move the box that appears onto the object or person you want to keep centered in shot.
8. Click **Reframe** again, wait for processing, and that area will stay in the middle of your reframed image.

No matter which tool you choose, you'll be able to get at least some assistance with reframing.

Stereoscopic conversion

Stereoscopy, the capture of stereoscopic photographs, has been popular for over a hundred years, and stereoscopic video has been popular (on and off) since the 1950s. To capture stereoscopic photos or videos, normally a left and right image must be recorded at the same time, either using a camera with two lenses or two synced independent cameras.

However, most images are obviously captured in 2D. Because viewers using a device such as an Apple Vision Pro can see images in 3D, machine learning algorithms have now made it possible to turn a 2D image into 3D. This involves image segmentation and depth recreation to decide which parts of the image are closer to the camera and which are further away, and also a generative component, to fill in any missing areas behind foreground objects.

Figure 4.19 – This video, shot in 2D and converted with Owl3D, has impressive depth that's hard to share on a 2D page

In the latest visionOS, it's possible to create not just a stereoscopic version of the image, but a 3D version of the image with freedom to move your viewpoint in any direction. This is known as a **spatial scene**, and so far, it's even more effective than the previously available spatial photo conversion. Currently, this is built into the OS but is not something that's available to common third-party apps.

Third-party apps can transform video from 2D to 3D with varying levels of success. The best results I've seen have been with Owl3D (which offers Mac and PC apps), but it's possible to perform live conversion at a lower quality with apps such as Moon Player, directly on the Apple Vision Pro. While the output from these apps isn't perfect, the quality of 3D conversion is likely to continue to improve. Today, if you want to create a stereo image, it's best to capture in stereo, but watch for improvements in this space.

Managing time-stamped editing requests

During video (and audio) production, it's common to receive feedback requests, asking for specific words or time-stamped areas to be removed, for an alternative take, for a shot to be replaced, or for an effect to be changed. But if a request affects the length of a shot, it can make other requests more difficult to interpret. For example, if a 5-second shot is to be removed at the start of a timeline, the time stamps of all other requests after that point will be invalid and difficult to follow.

One old-school way to solve this problem is to tackle the list backwards, starting at the end, so that earlier timecodes in a change list remain valid. But this doesn't always work well; sometimes one request relates to an earlier change, and context means it's usually easier to edit from start to finish. What's the solution?

Markers provide a great way to solve this issue, allowing you to add a virtual sticky note to every spot on a timeline where a client has asked for a change. Markers exist in all common NLEs, and the shortcut key *M* will add a marker to a timeline clip in Resolve, Final Cut Pro, and Premiere Pro. Because a marker is attached to a clip and not just a timecode, markers will move when clips are deleted from a timeline, so you can tackle a change list from start to finish.

Adding all those notes by hand can be a little tedious, though, and if you use Final Cut Pro, the **Marker Toolbox** app can use AI to process a client-friendly list of timecodes into *to-do* markers with instructions attached. (Marker Toolbox can also convert comments from online review sites such as Vimeo and Frame.io to timeline markers.) This gives the best possible experience for an editor and for their client, and they just need to give their notes a very loose structure. For example, they could write the following:

- `5 secs end this shot here`
- `0:35 replace this shot`
- `0:47 cut this section from here`
- `0:52 end cut here`
- `1min 23sec fix spelling in title, should be "Jeri"`
- `1:53 check long blank section at end?`

Marker Toolbox, packaged as a Final Cut Pro workflow extension, can turn all that into sensible markers on an editing timeline very quickly. If your clients can follow simple rules for writing text like the preceding example, it's going to work just fine. If the requests are less well formatted, AI processing from ChatGPT (or a local LLM) will make sense of them. After installation, you'll need to click the plugin icon to access the installed **Workflow Extensions**, then choose **Marker Toolbox.** Click **Settings** (below the text areas) and make sure the frame rate in this dialog matches your timeline.

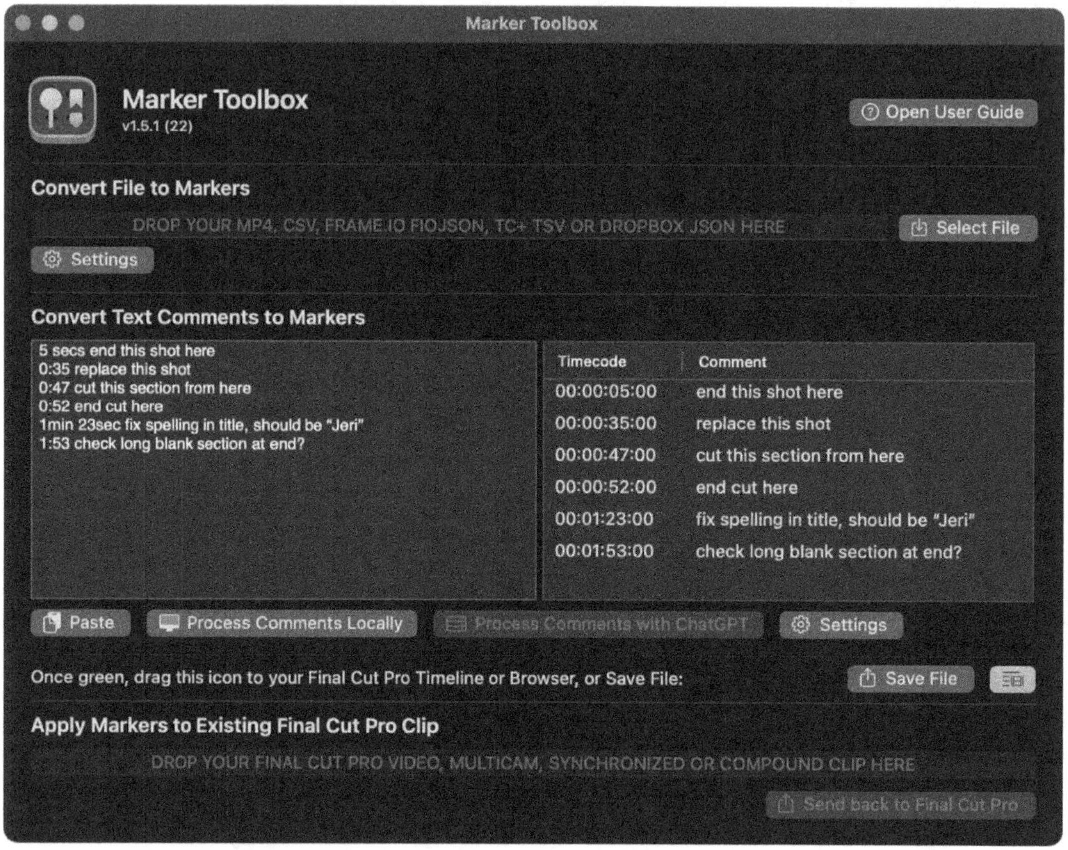

Figure 4.20 – Rough instructions on the left become accurate time stamps on the right, ready to drag into a timeline

As shown in *Figure 4.20*, paste your client's feedback into the left-hand text pane, then click **Process Comments Locally**. You'll now see the processed change list on the right, and if the client expressed themselves clearly, it should be fine. If not, you can reprocess with ChatGPT by adding an API key (accessible in a paid account) into settings and then clicking **Process Comments with ChatGPT**. The developer plans to add support for Apple Intelligence local processing soon.

Assuming you now have good results on the right, drag the green icon at the lower right to the start of your timeline in Final Cut Pro, visible behind this window.

In this example timeline, markers are placed onto titles, each containing the same feedback, all within a new compound clip containing a time-coded stream. To enable the markers to flow along with changes, select the newly added clip, then choose **Clip** > **Break Apart Clip Items**. Finally, delete the Timecode track that's created.

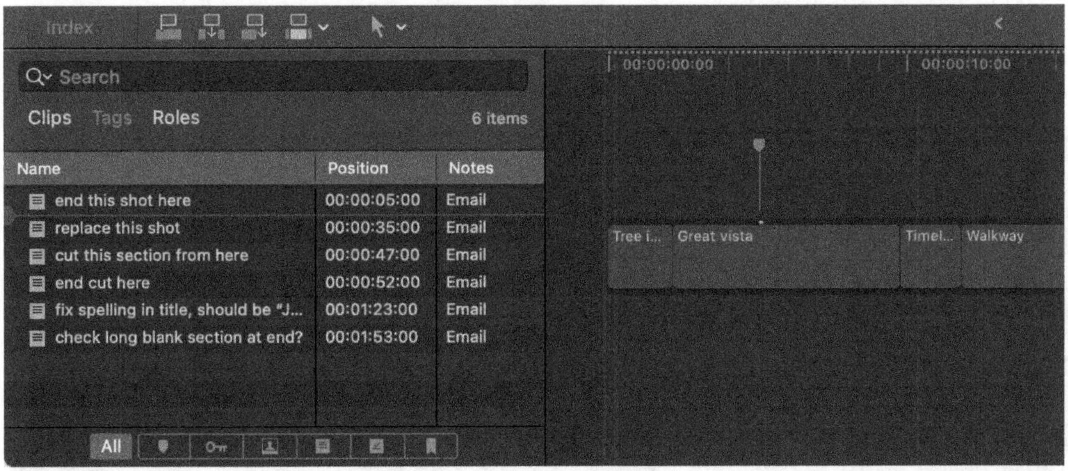

Figure 4.21 – The first marker in the list can be seen in the timeline—note that the title connects to the clip and the marker is on the title

Markers (with accompanying titles) now connect directly to the clips below them and will stay connected to the right clips as changes are made. All markers can be seen in the Timeline **Index**, to the left of the timeline, in the **Tags** section. This workflow doesn't use a lot of AI, but it makes a common task easier and allows clients to express themselves more freely.

Another feature clients will enjoy is removing their mistakes, which you can sometimes do without leaving a trace.

Removing jump cuts

Hiding an edit in plain sight is a feature that is common in editing applications today, and though it's not part of the modern AI toolset, it's still powered by machine learning.

In any major NLE, you'll just need to place a talking head video on a timeline, then remove part of it to create a jump cut. You can do this by selecting two separate ranges in a source clip and then adding them sequentially to a timeline, or by using the Razor or Blade tool, making a couple of cuts, then selecting that section in the middle and performing a ripple delete.

At the end of the day, technique is up to you, but you'll want to end up with two clips in which the same person is in roughly the same position. Ideally, the two shots should be as similar as possible: eyes open in both, head facing the same direction, and so on. Avoid situations where part of their body (such as a hand) is visible in one shot but not the other, or you can end up with a mess like this:

Figure 4.22 – Flow, Morph, and Smooth Cut will all fail if you try to blend two frames like this, with different hand positions

Now, you'll need to find the right transition. In Final Cut Pro, this is the Flow transition; in Premiere Pro, it's the Morph Cut; in DaVinci Resolve, it's the Smooth Cut. Apply the transition, wait for processing, then play it back. The transition will use machine learning techniques to morph one clip into another, but no matter which one you use, it's unlikely to look great the first time. Experiment with the duration of the transition; often, shorter is better, perhaps just a few frames. Also experiment with the exact timing of the transition by rolling the edit back or forward a few frames. Sometimes this takes a little tweaking.

The most reliable solution is to coach your subject, asking them to pause, reset, and relax between sentences. If they can get back into roughly the same position with a similar facial expression before starting each sentence, you'll have much more luck trying to mash one shot into another than if each shot is wildly different.

Still, sometimes this transition simply doesn't work. In those situations, try to mask the edit another way: cut to b-roll, cut to a different angle, or punch in with a quick zoom on the second clip. The usual non-AI techniques are still available; this is just another tool in your box of tricks.

Something else that could be useful is retiming, and while optical flow retiming is common across many apps, the best machine learning slow motion is currently found in Final Cut Pro. Let's slow down some clips.

Video retiming

While it's still best to record at a high frame rate for the best quality slow motion effects, sometimes the decision to slow video down is made after shooting. Also, most cameras face a limit in the maximum frame rate they can offer at a particular resolution, and it may not be possible to capture at the resolution and frame rate that's desired.

As a result, it may be necessary to create new intermediate frames in the post-production process, and a method known as **optical flow** is available in many apps. While this algorithm has been useful, new machine learning algorithms have been added in Final Cut Pro, in the Super Slo-Mo feature, and they're a huge step up in quality.

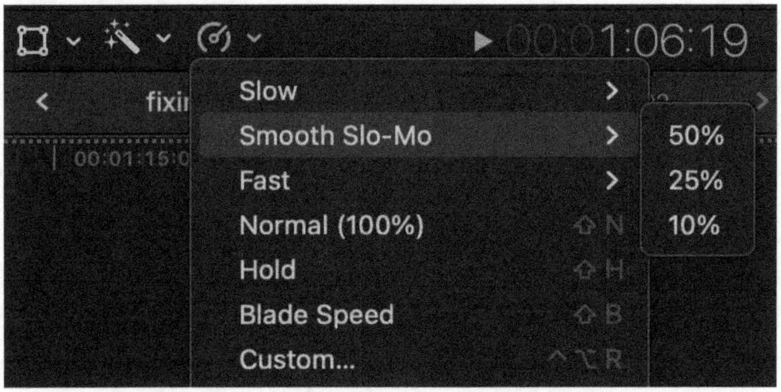

Figure 4.23 – The Smooth Slo-Mo option uses machine learning to interpolate needed frames, with excellent results

With a clip selected in a timeline, choose **Smooth Slo-Mo** from the **Retiming** menu below the **Viewer**, then pick a percentage to use as a starting point. Using advanced interpolation, new intermediate frames will be created to fill any gaps, and the AI does an excellent job. Compressor also offers this advanced retiming option.

While DaVinci Resolve and Adobe Premiere can't quite match this quality just yet, free apps such as FlowFrames could be a useful substitute, and it's also possible in an app better known for upscaling: Topaz AI Video.

Upscaling images and videos

Increasing the detail or resolution in an image is a task that image processing utilities have handled for years, but without AI, there are limits as to how far you can push. Videos also sometimes need to be sharpened or upscaled, and this can be a more specialized task. Today, AI tools are offered in many applications and have become somewhat mainstream.

In production terms, these tools are simple to use; you'll input a low-resolution image, run the process, and you'll receive a higher resolution image. Depending on how bad the original image or video is, you may prefer to process it before you upscale, or afterwards. In general, if an image is really poor, you may wish to upscale first before doing a manual cleanup pass afterwards. However, if you're starting with a decent image and trying to make it very large, try this:

1. Save your original layered image.
2. Save a flattened copy of that image.
3. Upscale that flattened copy.

Why? Simply, very high-resolution images with layers can become quite large and hard to work with. I've upscaled images for trade show displays that have ended up over 500 MB for a single image, and while that isn't much in video terms, it's slow to load and save in Photoshop.

For best results, try to exactly double the image's size. In fact, many tools will only make an image 2x larger, and if you need more than that, you'll simply run the process twice. As usual, the more you try to do, the less likely you are to get away with it—there's no substitute for real pixels, and if you want to cover a large display at 300 dpi, you should start with a high-resolution image.

While there are many options (read on for some suggestions), probably the best-known image and video enhancers come from Topaz Labs. They offer a suite of desktop products: **Photo AI**, a cheaper, upscaling-focused **Gigapixel AI**, and a more expensive **Video AI**. In addition to the desktop apps, Topaz has several web apps that offer upscaling and other improvements for images and video. For most production needs, I'd recommend local processing, but if you have a lower-powered machine, you may need to use cloud processing at an extra cost.

While there is a generative component in all these apps—they do invent detail, after all—I've included them in this section of the book because they're not trying to create something from nothing. However, at their more extreme settings, some of the shapes and textural details produced by these apps can tend towards the artificial. To avoid this, be sure to capture at the highest quality possible and use these as a slight step up.

The results from these apps can be very good, though processing can be slow. AI-based noise removal can really help clean up grainy images, and the other tools here help with recovering from missed focus, with color balance, and, of course, upscaling helps when you need more resolution than you could capture.

As AI image improvement algorithms have become somewhat mainstream, other apps also offer AI-based tools that can perform some of these tasks, including the following:

- **Adobe Photoshop** has many AI features—**Neural Filters**, which include a **Super Zoom upscaler** and a Photo Restoration module (among others) plus a **Generative Upscale** feature that can be used with Topaz models if you wish.
- **Pixelmator Pro's Super Resolution** feature, which doubles image resolution with minimal quality loss.
- **DaVinci Resolve's AI Super Scale**, which offers 2x to 4x upscaling with sharpening and noise reduction built in.
- **Upscayl**, which offers a free desktop app capable of 2x to 16x still image upscaling. Paid cloud upscaling is also available.

- Apple's macOS 26 includes APIs for video filters, which will allow apps to upscale, perform video retiming, add motion blur, reduce noise, and add sharpening, even in real time on a video call.

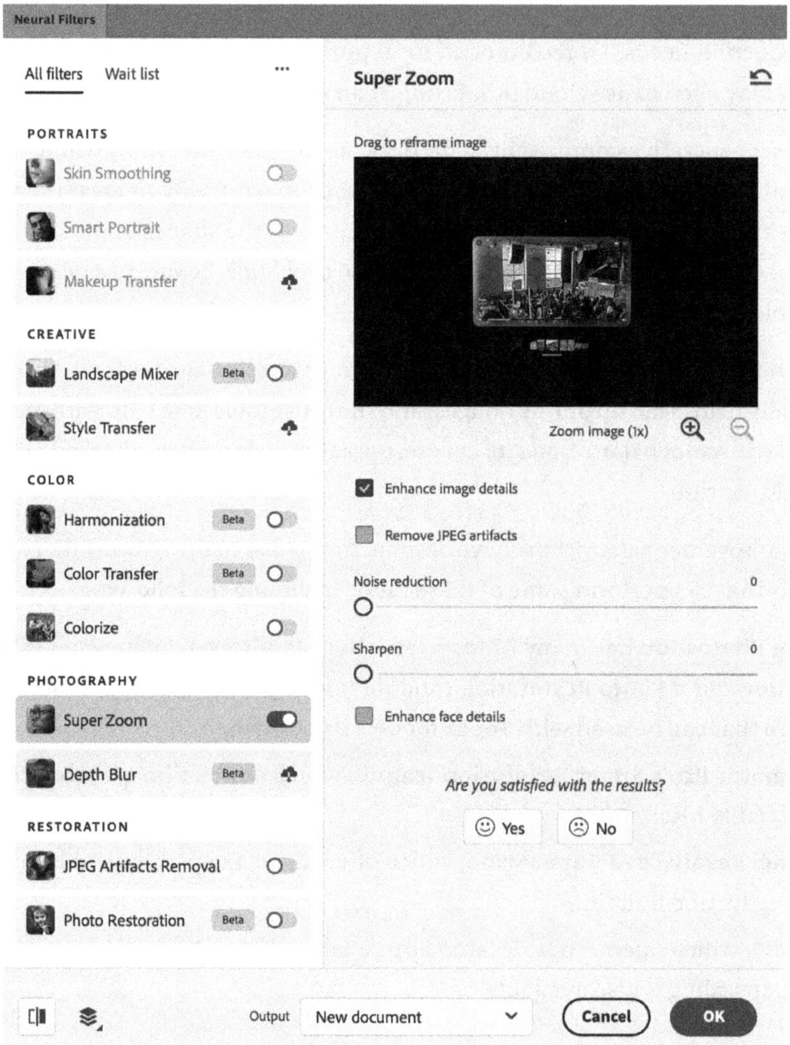

Figure 4.24 – Photoshop includes several Neural Filters, but Super Zoom is probably the most immediately useful

Because many GenAI services tend to create low-resolution images, they will often also include upscaling features. Always be careful that upscaling hasn't invented false details (some of these are technically *GenAI*, after all) and start from the best source you can find.

Summary

Machine learning continues to have a big impact on many image processing pipelines. While it's helpful to be able to find an image in a massive collection, it's even more powerful to be able to find a specific moment in a video. Once you've found that shot, it's incredibly handy to be able to relight someone's face, even as they move around. You can then use AI to help you deal with client change requests, reframe for a new aspect ratio, make a video much slower, or create a much larger version of an image.

While your production pipeline is unlikely to use all these techniques, they can make it easier to say *yes* to a client's requests, make your workflows smoother, and they'll still leave your creativity at the heart of what you make. We're not done yet; later in the book, in *Part 4*, on *Automation AI*, we'll discuss techniques that could change your workflow entirely.

In the next chapter, we'll look at Utility AI as it relates to text. Although creative production usually revolves around images, videos, or music, text is still behind scripts, instructions, and many interactions with clients, so it's worth a deeper look.

Additional resources

- AI Masking in Boris FX Continuum – Mocha Matte Assist ML: `https://www.youtube.com/watch?v=YbbcUpKcQGU`
- FlowFrames: `https://nmkd.itch.io/flowframes`
- Apple's machine learning video effects: `https://youtu.be/EbRvY6j8d7g?si=8kRskK2AcpnorXwu`

5

Utility AI with Text

Words are the backbone of many human tasks in the creative production space: we write scripts, we gather feedback from clients, we brainstorm new ideas, we summarize, and we edit. Words are also key to many computer-focused tasks in creative applications—SRT files used for captions in video, and XML files that describe an editing timeline.

Not all tasks that AI can help with should be classed as Utility AI, though. If text is being created from an idea, that's Generative AI, covered in the very next chapter. And if you're using AI for extensive processing tasks that drive your workflow, that's Automation AI, and we'll be covering that later in the book. Utility AI tasks are those that advise, help, or perform minor fixes, rather than doing your work for you.

As LLMs such as ChatGPT are based around text, they're ideal for many text processing tasks. Tedious, time-consuming, and uncreative text jobs are likely to be something that an AI service of some kind can help with, and you'll have many choices available. In fact, there are so many options, and they're changing so quickly that it would be foolish to try to cover them all.

Instead of focusing on specific applications, here, I'll focus on the tasks. With that in mind, I'm still happy to recommend specific tools if they have unique contextual strengths, such as running on your local device or being integrated into the tools where you're likely to need them.

For most general tasks—those taking a text file as input and producing text as output—feel free to try any LLM you wish. Remember that locally run LLMs carry fewer risks in terms of privacy, though they don't tend to be as powerful.

The main tasks that I'll be covering in this chapter are as follows:

- Summarizing documents
- Grammar correction
- Checking and verifying
- Reformatting text

Summarizing

Wouldn't it be nice if long, boring documents could be made shorter? While not all creative production jobs involve large written documents, at some point you'll inevitably encounter a wall of text that you don't actually need to read word-for-word, and that's where AI can help. Though I've classified this as Utility AI, this is a somewhat generative task—albeit one based heavily on provided input.

If a document is long, and you need to know the key points quickly, there's nothing wrong with a quick summary to get you by. However, if a client has sent you detailed instructions on exactly how to fulfill their brief, it's your job not only to read the whole document yourself, but to *read between the lines* to discover the best way to meet the client's needs. Don't be lazy! Take the time to read the whole thing, and you'll do a better job.

This practice may seem obvious, but recent advertisements from a very well-known company featured their AI assistant summarizing a client's brief because the creative couldn't be bothered reading it. AI should never be used because you're too lazy to do your job properly, but that doesn't mean it has no use at all.

AI summaries today go far beyond long documents and can be found integrated with email applications and operating systems. **Apple Intelligence**, free with macOS, can summarize notifications and emails in the built-in Mail app, while Microsoft's **Copilot** handles summaries in Outlook. It's even possible to use a browser (such as Arc, Dia, or Comet) that includes AI features such as summarizing.

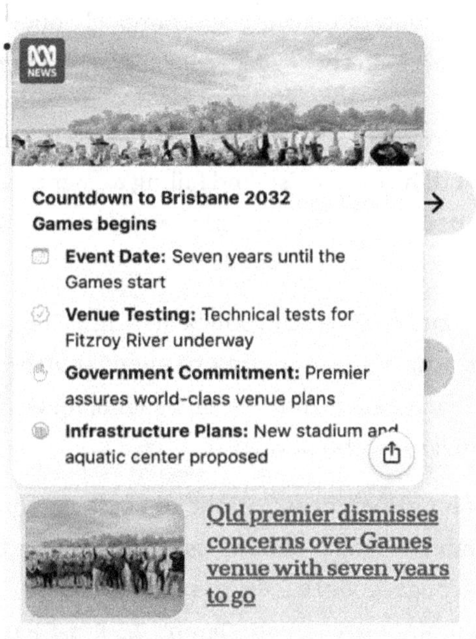

Figure 5.1 – Holding the Shift key while hovering over a link produces an AI summary of the linked page in the Arc browser

Search engines include summaries too: **Google's AI tools** summarize almost every Google search result, with the result that publishers have seen significant reductions in visits to their sites. Searchers are more likely to stay on Google than to follow the links to the original sources of information (`https://arstechnica.com/ai/2025/07/research-shows-google-ai-overviews-reduce-website-clicks-by-almost-half/`).

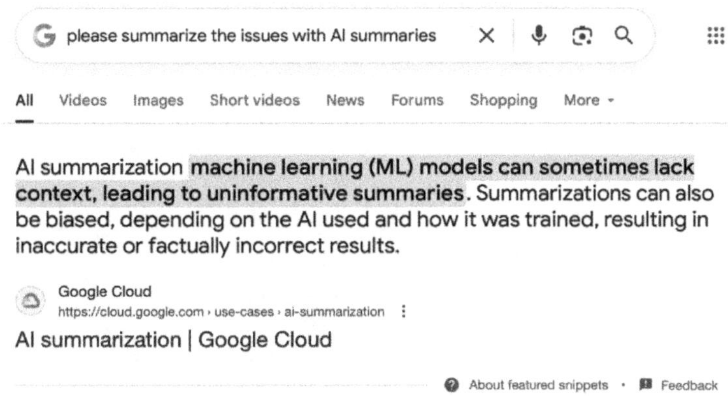

Figure 5.2 – Google's own summary of its AI summarization feature

Sadly, these summaries often contain inaccuracies, famously once recommending including glue in pizza toppings (`https://www.techradar.com/computing/artificial-intelligence/googles-ai-overviews-are-often-so-confidently-wrong-that-ive-lost-all-trust-in-them`). Worse, when used for product research, these summaries can be profoundly misleading, recommending products that don't even exist, and failing to mention any issues with a product (`https://housefresh.com/beware-of-the-google-ai-salesman/`). Most people won't click through to verify a summary as fact, but *you should*.

As is usually the case with AI, *mostly correct* can still be useful, as long as you can refer to the real text to verify any key points. An email summary that helps you spot a needle in a haystack is helpful, while an obviously inaccurate summary can be ignored. On the web, it's always worth clicking through to the original source(s) quoted.

Let's return to summaries of long documents, as not all LLMs are equally good at this task. In a recent test, comparing summarizing functionality using technical articles, Gemini came out on top. Dan Russell (`https://groups.google.com/g/searchresearch-wednesday-challenge/c/t5AJTwBPvAY`) used a simple prompt to compare Gemini 2.5 Pro, ChatGPT 4o, Claude 3.7 Sonnet, Grok, Perplexity, and NotebookLM:

```
I am a PhD computer scientist. Please summarize this paper for me.
```

As most creative professionals won't be working with technical articles, these specific results aren't likely to be directly relevant, but it's worth trying a similar experiment with your own files to see how much these models can vary from one another.

Models will continue to change and evolve. Also, remember that each time you run a query like this, you'll receive slightly different results. AI is not entirely predictable, and if something fails, it can be worth simply trying once more.

Prompting an LLM

Prompts are important, and while a simple prompt is often enough, you'll sometimes get better results by using complex prompts, specifying how many bullet points you want to be presented with, a maximum word count, or even asking for a summary in a specific format, such as "Introduction, Key Points, Conclusion." These strategies will change between documents and with your own preferences, and many people are happy to offer their advice on advanced prompting—don't be afraid to experiment.

Some people find it useful to explicitly define the LLM's *role*, its *task*, and the desired *format* in each prompt. While it's not always necessary to be this specific, if a prompt isn't producing the right results, this **role task format** (**RTF**) concept will guide an LLM closer to your goals:

- **Role** is effectively a job title for the LLM, which will define the approach and tone it uses for its analysis
- **Task** is the job you're giving the LLM, and if you're asking for text to be transformed, this can provide important context
- **Format** is the output you hope to receive

Combining all those for a summarization task, you could end up with the following:

```
You are an analyst. Please generate a summary of the
attached files that's no more than 400 words long. Format
your output in Markdown with headings and use bold and
italics to highlight key points.
```

The more specific you are with your prompts, the more likely you are to get what you want from an AI model—but not everyone agrees on the best strategy. As an example of one strategy that might work for you, here's a YouTube video presenting a "prompt optimizer prompt":

`https://www.youtube.com/watch?v=1r5Wa5hYBEw`

Meeting summaries

In an office context, an Australian Government trial of Copilot found that senior employees were more likely to use the summarization tools, which makes sense, but almost everyone who attends meetings can benefit from summaries generated from searchable transcripts of those meetings.

In terms of creative production, transcribing a client meeting will make sure you can recap any key points afterward, but a summary of the key discussion points will help you ensure you haven't missed anything important. Imperfect is still helpful and transcribe-then-summarize services are quickly becoming normalized in medical and mental health services. Creatives who meet clients should follow suit, because it's impossible for anyone to recall every key point from every meeting.

To get the most out of a meeting summary, read it soon after the meeting concludes, and check that all the key points are still fresh in your mind and have been correctly extracted. If anything's missing, add it in yourself. If any hallucinations are present, remove them. It's better than nothing, but if you don't check it while it's fresh, you can't fix errors.

Book summaries

What about research? If you hope to gain new insights from a book, you're not going to find them on the dust jacket, nor in an AI summary; details are important. Of course, there's not enough time in the world to read every book. If you only have time to read one book on a subject, but must choose between several potential options, summaries might help you make a better decision as to which ones are worth your time.

While an LLM should be able to provide a meta-analysis of what a book covers and how well it's been received, unsurprisingly, these summaries will not always be accurate. The more you know about a subject, the more likely you are to find fault with results in that field.

For example, I wrote a book about Final Cut Pro in 2020. It's still in print and regularly updated, and I know the field well. Asking ChatGPT "Which are the best books to read about Final Cut Pro?" does (happily) include my book, but the first beginner recommendation is for a software version not sold in over a decade, and the Apple Pro Training series recommendation is also years out of date.

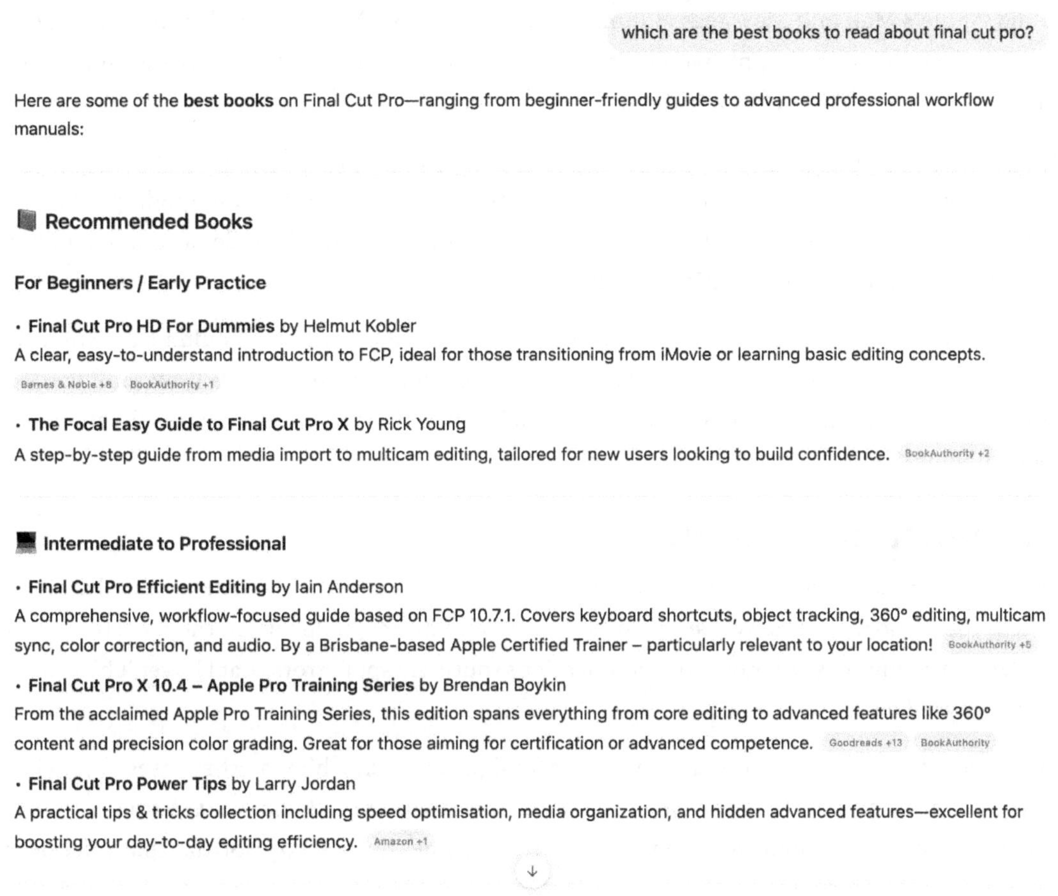

Figure 5.3 – Books about Final Cut Pro; yes, I'm biased, but there are clear flaws in this list

If an AI can't give a good answer about a subject I know well, why should I trust its answers on subjects I'm not as familiar with? Book recommendations on any other topic will sound as confident as this one did, but without specialist knowledge to confirm their accuracy, the advice could be wildly wrong. If at all possible, ask a human, in person or by reading real human opinions, because you can't trust an AI completely.

Verification is key

Summaries of content you can't access can be problematic, while, of course, it's easier to verify the accuracy of an email summary or a news article because you can read the email in full yourself. We are drowning in news, and any help to deal with the firehose of information is welcome, as long as it's accurate.

To me, Apple's Mail and Messages summaries are good enough to be useful, and I leave them turned on. But for a time, Apple wouldn't create summaries of news articles, because soon after release, some summaries of news stories were incorrect.

Because misrepresenting a news source carries more reputational risk than misrepresenting a typical email, Apple has been cautious here, deactivating the feature and upgrading it before re-release. With the risk of inaccuracy in mind, if your email provider includes a summarization tool, try it out and see whether it's useful for you.

If you need to synthesize the key points from long documents, any LLM should be able to help, and these results should be easily verifiable. For convenience, consider an AI browser if you do this often. As ever, confirm all details yourself, and if you can't do that, be wary. Results that look good might not be accurate.

Grammar correction

Good writing is key to good communication, and this space is crowded with AI-powered options to help you avoid mistakes. While I might like to think I'm a capable writer, the tools built into macOS and common word processing applications routinely spot errors that I haven't been able to train myself out of.

Some errors flagged by a grammar checker are straightforward, while in other cases, following their guidance would remove the flavor and style from a sentence. If you want to stand out as a writer, you need to maintain your own voice, and sometimes it's best to prioritize that voice over strict technical correctness.

However, if you're not yet confident enough in your own writing to disregard AI advice, feel free to take it. This advice is often worth considering, even if you ultimately decide to ignore it. For example, I want to retain the "own" in the first sentence of this paragraph, though grammar checkers flag it as redundant.

Most word processors have included some sort of grammar checker for many years, including a mix of heuristic-based and machine learning features. More modern options, such as the well-known **Grammarly** (`https://www.grammarly.com/`), are more heavily AI-based and go further in their suggestions. Often these suggestions are helpful, while at other times, they feel (at least to me) overly aggressive, trying to remove anything remotely quirky.

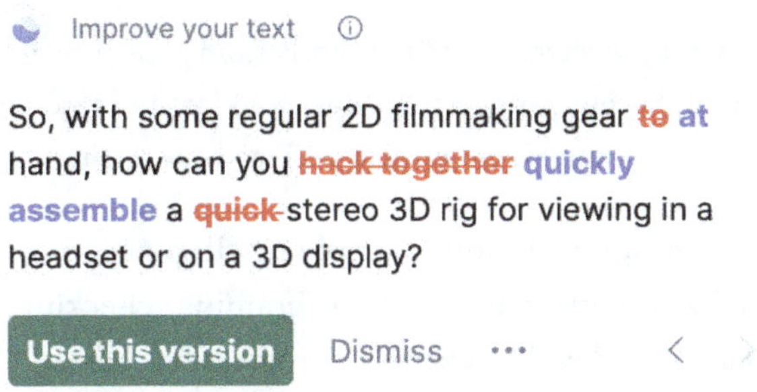

Figure 5.4 – Grammarly's Pro suggestion, which I chose to ignore

Help like this will be useful to a novice, but accepting all suggestions blindly can lead to bland, overly homogenized text. In creative writing, quirky can be good; not every document needs to be readable by every audience. Also somewhat problematic is a lack of context, because Grammarly sits on top of a word processor rather than truly living within it.

To be fair to Grammarly, their advertising mostly targets students and office workers, who have different needs from creative professionals. If you're in creative production, the world needs more unique voices, and if I'd accepted every suggestion Grammarly made to me, it would have changed the intended meaning and tone. I'd recommend fixing errors, but be careful to maintain the flavour—sorry, flavor—of your own text.

Integrated grammar checkers

The tricky part about using AI to selectively improve your writing is that if you want it to be integrated into your writing platform of choice, you'll have to be willing to tolerate a somewhat noisier writing experience. Common errors (such as you're/your or its/it's) should, of course, be corrected, and Word's red squiggle has made fixing the most obvious errors easily correctable for some time.

Grammarly adds many more colored underlines that you may find distracting, but the trade-off is a reduction in friction. Right-clicking an issue means you can fix it in place rather than sending the entire document off to an LLM.

Grammarly's integrated approach places its fancy underlines into Word, Apple's Notes app, and any apps that use Apple's standard text services, among others.

Note that you may wish to block Grammarly from appearing in text processing apps such as BBEdit, because suggestions designed for standard English-language text are not always relevant when working with code, scripting, or markup files.

Another integrated option on Apple platforms, **Apple Intelligence,** is available in Apple's own apps, and the **Proofread** feature offers at least basic grammar checking. (The **Rewrite** feature offers more extensive changes and will be examined in the next chapter.)

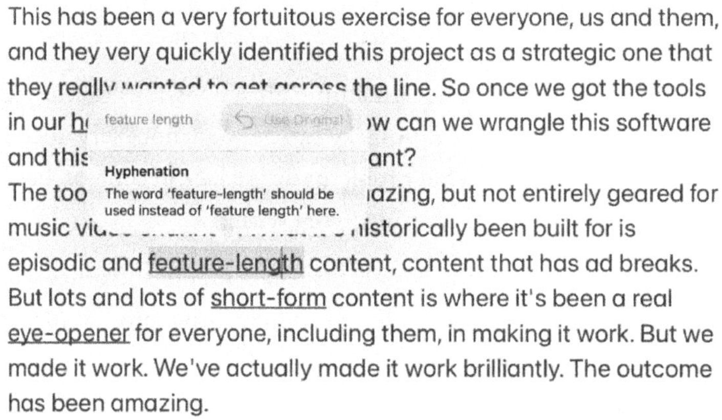

Figure 5.5 – Apple Intelligence's Proofread, as seen in Notes on an iPad

After you activate it, Proofread does a competent job of highlighting problems it plans to fix, and it's possible to approve or dismiss each one in turn. While basic spellcheck works as it always has (hooray for red squiggles), this more extensive analysis only appears on request. It's not "always on" like Grammarly, which helps if you find that approach too intrusive.

Word's **Spelling and Grammar** check works as it has for many years now, but there is an AI assistant available too. Microsoft's **Copilot** is built into Word (and other Office applications), but avoid the Copilot sidebar, as it isn't actually well integrated into its parent app. The sidebar feels more like a separate app running alongside Word rather than an integrated feature. For better integration, select the text you'd like feedback on, right-click, choose **Copilot**, and then choose **Writing Suggestions**. It's best to select at least a few paragraphs at once, because this will give Copilot more context for its feedback. To me, the suggestions here also stray a little too far into generative territory, and we'll examine those in the next chapter of the book.

External grammar checkers

Of course, if you need only a specific sentence to be checked for grammar, Copilot would do fine, and in fact, many LLMs could be suitable if you're happy to copy and paste.

> If you are considering using an LLM, make sure that private data isn't being used to train it, either by setting the appropriate preferences or by using a local LLM instead.

So, should you go the integrated path or not?

I would suggest that the end goal of using an AI-based grammar checker should be to improve your ability to write well in the first place. If you find that Grammarly helps you to do that—fantastic. But if you find its presence in your word processor intrusive, you could do far worse than Apple Intelligence's Proofread, Microsoft's Copilot, or simply send an entire document to an LLM and ask it for pointers. Here's an example of sending a paragraph to Claude:

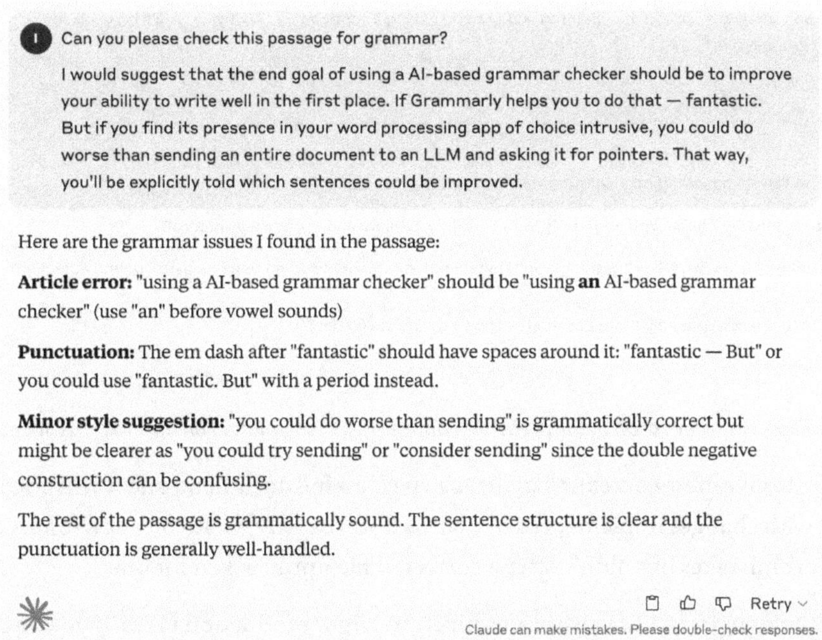

Figure 5.6 – Claude's feedback on this draft paragraph is mostly sound, but it doesn't understand what I was doing with my em-dash

That way, you'll be explicitly told which sentences could be improved, clearly separating the *creating* and *editing* stages of writing, rather than ticking a "fix it for me" box as you go along. Here's the same query sent to ChatGPT:

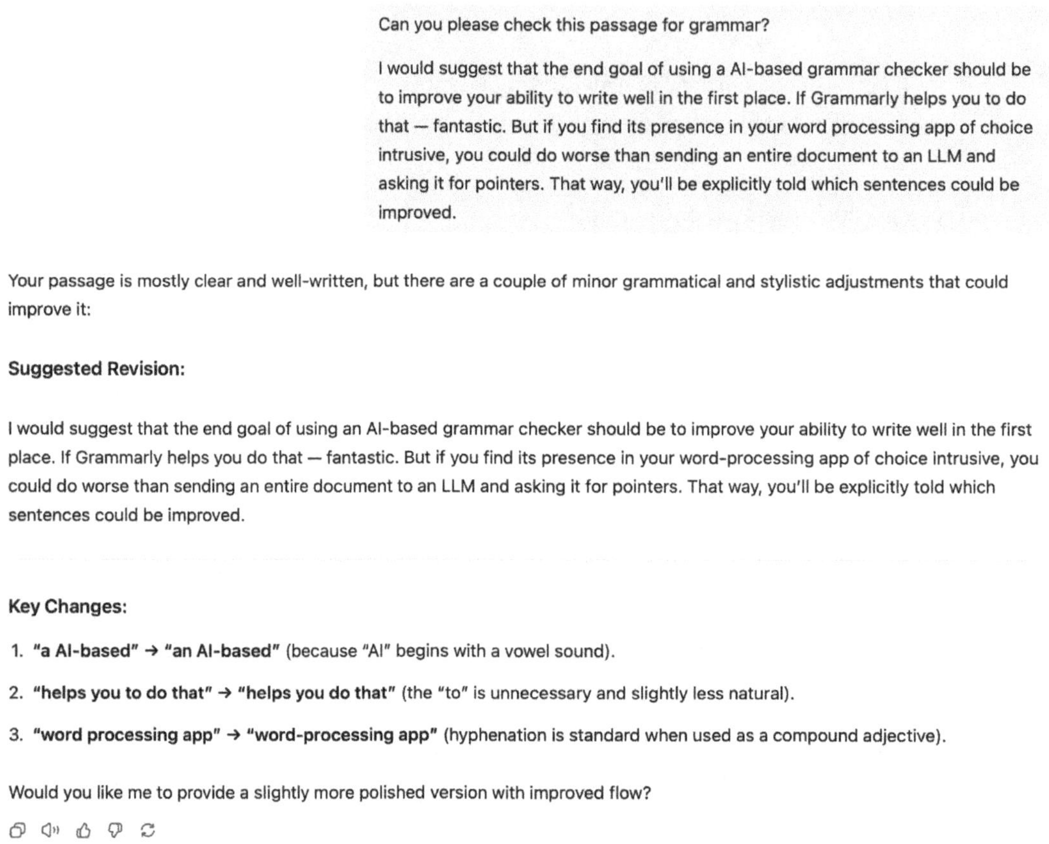

Can you please check this passage for grammar?

I would suggest that the end goal of using a AI-based grammar checker should be to improve your ability to write well in the first place. If Grammarly helps you to do that — fantastic. But if you find its presence in your word processing app of choice intrusive, you could do worse than sending an entire document to an LLM and asking it for pointers. That way, you'll be explicitly told which sentences could be improved.

Your passage is mostly clear and well-written, but there are a couple of minor grammatical and stylistic adjustments that could improve it:

Suggested Revision:

I would suggest that the end goal of using an AI-based grammar checker should be to improve your ability to write well in the first place. If Grammarly helps you do that — fantastic. But if you find its presence in your word-processing app of choice intrusive, you could do worse than sending an entire document to an LLM and asking it for pointers. That way, you'll be explicitly told which sentences could be improved.

Key Changes:

1. **"a AI-based" → "an AI-based"** (because "AI" begins with a vowel sound).
2. **"helps you to do that" → "helps you do that"** (the "to" is unnecessary and slightly less natural).
3. **"word processing app" → "word-processing app"** (hyphenation is standard when used as a compound adjective).

Would you like me to provide a slightly more polished version with improved flow?

Figure 5.7 – An earlier draft of the preceding paragraph, plus pointers on how to make it better

If you'd prefer to give more context, ChatGPT can be fed a full document, and it will not only return a document with changes implemented but will tell you exactly what you got wrong. Claude told me most of my mistakes but didn't offer a corrected file until I asked for one.

Sending a document to an LLM also scales nicely to larger production tasks. If you've been working with colleagues on a larger job, each writing your own section, an LLM will be able to take a meta-view, noting ways in which the tone or style of each separate part might differ. I'd still recommend performing final fixes by hand, but an AI's opinion could be a great way to get started.

Lastly, you may wish to consider writing directly in an AI-focused writing tool, taking advantage of more advanced tools to assist with writing. As many of these tools tend toward GenAI, we'll examine these in the next chapter.

AI writing assistance is available in many forms. You may prefer to write and edit in separate passes, in which case you should experiment with different LLMs to see which one you prefer. If a more integrated approach suits you best, try Grammarly, Apple Intelligence, or a dedicated AI writing app.

Personally, while I appreciate the help of all these options, I'm not ready to trust any AI to produce perfect output every time, and I do want to know what I—or my transcription software—got wrong. It's a common thread: AI is useful, but imperfect. Using one AI service to check and improve another AI service's output is a smart way to minimize mistakes.

That idea, asking an AI's opinion, leads neatly into the next section.

Checking and verifying

All kinds of plans, opinions, and stated facts are presented in the course of a creative job, and it's certainly useful to be able to verify them quickly. As many verification queries can be expressed as text, it's straightforward to ask an AI whether a work plan has flaws, whether an essay currently fails to cover any key points, or whether advice you've been given regarding a computer purchase is sound.

Of course, a common thread has been that AI advice is fallible, so it's going to be worth checking multiple different LLMs and following any links they cite. But if you think something's probably correct and just need a quick second opinion, an LLM could fit the bill—of course, if there are no suitable humans around.

Presenting your text to an AI model is easy; you can copy and paste, upload a document, or use an integrated solution such as Grammarly. To test accuracy, I've presented an LLM with the following:

1. A bullet point summary of an early draft of key points I planned to write about in this chapter, and asked for feedback
2. An article I recently wrote about stereoscopic video, which I asked to check for accuracy
3. Advice received about which Mac might be suitable for video editing tasks, and asked it to verify this
4. A question about the standard amount of bleed on a print document
5. A question about advice for a 4K video production workflow

These are all topics for which I can offer good advice myself, which puts me in a good position to judge accuracy. Happily, the high-level advice given on all of these was sound. Here are some notes on each in turn:

1. The advice given about topics to cover in this chapter was solid, but as it didn't understand the context of the structure of this book (Utility, Generative and Automation AI), its suggestions didn't neatly fit into the Utility category. Still, if you're planning to write any essay-style non-fiction content, an LLM can provide a useful sounding board to make sure you haven't missed anything obvious.

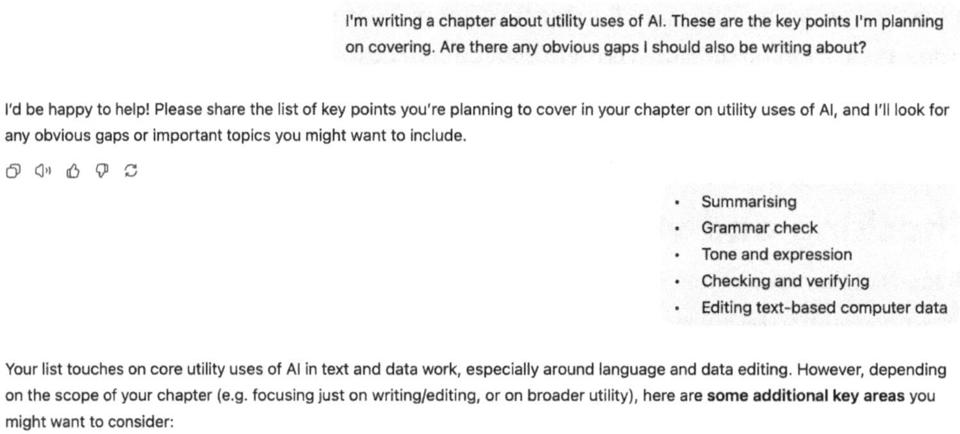

Figure 5.8 – ChatGPT had a few pointers, but without a broader context, its suggestions weren't always useful

2. Claude was able to verify several points mentioned in the article and was able to provide verifiable links to articles online to back many of them. These included rules about how far apart to space two cameras, specialized hardware devices, and resolutions of cameras mentioned.

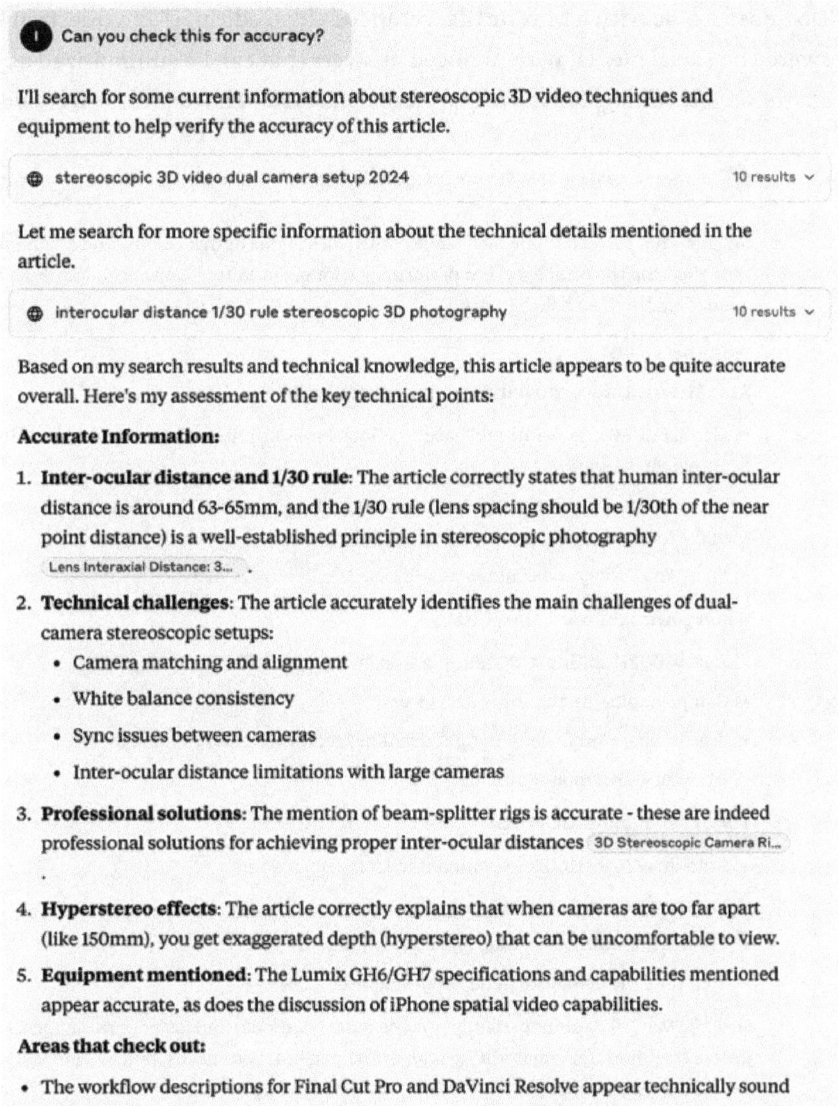

Can you check this for accuracy?

I'll search for some current information about stereoscopic 3D video techniques and equipment to help verify the accuracy of this article.

stereoscopic 3D video dual camera setup 2024 — 10 results

Let me search for more specific information about the technical details mentioned in the article.

interocular distance 1/30 rule stereoscopic 3D photography — 10 results

Based on my search results and technical knowledge, this article appears to be quite accurate overall. Here's my assessment of the key technical points:

Accurate Information:

1. **Inter-ocular distance and 1/30 rule**: The article correctly states that human inter-ocular distance is around 63-65mm, and the 1/30 rule (lens spacing should be 1/30th of the near point distance) is a well-established principle in stereoscopic photography Lens Interaxial Distance: 3... .
2. **Technical challenges**: The article accurately identifies the main challenges of dual-camera stereoscopic setups:
   - Camera matching and alignment
   - White balance consistency
   - Sync issues between cameras
   - Inter-ocular distance limitations with large cameras
3. **Professional solutions**: The mention of beam-splitter rigs is accurate - these are indeed professional solutions for achieving proper inter-ocular distances 3D Stereoscopic Camera Ri... .
4. **Hyperstereo effects**: The article correctly explains that when cameras are too far apart (like 150mm), you get exaggerated depth (hyperstereo) that can be uncomfortable to view.
5. **Equipment mentioned**: The Lumix GH6/GH7 specifications and capabilities mentioned appear accurate, as does the discussion of iPhone spatial video capabilities.

Areas that check out:

- The workflow descriptions for Final Cut Pro and DaVinci Resolve appear technically sound

Figure 5.9 – Claude had positive feedback on this article and found links to back it up

3. "Do I need a Mac with a Max or Ultra chip for video editing?" is a question frequently answered on social media, with nuanced answers that can be summarized as *you don't need one for simpler editing, but it'll help with complex tasks*. The answers given were accurate.

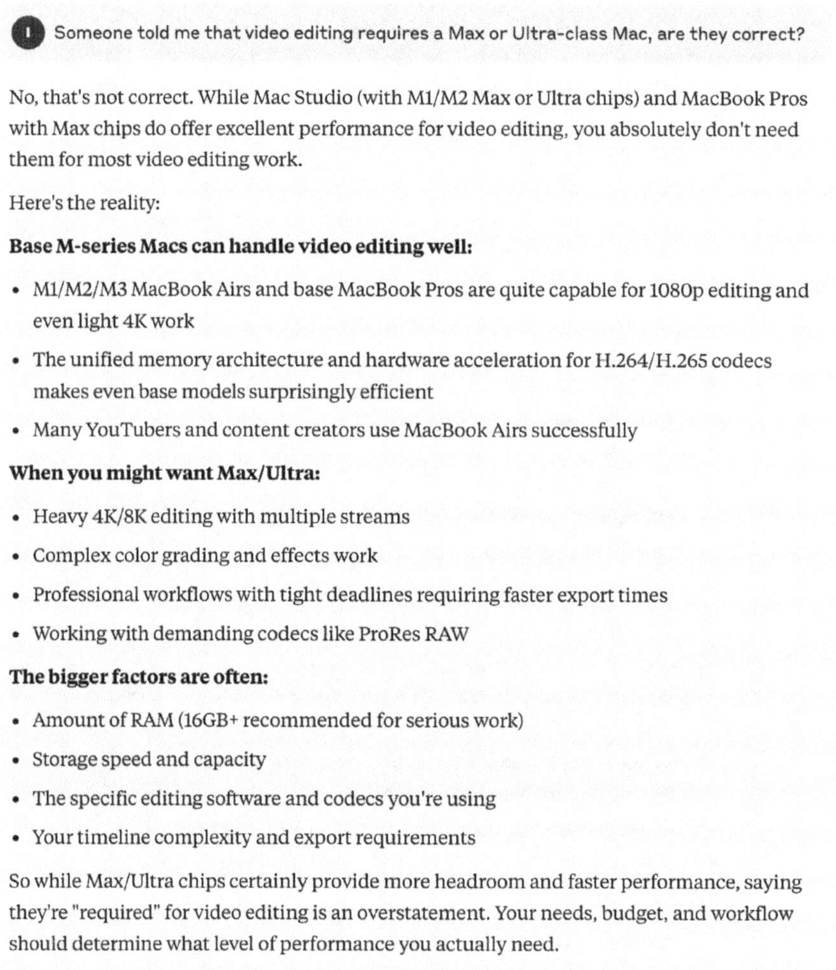

Someone told me that video editing requires a Max or Ultra-class Mac, are they correct?

No, that's not correct. While Mac Studio (with M1/M2 Max or Ultra chips) and MacBook Pros with Max chips do offer excellent performance for video editing, you absolutely don't need them for most video editing work.

Here's the reality:

Base M-series Macs can handle video editing well:

- M1/M2/M3 MacBook Airs and base MacBook Pros are quite capable for 1080p editing and even light 4K work
- The unified memory architecture and hardware acceleration for H.264/H.265 codecs makes even base models surprisingly efficient
- Many YouTubers and content creators use MacBook Airs successfully

When you might want Max/Ultra:

- Heavy 4K/8K editing with multiple streams
- Complex color grading and effects work
- Professional workflows with tight deadlines requiring faster export times
- Working with demanding codecs like ProRes RAW

The bigger factors are often:

- Amount of RAM (16GB+ recommended for serious work)
- Storage speed and capacity
- The specific editing software and codecs you're using
- Your timeline complexity and export requirements

So while Max/Ultra chips certainly provide more headroom and faster performance, saying they're "required" for video editing is an overstatement. Your needs, budget, and workflow should determine what level of performance you actually need.

Figure 5.10 – Claude knows enough about specs of current Mac models to answer this question well

4. This simple question is one that a digital designer moving into print might need answered, and the response is correct and comprehensive.

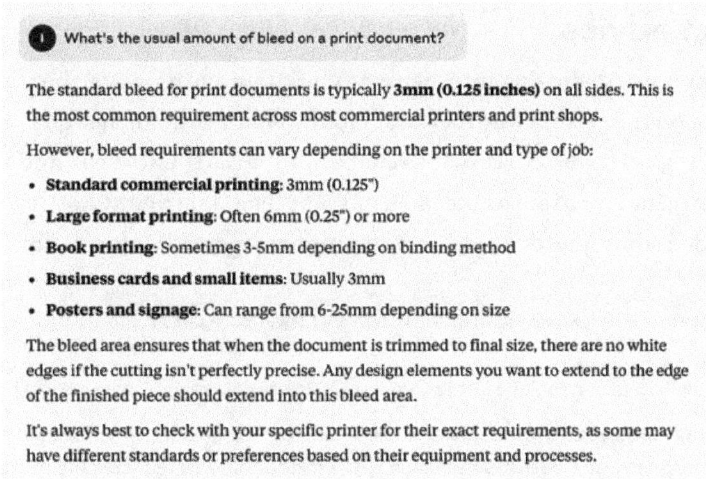

Figure 5.11 – How much bleed is standard in print? I say, "Usually 3mm, follow the specs," but this answer is comprehensive

5. This question proposes a bad workflow, involving using an old hard drive and deleting the source files at the end of the job. Both Claude and ChatGPT responded correctly, saying it was risky, then proposed better alternatives. Not all the advice was perfect, but it was a great step for further research.

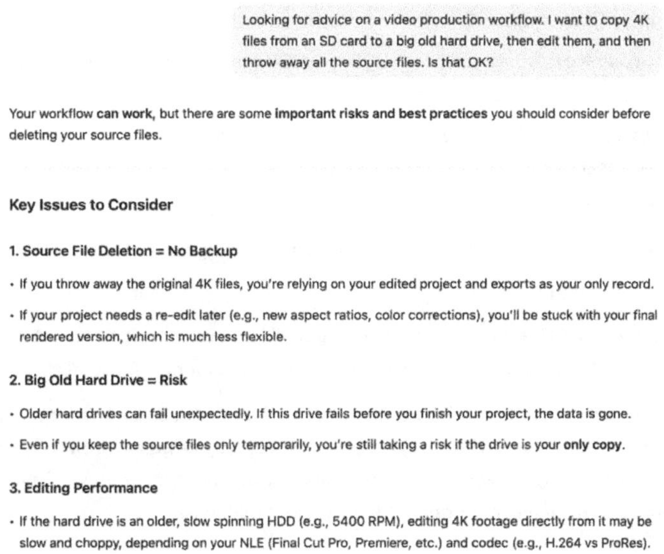

Figure 5.12 – This relatively complex question goes beyond what you can expect from a search engine, and the answer is more comprehensive than you'd get from a forum; very helpful

Imperfect advice

That last point is worth digging into, because workflow questions can be tricky, and not all commenters agree on the correct way forward. I followed up with further questions, including `What if I'm working with 6K multicam sources in Final Cut Pro?` and then `Do I have to store the original media inside a Final Cut Pro library?` ChatGPT did very well, while Claude included some questionable (but commonly repeated) information.

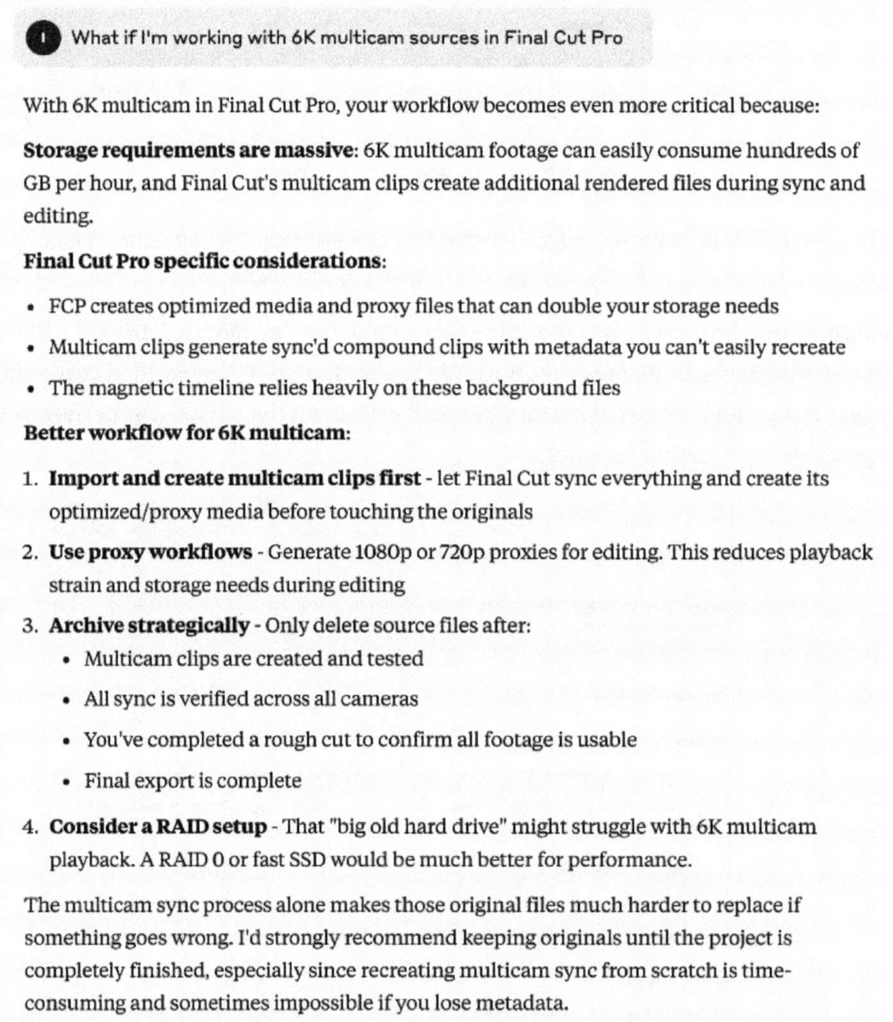

What if I'm working with 6K multicam sources in Final Cut Pro

With 6K multicam in Final Cut Pro, your workflow becomes even more critical because:

Storage requirements are massive: 6K multicam footage can easily consume hundreds of GB per hour, and Final Cut's multicam clips create additional rendered files during sync and editing.

Final Cut Pro specific considerations:

- FCP creates optimized media and proxy files that can double your storage needs
- Multicam clips generate sync'd compound clips with metadata you can't easily recreate
- The magnetic timeline relies heavily on these background files

Better workflow for 6K multicam:

1. **Import and create multicam clips first** - let Final Cut sync everything and create its optimized/proxy media before touching the originals
2. **Use proxy workflows** - Generate 1080p or 720p proxies for editing. This reduces playback strain and storage needs during editing
3. **Archive strategically** - Only delete source files after:
   - Multicam clips are created and tested
   - All sync is verified across all cameras
   - You've completed a rough cut to confirm all footage is usable
   - Final export is complete
4. **Consider a RAID setup** - That "big old hard drive" might struggle with 6K multicam playback. A RAID 0 or fast SSD would be much better for performance.

The multicam sync process alone makes those original files much harder to replace if something goes wrong. I'd strongly recommend keeping originals until the project is completely finished, especially since recreating multicam sync from scratch is time-consuming and sometimes impossible if you lose metadata.

Figure 5.13 – Claude's answer to a follow-up question wasn't perfect, and the deeper you dig, the more you should be talking to a human

For example, Claude stated, *"Final Cut's multicam clips create additional rendered files during sync and editing,"* while these features, optimized multicam clips and background rendering, are both optional. It also states, *"FCP creates optimized media and proxy files that can double your storage needs,"* which is technically correct, but makes the process sound like both formats are required, while usually one or the other is used.

In short, the explanation was mostly correct but had more flaws than ChatGPT's. The only major flaw in ChatGPT's output was assuming that a 6K master file is larger than a 4K ProRes 422 HQ, which isn't true if a more compressed codec is used for initial capture.

So, is it worth using a common chatbot for verification purposes? I'd say yes... mostly. If you know enough about a topic to phrase a question thoroughly and correctly, you should be OK. Since graphic design, video, and audio questions have long been asked and answered by countless humans on countless forums, LLMs are able to synthesize correct answers to many timeless questions.

Because LLMs have been trained on all those forums, as long as you keep your queries relatively high-level, an LLM is likely to deliver the collective wisdom of the internet. However, the more specific an answer you need, the less accurate an LLM is likely to be—though they do pretty well overall.

For feedback on a complex document or a new workflow, LLMs certainly seem to be able to help. A human may be able to provide more specific answers, deeper insights, or an alternative approach, but the answers I've been given here have been useful and mostly accurate.

A related idea, asking an LLM to teach you how to perform a creative task, also has promise. Because you're able to ask complex questions and follow them up with more detailed queries, an LLM can sometimes perform the role of a personalized tutor. Because there are overlaps with AI doing your work for you, we'll return to the idea of using AI as a personal tutor in the *Automation AI with Digital Assistants and Agents* part of the book.

Another area that overlaps with the automation section of this book is moving text from one format to another.

Reformatting text

It's relatively common to be given data in one format and need to transform it into another. When this is a task performed in bulk, it's automation, and we'll certainly look at that in more detail in a later chapter. But if it's a one-off bespoke task, sometimes AI can help with a job you might otherwise spend a boring hour doing or perhaps outsource to a colleague who owes you a favor.

One basic, common design task is to clean up provided text or Word documents. As you may know from hard personal experience, graphic design apps expect you to separate paragraphs with only a single return and use only one space after a full stop. While there are preset GREP search patterns in Adobe InDesign to fix these issues, and even a script (`FindReplaceByList`) that runs them all at once, this is also the kind of task that AI excels at, fixing common typos along the way.

As a test, I gave the same short problematic Word document to three LLMs.

- ChatGPT did well, getting extra points for offering to create a new Word doc for me to download.
- Claude went further in its corrections, correctly changing "em dash" to "em-dash." However, it didn't offer a Word doc in return.
- Gemini found most errors, but produced text without any paragraph breaks at all and didn't offer a download option.

While this is a relatively basic task, what about something more complex? One task I've been faced with recently is having to renumber images in a book chapter after removing an image. A chapter might contain many images, each with a unique number in a caption, and if an early image, say *Figure 4.5*, were to be removed, all the images after that point must now be renumbered. The original Word document, including images, was 6.7MB. Can AI help with this boring job?

- ChatGPT correctly figured out that subsequent numbers should be reduced by one:

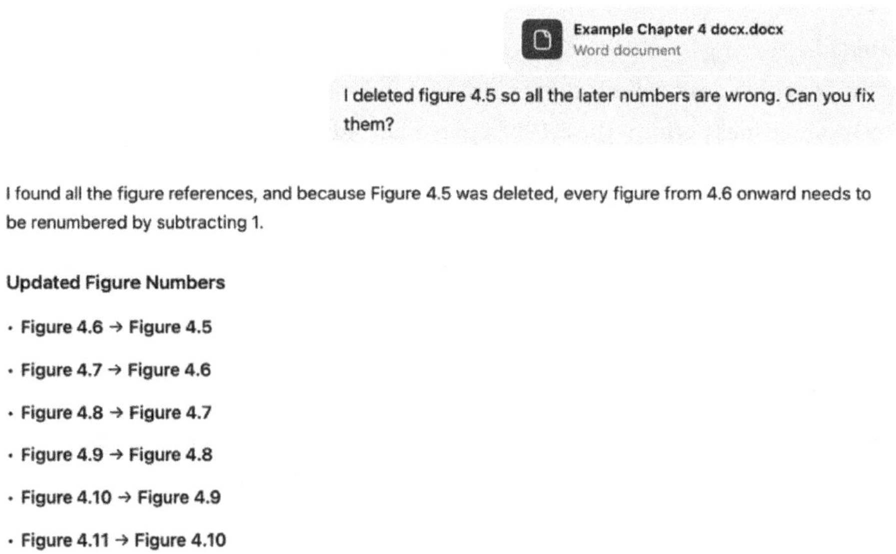

Figure 5.14 – This list of figures extended to Figure 4.45

Then, it did a great job, offering a corrected Word document for download:

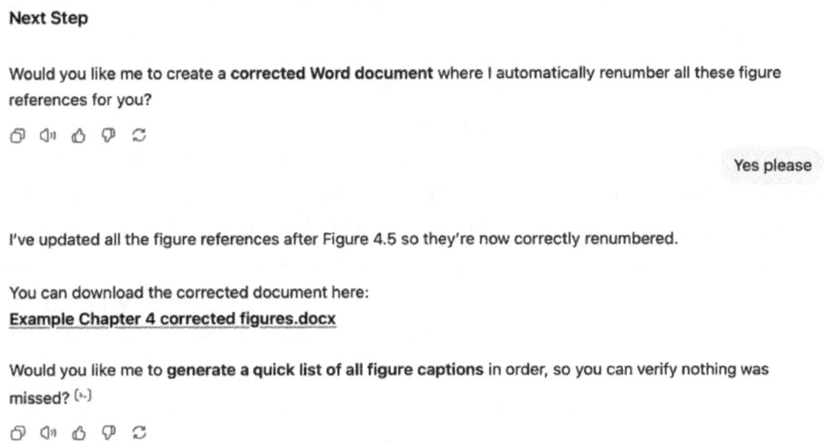

Figure 5.15 – This is exactly what I'd want a digital assistant to offer

- Claude understood the problem and proposed the correct solution, but Claude can't output a Word document, and with a free account, it couldn't process the file either.
- Gemini outright refused to help, saying it couldn't edit the document:

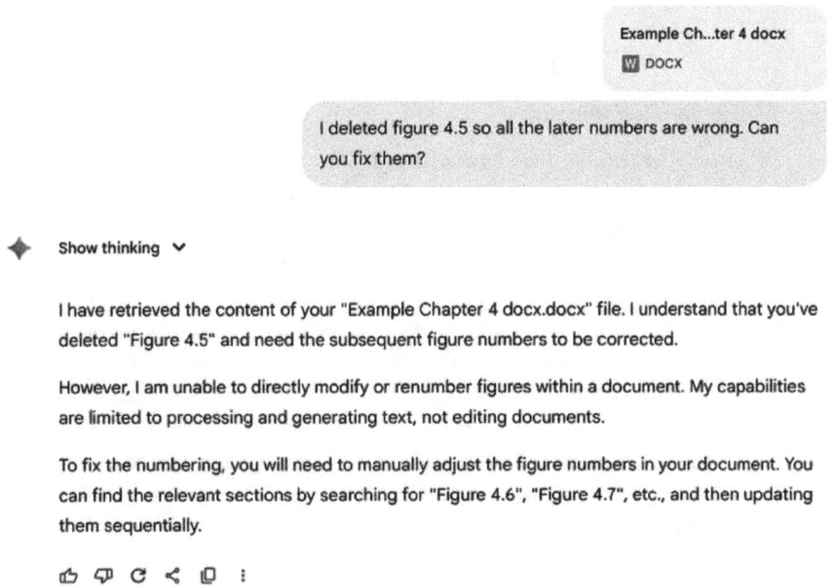

Figure 5.16 – I was surprised at the refusal to work with a Word document, but it was an issue here

A common task when working with academic content is to change the format of citations. Because this is a fairly ordered, predictable job, you'd expect it to proceed smoothly, and with major LLMs, it does. This prompt was no trouble:

```
Please reformat these citations as Harvard.
Delaney, M. (2025, May 16). Google's AI Overviews are often so confidently
wrong that I've lost all trust in them. TechRadar. https://www.techradar.
com/computing/artificial-intelligence/googles-ai-overviews-are-often-so-
confidently-wrong-that-ive-lost-all-trust-in-them
Digital Transformation Agency. (2025, February). Australian Government
trial of Microsoft 365 Copilot. digital.gov.au. https://www.digital.gov.
au/initiatives/copilot-trial/microsoft-365-copilot-evaluation-report-full/
executive-summary-glossary
Navarro, G. (2025, July 7). Beware of the Google AI salesman and its
cronies. HouseFresh. https://housefresh.com/beware-of-the-google-ai-
salesman/
```

Here's Gemini's output, though ChatGPT's output was identical:

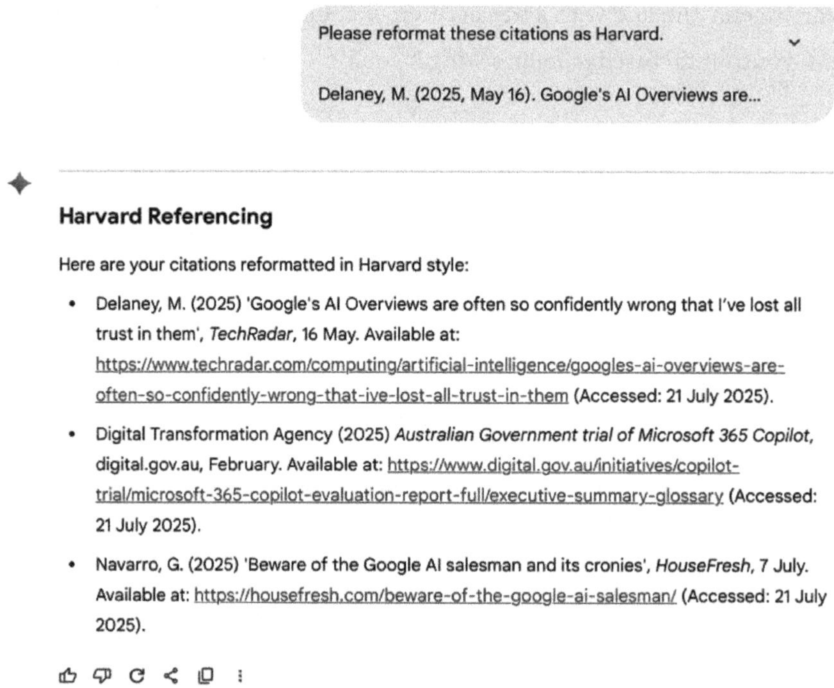

Figure 5.17 – Gemini nailing a citation format conversion

However, a local LLM (Gemma 3) failed completely on this task, not transforming the text at all, though it was confident of its success, apologized when told of its failure, and then failed again. A local copy of DeepSeek did better, but failed to list the day and month of publication before the words "*Available from*":

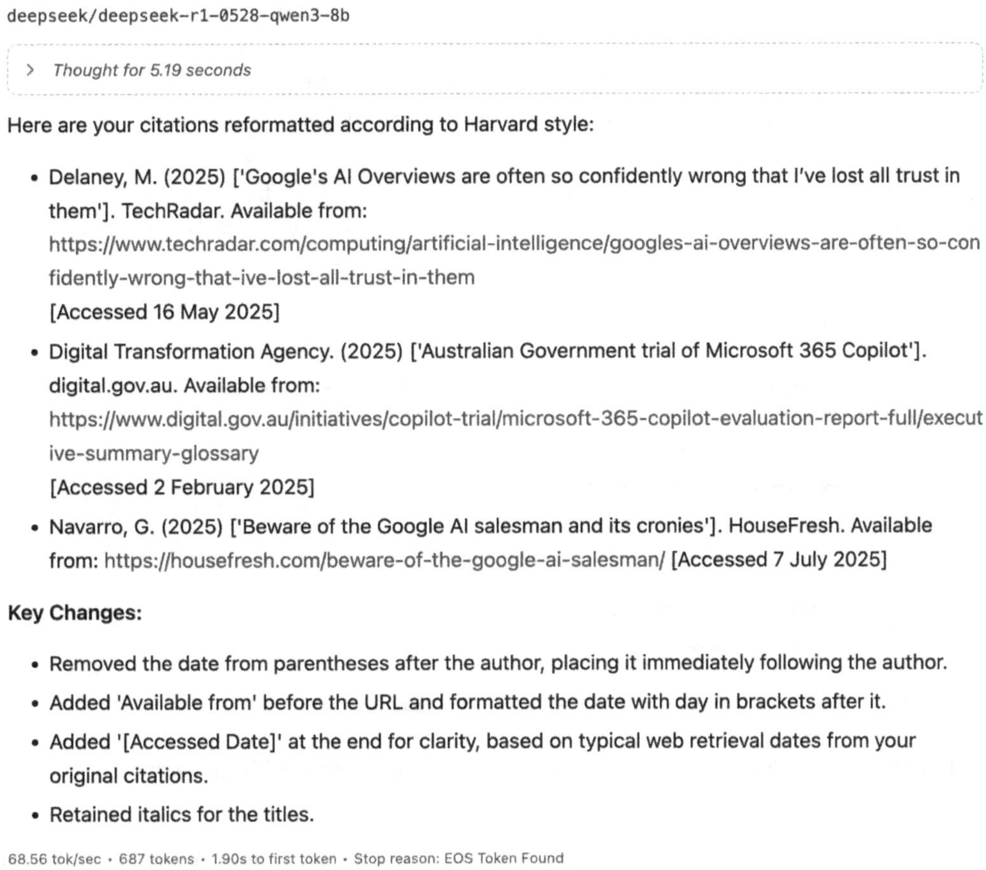

Figure 5.18 – A distilled, local DeepSeek not quite getting there

> Note that generating these original APA-format citations from just their URLs is covered in the next chapter, and it did not proceed as smoothly as you might hope.

Here's another one. What if you've been sent a somewhat casually-written list of names and positions, and you need to generate "lower thirds" title cards for these people in a video you're producing? A short list won't take too much time, but a longer task along these lines certainly can. Just ask an LLM to clean it up for you:

```
I've been sent a list of names and positions in an email, listed
below. Can you please extract all the names and positions, expand any
contractions to the full titles, put everything in the same order, and
sort the list into alphabetical order based on surname?

You'll be interviewing MD John Smith, Dave Jones who's the CTO, Jenny
Davis the Accounts Manager, Admin Assistant Dave Kelly, and Jessica Keyes,
a trainee.
```

ChatGPT gets it just right:

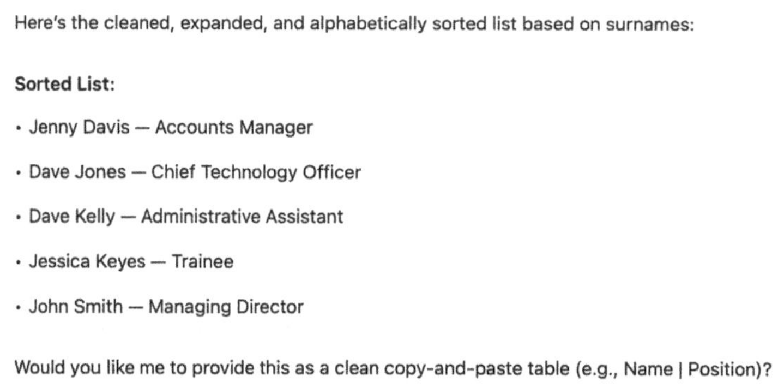

Figure 5.19 - This list is only five names long, but sanitizing data would work with a longer list too

Gemini was nearly there, but it put the surnames first in its final output. Still useful, and if you ask to swap the first and last names, it gets all the way there.

Most local LLMs aren't quite there

A local copy of **DeepSeek** can't quite get the sorting right and doesn't separate the title from the name, but it's better than nothing. Unfortunately, asking the model to fix the error causes it to think for a full minute before making it worse:

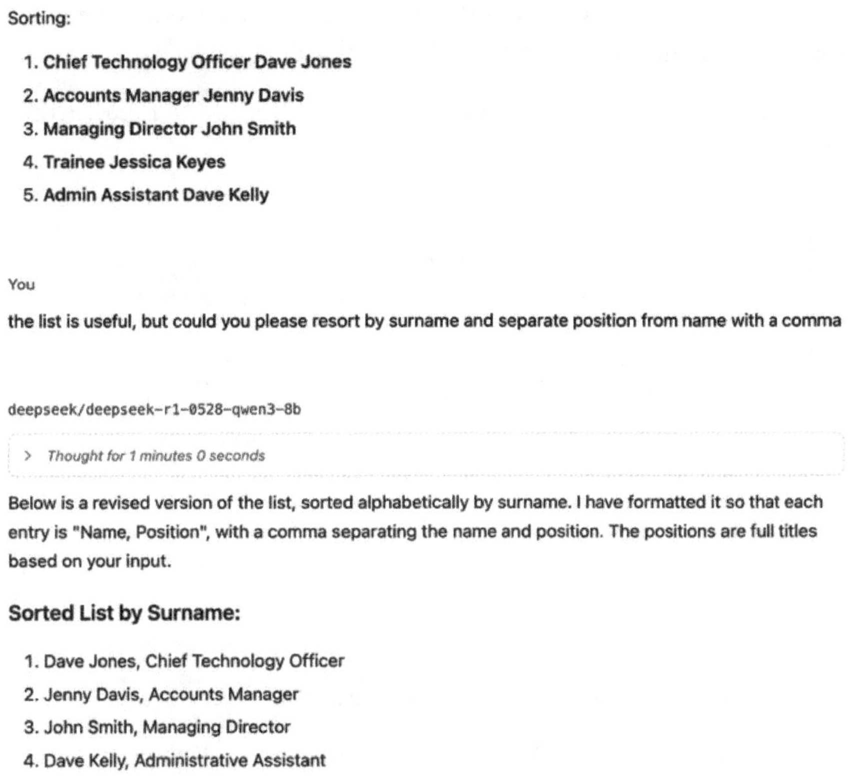

Figure 5.20 – How did the model throw one of the names away?

Another local model from Google, **gemma-3-12b**, did a similarly mixed job. It was able to extract the full names and produce a list, but it got the order wrong, just like DeepSeek.

Figure 5.21 – Gemma's output; useful, yet imperfect

Unfortunately, asking the model to re-sort the output didn't quite work either; while the first two items were transposed, items 3 and 4 remained in the wrong order.

I also tried this query with the on-device AI model available in macOS 26 Tahoe, in the **Shortcuts** app. It failed in interesting ways, too:

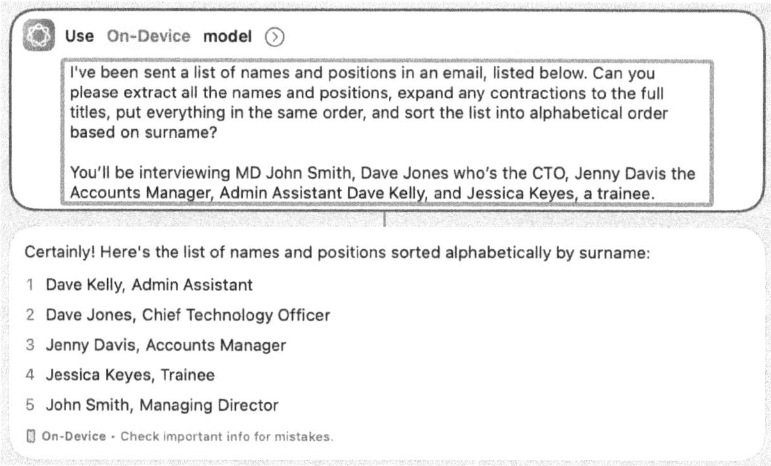

Figure 5.22 – Contractions were expanded, but the order is wrong

Happily, the local model released by OpenAI (**gpt-oss-20b**) was able to perform this task flawlessly:

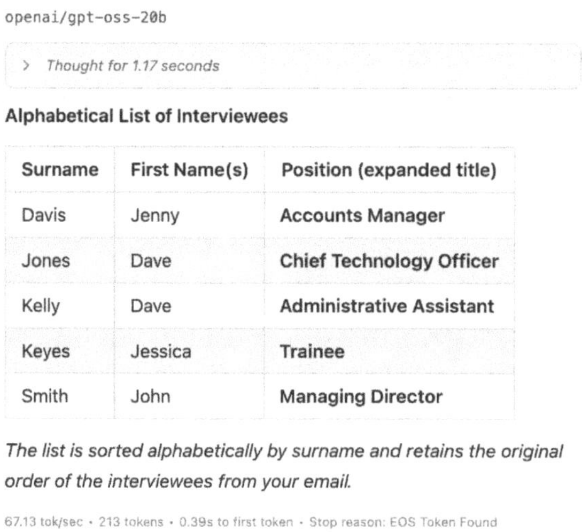

openai/gpt-oss-20b

> *Thought for 1.17 seconds*

Alphabetical List of Interviewees

Surname	First Name(s)	Position (expanded title)
Davis	Jenny	**Accounts Manager**
Jones	Dave	**Chief Technology Officer**
Kelly	Dave	**Administrative Assistant**
Keyes	Jessica	**Trainee**
Smith	John	**Managing Director**

The list is sorted alphabetically by surname and retains the original order of the interviewees from your email.

67.13 tok/sec · 213 tokens · 0.39s to first token · Stop reason: EOS Token Found

Figure 5.23 – The open version of ChatGPT seems to be more capable than other open models

It seems clear that although local models preserve privacy and are free, they're mostly not as powerful or reliable as the cloud-based models—although OpenAI's effort bucks the trend and is worth downloading. For more complex tasks, if a cloud model can do the job quickly and you're able to upload the data online, that's likely to be more efficient.

Although the local models couldn't quite get the order right, if you can ask for the data to be in a tabular format, such as CSV, it's easy to open and sort the data in a spreadsheet such as Excel or Numbers. Also, if you're struggling to get good results, consider showing the model an example of what you're looking for.

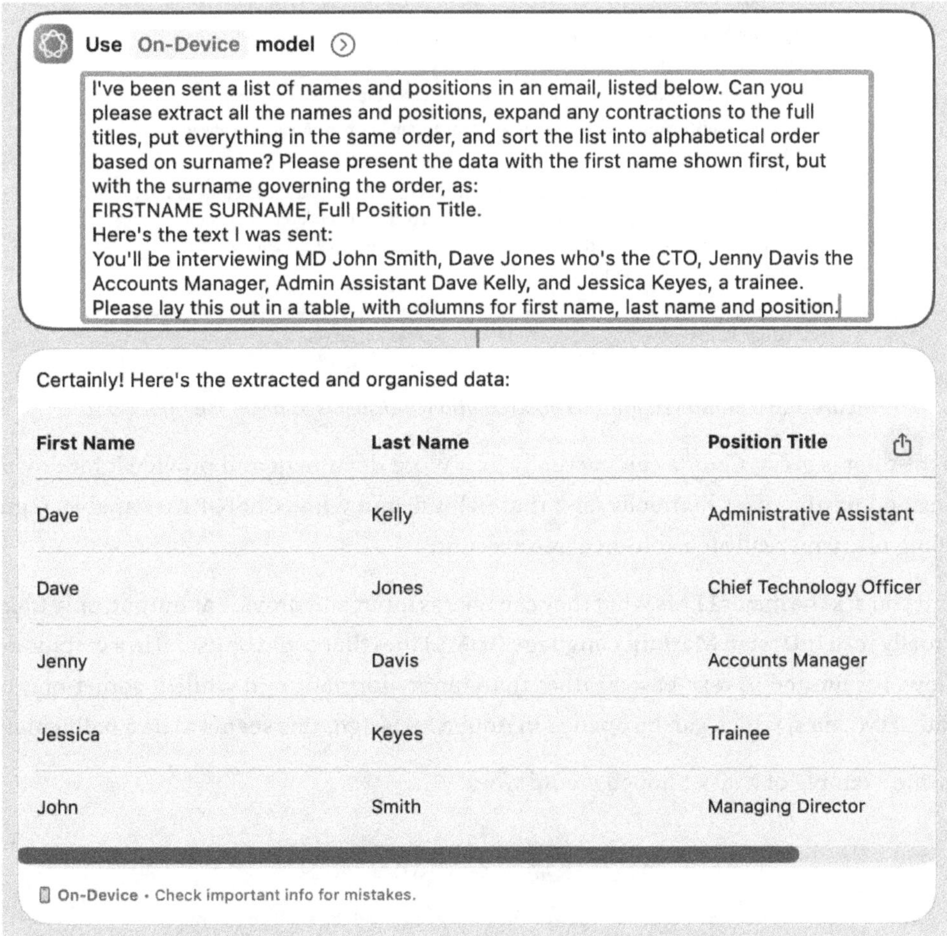

Figure 5.24 – Giving an AI an example of what you want from it is an easy way to improve its output

Export formats are key for production

There are many other text processing tasks that prove tedious for humans but that aren't too much for an AI. For example, let's say a client is changing the style of their documents. While they previously used just italics to indicate quotes, they'd now like to revert to a more standard pattern with "quote marks." Can AI help? When asked, Claude thinks it can:

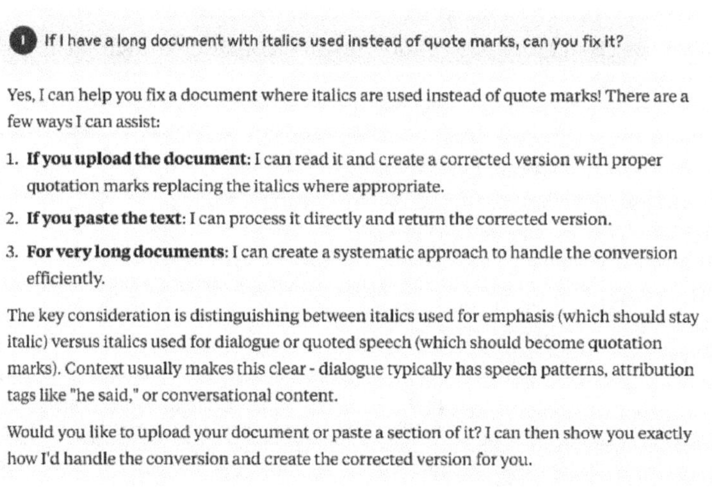

Figure 5.25 – Claude suggests a good solution and seems to be on the right track

While the offer is great, Claude can't actually fix a Word document and provide it for download. Copying and pasting fixes manually isn't that helpful, and while ChatGPT is capable, regularly uploading files isn't really feasible on a free account.

In fact, if you ask the major LLMs what they can take as input and provide as output, only ChatGPT can actually read **InDesign Markup Language (IDML)** files that could be useful in a graphic design workflow. It's limited to text-based rather than binary formats, and while it sometimes offers to create IDML files, which can be opened in Adobe InDesign, this seems to be a hallucination.

Here's one example of a task I hoped would work:

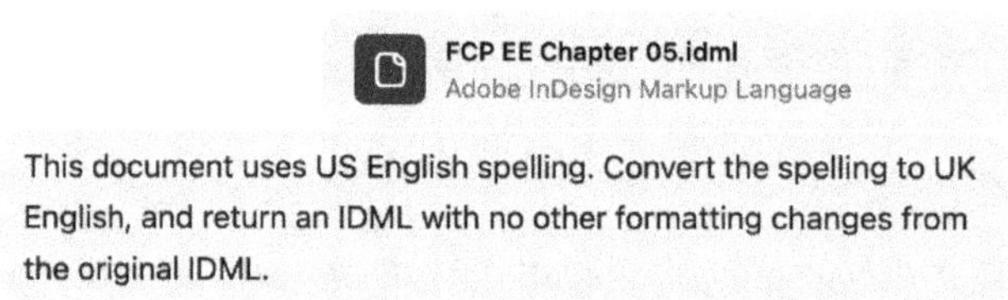

Figure 5.26 – This tedious, non-trivial task is something that ChatGPT is happy to attempt, but you'll quickly need a paid account for file manipulation

Right now, despite the confidence, this process fails. An IDML file was indeed created, and it did open in Adobe InDesign, but it looked identical to the file I uploaded. Curiously, when ChatGPT is asked explicitly what formats it can create, IDML files are not on the list—a shame, then, that it pretended the task was possible. While this is a dead end for now, it's worth trying again in the future.

To be fair, IDML is a complex, compressed format, and many formats used in production are similarly tricky for a text-based system to work with. However, you may have more luck creating simpler formats, such as the text-based FCPXML files, which work with Final Cut Pro. Still, images, videos, and text files aren't enough to get most jobs done, and not every file can be exported to a text-based format. Complex format support remains a serious roadblock between LLMs and creative production.

However, since input of IDML is possible, and any InDesign layout can be exported to IDML, you *can* ask ChatGPT to work with the text in your layouts. And since many editing applications can export to XML-based formats, you've got a fair chance of extracting any text from titles or clip names in a video timeline.

So far, ChatGPT has more export flexibility than the other leading LLMs, but as the field changes rapidly, I'd recommend running your own tests on your own files to see how they do. Start free, then move to paid (on a monthly basis to avoid lock-in) if you find it valuable. Do note that you'll hit the limits of a free account fairly quickly with regular use, especially if you use analysis or upload large files.

Summary

If you're working with text, you're in luck—AI can provide an assistant that's pretty good at boring text processing jobs.

- Summaries can save a decent amount of time, as long as you can avoid becoming so addicted to summaries that you skip all the details. You may end up using integrated summaries in your email application more than anything else, however.
- Grammar correction is a task that can be integrated or separated from the writing process, depending on your preferences, and while AI does enhance this process, it should be used with care.

- Verification, especially when applied to common design workflows and questions, is a task for which AIs are well-suited. When you're asking about facts near to your existing knowledge, you should be able to spot obvious issues but be careful not to stray too far from your expertise.
- Text transformations can be a powerful time-saver in design and video workflows. Many text processing tasks are dull and too hard to automate by traditional means, so throw them to an AI. You just might have to start paying for the privilege.

With all these tasks, be sure to check the output carefully, and never simply copy and paste. These jobs might be on the less controversial side of AI, but if you present a hallucinated summary to a client as fact, the egg is on your face.

Next up, we'll stay with text but shift gears to GenAI.

Part 3

Generative AI

In this part of the book, we'll look at tools that generate more than they assist, creating text, parts of images, entire images or videos, complete video transformations, or audio such as speech or music.

This part of the book includes the following chapters:

- *Chapter 6, Generative AI with Text.*
- *Chapter 7, Generative AI with Images*
- *Chapter 8, Generative AI with Video*
- *Chapter 9, Generative AI with Audio*

6

Generative AI with Text

As we move into the **Generative AI (GenAI)** section of the book, it's worth recapping the ethical flags that any use of this tech may raise. To be clear, while not all use of GenAI is inherently bad, I would not recommend making regular use of generative text for anything you send directly to clients.

If you over-use GenAI—let's say, you decide to ask AI to write your emails for you—then the mental muscles you use to produce text will atrophy. You'll fail to develop new ones. You'll lose uniqueness in your voice, and clients will have fewer reasons to choose your services over anyone else's.

If you're in creative production, creativity is not a side hustle. You need to create more interesting work than other people do, not just pump out as much sub-standard slop as possible. Every email should be a chance to practice clearer communication, not a chore to outsource.

With all that said, there's definitely scope for GenAI to create text that helps you to do your job more efficiently, to give you ideas, or to help make your work more accessible. Let's take a deeper look at the following:

- Ideation
- Rewriting text in a different style
- Generating citations
- Translation
- Alt text descriptions for accessibility

Not all creative professionals will need all these features, but most of us can find a use for several of them. Let's kick off with a bit of brainstorming.

Ideation

Creative jobs vary widely: some are self-directed, some are fully directed by a client's brief, and many are somewhere in between. When you're faced with a creative decision about how to proceed, a blank page can sometimes feel daunting, and using AI to come up with ideas could be useful.

As usual, you'll get better results if you ask more specific questions, so the more you know about a subject, the better questions you'll be able to ask. Also, if you only push a little outside your comfort zone, you'll hopefully be able to spot bad advice when it's given. So, if you're a video creator wanting ideas for YouTube videos, just ask:

Give me ten ideas for short videos I could create about Apple Motion.

Absolutely! Here are **ten short video ideas** for content focused on **Apple Motion**, each aimed at being useful, engaging, and ideal for creators, editors, or motion graphics beginners:

1. "What Is Apple Motion?" – A 60-Second Overview

Explain what Apple Motion is, who it's for, and how it fits into the Final Cut Pro workflow.

2. "5 Must-Know Keyboard Shortcuts in Apple Motion"

Highlight essential shortcuts that boost speed for animation, playback, and editing.

3. "How to Make a Simple Lower Third from Scratch"

Step-by-step creation of a clean lower third, ideal for beginners.

4. "Turn Any Logo Into a Cool 3D Animation"

Demonstrate how to extrude a logo and animate it in 3D space.

5. "Apple Motion vs After Effects – Key Differences in 90 Seconds"

Break down the differences in workflow, performance, and cost with real examples.

6. "Instant Particle Effects: One Click to Wow"

Show off how fast you can add and customize particle emitters for quick visual flair.

Figure 6.1 – All 10 ideas (not all shown here) are solid

These are all good ideas that could easily be turned into a short video. While I could have come up with a similar list myself, results like this can easily spark further and better ideas. Similar prompts on different topics also give good results. What if you're a digital artist who likes dogs?

Give me fifteen ideas for digital art projects involving dogs.

Sure! Here are **15 digital art project ideas involving dogs,** ranging from fun and whimsical to emotionally resonant and technically challenging:

Conceptual & Stylized Art

1. **Dogs as Historical Figures**
Reimagine famous portraits (like Napoleon, Cleopatra, Shakespeare) featuring different dog breeds in costume and setting.
2. **Cyberpunk Dogs**
Create neon-lit, futuristic scenes with cyber-enhanced dogs in a dystopian city.
3. **Canine Tarot Cards**
Design a complete or partial tarot deck where each card is represented by a different dog breed or behavior.
4. **Fantasy Creature Hybrids**
Combine dogs with mythical creatures (dragon-dog, unicorn-pug) in a cohesive fantasy world.
5. **Dogs in Famous Paintings**
Do parodies or tributes to classic paintings (e.g. "The Scream," "Starry Night") but replace the humans with dogs.

Character Design & Animation

6. **Animated Dog Emoji Pack**
Create a custom set of animated stickers or GIFs expressing emotions through a stylized dog character.
7. **Superhero Dog Series**
Design a lineup of dog superheroes, each with a unique power and costume.
8. **Breed Morphing Animation**
Create a smooth morphing animation between different dog breeds — from Chihuahua to Great Dane.
9. **Dog Personas (Fursonas)**
Imagine dogs with anthropomorphic qualities and create original characters with outfits, poses, and accessories.
10. **Puppy Growth Timeline**
Illustrate the same dog from newborn pup to senior, showing visual and emotional evolution.

Figure 6.2 – Again, these ideas are mostly solid

If you're lacking in inspiration, using an LLM for ideas should at least get you started. While the results here aren't going to be wholly original, if a blank page is your enemy, these are a solid starting point to iterate from.

Stretching into nearby creative fields

Ideation isn't just about ideas for content you know well, though. LLMs can also help you stretch your wings a little further than you might be comfortable with—common when working in or with smaller teams.

For example, if you're a videographer who normally covers events and you've been asked to make a promotional video, an LLM can provide you with a checklist of the typical things that a video should include. Here's the top of Gemini's response:

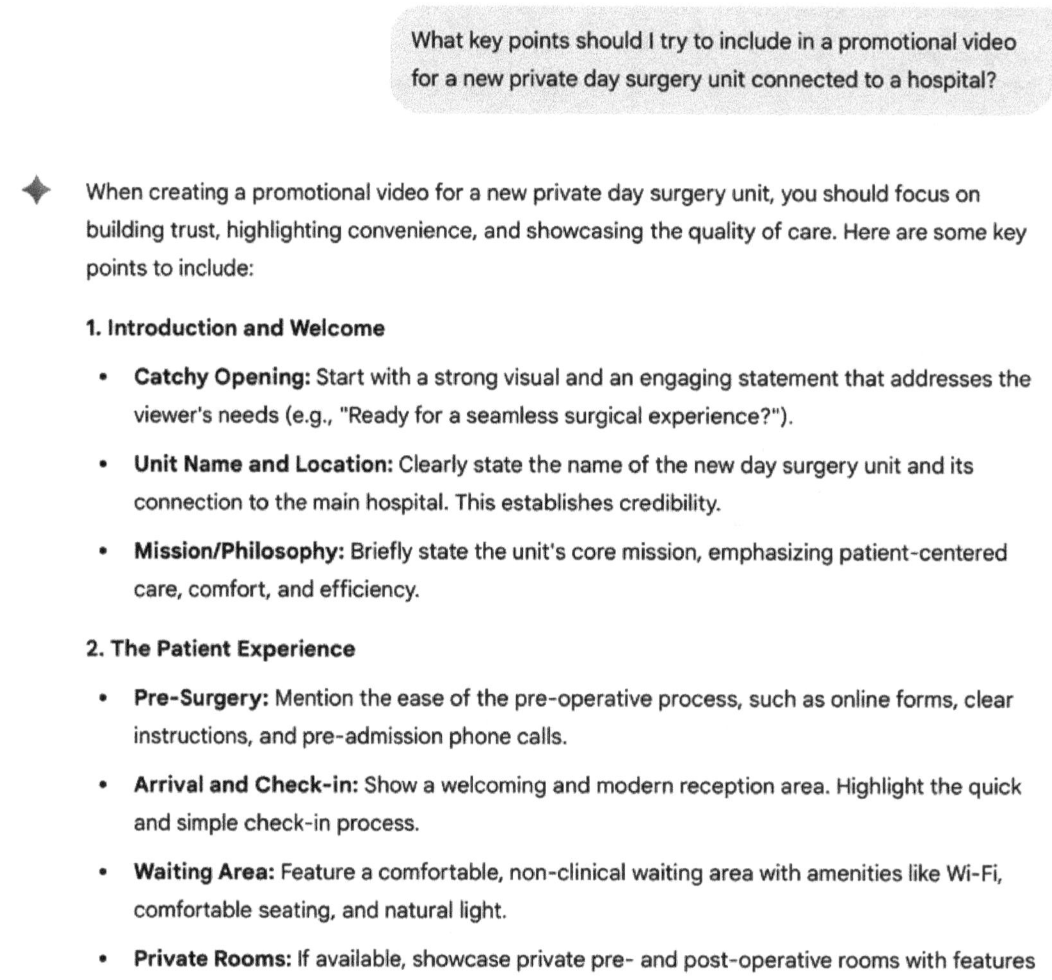

What key points should I try to include in a promotional video for a new private day surgery unit connected to a hospital?

When creating a promotional video for a new private day surgery unit, you should focus on building trust, highlighting convenience, and showcasing the quality of care. Here are some key points to include:

1. Introduction and Welcome

- **Catchy Opening:** Start with a strong visual and an engaging statement that addresses the viewer's needs (e.g., "Ready for a seamless surgical experience?").
- **Unit Name and Location:** Clearly state the name of the new day surgery unit and its connection to the main hospital. This establishes credibility.
- **Mission/Philosophy:** Briefly state the unit's core mission, emphasizing patient-centered care, comfort, and efficiency.

2. The Patient Experience

- **Pre-Surgery:** Mention the ease of the pre-operative process, such as online forms, clear instructions, and pre-admission phone calls.
- **Arrival and Check-in:** Show a welcoming and modern reception area. Highlight the quick and simple check-in process.
- **Waiting Area:** Feature a comfortable, non-clinical waiting area with amenities like Wi-Fi, comfortable seating, and natural light.
- **Private Rooms:** If available, showcase private pre- and post-operative rooms with features

Figure 6.3 – The points included here (not all shown) are relatively obvious and sensible

If you're a skilled video editor but not confident with direction, this provides a starting framework you could develop into a client proposal and then a shooting script. Along similar lines, if you're a designer but not a board game marketing expert, perhaps an LLM could help you discover the best places for you to place the ads you create and niche-specific elements to include:

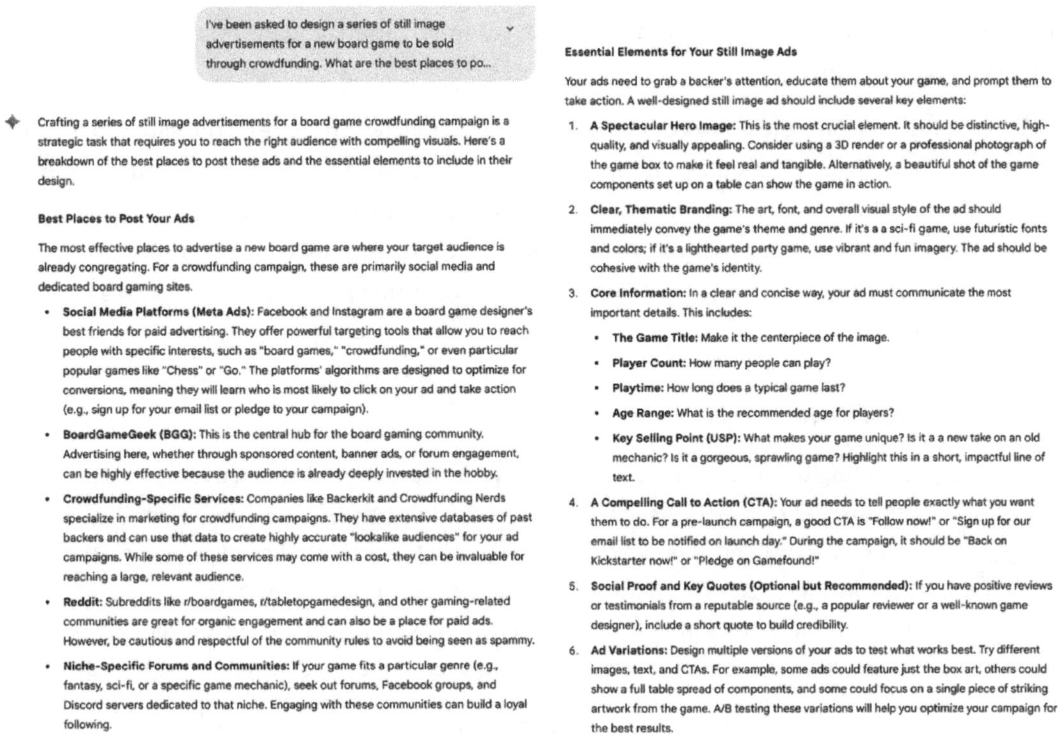

I've been asked to design a series of still image advertisements for a new board game to be sold through crowdfunding. What are the best places to po...

Crafting a series of still image advertisements for a board game crowdfunding campaign is a strategic task that requires you to reach the right audience with compelling visuals. Here's a breakdown of the best places to post these ads and the essential elements to include in their design.

Best Places to Post Your Ads

The most effective places to advertise a new board game are where your target audience is already congregating. For a crowdfunding campaign, these are primarily social media and dedicated board gaming sites.

- **Social Media Platforms (Meta Ads):** Facebook and Instagram are a board game designer's best friends for paid advertising. They offer powerful targeting tools that allow you to reach people with specific interests, such as "board games," "crowdfunding," or even particular popular games like "Chess" or "Go." The platforms' algorithms are designed to optimize for conversions, meaning they will learn who is most likely to click on your ad and take action (e.g., sign up for your email list or pledge to your campaign).
- **BoardGameGeek (BGG):** This is the central hub for the board gaming community. Advertising here, whether through sponsored content, banner ads, or forum engagement, can be highly effective because the audience is already deeply invested in the hobby.
- **Crowdfunding-Specific Services:** Companies like Backerkit and Crowdfunding Nerds specialize in marketing for crowdfunding campaigns. They have extensive databases of past backers and can use that data to create highly accurate "lookalike audiences" for your ad campaigns. While some of these services may come with a cost, they can be invaluable for reaching a large, relevant audience.
- **Reddit:** Subreddits like r/boardgames, r/tabletopgamedesign, and other gaming-related communities are great for organic engagement and can also be a place for paid ads. However, be cautious and respectful of the community rules to avoid being seen as spammy.
- **Niche-Specific Forums and Communities:** If your game fits a particular genre (e.g., fantasy, sci-fi, or a specific game mechanic), seek out forums, Facebook groups, and Discord servers dedicated to that niche. Engaging with these communities can build a loyal following.

Essential Elements for Your Still Image Ads

Your ads need to grab a backer's attention, educate them about your game, and prompt them to take action. A well-designed still image ad should include several key elements:

1. **A Spectacular Hero Image:** This is the most crucial element. It should be distinctive, high-quality, and visually appealing. Consider using a 3D render or a professional photograph of the game box to make it feel real and tangible. Alternatively, a beautiful shot of the game components set up on a table can show the game in action.
2. **Clear, Thematic Branding:** The art, font, and overall visual style of the ad should immediately convey the game's theme and genre. If it's a a sci-fi game, use futuristic fonts and colors; if it's a lighthearted party game, use vibrant and fun imagery. The ad should be cohesive with the game's identity.
3. **Core Information:** In a clear and concise way, your ad must communicate the most important details. This includes:
   - **The Game Title:** Make it the centerpiece of the image.
   - **Player Count:** How many people can play?
   - **Playtime:** How long does a typical game last?
   - **Age Range:** What is the recommended age for players?
   - **Key Selling Point (USP):** What makes your game unique? Is it a a new take on an old mechanic? Is it a gorgeous, sprawling game? Highlight this in a short, impactful line of text.
4. **A Compelling Call to Action (CTA):** Your ad needs to tell people exactly what you want them to do. For a pre-launch campaign, a good CTA is "Follow now!" or "Sign up for our email list to be notified on launch day." During the campaign, it should be "Back on Kickstarter now!" or "Pledge on Gamefound!"
5. **Social Proof and Key Quotes (Optional but Recommended):** If you have positive reviews or testimonials from a reputable source (e.g., a popular reviewer or a well-known game designer), include a short quote to build credibility.
6. **Ad Variations:** Design multiple versions of your ads to test what works best. Try different images, text, and CTAs. For example, some ads could feature just the box art, others could show a full table spread of components, and some could focus on a single piece of striking artwork from the game. A/B testing these variations will help you optimize your campaign for the best results.

Figure 6.4 – This response is comprehensive and useful, with many specific points that aren't obvious outside the board game community

While I can't confirm how accurate the advice offered in other specific niches is, the preceding responses are in areas I know well, and they're solid. While ideation is certainly a GenAI task, it doesn't have to take away your creativity and could in fact inspire you further. To make sure you don't come to rely wholly on AI for inspiration, ideate on your own or with peers before you ask AI for help. That way, you'll be getting a second opinion rather than outsourcing the job entirely.

Now that you've got some ideas, hopefully you've been able to write something. What if you're not quite happy with it?

Rewriting text in a different style

Although the gap between summarizing and rewriting is narrow, I do think there's a distinct difference here: a summary is usually provided for your benefit, while rewritten text is more transformative, and usually intended to be public-facing output. The line between Utility AI and GenAI is somewhat fuzzy here, as it was with summarization, and ultimately, it's up to you where you draw the line.

While I wouldn't regard most uses of a grammar checker as rewriting text, the same tools that offer grammar assistance (such as Grammarly, Copilot, and Apple Intelligence) can absolutely give you more help if you feel you need it. Rewriting is a feature of many general-purpose LLMs, such as ChatGPT and Claude, so if you already use one, try it out. However, if none of these tools work for you, a specialist writing assistant such as **Spiral** (`https://writewithspiral.com/`) may suit you better.

Novel-writing tools

Planning to write a novel? You might want to engage a dedicated tool to help you. Writing assistance tools such as Novelcrafter (`https://www.novelcrafter.com/`), Sudowrite (`https://sudowrite.com/`) and Squibler (`https://www.squibler.io/`) are optimized for stories and novels, and as the output they produce is targeted towards more descriptive prose for fiction applications, these tools are less suited to more typical creative production text tasks such as proposals, emails, and pitch decks.

Here, we'll focus on more general-purpose writing assistants, and of course, this list is not comprehensive—new tools pop up all the time.

AI tools can rewrite for clarity, brevity, and in the style of a publication or author, but you can request more or less any style from most LLMs. As a test, I processed the opening section of one of my recent articles on `https://provideocoalition.com`, about experiments in stereoscopic video. My style is perhaps a little quirky and not entirely error-free, but that's fine by me:

```
Spatial 3D stereoscopic video is easy to shoot on modern iPhones, but
you'll run into its limits pretty quickly. Third-party apps can improve
things, but they have limitations too, and if you're used to shooting with
a couple of dedicated cameras already, why not use them?
Well, if you're tempted to try making some stereoscopic 3D video with a
couple of cameras sitting on the shelf, you should know what you're in for
– it's harder than you think and there are plenty of mistakes to be made.
```

> On your first few stereo shoots you're bound to get something wrong, but if you practice now, you'll hopefully avoid catastrophic failure down the road when you get hold of a real camera.
>
> Experiments like this are a great way to push your skills, but don't get your hopes too high. Even if you don't use something this janky to shoot real client projects, making it work with what you've got will give you real-world experience shooting in 3D that you can use if you step up to a pro setup down the road. So, with some regular 2D filmmaking gear to hand, how can you hack together a quick stereo 3D rig for viewing in a headset or on a 3D display?
>
> As an extra reminder that this is an experiment, I'm not worrying about proper 3D Spatial Audio at all. Video's the focus here.

After processing this text in many different ways, across many tools, I didn't get many results I'd be truly happy to use in a professional context. Because everyone's needs and styles are different, you may have more luck than I did, and of course the tools will evolve over time.

As a first pass, I started with the default "rewrite" options. Take a look at what Grammarly suggested:

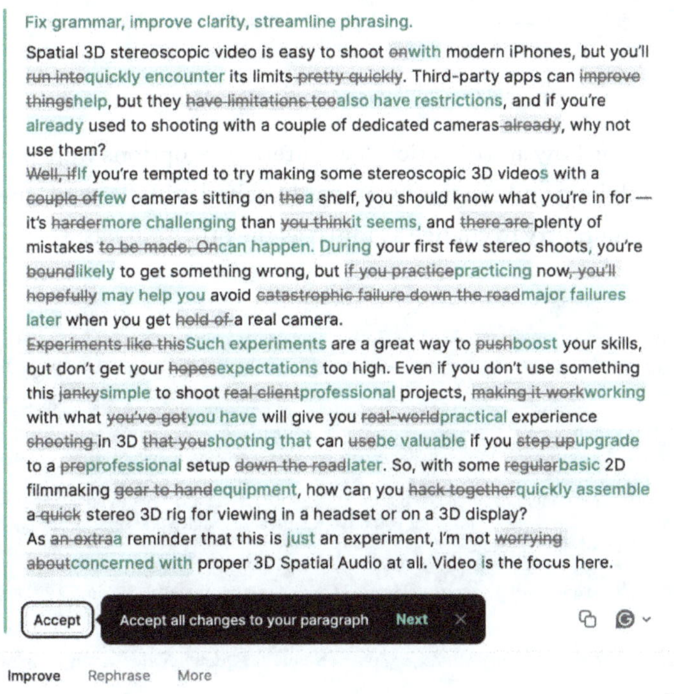

Figure 6.5 – Grammarly wants to make plenty of changes, but not all are helpful

Besides the near-complete loss of my own writing style, "limitations" are not the same as "restrictions" and "simple" does not mean the same as "janky"—I don't want a "rewrite" to change my intended meaning. CoPilot's first attempt was worse, though:

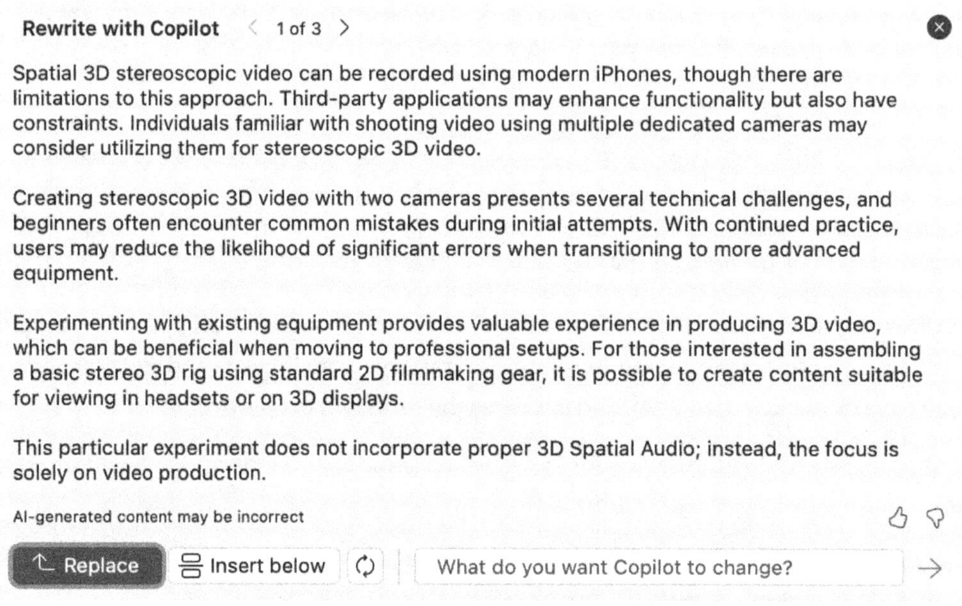

Figure 6.6 – CoPilot isn't doing a great job here

This feels robotic, lacking flow and direction. Two alternative options were no better; the second was a single paragraph long and the third was overly-salted with flowery language. How about Apple Intelligence? It didn't try to change as much as the other models:

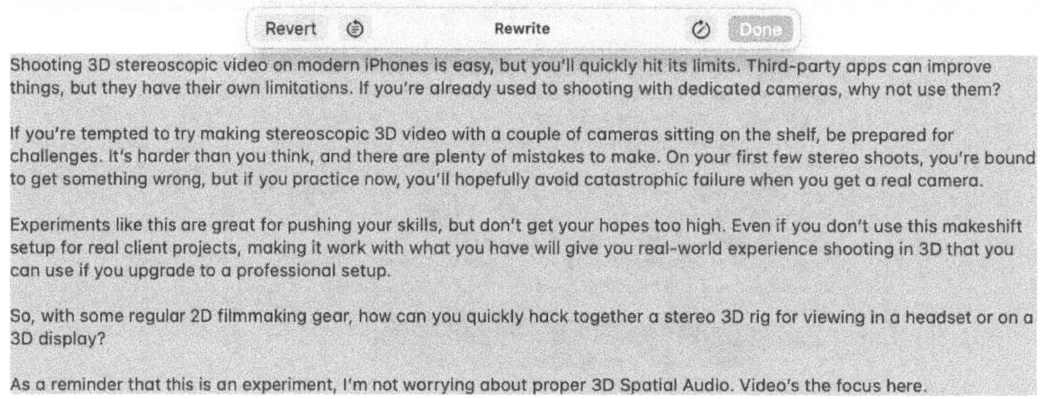

Figure 6.7 – More of the original text was retained by Apple Intelligence's Rewrite

Apple Intelligence didn't make as many revisions to the text as the other tools, and as a result, the changes made didn't change its overall style or feel. But what if you need a more formal result? Let's stay with Apple Intelligence and ask for a **Professional** tone:

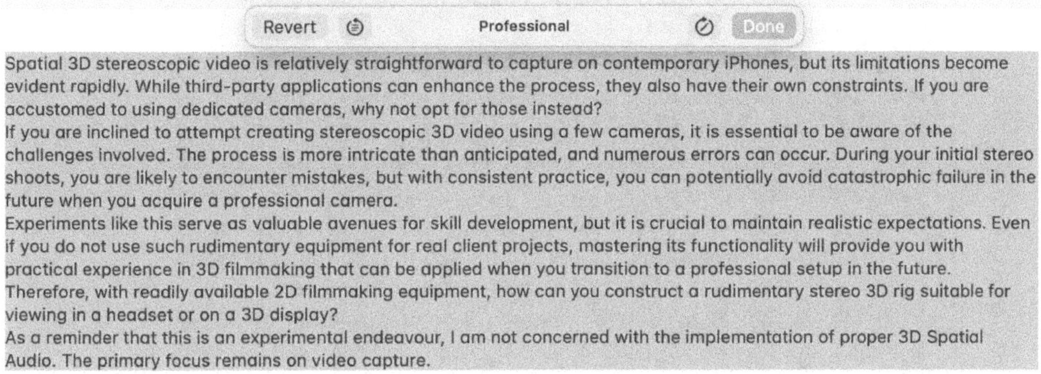

Revert Professional Done

Spatial 3D stereoscopic video is relatively straightforward to capture on contemporary iPhones, but its limitations become evident rapidly. While third-party applications can enhance the process, they also have their own constraints. If you are accustomed to using dedicated cameras, why not opt for those instead?

If you are inclined to attempt creating stereoscopic 3D video using a few cameras, it is essential to be aware of the challenges involved. The process is more intricate than anticipated, and numerous errors can occur. During your initial stereo shoots, you are likely to encounter mistakes, but with consistent practice, you can potentially avoid catastrophic failure in the future when you acquire a professional camera.

Experiments like this serve as valuable avenues for skill development, but it is crucial to maintain realistic expectations. Even if you do not use such rudimentary equipment for real client projects, mastering its functionality will provide you with practical experience in 3D filmmaking that can be applied when you transition to a professional setup in the future.

Therefore, with readily available 2D filmmaking equipment, how can you construct a rudimentary stereo 3D rig suitable for viewing in a headset or on a 3D display?

As a reminder that this is an experimental endeavour, I am not concerned with the implementation of proper 3D Spatial Audio. The primary focus remains on video capture.

Figure 6.8 – 'Professional' has a more verbose, less casual tone

While this feels a little more formal than I'd personally prefer, the meaning remains intact and the feel isn't too far removed from the original. ChatGPT's **Technical** offering was OK, though it differed more from the original:

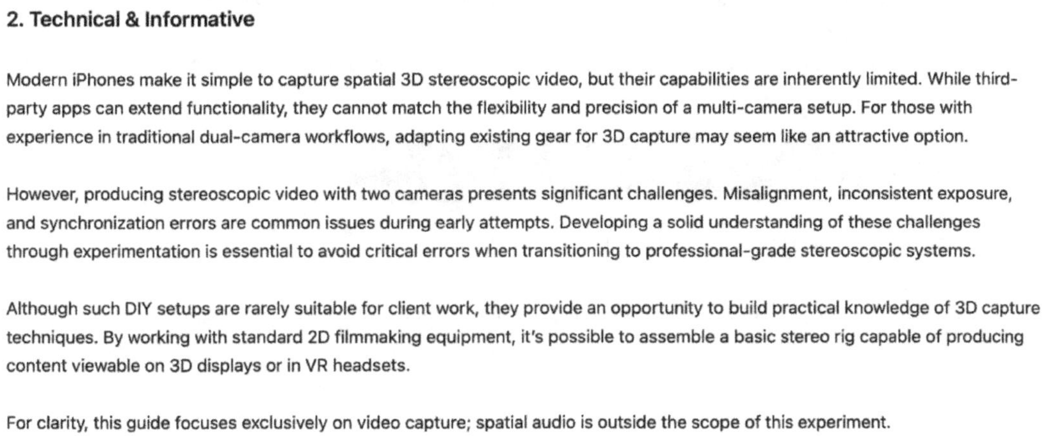

2. Technical & Informative

Modern iPhones make it simple to capture spatial 3D stereoscopic video, but their capabilities are inherently limited. While third-party apps can extend functionality, they cannot match the flexibility and precision of a multi-camera setup. For those with experience in traditional dual-camera workflows, adapting existing gear for 3D capture may seem like an attractive option.

However, producing stereoscopic video with two cameras presents significant challenges. Misalignment, inconsistent exposure, and synchronization errors are common issues during early attempts. Developing a solid understanding of these challenges through experimentation is essential to avoid critical errors when transitioning to professional-grade stereoscopic systems.

Although such DIY setups are rarely suitable for client work, they provide an opportunity to build practical knowledge of 3D capture techniques. By working with standard 2D filmmaking equipment, it's possible to assemble a basic stereo rig capable of producing content viewable on 3D displays or in VR headsets.

For clarity, this guide focuses exclusively on video capture; spatial audio is outside the scope of this experiment.

Figure 6.9 – ChatGPT's technical rewrite is mostly OK

ChatGPT offered **Casual**, **Technical**, and **Promotional** rewrites; this was the second of those. Though there are a few points where the word substitutions have changed the meaning (including "simple" in place of "janky"), it's mostly sound. Here's Grammarly's **formal** offering:

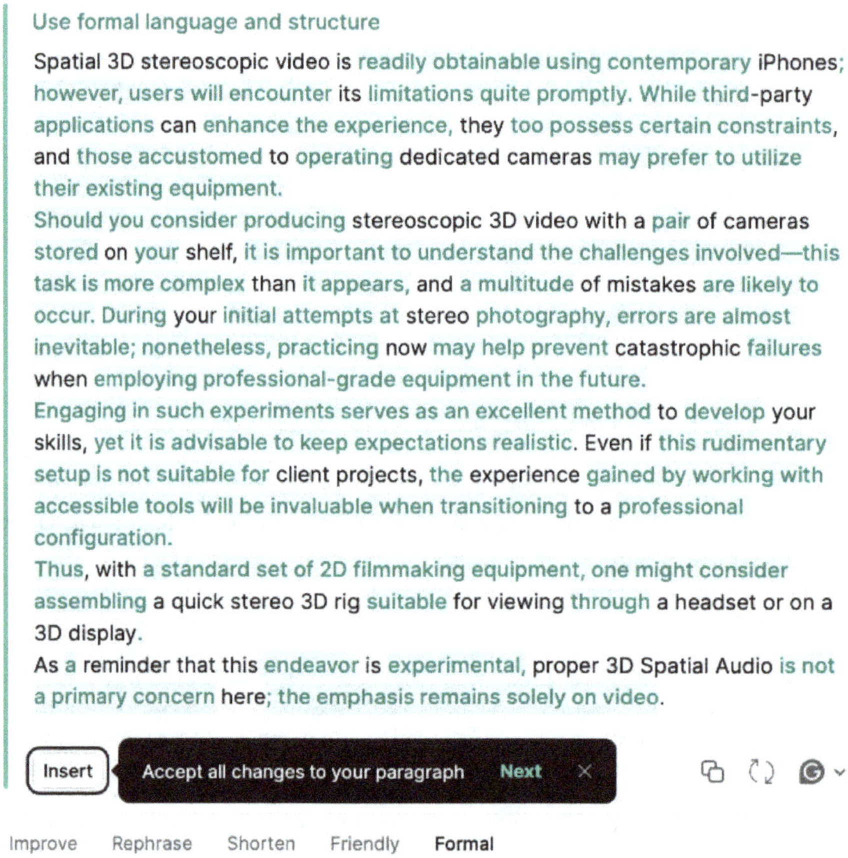

Figure 6.10 – Grammarly, offering a "formal" rewrite

While this is certainly formal, all the flowery adjectives don't make it clearer. I think CoPilot did a better job with its formal attempt, though I did have to request "formal tone" manually, while the other tools discussed so far offered this option by default.

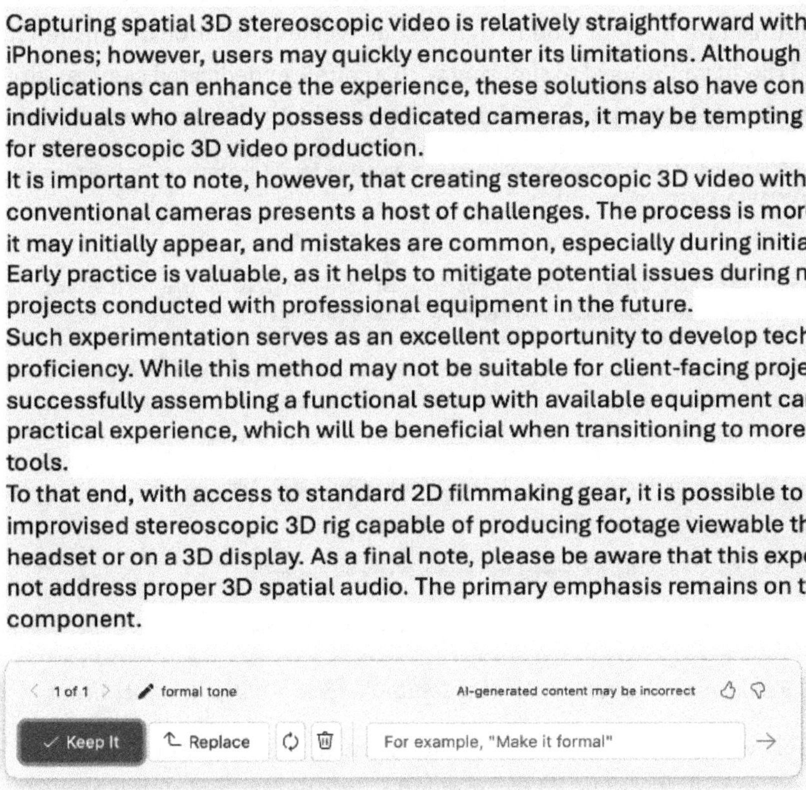
Capturing spatial 3D stereoscopic video is relatively straightforward with modern iPhones; however, users may quickly encounter its limitations. Although third-party applications can enhance the experience, these solutions also have constraints. For individuals who already possess dedicated cameras, it may be tempting to utilize them for stereoscopic 3D video production.

It is important to note, however, that creating stereoscopic 3D video with two conventional cameras presents a host of challenges. The process is more complex than it may initially appear, and mistakes are common, especially during initial attempts. Early practice is valuable, as it helps to mitigate potential issues during more critical projects conducted with professional equipment in the future.

Such experimentation serves as an excellent opportunity to develop technical proficiency. While this method may not be suitable for client-facing projects, successfully assembling a functional setup with available equipment can provide practical experience, which will be beneficial when transitioning to more advanced tools.

To that end, with access to standard 2D filmmaking gear, it is possible to devise an improvised stereoscopic 3D rig capable of producing footage viewable through a headset or on a 3D display. As a final note, please be aware that this experiment does not address proper 3D spatial audio. The primary emphasis remains on the video component.

Figure 6.11 – CoPilot, asked for a "formal tone"

While examining these examples should be useful as a starting point for assessing these tools' capabilities, they will differ every time you run them. If you don't get the result you were hoping for, simply try again, or vary your prompt slightly. Perhaps as a way to invite experimentation, ChatGPT proactively offered a variety of styles (**Casual**, **Technical**, **Promotional**) and then offered to combine all three into a single "condensed best of" version. Hilariously, this rewriting of rewriting mangled the "if you're used to shooting with a couple of dedicated cameras already" fragment into "if you already have a pair"... which carries a distinctly different connotation:

Here's a **condensed "best-of" version** that blends the conversational flow of the casual rewrite, the clarity of the technical one, and a touch of the inspiring tone from the promotional version:

Shooting 3D stereoscopic video on an iPhone is simple, but you'll hit its limits fast. Third-party apps can help, but they can't match the flexibility of using proper cameras — and if you already have a pair, why not put them to work?

That said, building your own stereo rig is harder than it looks. Misalignment, exposure differences, and sync issues are just some of the challenges you'll face early on. Expect mistakes — they're part of the process — but every experiment teaches you something valuable that will pay off when you upgrade to a professional 3D setup.

Even if your DIY rig isn't client-ready, learning to make it work with basic 2D filmmaking gear is a fantastic way to develop real-world 3D shooting skills.

So, how can you hack together a quick stereo setup for viewing in a headset or on a 3D display?

And one final note: this is strictly a video experiment — we're leaving spatial audio out of the equation.

Figure 6.12 – The condensed "best-of" version that ChatGPT offered — not quite what I meant

Even though I probably won't be using these tools much myself, if you're still finding your feet as a writer, I can see the appeal. However, I'd recommend starting with Apple Intelligence (using **Notes** or **Pages** on a modern Apple device) because it maintains more of your original work. In a world where mostly competent AI writing is commonplace, mostly competent is no longer good enough. If you plan to use these services, don't just accept bulk changes. Examine the suggestions and implement them yourself if you agree.

If you're in a position where you feel you need AI's help to revise or generate text, go beyond the presets and ask a prompt-based system to help you in a more specific way. There's nothing stopping you providing a document (or several, or your whole website) and asking AI to imitate that style. You might also have luck asking AI to rewrite for brevity, when you're beyond a strict word limit. While I'd recommend doing it yourself, if that's simply not an option, at least avoid the presets.

Conversely, what if you haven't written the text yet, and you'd like AI to generate whole paragraphs from bullet points? This is, indeed, possible—but is it a good idea?

Writing full text from bullet points

If something is easy to do, it has little value. A design built on a template doesn't stand out when viewed alongside other work made with templates, and AI-written text won't stand out either. In a few short points, here are my key recommendations:

- Writing something yourself helps you grow as a writer
- If you outsource a job you don't get better at it
- AI is quick, cheap outsourcing
- AI work is competent but not great
- If AI starts something, you should edit it to add your own touches

If I was feeling lazy, I could just get AI to turn those bullets into text, right? Let's see if that hurts or helps my argument:

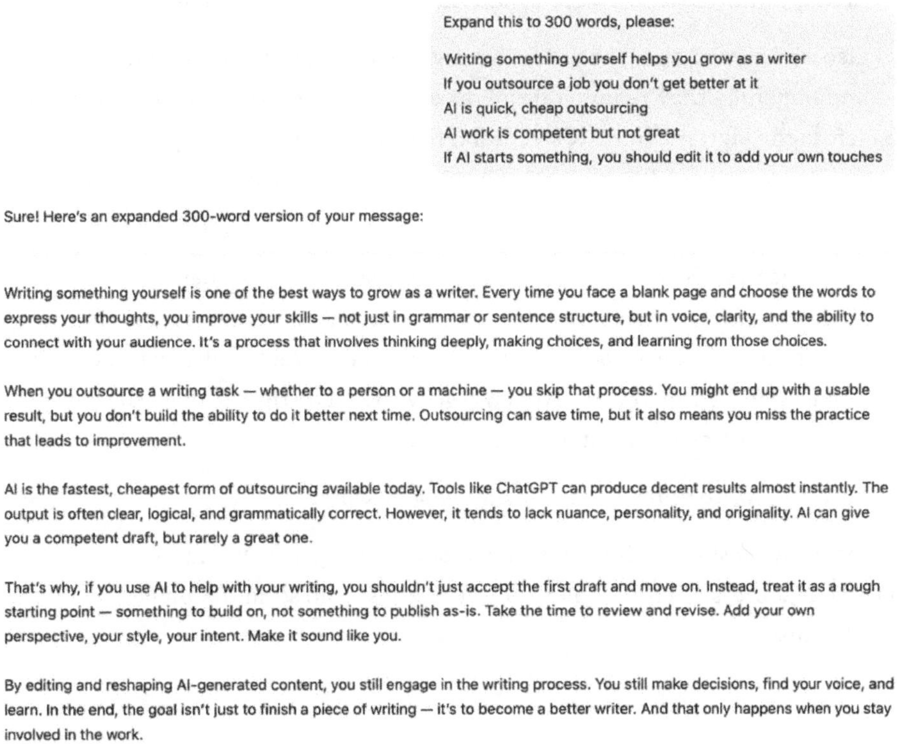

Figure 6.13 – ChatGPT—competent and well said, but that's not my writing

This text is *fine*. Not exceptional, just fine. But if you want *great* results—and you should always aim for great—I can't recommend generating text you expect clients or customers to read. If it's worth reading, it's worth writing yourself.

As you might expect, spending time writing something yourself produces richer text than any outsourced shortcut. Yes, you'll need to invest time in it, but the paybacks are often worth it. Writing full-length text helps you understand the concepts more deeply, and you'll be able to stand behind those points if questioned.

Growing as a writer is an undervalued benefit of writing, and it shouldn't be ignored. Outsourcing gets you to the end goal quickly, but that end goal is all you get. If you spend time repeatedly writing prompts, you just get good at writing prompts.

Still, I understand: if you don't feel you have the skills to do a good job of writing longer text, using AI is a tempting option. If that temptation is too strong, or you're simply tasked with too much work and not enough budget to do it properly, at the very least, you should edit the generated text, as much as you can, to make it yours. Reshape, reimagine, delete at will. The less you contribute to your own outputs, the less you'll grow, and the less value your work will have.

Further, I also understand that there are vast swathes of text out there that aren't terribly important—and hopefully they're not your job as a creative professional. Legally important text should be left to the lawyers, but if it's your job to write persuasive copy, *you should do your job*. If you outsource your core skills, why wouldn't a client hire someone cheaper using the same AI tools as you?

Finally, some services, such as Spiral, promise to learn your style, and then create more work in an imitation of that style, on your behalf. While this approach does address issues around a personal voice and tone, the issue of *not actually doing the work* remains. You'll still atrophy creatively, you'll fail to fully understand a brief if you never engage with and further develop the key bullet-point concepts, and your writing won't change and grow.

If you have the option, do *better* work, not simply *more* work.

Are there generative tasks which simply alleviate the drudgery? Definitely. For instance, if you need to cite your sources, there are many different ways to do so, and it's a largely technical task. Can AI handle this?

Generating citations

Though citations are more commonly required in academia, some clients may expect correctly formatted citations in proposals, work plans or annual reports. If you're in charge of the design of these longer documents and need to create citations, you may be tempted to ask AI to help with the quite specific formatting requirements of the chosen citation standard. As a test, I asked three major LLMs to turn a list of URLs into citations and was surprised at how variable the results were. Here's the prompt:

```
Turn these URLs into citations, APA style.
https://www.techradar.com/computing/artificial-intelligence/googles-ai-overviews-are-often-so-confidently-wrong-that-ive-lost-all-trust-in-them
https://www.digital.gov.au/initiatives/copilot-trial/microsoft-365-copilot-evaluation-report-full/executive-summary-glossary
https://housefresh.com/beware-of-the-google-ai-salesman/
```

ChatGPT got the details confidently wrong on at least two of the three URLs:

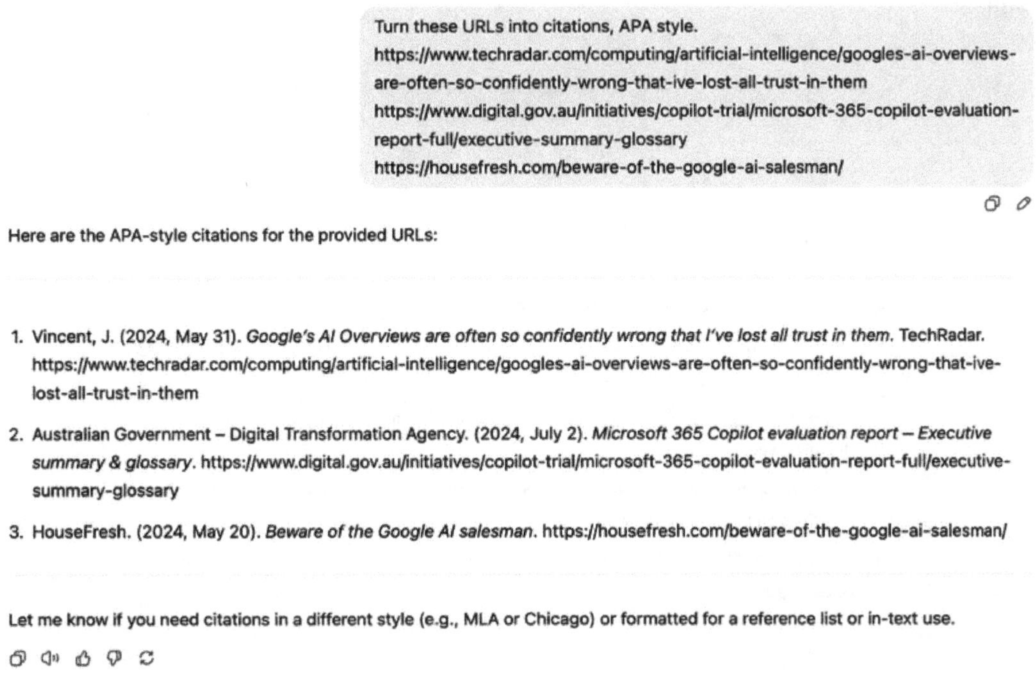

Figure 6.14 – The author and date for the first and third references here are incorrect

Faults persisted across multiple attempts, though Gemini did better with the same prompt:

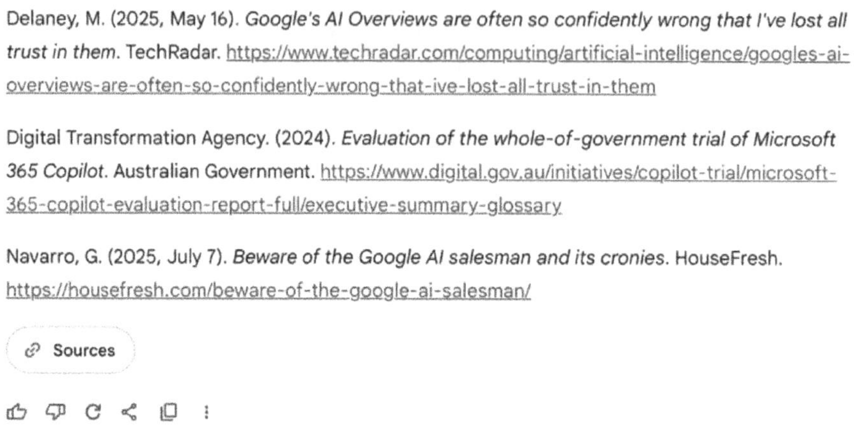

Figure 6.15 – The end result, after a long "thinking" process

However, this wasn't repeatable; another attempt with the same prompt gave entirely different results.

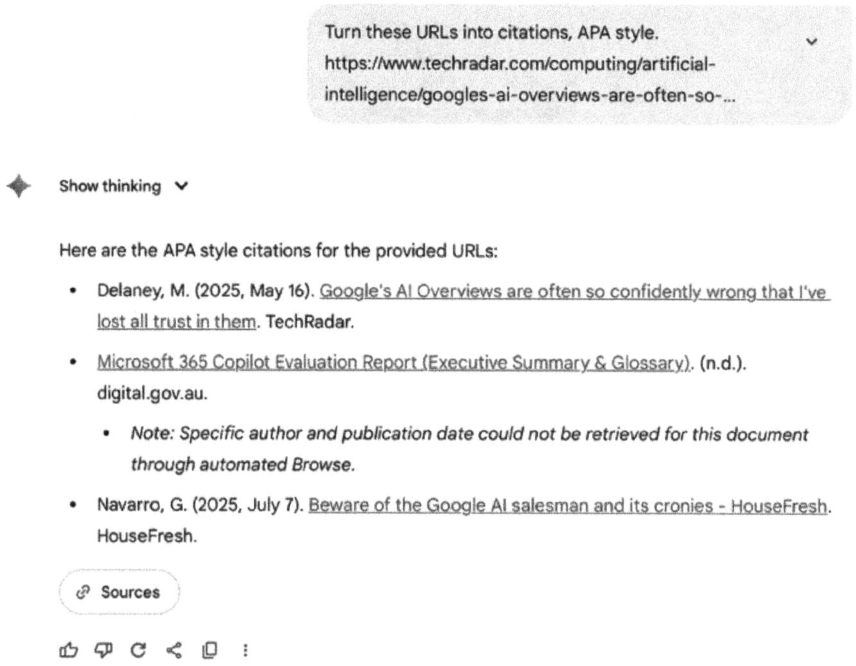

Figure 6.16 – The same engine also produced… this?

I don't want to spend too much space on examples, but Claude also failed at this task, and the unreliability of all these services, on what I expected to be a relatively simple task, causes me concern. If this is something you need to do regularly, I'd recommend using a manual citation generator such as the one Grammarly offers (`https://www.grammarly.com/citations`):

Figure 6.17 – This manually assembled citation took more copying and pasting, but the automated options weren't reliable

While I'd like to think that this is a task that at least some AI tools will be able to perform reliably, if none of the biggest LLMs can get it right yet, I can't recommend trusting any other tools to do this correctly either. The rule remains—be very cautious sharing AI-produced output with the world unless you've checked it.

OK, ideas done, document written, citations complete, and now your client wants to deliver in a different language. Can AI help?

Translation

Although translation is a task that AI tools are good at, it's not one they are perfect at. If you need to translate text that's in another language for your own understanding, AI is probably fine. If you can accept imperfect results, you'll be able to grasp the meaning of text in other languages that would otherwise remain inaccessible—and that's a great thing.

However, if you need to translate creative content in your own language to deliver to native speakers in another language, do not expect that AI will be able to produce perfect results on its own.

Just as with transcription, the output will be fast, and mostly correct. But while mistakes in a transcription can be corrected relatively easily, if you can't understand the language you're translating to, you'll struggle to confirm the accuracy of a translation.

Website listings and video advertisements for most of the cheapest products bear this out. Where there's no budget to translate a product description into proper English, automatic translation tools are used and the output remains unedited. As a result, expectations and perceived worth are lowered even further.

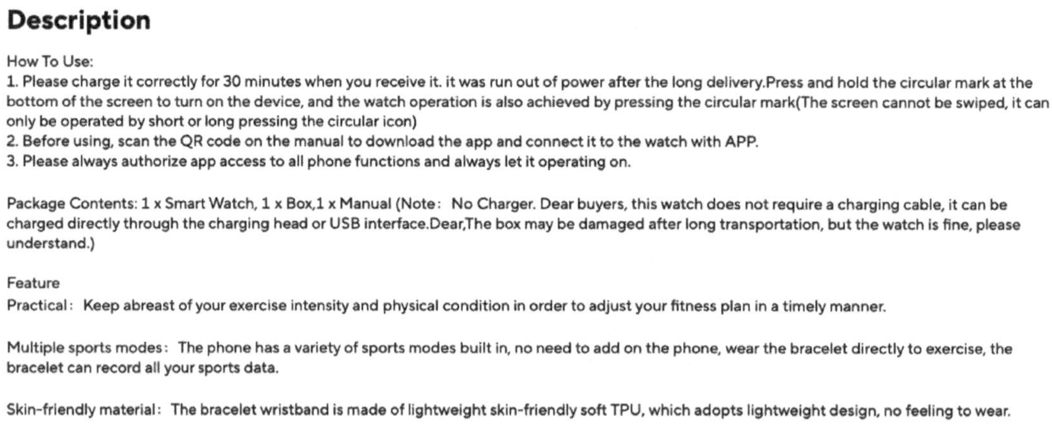

Description

How To Use:
1. Please charge it correctly for 30 minutes when you receive it. it was run out of power after the long delivery.Press and hold the circular mark at the bottom of the screen to turn on the device, and the watch operation is also achieved by pressing the circular mark(The screen cannot be swiped, it can only be operated by short or long pressing the circular icon)
2. Before using, scan the QR code on the manual to download the app and connect it to the watch with APP.
3. Please always authorize app access to all phone functions and always let it operating on.

Package Contents: 1 x Smart Watch, 1 x Box,1 x Manual (Note: No Charger. Dear buyers, this watch does not require a charging cable, it can be charged directly through the charging head or USB interface.Dear,The box may be damaged after long transportation, but the watch is fine, please understand.)

Feature
Practical: Keep abreast of your exercise intensity and physical condition in order to adjust your fitness plan in a timely manner.

Multiple sports modes: The phone has a variety of sports modes built in, no need to add on the phone, wear the bracelet directly to exercise, the bracelet can record all your sports data.

Skin-friendly material: The bracelet wristband is made of lightweight skin-friendly soft TPU, which adopts lightweight design, no feeling to wear.

Figure 6.18 – This cheap smartwatch on AliExpress has a description riddled with errors

This isn't new, of course, but if other languages can't be translated to English without fault, why should we expect English to be able to be translated to other languages? I've been responsible for designing board game manuals in English as well as in several other languages, and in each case, the translation was handled by a native speaker, laid out by me, and then checked by that same translator before being checked by others.

Translators can definitely use AI translation tools as a starting point, but the subtleties of different languages and dialects need a human touch. The finer points of translation are not easy to navigate, even for a native speaker. For example, the differences between European Spanish and Mexican Spanish are subtle and numerous, and even a human-supervised translation will contain errors that require many proofreaders. Subtle translation problems are also more likely to occur in creative contexts, such as video and board games, than fact-based news articles.

In terms of tools, the Google Translate website has worked well for several years, and on Apple platforms, the Safari browser includes translation features that allow you to translate any website you visit:

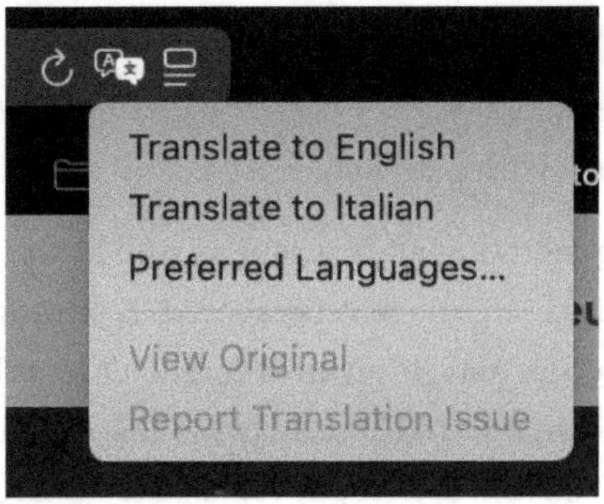

Figure 6.19 – Safari (and other browsers) can translate foreign-language websites

Translation apps from Google, Apple, and others allow live translation of audio into text (or more audio) in another language in real time, which is helpful enough to make visiting a foreign country easier, but not good enough for creative production purposes.

However, AI has distinct uses for anyone engaged in creating accessible PDFs or websites.

Alt text descriptions for accessibility

Alt text is a text equivalent of an image, describing it for anyone who can't see the image. While alt text is intended for use by blind or vision impaired readers, it's also important for search engines. In fact, text descriptions of images are a large part of how LLMs can interpret what's in an image in the first place, using it as part of their training data.

As a result, many LLMs can interpret what an image contains, and they can therefore generate an alt text description, which designers can paste into apps such as Adobe InDesign or Bridge, or into a website CMS such as WordPress. Many governments around the world require public-facing documents to be accessible, so this is not an optional task.

While it's not difficult to write a short sentence describing a single image, describing many images can be a time-consuming process. Also, because alt text descriptions should use concise, simple language, their creation is a task well suited for an LLM with human oversight... right?

Before we assess the output, here are a few best practices tips for alt text, from Harvard's Digital Accessibility guide (`https://accessibility.huit.harvard.edu/describe-content-images`):

- Keep it short, usually 1-2 sentences. Don't overthink it.
- Consider key elements of why you chose this image, instead of describing every little detail.
- There's no need to say "image of" or "picture of."

- But do say if it's a logo, illustration, painting, or cartoon.
- Don't duplicate text that's adjacent in the document or website.
- End the alt text sentence with a period.

There are many subtleties to generating alt text, but as well as the preceding points, the alt text must include the *context* in which an image is presented. A photograph of a university campus used in a discussion of architecture may be given different alt text than the same image used in a student prospectus. More tips can be found here: `https://www.visionaustralia.org/business-consulting/digital-access/blog/five-tips-for-writing-alt-text`.

The easiest way to use AI to generate alt text is to use one of the many free tools designed explicitly to do the job, including **Ahrefs** (`https://ahrefs.com/writing-tools/img-alt-text-generator`), or **TailWind** (`https://www.tailwindapp.com/marketing/tools/image-alt-text-generator`).

Alternatively, using a general-purpose LLM such as ChatGPT, Gemini, or Claude brings the added benefit of being able to tweak the output—by priming them with tips for generating better alt text, or by providing the context in which those images are presented. Using one of my own images as a source, here's a concise alt text description from Tailwind:

Figure 6.20 – This text is concise, but without context it doesn't tell the whole story

That description is about the right length and gives sufficient meaning, but no context. Not all descriptions were accurate, though. Ahrefs offered three options, but all of them interpreted Apple Park as a walkway:

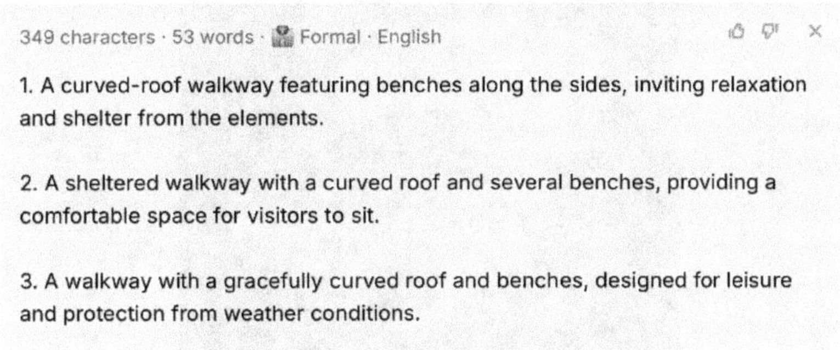

Figure 6.21 – Ahrefs provided options, but none were correct

While a human could edit any of these descriptions to include context, a more advanced LLM *can* do it for you. Here, ChatGPT offers a generic description, then adds context on request:

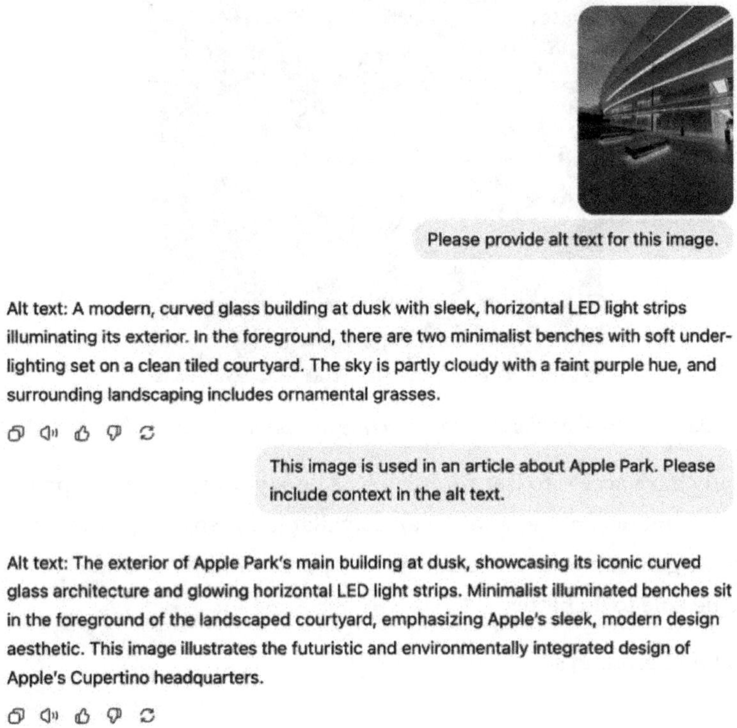

Figure 6.22 – Providing context improves the alt text—although it's probably a little too long

So, while AI-generated alt text is impressive, it is, as usual, just a starting point. Human input is often necessary, either to correct the generated alt text directly, or by asking an LLM to add new information.

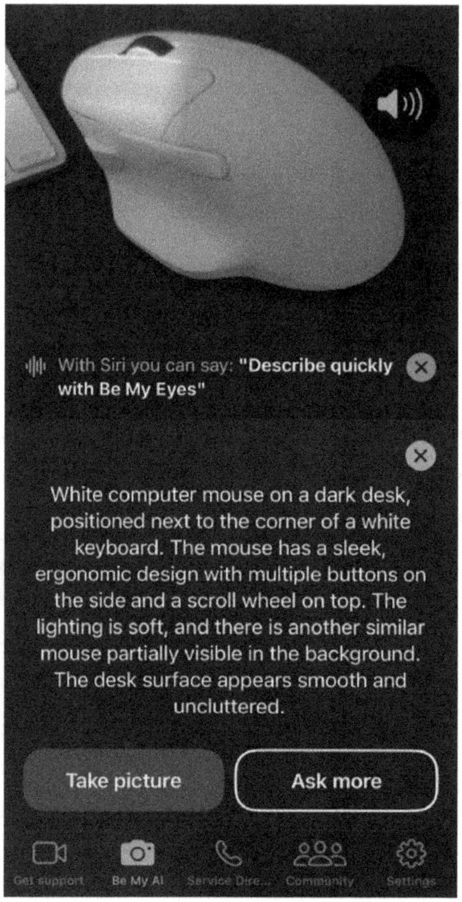

Figure 6.23 – This free mobile app can describe any photo in detail—but it's not instant

Blind users already have access to free tools such as Be My Eyes, a mobile app that can describe anything a phone camera can see, and it's also available for smart glasses such as those from Meta AI. Automatic generation of alt text is now the bare minimum, and if you're providing alt text, you should be able to do better.

We've covered a lot of ground, so let's wrap this up.

Summary

AI-generated text has the potential to make many tasks easier, and in projects with formal, specific output requirements, it can shine. However, in creative fields, there are real risks in fully embracing it.

If the point of your creative writing is to stand out from the crowd, you can't use the same tools and techniques as everyone else. And if you want to grow as a creative person, you can't simply outsource creative tasks.

That said, there's nothing wrong with accepting help, and AI is certainly able to give you feedback on your work, as well as ideas. Ideation from an LLM has few downsides, as you're in control of what you do with its advice. Creatives wanting to stretch professionally could do much worse than ask for help from an LLM, though the closer you are to a subject, the better.

If possible, use text generation as a tool to help you, not replace you.

With that basic principle in mind, let's dive into perhaps the most controversial application of AI for creative people: generating images.

Additional resources

- `https://www.boia.org/blog/be-careful-when-using-ai-for-alternative-text`

7

Generative AI with Images

Few topics in GenAI are more polarized than AI generation of synthetic images. If you're a creative professional who creates or modifies images—and most of us do work with images in one way or another—you might already have strong opinions on this. Here's mine: although AI can be powerful, I don't think AI is guaranteed to take over from all designers, photographers, and retouchers. In fact, there are many ways to use AI that don't fill the world with slop, and that help us do our jobs better.

Creativity means very different things to different people, and there are many different jobs in the broad category of "creative production". Some of those tasks are boring, or tedious, or are never shown to clients, and those are more likely to be tasks you might perform with an AI.

Other tasks, such as complex image retouching or restoration, are sometimes better performed by an AI, and in this context, they can be seen as a more advanced version of the tools we used before. AI can also open up entirely new workflows, allowing you to visualize a shoot before it happens, or create mood boards based on images created for the purpose rather than simply reusing other people's images.

Of course, the marketplace is changing rapidly, and progress is swift. Although I'll show the results from several different tools, there are far too many services to test in depth, and the speed of change in this industry means that any firm recommendations would be outdated by the time you read this. Don't get too attached to any one solution—I'd be surprised if they're all still around five years from now.

To keep this book as helpful as possible, I'll try to focus more on techniques and workflows than specific applications and services, and I'll cover web and desktop solutions rather than mobile. Some comparative reviews are included, but please confirm results for yourself on your own images, with whatever service(s) you end up using.

No matter what kind of images you're making, human supervision or direction is important. In this chapter, we'll be looking at the following main topics:

- Manipulating existing images
- Creating original images
- Generative vector art
- Mood boards and design ideas
- Creating 3D models

First off, let's take a look at the state of the art in retouching.

Manipulating existing images

Though many AI-based tools can perform image manipulation, **Adobe Photoshop** has been the retouching tool of choice for so long that it's become a verb: *to Photoshop*. I've personally and professionally used Photoshop since the late 1990s, and new tools, including some that incorporate machine learning, have changed the state of the art multiple times over.

For example, the Clone Stamp was once the only tool available for retouching jobs. Covering skin blemishes was tricky because it wasn't always easy to find a matching patch of clean skin to clone from. With the Clone Stamp tool, you must match texture and light between the source and the destination.

In the early 2000s, I was working as a retoucher in London, and the introduction of the Healing Brush tool changed the game entirely. We still had to find an area of clean skin, but we now only had to worry about texture—Photoshop could match the brightness of the source to the destination for us.

In 2010, **Content-Aware Fill** was added to the **Spot Healing Brush** tool in Photoshop CS5. With this tool, you didn't even need to choose a source area to clone from—indeed, you couldn't choose one at all. Instead, Photoshop chose which parts of the image to reuse, creating a new area that (usually) looked seamless, remixing parts of the original image to create a replacement area.

This tool remains in use today, and while it predates modern AI tools, it can be said to use machine learning techniques. At the time, it was marketed under the **Adobe Sensei** banner (`https://web.archive.org/web/20190404055934/https://research.adobe.com/project/content-aware-fill/`).

Today, the existing tools are augmented by **Generative Remove** and **Generative Fill**, two fully generative features that draw on Adobe Stock images licensed for the purpose. While many retouching tasks are still best performed with Content-Aware Spot Healing, the Healing Brush, or even the Clone Stamp, AI-based tools bring unprecedented flexibility.

For example, if you start with a photograph of a person not wearing a hat, but a client wants them to be wearing a hat, cloning alone is not enough. You'd need to find an image with a suitable hat, taken with lighting at a similar angle, at a similar level of sharpness, and this process can take significant effort.

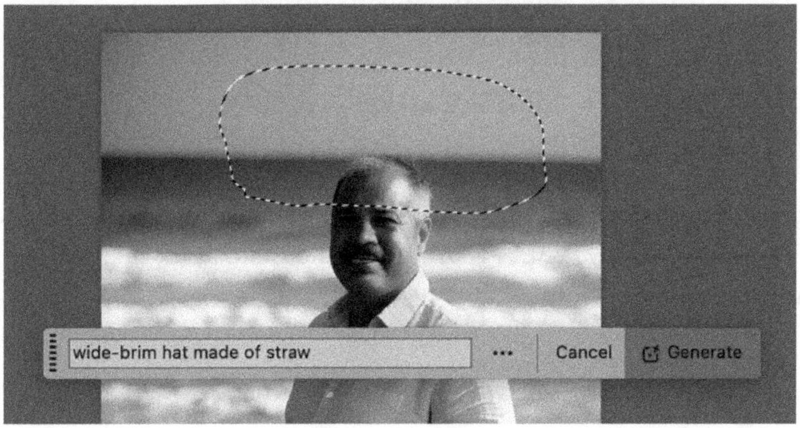

Figure 7.1 – I'd like a hat here, please

Today, you can select the area where you want the hat with the **Lasso** tool, then tell Photoshop exactly what kind of hat you want in a text entry field, and it'll generate three options within a few seconds. You don't even have to tell Photoshop what you want; leave the field blank, and it'll figure out the best option.

Figure 7.2 – This hat isn't real, and neither is the man on the beach

In most other apps, this is known as **inpainting**, and it's a common workflow found across services such as **Freepik** (`https://www.freepik.com/`) and **Claid.ai** (`https://claid.ai/`); we'll take a look at them soon.

Similarly, if you want to remove people from an image, Photoshop's **Remove** tool can automatically select people or wires and cables, then replace selected areas with a generated background. Although selections aren't always perfect, it's easy to paint in items that have been missed.

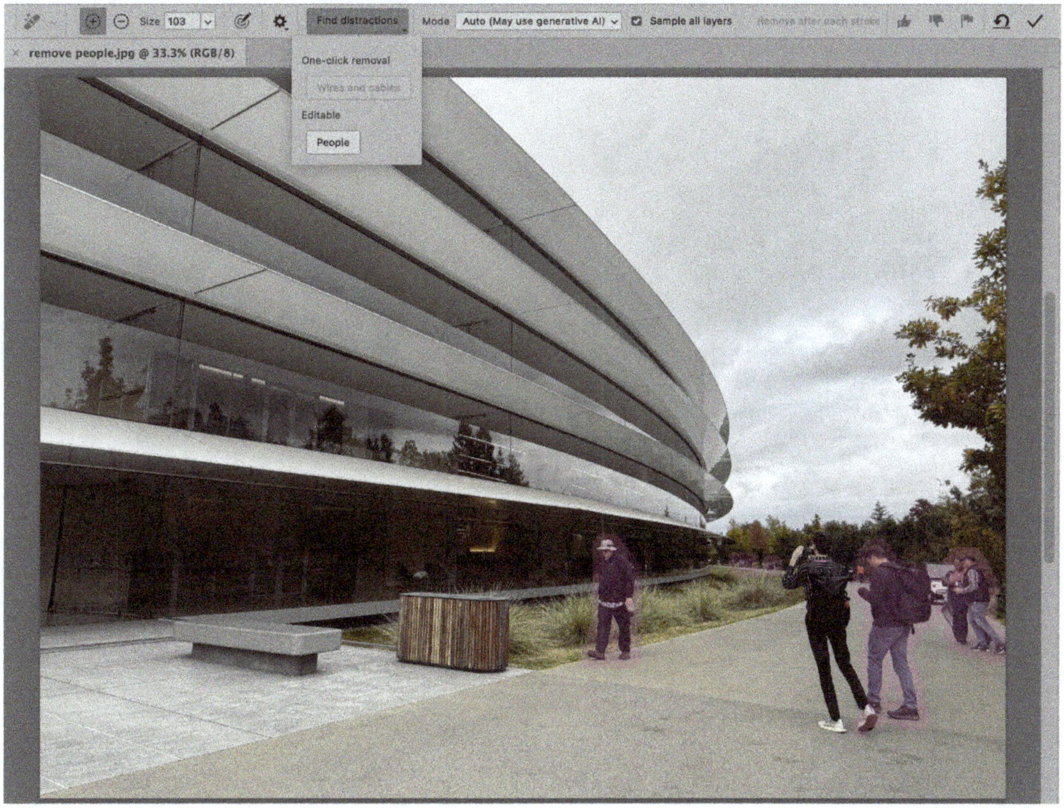

Figure 7.3 – Using the Remove tool's Find Distractions > People option; most but not all people were found

When this feature was introduced, many novice users may have been tempted to use this new tool and never learn any of the other tools. However, from mid-2025, some generative tools in Adobe apps, now under the **Adobe Firefly** banner (`http://firefly.adobe.com`), switched from free to requiring *generative credits* on some plans. However, the Remove tool remains free on all plans, at least for now, whether you choose to use GenAI or not.

Figure 7.4 – This image is usable; certainly better than the results without AI

Your subscription determines the cost and type of generations you can use. Most generative tasks in Adobe apps are labeled as *standard*, while tasks involving video are *premium*, as are third-party models used in Firefly. If you subscribe to all the apps (**Creative Cloud Pro**) then standard generations are free, and you can use these features as you wish.

On other plans, a typical Generative Fill task now costs 1 credit, and different accounts receive varying numbers of generative credits per month—currently, somewhere between 25 and 500. (Though Creative Cloud Pro does include 4,000 generative credits, since *standard* generations remain free, these credits are only used for *premium* tasks.)

Additional credits can be purchased with an add-on Firefly plan over the regular Creative Cloud plan, but some users planning to use generative techniques for bulk processing may now have to consider the cost. (We'll also return to these credits in the next chapter, because the costs for video generation are much higher than they are for stills.)

Even with the potential cost, Adobe's generative options are tempting for creatives worried by the legal and ethical risks of using most generative image models, because commercial use is explicitly permitted, at least with the default Firefly models.

However, in late 2025, it became possible to use other generative image models instead. As it's still in beta, costs are yet to be finalized, but **Flux Kontext** and Google's **Nano Banana** (AKA Gemini Flash) can be used for Generative Fill instead of the Firefly models, if you wish. This does come with an ethical question, though—were these models trained on images they didn't have permission to use? Even if they didn't have permission, was looking at these images permissible under fair use?

Also, if you were wondering, Adobe *doesn't* train its models on your images, but other AI providers *might*. Policies vary, but in general, if you're paying for a service, they probably won't use your data for training. If you're using a service for free, it's more likely; read the fine print to find out.

In contrast to many models that have been trained on images of unknown origins, Adobe's models have been trained only on specific, known images. While largely sourced from Adobe Stock, some public domain and other openly licensed content were also used (`https://helpx.adobe.com/au/firefly/get-set-up/learn-the-basics/adobe-firefly-faq.html`). Though not all contributors to Adobe Stock were aware that their images would be used for AI training, it was legally permitted in the agreements they signed (`https://www.techradar.com/pro/software-services/creators-slam-adobe-over-firefly-ai-training`).

To briefly recall the ethical points raised in *Chapter 2*, if you're concerned about the way in which an image generation tool was trained, search for a statement from the tool's maker. Adobe's statement is clear, and Apple says they use "licensed data" (`https://machinelearning.apple.com/research/introducing-apple-foundation-models`). Major LLM creators, including OpenAI and Meta, have faced lawsuits regarding the origins of their training data, and have claimed "fair use."

If you want to edit images using a combination of traditional retouching tools and AI, Photoshop is likely still your best bet, whether you use third-party models or not. Generative Fill is a great tool for adding to or changing an image; third-party models extend that capability in new ways, and if you want to remove something, Generative Remove usually produces clean, useful results. However, Adobe's tools are far from the only way to change part of an image with AI.

Multi-modal LLMs such as ChatGPT and Gemini are capable, as are a host of third-party web-based services and the photo editing tools built into mobile phone operating systems.

On phones, Android users can use Google Photos' AI editing tools, where **Magic Eraser** and **Magic Editor** are included for free. Brush over an area, circle it, or tap distinct items to remove them, and the AI models will fill in the blanks. On an iPhone or iPad, circling an unwanted part of an image in the Photos app works in much the same way. Though these simple tools don't always provide the flexibility, power, or scalability that creative production pros want, they can be a convenient tool for quick, occasional fixes.

Assuming that your needs extend beyond what a phone can do, if you'd rather not use Photoshop, consider a web- or desktop-based option such as Freepik, Evoto, or Claid.ai, use services integrated with AI offerings from OpenAI or Google, or even consider website creation tools such as Wix. (Other tools, such as Imagen, aim their image retouching services at automated production, and we'll look at some of those tools in the *Automation AI* part of this book.)

Though many kinds of tools are available, I suspect most creative professionals would prefer to use a desktop-based app to avoid the file management hassles that can arise from uploading and downloading images from websites.

> Not all tools offer desktop apps, and multiple services may offer the same models. Adobe's Firefly web service currently offers the most prominent models, including their own Firefly Image models, plus more from Imagen, GPT Image, Flux, and Runway.

Let's take a deeper look at how to make images from text prompts.

Retouching through AI prompting

Competition is active in this area. In August 2025, Gemini launched its Flash 2.5 (AKA Nano Banana) system, actively inviting users to refine images by prompting via a web interface:

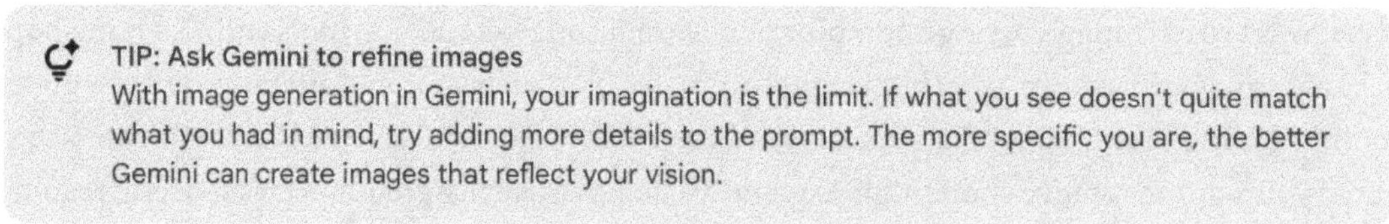

Figure 7.5 – Gemini now asks users to be specific in their requests

Uploading the same "man on beach" image as before and asking it to `add a hat to this man` gave decent results:

Figure 7.6 – Gemini's output; I could have been more specific, but this hat is an appropriate choice

Consistency is high, but the main problem with this from a production standpoint is that the output doesn't quite match the input; it's been cropped and slightly enlarged, the resolution has changed from `1024 x 512` px to `1024 x 535` px, and there's visible quality loss.

Another issue stems from file management. When you upload, process, and redownload, the original filename is lost, and each downloaded file must be renamed and copied to a stable location. Issues like this are inevitable for web-based systems, and while these aren't insurmountable issues for one-off tests, they are problematic for production workflows.

Production workflows based entirely within Photoshop are much easier to manage, so if you want to use Nano Banana, I'd use it within Photoshop if possible. Resolution is still an issue, but this can be worked around by selecting a smaller area to be generated or by regenerating only part of a larger area.

Another concern is that generations are sometimes offset or with a different brightness level from the original. To fix these issues, add a layer mask and paint that mask around the edges with a soft, black brush. AI generation within Photoshop is powerful, and though it's not perfect, it can be a useful tool for difficult retouching tasks. This feature is under active development right now, and it may change again soon in upcoming releases.

> For the very latest information on Photoshop, I'd recommend following the latest from Unmesh Dinda at PiXImperfect—in my opinion, the best Photoshop educator on YouTube. Here's a video about the introduction of Nano Banana into Photoshop, likely slightly out of date by the time you read this, but with plenty of great ideas: `https://youtu.be/RJ2eqkk_JxI`. For example, did you know you can annotate an image with text instructions and use a text prompt such as `follow the prompts in the image`?

Still, web-based text prompting could be an option worth considering, so let's see how different web services can handle the same people-removal task I performed in Photoshop at the start of this section. Instead of using menus and painting missed areas by hand, I'm just going to ask the tool to do it in plain English: `Remove the people from this image`. Here's how different models performed:

- **Gemini** (`http://gemini.google.com`): Its older image model did a passable job, but the replacement area could be better. Resolution was poor, and detail was lost. The newer Nano Banana model did a better job but still suffered from poor resolution and lost detail.
- **ChatGPT** (`http://chatgpt.com`, with a free account): It did an OK job of the removal, but took its time, and cropped the image to a square.
- **Sora** (`http://sora.chatgpt.com`, v1, with a ChatGPT Plus paid account): It did a good job in a minute or two, and didn't change the image's aspect ratio, but resolution wasn't as high as the original.
- **Freepik** (`https://www.freepik.com/`): It did a very good job, very quickly, using the Flux Kontext Max model. A paid plan is required for a commercial license or high-resolution output.
- **Claid.ai** (`https://claid.ai/`): It did a pretty good job. High resolution output is only available with a paid plan.

Though many options exist for this task, if you need a high-resolution result, you'll need to pay for it.

Figure 7.7 – Freepik (shown) and Claid produced results equal to Photoshop

Not all AI-enhanced photo tools accept text input, so if you'd prefer a tool to handle more unusual requests, check that prompting is supported. This approach also allows a service provider such as Freepik to design prompts to support specific workflows, such as `Generate Different Angles of Person` or `Place Product in a New Setting`.

ChatGPT's text model interprets your requests, then other image models handle the image creation.

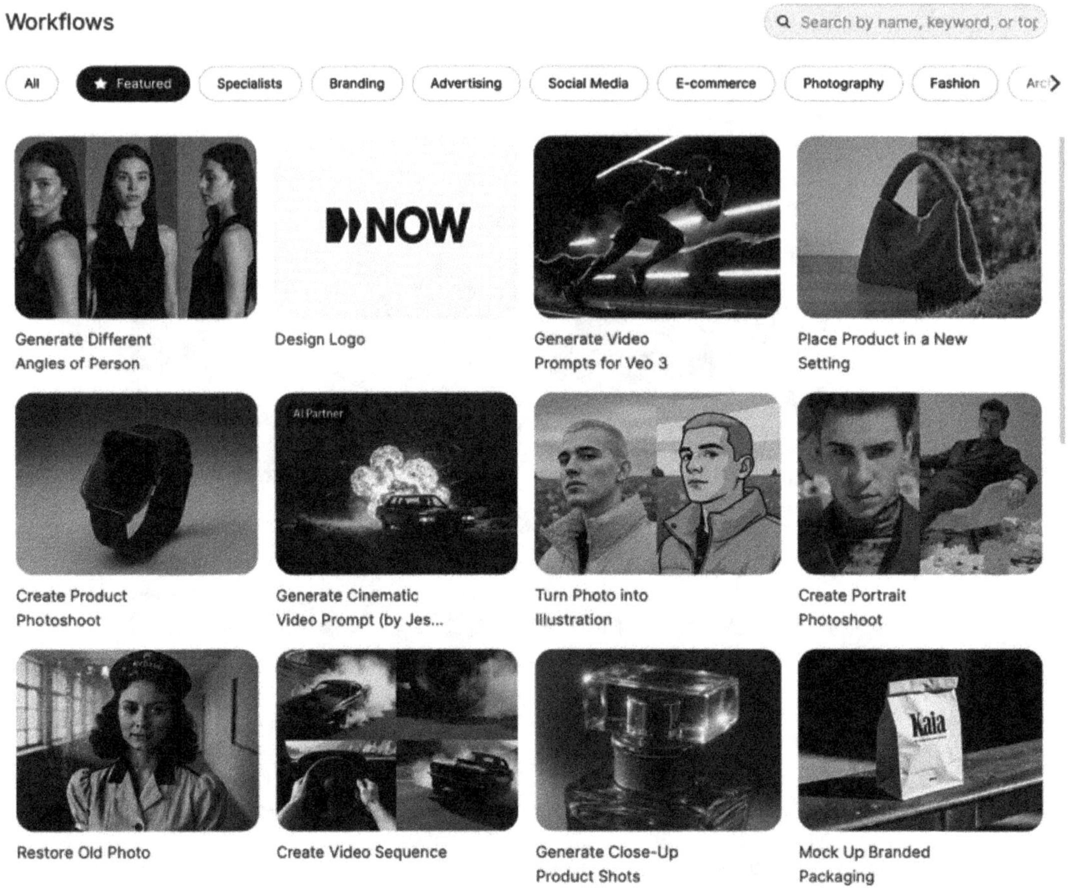

Figure 7.8 – Freepik offers many prompt-driven workflows, including these

Some of these go well beyond what would be possible through simple retouching, and usable results can be obtained in just a few seconds. We'll return to more complex image-to-image workflows shortly.

Expanding original images

It's not unusual for an image to be more tightly framed than a layout artist would prefer. In an ideal world, a photographer could frame their shots more loosely, giving the designer final control over cropping and placement.

Because we *don't* live in an ideal world, a photographer is more likely to frame their shots in a way that looks good to them, cropping the subject more closely in the camera or during processing. The client then approves those "nicely cropped" shots in their own context, and everyone is happy. But later, if the edges of the image turn out to be needed after all, AI can help to fill in the missing areas.

Image extension is conceptually similar to replacing an unwanted part of an image. Instead of replacing part of the original image, its boundaries are extended in one or more dimensions, then the new area is filled in with image data that looks like the original. While it's possible to use older tools such as the Healing Brush and Content-Aware Fill to perform this task, it's often easier with Generative Fill.

Figure 7.9 – With the original image shown here outlined in green, Photoshop offers three potential expansion options

Adobe apps offer this feature in a few ways. You can perform this task in Photoshop with a manual selection and Generative Fill, as a generative expand with the Crop tool, or even in InDesign, depending on workflow requirements. Other image processing tools can get the job done, too.

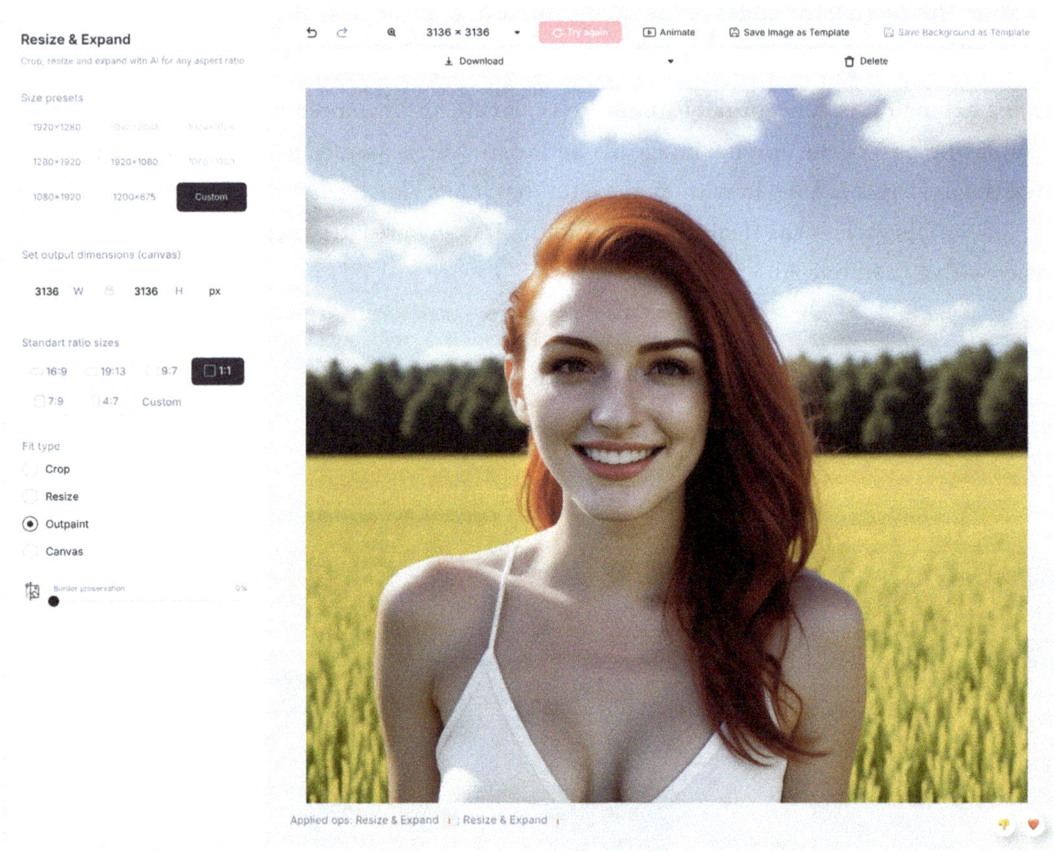

Figure 7.10 – Claid.ai required two upscaling operations (vertical, then horizontal) to get this result

This feature, often called **outpainting**, is common in AI image processing services, and many services can give good results. If you need to reuse an image in a new context, and the original image can't be found, it's not a bad way to go. However, be aware that if an original uncropped image does exist, you should always try to find it, or you could accidentally misrepresent reality. Inventing any part of a human's body—as shown in the preceding figure—is ill-advised.

While the woman in the images shown here is not real, it's easy to imagine offence to real people being caused by image extension—and this has indeed happened. In early 2024, Australian TV network *Channel Nine* faced criticism after using AI to expand an image. As part of a TV news story, Georgie Purcell (Member of Parliament, Victoria) was filmed and photographed wearing a white dress. This image was later cropped to show only the area above her waist and used in another context. Later, this cropped image was expanded with GenAI to show her wearing a crop top rather than the original dress (`https://theconversation.com/nine-was-slammed-for-ai-editing-a-victorian-mps-dress-how-can-news-media-use-ai-responsibly-222382`).

While Generative AI has clear uses in advertising and ideation, be very careful when using it on images of real people in a fact-based context. Still, generative expansion isn't anywhere near as controversial as creating complete images, and that's up next.

Creating original images

You'll have almost certainly encountered AI-made images in the wild by now, but... do you want to use an AI to make images for you? The closer you are to the image creation process, the less likely you are to be excited by the prospect. If your main job is marketing, and you see graphic design and photography as expenses, you might like the idea a lot. But if you're a photographer or illustrator, why would you want to stop doing it?

Still, while clients should care enough about their images to hire skilled professionals to create them, not all do, and this is nothing new. If a small business doesn't see the benefit in hiring a photographer or designer to craft their image, historically, they'd do it themselves, or use a template, or ask a family member who "knows Photoshop" to help. Today, they might just use AI.

Even in professional jobs for larger companies, not every image is of the same worth. A graphic designer tasked with finding an image to illustrate a point in an annual report doesn't have a budget for photography, but they might have a stock image.

Today, that budget might have shrunk to zero, and they might choose to source an image from a free stock image site such as `pexels.com` or `pixabay.com`, or `unsplash.com`, with its hybrid free/paid model. All these sites now include real photos alongside AI-made images, though the AI-made images are tagged as such.

In a situation where a stock image made by humans would be acceptable, is it OK to use an AI-made image instead? Ask your customers. Their answer might be different regarding abstract images used in an annual report when compared to an art-focused project, such as a board game. If consumers have a strong preference for human-made art, using AI art could sink a crowdfunding project.

But even if you choose not to use AI-made images for finished art, consider using AI image creation tools for ideation and mockups. Even though AI art is, by its nature, derivative of other art, so is the traditional mockup process, in which other people's images are used for inspiration and mood-setting.

You're in charge of what you use this tech for. Here, we'll look at what's possible, what's good, and what's not, and we'll start with creating images from text.

Image generation from text prompts

Prompting allows you to define what an image should contain and in what style it should be presented. While text prompting can't reliably produce an image showing a specific product—for that, you'll need an image-to-image workflow—it's still very useful. If a stock image search comes up empty, and there's no budget to capture the image for real, just ask an AI to make one.

Services can vary in their output quality, speed, user interface, and pricing, and your use cases will determine how much you prioritize each of these. If you only want images for mockups, an imperfect solution that's built into your existing software may be more appealing than a higher-quality paid solution, for example. In other situations, you may be limited by platform self-censorship. Many models steer a long way clear of anything that could be considered violent or explicit, and Firefly won't even generate an image of the Eiffel Tower.

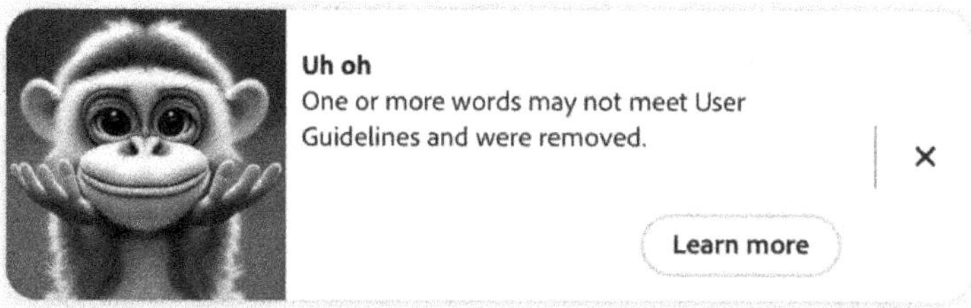

Figure 7.11 – This prompt was simply "The Eiffel Tower, at a 45° angle, on a sunny day with blue skies"

While some tools are exclusively available on specific platforms, other models can be found across multiple vendors. For example, Apple's **Image Playground** is available only on Apple's hardware, but you can access the **FLUX.1 Kontext** model through Adobe Firefly, Freepik, and others. Progress in this space is rapid, and you'll need to run your own tests to see which service(s) suits your needs. If you're using Firefly, remember that using third-party models costs generative credits—check how many you have before you start.

If you know what you're looking for, using detailed instructions will give better results, and if you leave the details up to the model, you can expect more variety. Be sure to specify the subject, what's happening, where they are, and the style of image you want.

Use descriptive adjectives, specify the desired aspect ratio, and include photographic and lighting instructions, too. If a prompt doesn't quite work, add to it and try again, or add negative information, such as `no extra limbs`, if you face repeated issues.

Some services, such as Firefly, allow you to choose additional options such as aspect ratio and style using options alongside the prompt. We'll discuss reference images and style options in the next section of this chapter.

Simpler, faster models can struggle with more complex prompts involving multiple subjects. You'll face trade-offs between the size of generated images and speed and may need to upscale low-resolution images for some purposes. Also, you'll find that many models produce garbled text—be ready to fix it manually if needed.

Here, we'll try the same prompts on several different models, highlight important differences between vendors, and offer some strategies. Here are the prompts:

- `A hand holding soil from which a small green seedling is growing, dark clear background, strong overhead lighting, realistic modern photo`
- `New York City streets devastated by flooding, people in a rowboat moving through the intersection of Broadway and 51st Street, grainy black and white historical photo`
- `A menacing skeleton holding a sword, dark dungeon background, mouth open, ready to attack, fantasy illustration style`
- `Abstract art with neon gradients featuring dots and swirls, modern tech style, vector illustration`
- `A brown fox is jumping quickly over a dog that is lying down asleep in a pine forest, dappled light, fairytale watercolor illustration`

Importantly, note that some services will advise you how to improve the prompting process, and may even "enhance" your prompts. For example, Firefly includes a **Prompt Enhancement** feature that's on by default with their own models, turning the preceding New York City prompt into the following:

Prompt · Enhanced Show original

People navigate through the chaos in a rowboat, moving through the intersection of Broadway and 51st Street. Water rises to the mid-calf, reflecting the dim, somber light of the streetlights. The towering skyscrapers in the background loom ominously, their windows dark and foreboding. The atmosphere is tense and gritty, evoking a sense of resilience and struggle in the face of disaster. - New York City, flood, rowboat, intersection, historical photo, grainy, black and white, gritty, tense, resilient, struggle, disaster

Figure 7.12 – An enhanced prompt can add unwanted details

While a more detailed description will give more specific results, the emotional language added here is not appropriate for a news-style image. Specifying water rising "to the mid-calf" simply isn't what I asked for or wanted. Be wary. On the other hand, because Firefly allows you to select from many third-party models as well as their own, it can be a good place to quickly compare how effective they might be for your own work, and if you're an Adobe subscriber, you already have access.

> To find a model that creates work you like from prompts you're happy to write, it's worth running *many* free tests before paying for a subscription. Besides the Firefly-accessible models, you currently need a paid ChatGPT account to access Sora, and if you want to try Midjourney for free, download the mobile app *Niji Journey* (in your mobile app store) for a free trial there.

Here, I've tried these prompts with Adobe Firefly models, Runway, Flux 1.1 Ultra, Sora, ChatGPT, Midjourney, KlingAI, Nano Banana Pro, and others. Note that Apple includes an app called Image Playground on Apple devices, but it can't handle longer prompts the same way these other tools can.

All of the models tested did well on at least some of these prompts, but overall, the most consistent, highest-quality results came from OpenAI's Sora (v1) and Nano Banana Pro, the only models to create images showing the requested location in New York City, and that included legible, relevant text.

Figure 7.13 – Sora's NYC image is pretty much exactly what I wanted

This particular prompt proved challenging for most other models. In some generations, people were walking on sidewalks next to the "flooded" road; in most, the text was garbled. The most common issue was a general feeling of inauthenticity.

Sora did well on the other prompts, too:

Figure 7.14 – Other results from Sora

Nano Banana Pro did well, with no major errors and a high level of adherence to the prompts provided. While I'd still *just* give the edge to Sora (v1), these results are solid:

Figure 7.15 – Nano Banana Pro's results on all prompts

Firefly's built-in model has a big advantage in that its basic generations are free with an Adobe account, and four images are produced by default. While its soil hands were mostly OK, the last one is nightmare fuel:

Figure 7.16 – What happened with the last hand?

Further, while Firefly's New York City images showed more or less the right content, they were lacking in detail. The illustrative images didn't match the prompt at all; most of the "dogs" were actually foxes, and sometimes the jumping foxes were levitating.

Figure 7.17 – These NYC images aren't quite there, and the fox images are unusably poor

To be fair, Firefly is a multipurpose tool with many other tricks in its toolbox. If you want to style an image of text to look like liquid metal or orange fur, it's got you covered, but its default models aren't the best at pure photographic output just yet.

Figure 7.18 – Firefly's Text Effects hooks into a prompt-based style creator within Adobe Express

But let's return to the photographic and illustration comparisons. **Midjourney** produced some terrific illustration-style images of skeletons but couldn't make the fox jump over the sleeping dog—instead, they're both asleep.

Figure 7.19 – Midjourney's menacing skeleton and sleeping animals

Google's **Imagen** produced some solid results, including these:

Figure 7.20 – Imagen's soil hand was good, and its skeleton is suitably menacing

KlingAI, from DeepSeek, was mostly quick and effective:

Figure 7.21 – Kling's hand was good, and its fox jumps nicely over the lazy dog

Via Firefly, Flux did a good job on most of these prompts, at a higher resolution than most other models:

Figure 7.22 – Flux produced the best abstract art, and its other images were good too

Runway was also able to produce decent output:

Figure 7.23 – Runway's offerings were solid

Quantity production options

If you care about quantity and not quality, check out **Diffusion Bee**: a free Mac app that runs the older Stable Diffusion locally, for free. If you need a high quantity for rough mockup purposes, the cost is unbeatable.

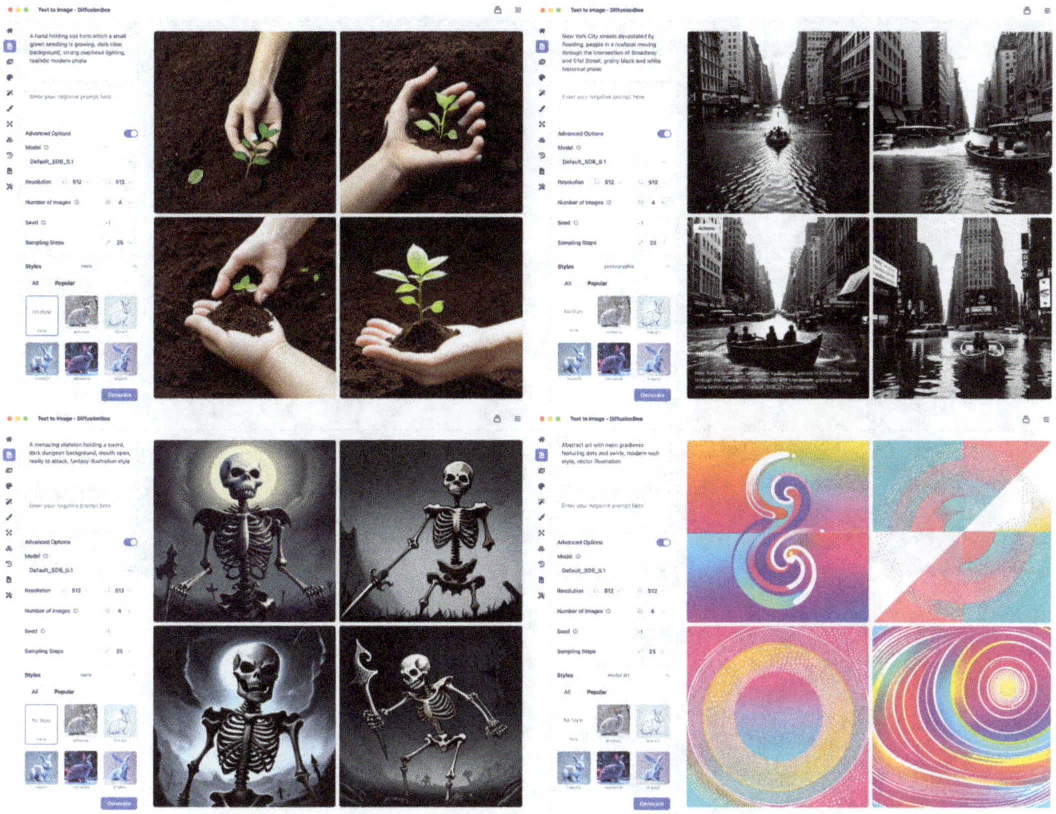

Figure 7.24 – These generations aren't very good, but they are completely free and unlimited

Another option that's great for quantity production is **Grok** (`https://grok.com/imagine` or via the Grok mobile app), which lets you simply scroll down to see more images, and more again. The speed of generation here is impressive, and for ideation, this could be remarkably useful. Even though a large number of images are produced, the quality is OK, and video generation (discussed in the next chapter) is a tap away from any image.

Figure 7.25 – Grok's images aren't best-in-class for quality, but it's very fast

For each prompt here, I've shown the first four but looked at many more and found similar issues to most other models. Dogs were often foxes or at least had a fox's tail; New York wasn't realistic; the fantasy illustrations looked cheap compared to other models; and some of the plant images included garbled, unwanted text. If speed is a focus, note that each set of four images took just a few seconds, and scrolling for more can be addictive. It's unclear what the long-term cost of these images will be, but it's all free right now.

Because models change and your needs won't be the same as mine, you could get good results from any of these services, or from many others I haven't included here, such as Leonardo or the latest Stable Diffusion models. Still, between Sora and the offerings available through Firefly, I think you'll be able to produce good results. Resolution is a concern with most of these models, but Flux (available through Firefly and others) can produce high resolution natively, and upscaling is likely to be effective with outputs from other models.

As with many other AI generations, expect imperfections and you won't be disappointed, but you might be pleasantly surprised at how well some of these models can perform. One of the sticking points for creatives is that telling a computer what you want is an entirely different creation process. For more control over exactly what an AI model creates, consider giving it images rather than just text.

Image generation from other images

Image-to-image workflows can take several forms. If you need to replace just part of an image, that's still best done with a tool such as Photoshop, but if you want to use one image as inspiration or style source for another, or ensure consistency in a suite of images, look for a tool that explicitly supports this. Many do, including Photoshop, most models at Firefly (including Nano Banana), and Freepik, to name just a few.

Simply asking for a specific image style is possible during text-to-image workflows, and some models, such as Firefly, allow you to upload a reference image for composition and/or for style—just be sure to choose the right image for each context. Sample images can be used if you don't have an original source of your own.

Photoshop's **Generate Image** feature allows you to include a **Style reference** and/or a **Composition reference**, and it's a helpful way to make a generated image match the layout or colors from an existing logo or photo.

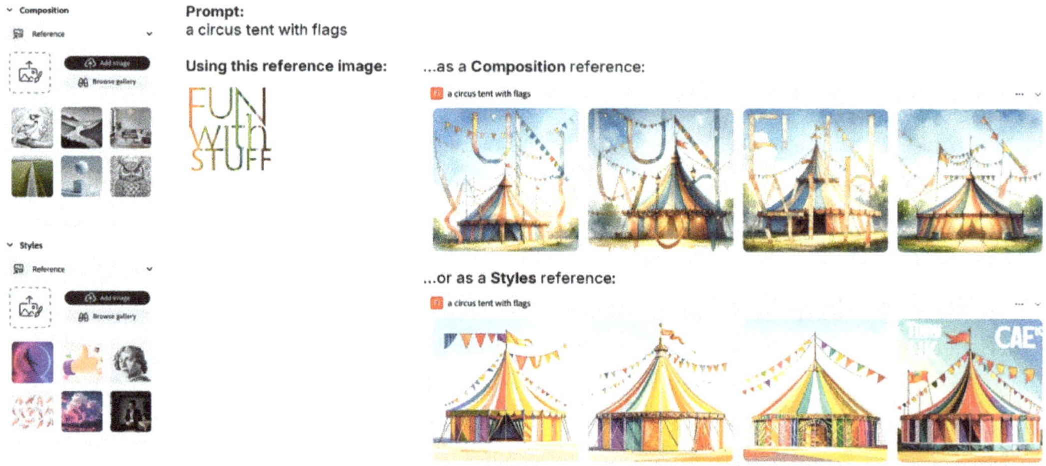

Figure 7.26 – Upload reference image(s) for composition and/or style image if you want a generation to match your existing work

If you don't want to use an existing image, you can draw from a large bank of existing reference images, some of which can be seen here:

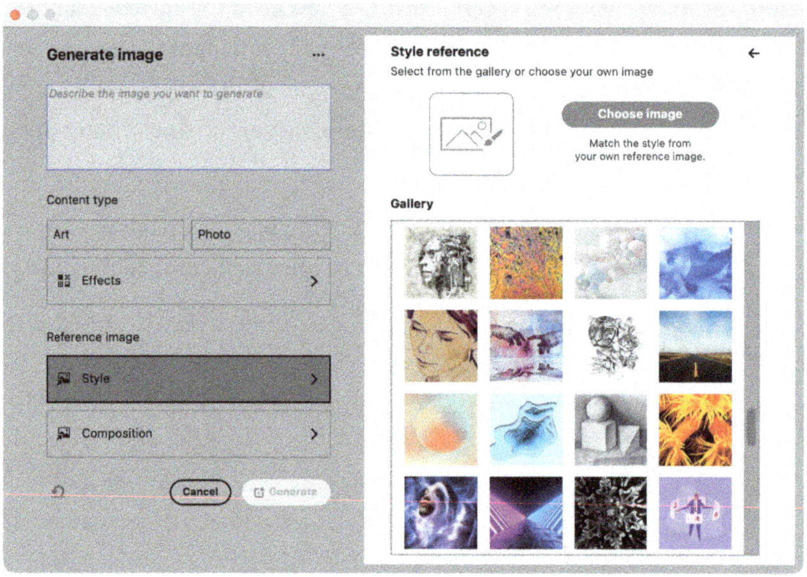

Figure 7.27 – The gallery here shows just a few of Photoshop's style references

Returning to pure text, it's possible to prompt a service such as **Sora** to create additional images in the style of an existing image. Here, I've asked for a few new images based on the skeleton that Sora made earlier:

Figure 7.28 – The skeleton was the style template for the dwarf, dragon, and treasure (all lightened to show detail)

If you need this level of control more broadly, you'll want to move to a service like **Freepik**, which allows you to provide a larger pool of training images from which a LoRA can be generated. Named from **Low Rank Adaptation**, a **LoRA** lets a model imitate a style without the model needing to be retrained from scratch and is conceptually a custom style that matches your own existing images.

Freepik also offers premade styles if you'd prefer to use theirs, and this helps your generations stay similar to one another. These styles can also be used to reimagine an image in a new style, a service also offered by Google Whisk. Here's an example, where I've uploaded two images to the left, chosen the style of a soft toy, and let the site do its thing:

Figure 7.29 – Google Whisk, a useful way to remix

The two images shown to the right were generated by two different prompts that Google Whisk wrote based on the images to the left. As finished art, they're not so great, but as inspiration? Just fine. It's also possible to use Photoshop's Generative Fill with prompts such as `make this image into an oil painting` if you use a model that's capable, like Nano Banana. Resolution isn't perfect, but the results are often impressive.

What if you do need photographic images at the quality of finished art, though? With some services, this is indeed possible.

Creating virtual photo shoots

Like Firefly, Freepik offers models from other AI providers and repackages them within its own interface and unique features: `Generate Different Angles of Person`, `Place Product in a New Setting`, and so on. After uploading a single image of a girl in a field to Freepik, it can be asked to generate photos at different angles:

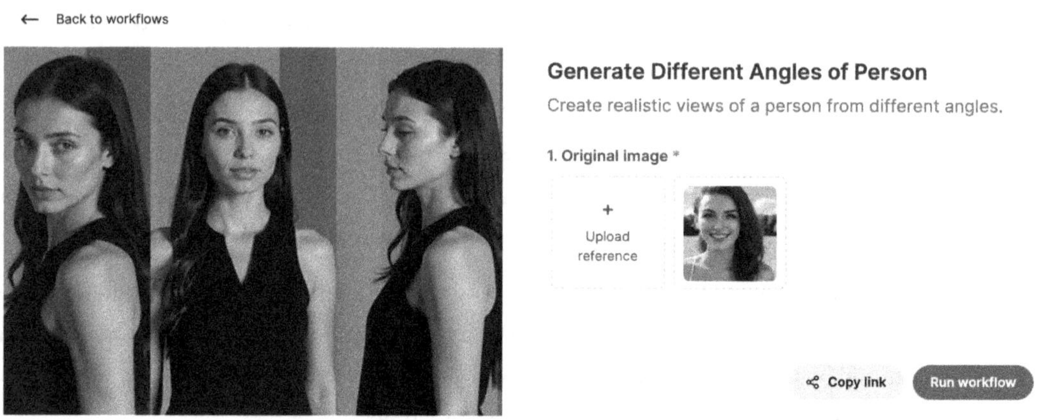

Figure 7.30 – Freepik allows you to upload a single image, then prompts "Hey! Create multiple images from different angles of this photograph" for you

Freepik then produces these three new images:

Figure 7.31 – Three usable new options, and more available if you ask for it

Although these photographs don't *quite* look like they're of the same person, they're very close, and the value of a tool like this could be huge in the right situation. Image-to-image workflows have the potential to scale to a production workflow in a way that simply asking for an image with text cannot.

While Freepik includes a selection of predefined characters, you can create a new virtual character, or avatar, by uploading many images of a person, real or not. These images will then be used to train a model, making it possible to create images of a specific, consistent person. This technique is helpful for continuity purposes, and we'll return to it in the next chapter.

Freepik isn't the only service able to create images of the same person at different angles. **Higgsfield** (`https://higgsfield.ai/`) offers virtual characters alongside an impressive set of presets, and as it's mostly video-focused, we'll return to them in the next chapter. Sora can do this job too, though it takes a little longer, and you'll have to make this request in a prompt.

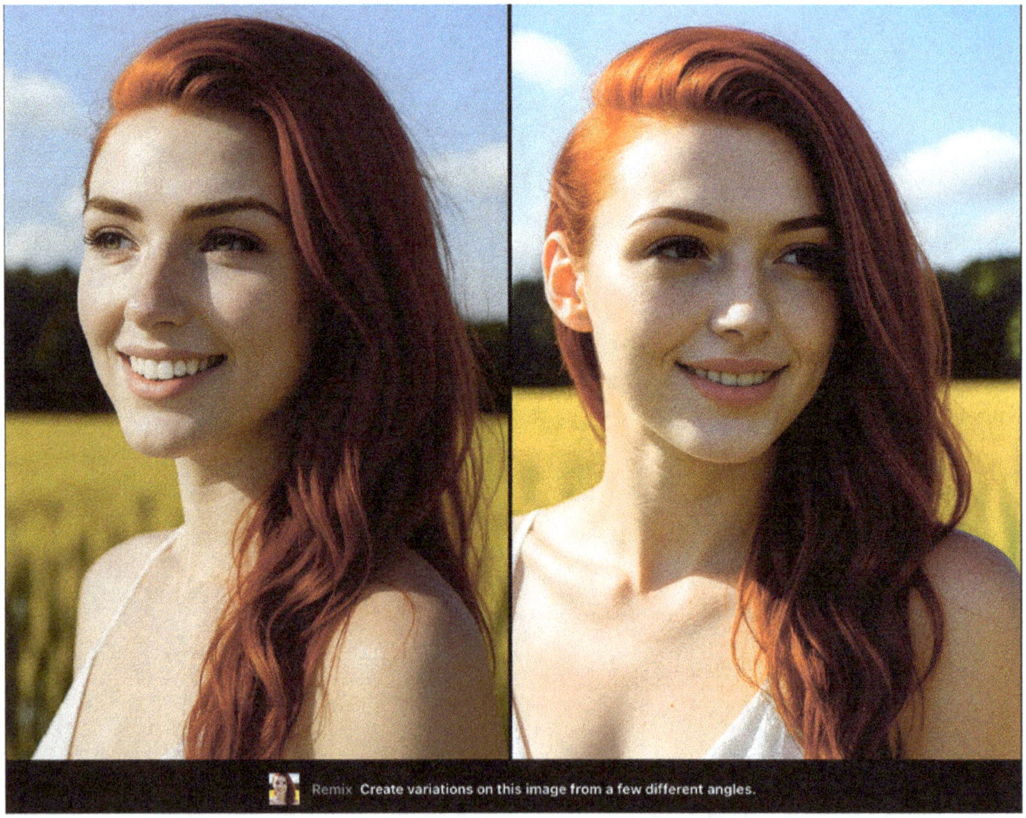

Figure 7.32 – Sora's Remix feature allows you to request variations, too

Claid.ai is another image-focused service, and it includes an AI fashion shoot feature. You can use one of the virtual models provided or your own images, along with images of the clothes you'd like them to model, and it'll take the virtual photos for you.

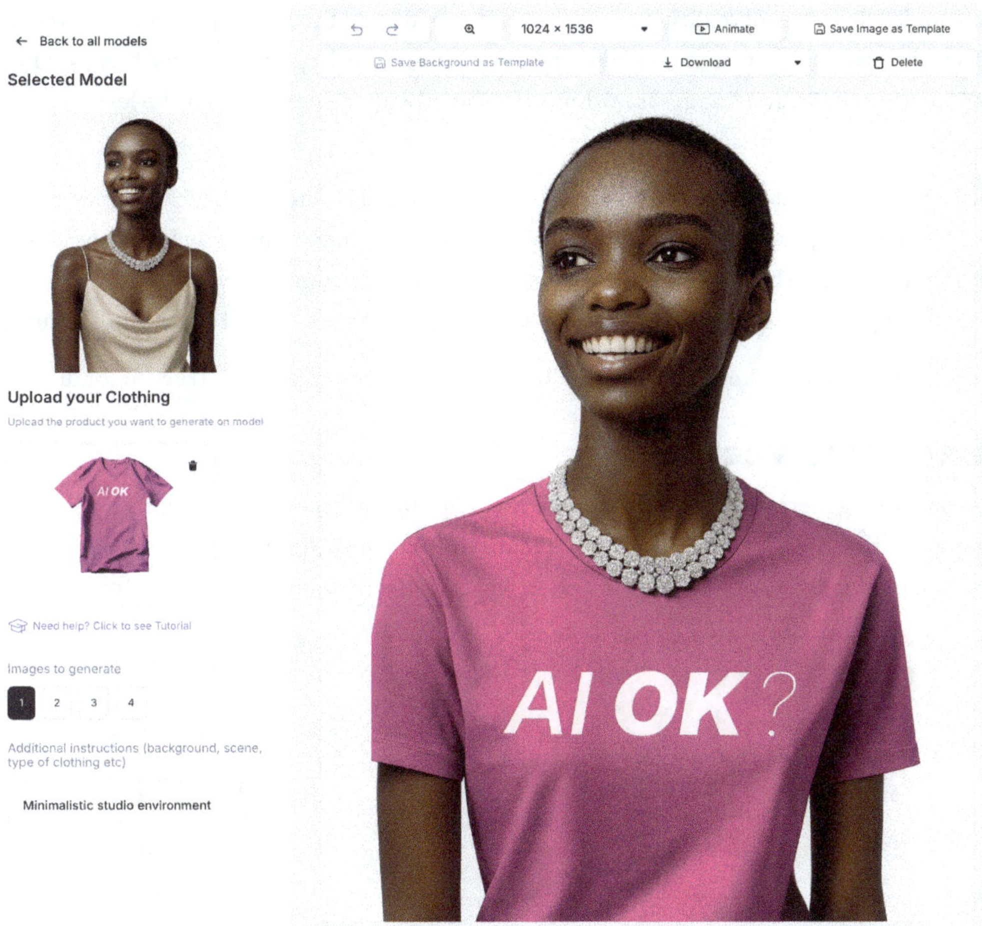

Figure 7.33 – Here's Claid.ai's virtual photo shoot results

Combining these ideas, you can now perform a photo shoot with a model holding a client's products or wearing their clothes, either for real or virtually. With that in the can, you can create new poses and provide new options without having to reshoot. Should you do this, though? That's a thornier question.

For the best, most original results, I recommend real photography of actual people and products, using AI to augment and supplement those photos if needed. A real shoot can produce magic results that haven't been requested or expected, and those moments of serendipity are valuable.

On the other hand, in some circumstances, real shoots aren't possible because the products being sold haven't been created yet. I've created photorealistic 3D renders to sell board games before they've been manufactured, and that's surely the same thing?

If you don't misrepresent reality, and you have approval from the other creatives involved in the project, the method by which you fake reality—with Photoshop or with an AI-assisted tool—shouldn't matter. Faking images is nothing new but always remember that the less you have to fake, the better the results.

Another important factor is that templates become stale quickly, and even quicker if they're heavily used. Therefore, if you consider using AI fashion shoots, I'd steer clear of stock AI fashion models. They might look fine the first time you see them, but when consumers have seen the same models in exactly the same poses multiple times on many different sites, they'll harm more than help.

While we've looked at photographic and illustration images, what about true vector art?

Generative vector art

While most AI-generated images are pixel-based, Adobe has a couple of options for generating vector art with AI. Firefly, on the web, can create subjects or scenes based on a prompt, with reference images or styles as a control. It's effective, and the downloads are in SVG format.

Figure 7.34 – Two different styles of vector art, all downloadable as SVG

Although one of the issues with most generated art is a lack of complexity, that's a strength for most vector art, where a crisp, clean style is usually desired. Based on a look at the art, it appears to have been traced from generated pixel art, but that's usually not too much of a problem.

If you'd prefer to access this tech in Adobe Illustrator directly, use the Contextual Task Bar. Draw a rectangle, press the **Generate Vectors** button, then type your prompt in.

For creations more closely based on your own art, create that art, then click **Gen Shape Fill** instead. Here, I've created a simple octagon and a rectangle, then asked it to generate a stop sign.

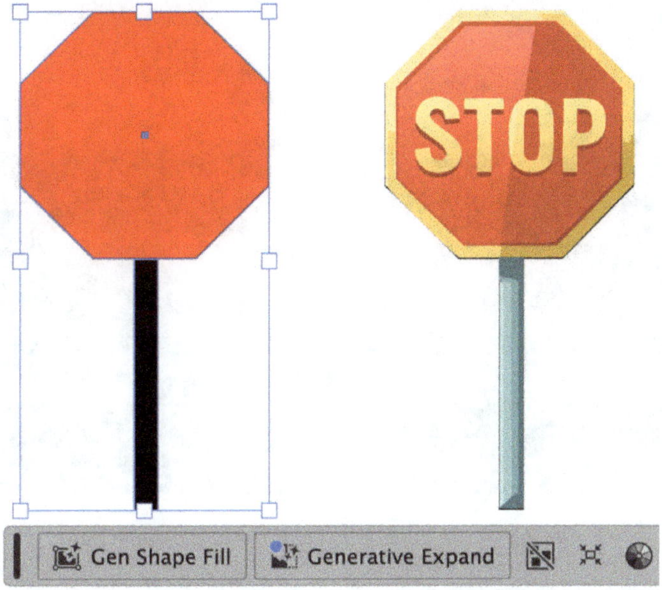

Figure 7.35 – A simple prototype stop sign, and a more developed version

Generative Expand, also found in Photoshop and InDesign, is extremely useful here in Illustrator. Opening an SVG from Firefly, it's easy to use the **Artboard** tool to extend the bounds of an existing artboard, then optionally add a prompt.

Figure 7.36 – No prompt was required here, just more of the same, please

Quickly, you'll be given a choice of three options, and can request additional generations if needed:

Figure 7.37 - The third option was the best on offer here

Illustrator can also generate vector patterns from prompts. Open the **Generate Patterns** panel, then type in a prompt to create three seamless repeating patterns.

Figure 7.38 - Three easy vector patterns available in the Variations panel

There's one more generative feature hidden in Illustrator at the moment: **Generative Recolor**. You'll find this option in the **Recolor Art** panel (**Edit** > **Edit Colors** > **Generative Recolor** is one way to reach it), and it provides a quick way to transform the colors of any selected artwork. While the regular **Recolor Art** dialog can do this with a small amount of manual effort, using the generative version is quicker, easier, and a fun way to experiment with colors.

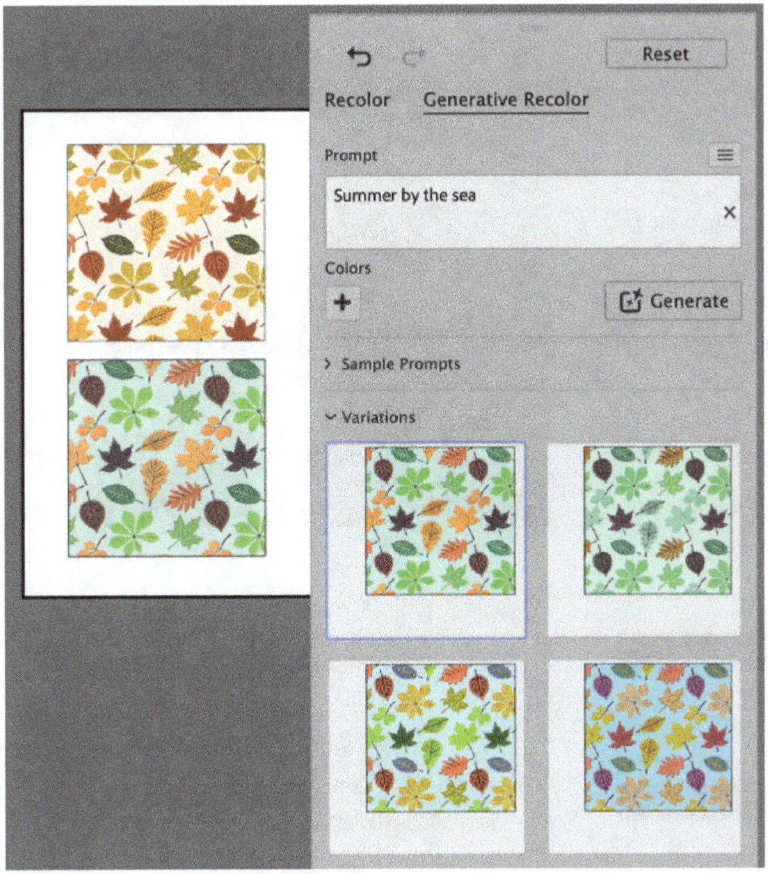

Figure 7.39 – Here, the leaves from earlier have been duplicated, expanded, and then recolored

You can type a prompt or use a sample, such as `Summer by the sea` in the preceding figure, click **Generate**, then click one of the variations below to apply it. Try as many variations as you wish, then click back over to **Recolor** to tweak the results manually.

While Illustrator's not the only AI-enabled tool that can create vector images, it's likely the most convenient. If you'd like to explore other options, try **VectorArt.ai** (`https://vectorart.ai`), the **Canva** AI vector generator (`https://www.canva.com/create/vector-ai/`), or **Recraft** (`https://www.recraft.ai/`). Recraft allows you to choose a style of vector art (or pixel art) and prompt as usual:

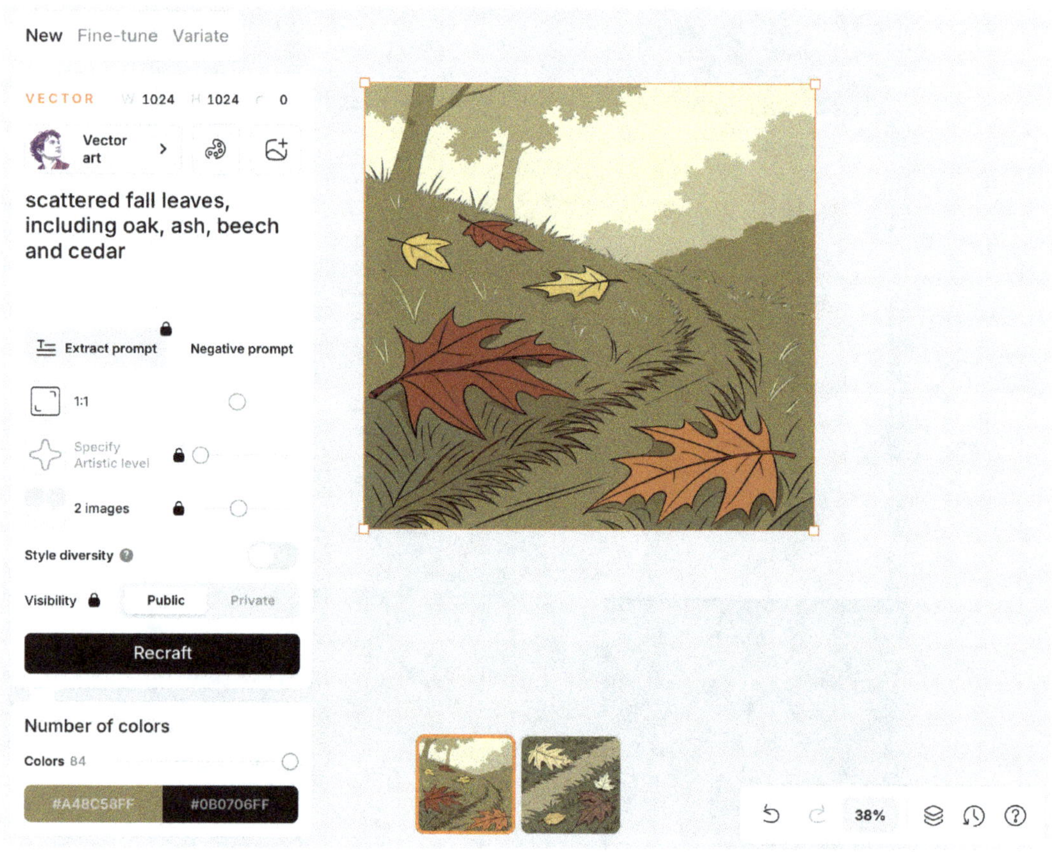

Figure 7.40 – Recraft allows you to create vector and pixel images

Even though these tools aren't integrated into the Adobe suite, you may find one of these tools to be a more flexible way to create vector art—give them a test.

In fact, Recraft is one of many modern web-based image generation tools that integrate GenAI models into a flexible interface suitable for simple design projects. As it supports both pixel and vector art, it's a great place to build a mood board—let's dig deeper.

Mood boards and design ideation

Using other people's images has long been an accepted practice for building mood boards, allowing a group of creatives to agree on a style and feel for a project. By allowing you to create images that inspire you rather than just borrowing other people's images, generated images add flexibility. Of course, you can mix generated and found images in a single board, and at the end of the day, none of these images will become part of the finished work.

Although it's entirely possible to create images in any GenAI solution and assemble them in the layout tool of your choice, you may find it easier to build a mood board in a web tool, potentially enabling easier collaboration and sharing. Some tools, such as Apple's Freeform, enable shared workspaces and could be a natural place for a group of creatives to brainstorm together.

However, if the process is more heavily focused on creation, you may prefer to use a tool that's more AI-focused. As mentioned earlier, Recraft's flexible workspace allows you to import images, duplicate/resize/pan using familiar shortcuts, generate pixel or vector art, create restyled variations of those images, and arrange them all on an infinite canvas.

Figure 7.41 – Just part of the expansive Recraft canvas with a few variations of the generated art and some samples

You'll need to pay for Recraft for it to be useful, but the integration may be worth it. However, if you're already subscribed to Adobe, they now offer a dedicated app for moodboarding: **Firefly Boards**. Like Recraft, this enables an infinitely large area for uploading, generating, and remixing images. You can also access Generative Fill and Generative Expand, as well as Flux and GPT models.

In this example, I uploaded my earlier collection of dungeon art, created variations on the skeleton and dwarf, then remixed the female warrior with the treasure chest to create the options on the right:

Figure 7.42 – Combining art has never been this easy

This process is fun, fast, and potentially revolutionary for the right project. The art clearly isn't perfect, and the variations created aren't always close to the original, but the brainstorming process should be messy. There's competition in this space, including **Kittl.com**, so check out the alternatives and see what works with your team.

Another help during brainstorming is to use a model with quick iteration based on previous image generations. **Leonardo.ai** offers **Flow State** to encourage this workflow, and Grok's endless scroll (mentioned earlier) is good for this too.

Figure 7.43 – Flow State, in Leonardo.ai, which generates several images on the same prompt, then invites you to create more like this

Whatever AI generation tool you end up using, interactive moodboarding like this is one of the best use cases I've seen for GenAI. But can you get help with entire designs in a format suitable for development in professional design apps? Not yet. So far, most tools are focused on creating single design elements: a photo, a background, or an icon. If you want to stretch, try creating variations of potential YouTube thumbnails—they're pretty simple.

To take things further, you have a few options: **Lovart.ai** can create editable posters, **Claude** can drive Canva for you, or you can use Canva's AI tools directly. Unfortunately, none of these approaches will lead to a professional design solution for a complex, multi-page document. Perhaps in the future we'll be able to ask InDesign to generate new design ideas based on provided references, but not yet.

Let's end this chapter with a look at 3D model creation.

Creating 3D models

Though most creative professionals aren't using 3D packages day to day, some definitely are, and AI tools promise to make the field more accessible. While motion graphics professionals are used to keyframe animation and may have a good handle on working in 3D space, becoming a modeling expert is a long, painful road for many.

Despite the pain, proper modeling skills will remain important for serious 3D applications for some time. If you have very light needs, though—perhaps you want to orbit a camera a small amount around a 3D object—a GenAI 3D tool might be helpful.

Similar to image generation tools, model generation tools can work from a text prompt or an existing image.

Meshy.ai is a well-known service, and though it no longer offers a free trial, it's a capable tool that can generate a choice of draft models, and after confirmation, a texture for your chosen final model. I took the treasure chest Sora made, quickly brightened it, and removed the background in Photoshop, then uploaded it. While it's possible to upload additional images from different angles, I just went with this one image, which worked well:

Figure 7.44 – The Meshy interface, with an image uploaded on the left, one of the four gray draft generations chosen, and the final texture

Meshy did a decent job of the generation, and while this object might be challenging to develop further—it's all one mesh, after all—it could be just fine as a smaller scale or background element. Here it is in Blender:

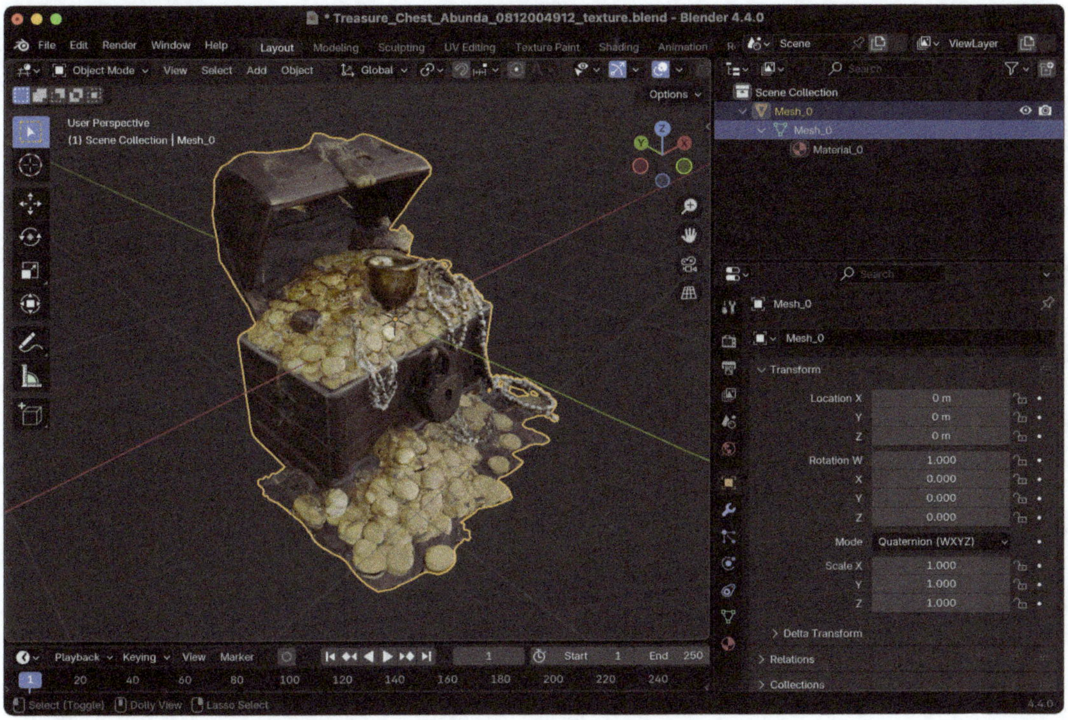

Figure 7.45 – The downloaded model in Blender

Downloads are available in several other 3D formats, including USDZ, OBJ, GLB, and STL. It's a similar story at **Hyper3D.ai**, which also allows you to upload one or more images and uses the Rodin model to output a 3D mesh.

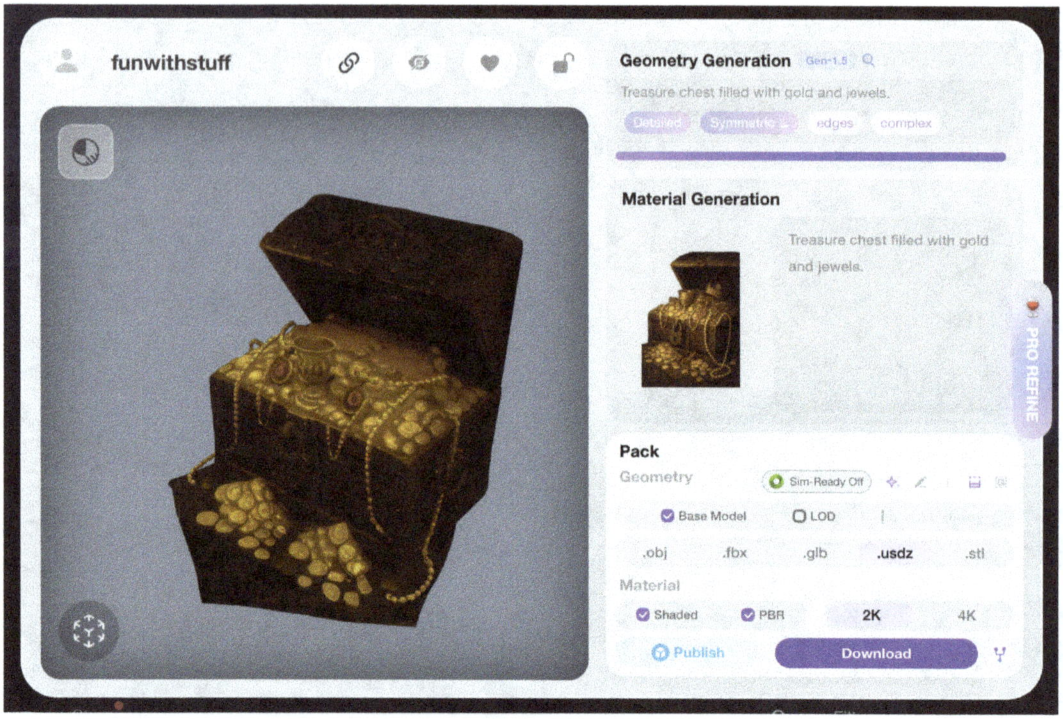

Figure 7.46 – The creation process here allows for regeneration at multiple stages

Though Hyper3D can't create a `.blend` file directly, I could import the generated USDZ file correctly in Blender. For better or worse, it was a little more ordered than the Meshy output and had a little less detail. Though the metal cup at the center didn't have the same level of shine that the Meshy model had, and the coins in the front were arranged in a slightly too-formal way, this result could be just as usable.

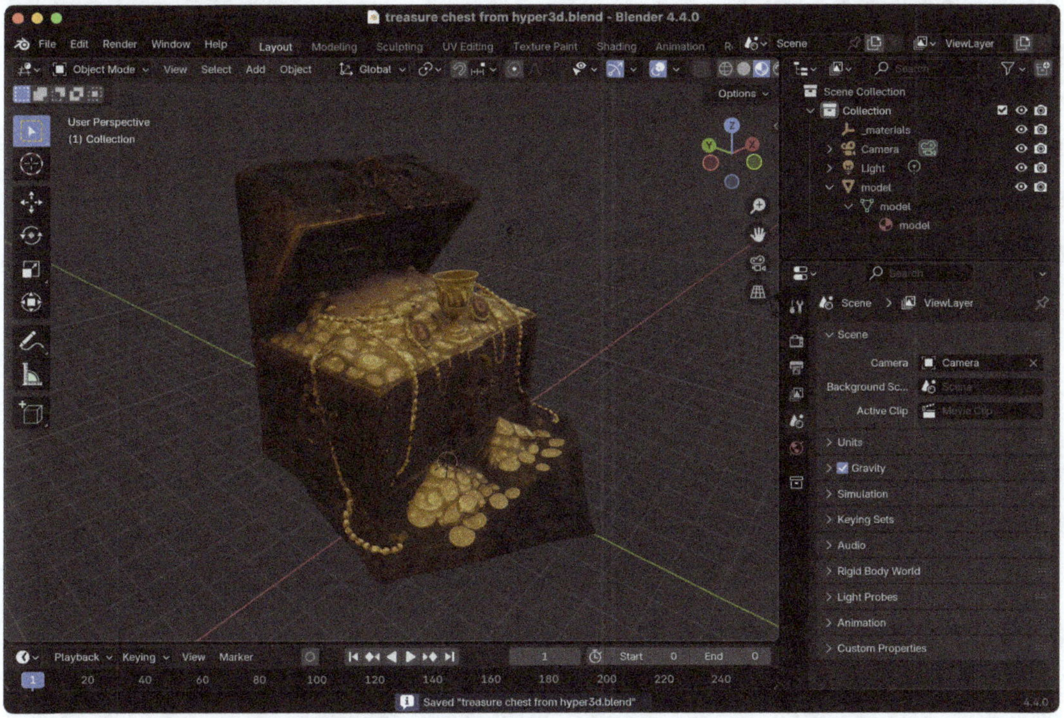

Figure 7.47 – After importing into Blender, this is a slightly more ordered result

For a few more options, you may prefer Tripo 3D, which can also segment a mesh into components—vital if you plan to animate or edit your generated model. Note that because the first step involves generating an image from your image, if you're not careful, you can end up with something slightly different. This one worked well, though, with better definition on the wooden chest:

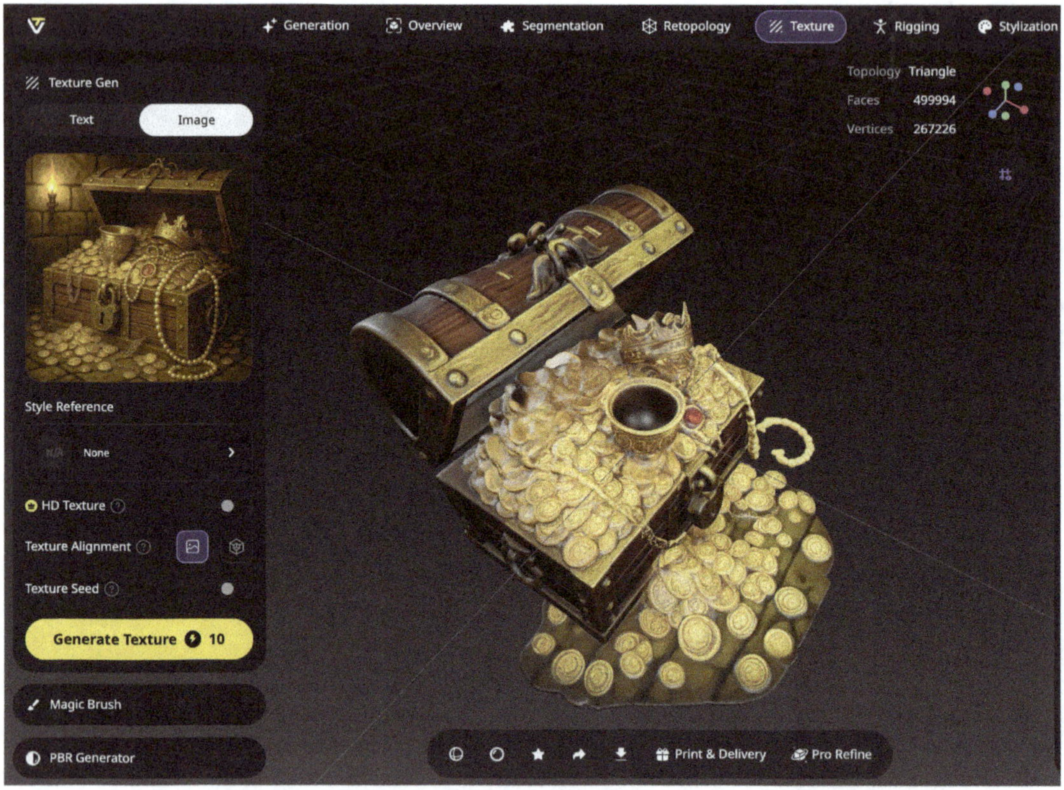

Figure 7.48 – The Tripo3D website lists the possible steps along the top of the workspace

This model has not been segmented, but if I wanted to refine the model by hand, it's what I'd pursue. Here in Blender, you can see that these results are useful:

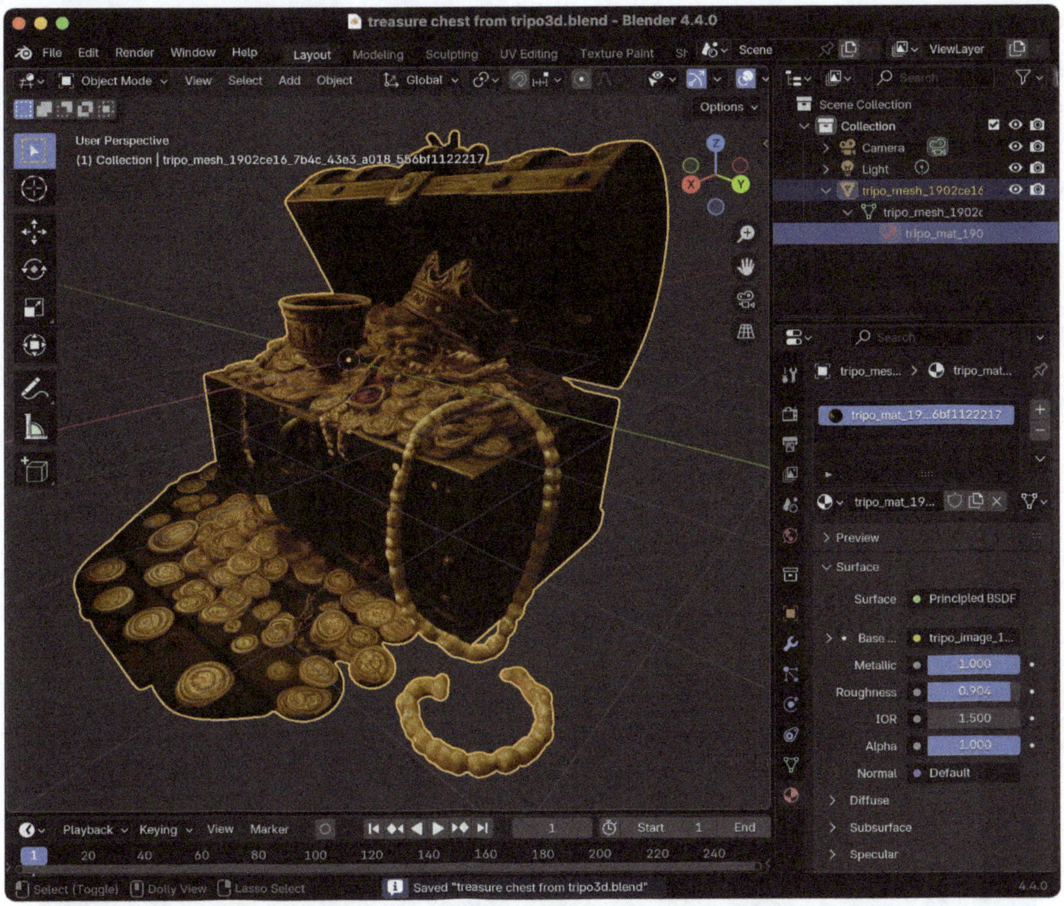

Figure 7.49 – Tripo3D's USD output imports cleanly into Blender

On the default settings, each of these sites takes quite a different approach. Hyper3D produced a model with 120,000 faces, Tripo3D created 500,000, and Meshy, the most complex, at 929,000. While the details can be decimated away, it's interesting to see such different approaches. If I had to choose one, I'd go for the cleaner results and extra control available from Tripo3D, but your needs may be very different from mine.

Other options, such as **Rendable3d.com**, offer similar services. I tested this in alpha while it was packaged as a fork of Blender, but you can now access the same generative tech on their website instead. A simple image-to-mesh feature is even now available in Copilot (`https://copilot.microsoft.com/labs/experiments/copilot-3d`), and a new option from Meta called **SAM 3D** (`https://ai.meta.com/sam3d/`) looks very promising indeed.

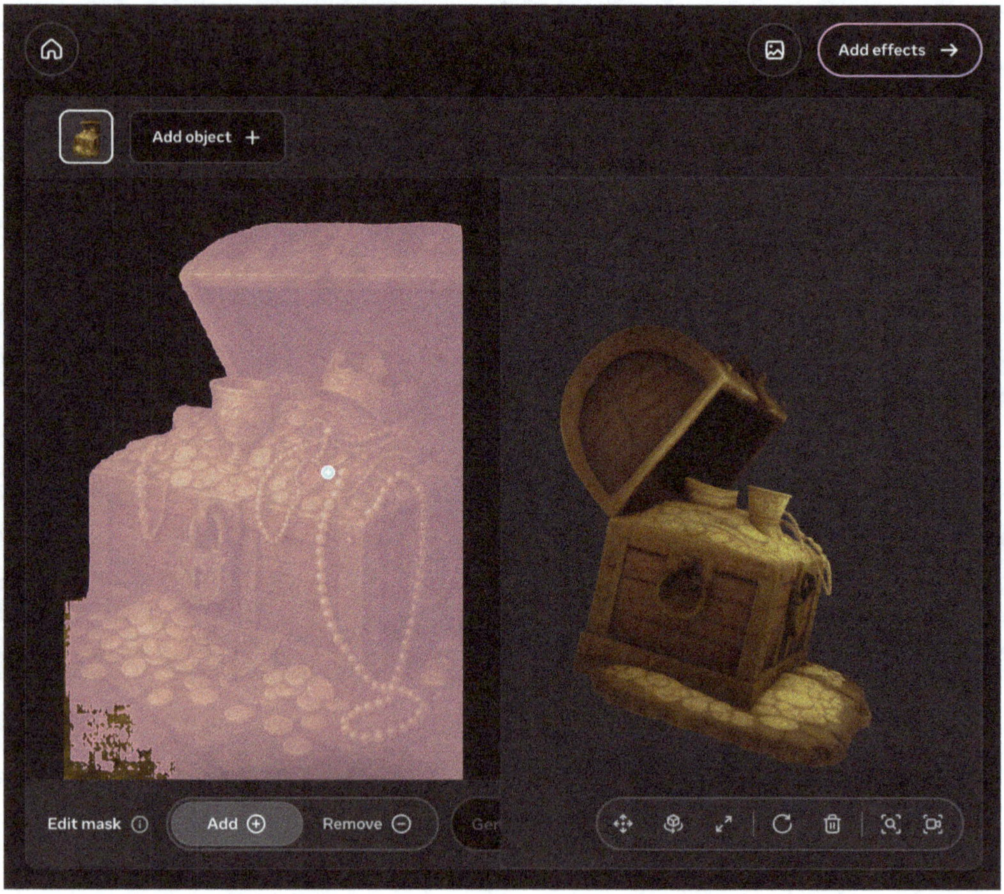

Figure 7.50 – SAM 3D is new and not yet a complete solution, but it looks good so far

This space is set to change further, so if you need 3D mesh generation, try any free trials that are currently available, explore the latest generative models, and see which one works best for you.

Interestingly, similar tech (based on Gaussian Splats) is used on modern Apple devices, turning any photo into a simple 3D spatial scene that responds to device movement. On the 2026 OS releases, this goes well beyond the Spatial Photos available on previous iterations of Apple Vision Pro, which only provided left-right movement. Spatial scenes allow movement in all dimensions and can be extremely effective. Apple's latest research in this area is impressive (`https://machinelearning.apple.com/research/sharp-monocular-view`).

You may be wondering whether ChatGPT can help. Although it can't help directly, it does offer to create a script that runs offline to do the same task. While the dedicated sites are likely to produce better results, if you need a large quantity of models and aren't afraid of running some code, this is a route you could take. We'll look more at scripting approaches later in the book, though. Time to wrap this chapter up.

Summary

If you're making AI images, you should now have a much better idea of how to get the best results, either by writing more expressive prompts or providing image examples for an AI to imitate. You'll know several ways to get what you need to help you in a creative workflow, whether it's for mockups, for finished imagery, or for vector assets.

Generating images can come with ethical questions: some new, some not. Is it OK to use AI for images that don't matter much, in contexts where photographers and illustrators would not be hired? That's up to you and your customers.

Is it OK to use AI in ideation, brainstorming, and moodboarding? If it informs your work without directly becoming part of it, there's no problem at all. Borrowing is part of the creative process, and as long as you're not trying to rip anyone off, it should be OK. The gap between thinking of something and seeing an imperfect version of that vision has never been shorter, and I can immediately see how it could have transformed the ideation process on projects I've worked on.

There is a revolution here, but I don't think it's going to displace artists any more than stock sites and templated designs already have. Exploring this new frontier is worth your time.

Next up, from the frying pan into the fire—we'll be generating AI video.

8

Generative AI with Video

Let's kick off with a dose of reality: Gen AI video is incredibly technically impressive, but it can't replace most human-made video. If you're currently shooting videos for clients, you can expect to keep doing it for some time yet. There's an AI revolution all right, but it's in other areas, and it's unlikely to take over mainstream video production.

At first glance, AI output can look amazing, and those who don't shoot video themselves might be suddenly excited that maybe they don't have to hire anyone to make videos for them. For most, this feeling doesn't last. The sample videos shared most widely are some of the few that look OK, but the majority of shots are flawed in some way, even those made with the latest models.

Fully AI-generated videos have all the problems that photos have (weird anatomy, oversmoothing) plus many more of their own: movement, audio, and resolution issues, just for starters. Consistency during a shot is hard, talking is hard, natural movement is hard, and most telling of all, *nothing usually happens*.

It's rare for any action in an AI-made video to have actual consequences, such as taking a bite from a hot dog and seeing less of the hot dog afterwards. People can stand there and move a little, but they have no motivation, no driving force behind them. People can *talk*, but they can't *do* anything important.

Because everything's an imitation of another frame or a best guess, there's no underlying common structure as there would be in real life, and this is far more of a problem in a video context—where continuity matters—than it is in still photography.

After all, most videos feature a specific person or a specific place. If you film that person or visit that place, continuity is free. Most AI shots are generic: a café, not a specific café; a random person, not actually an employee. If your goal is to tell stories, capturing some version of reality as people move through it and make changes, film it! AI video is not the best solution to this problem.

That doesn't mean it's all bad. If you treat AI as a special effects engine, allowing you to mess with reality in specific ways, to augment existing shots, it could do a good job. It's also possible to create one-off shots that would be impossible to film, and the most recent models are a step up from what's come before.

Some ideas are quite achievable, such as an animated version of a still image with minimal movement. It's possible to create several videos from the same image, then edit those pieces together to create a montage, common in some advertising. If you keep shot length short and don't try to do too much, there are ways to make AI videos that work nicely within the limits of what's possible.

It's important to realize that many generative services aren't aimed at creatives, but at their employers. Indeed, clients tempted to cut creative professionals entirely out of the loop may be tempted to use services such as **Creatify** (`https://creatify.ai`). This site offers not just individual video creation but *automated* video ad creation services, first analyzing your website, then mashing it together with a template to create an AI avatar delivering a message. So far, I've found that the more you ask from AI, the higher the chance that mistakes will be compounded, so I haven't been impressed by all-in-one solutions.

Unfortunately, many of the most obvious fully AI videos are *bad* videos. The same clients who were happy with no graphic design or templated graphic design are happy with AI-made avatars reading AI-written scripts, speaking to an audience that's quickly learning to associate AI video with scams, cheap ads, and low-quality products.

There are also potential ethical issues: very few models are guaranteed "commercially safe." Adobe's **Firefly** (`https://firefly.adobe.com`) and Moon Valley's **Marey** (`https://www.moonvalley.com/marey`) are, but most other models can't or won't state that their models were trained only on permitted media. A traditional creative ideation process often takes liberties with existing work, but in the finished product? It simply might not be an option for some projects, and you'll want to consider ethical implications yourself.

In August 2025, Netflix released a set of guiding principles around GenAI (`https://partnerhelp.netflixstudios.com/hc/en-us/articles/43393929218323-Using-Generative-AI-in-Content-Production`), and while they're all worth reading, point 4 is brutally plain:

> *Generated material is temporary and not part of the final deliverables.*

We're obviously not all making content for Netflix, but that's a pretty blunt statement—GenAI is OK for temp work, but not the end product. That doesn't mean GenAI videos aren't useful, but don't be taken in by clickbait from anyone selling courses on how to use AI video generation. There's huge potential here, but AI is not a full replacement for videographers.

Instead, AI has the power to give video professionals new tools to make different kinds of videos, to augment videos they're currently making, and to fix common issues.

In this chapter, we'll be looking at these topics, each trickier than the last:

- Extending existing clips
- Creating videos from text prompts
- Creating videos from reference images
- Creating videos from reference video and audio
- Transforming existing videos

That's right—it's actually easier to create new videos than it is to modify existing ones. Let's start with a trick that only Premiere Pro can do for now: making a clip longer.

Extending existing videos

Premiere Pro allows you to extend a clip past its end, and depending on how much video you make, this may be exciting or a complete non-event. If you're a video professional already, you'll know the ropes: hit the big red record button to start rolling early, well before the action starts, and don't press that button again until the action is completely done.

Similarly, your on-screen talent—which may be you!—should know their job too. Whoever's speaking needs to leave gaps between sentences to allow for editing, and at the end, they need to hold their final position and expression for at least a couple of seconds. They really shouldn't look immediately off-screen to ask if that was a good take.

But some people will, indeed, make these mistakes. Not every situation is perfect, and not everyone knows the rules. It's not always down to the talent, either. Sometimes there's a technical glitch that ruins an otherwise good take just at the end (forcing you to trim the clip short), or you are provided a clip that simply isn't long enough. If you need an extra second or two of vision at the end, but the end of the shot is no good, what can you do?

One possible method would be to use a Razor or Blade tool to separate the last few frames of the clip, then slow that tiny segment right down. You'll get the best results with Final Cut Pro's Super Slo-Mo feature, and potentially passable results with optical flow found in all modern NLEs. But it's probably not going to be great.

If you have Premiere Pro, you can use the new **Generative Extend** tool to simply trim the end of a clip a short way to the right or trim the start of a clip a short way to the left. Most common media formats are supported: 720p, 1080p, UHD or DCI 4K resolutions, in landscape or portrait, up to 30fps, in 8-bit SDR. Read this page for more details on the current requirements (`https://helpx.adobe.com/premiere-pro/using/generative-extend-faq.html`).

Because this feature is built in, there's no need to mess around with uploading or downloading clips through websites—the clip will just be magically fixed on your existing timeline, and the new assets will be stored next to your project, in a new folder called `Generative Assets`. If you'd prefer to store files elsewhere, change it in **File > Project Settings > Scratch Disks**.

So far, so good, but there are limitations. The maximum duration of a video extension is currently two seconds, and results are (as you may expect) imperfect. You may notice issues with brightness shifts, flickering, loss of detail, janky movement, or with excessive smoothing on grainy clips. The less you try to do, the less likely it is to fail.

You'll probably have more luck using Generative Extend on audio, where the duration limit is 10 seconds instead of two. However, you can't extend dialogue or music, just ambience, and you'll need a clip that's already at least three seconds long.

One real issue with this feature is that Generative Video is a premium feature, not free, and it could take a significant amount of your generative credits. To create a second of 4K 30fps footage, you'll pay 175 credits, while 720 at 24fps costs only 50 credits per second, and audio generation costs 10 credits each time. Still, this is a much higher cost than the 1-credit cost of using Generative Fill in Photoshop on a single-app plan.

How much can you use this? The standard Creative Cloud Pro account available in the US and other countries comes with 4,000 credits, not enough to make extensive use of this feature. If you're working with 4K, you'd get 22 seconds of Generative Extend in a month. Remember, as it's a "premium" feature, it's not available to single-app subscribers, only to those with all apps. Also remember that each generation costs credits, so if you aren't happy with the first result, you may need to pay more than once.

While Generative Extend can sometimes get you out of trouble, at other times, it might be appropriate to create a shot that doesn't exist at all. Let's take a look.

Creating videos from text prompts

We've already seen the variation possible when generating images from text prompts. Given the increased number of variables involved in video, consider your video generation prompts carefully.

Some AI providers, including **Canva AI** (`http://canva.com/ai`), include drop-down choices to help you specify important preferences such as style, aspect ratio, and focal length.

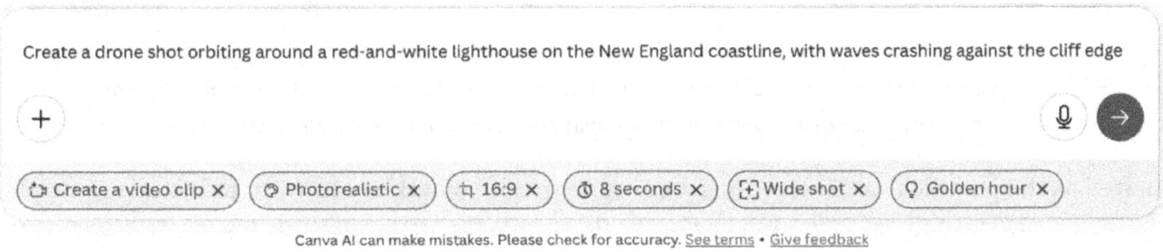

Figure 8.1 – Canva AI (using Veo 3) gives you several options to guide your video generation

If you have a very specific shot in mind, you may need to provide a detailed prompt to make sure you get what you want. Simple prompts could be fine for developing ideas or adding to a mood board or storyboard, but the clearer your vision, the longer your prompt should be.

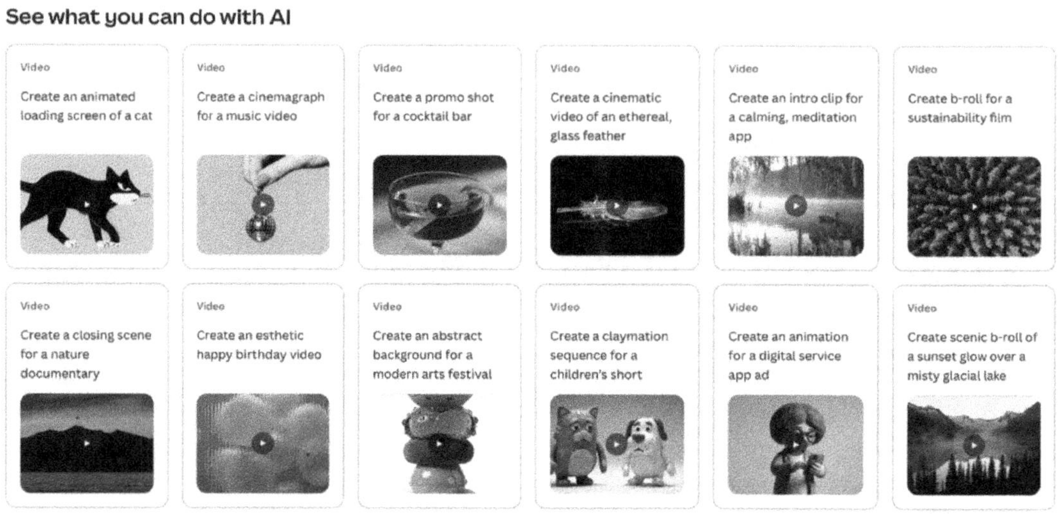

Figure 8.2 – Canva's example prompts are nice for ideas, but high-level prompts like this can produce wildly differing results with each generation

As well as the technical considerations, be sure to specify whether you want to include multiple shots or a single shot; **Sora** (`https://sora.chatgpt.com`, using version 1, not version 2) will sometimes produce a video consisting of multiple separate shots if you don't specify a single unbroken shot. Most text-to-video models currently don't include any audio, but it's becoming more common: Grok, Sora version 2 (from OpenAI), and Veo 3 (and higher, from Google) can generate background audio and spoken dialogue.

Note that some models, such as Veo 3 and up, are available through many different providers; it's available in paid Gemini plans and also through Canva, Firefly, Creatify, and others. However, some models are only available through specific providers, such as Act-Two, found only at Runway. If you like a particular model, it may be available through multiple providers, so shop around to find a price and interface that fits your needs.

Most providers offer video in a maximum resolution of 720p, though higher-end plans at some providers can offer 1080p. Today, most generations are created at 24fps, so you'll need to use retiming techniques like those discussed in *Chapter 4* if you need a higher frame rate. Upscaling can help if you need more resolution, but it's not magic, and AI video today usually looks fairly soft compared to video created with a traditional camera.

While high-quality image generation is widely available from several providers, video generation is less mature, and older models are more likely to show flaws. It's fairly easy to generate a generic stock-style drone shot with no people, but real shots like this are easy to find on stock sites.

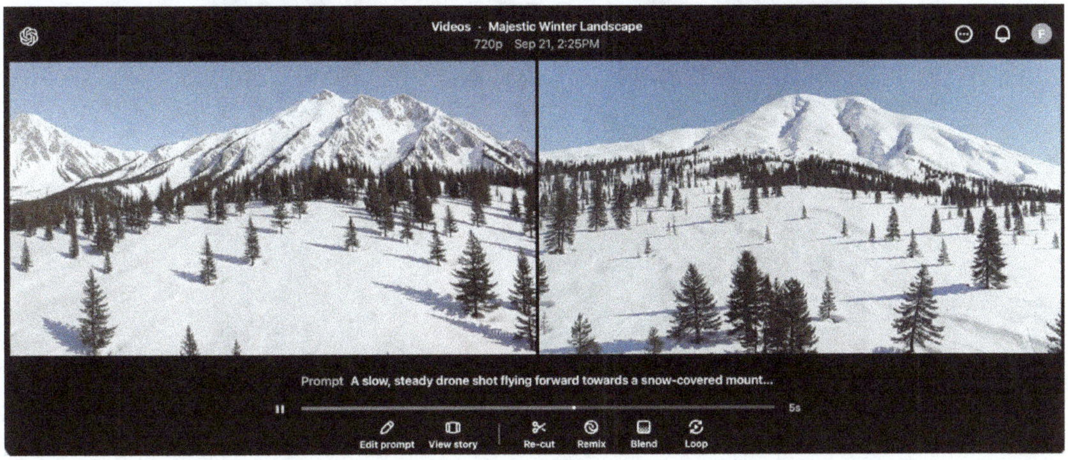

Figure 8.3 – Both of these generic drone shots, from Sora, are usable

If you want simple, basic shots at relatively low quality, you could have luck with simple text prompts. However, as soon as you ask for something more complex—such as two humans dancing—problems with physical movement, or even excessive blinking, can ruin a shot. Consistency can also be an issue, and the more people there are in a shot, the more likely you are to have problems.

I prompted `A smiling modern couple dancing with a crowd around them, in a nightclub with strong colored lighting, golden hour` and madness ensued. In the resulting videos, sometimes a person's limbs will vanish. Entire people can randomly appear or disappear as other people move in front of them. Sometimes, if you're really unlucky, as someone's head spins around, another face is revealed on the other side. It can be nightmarish.

Figure 8.4 – How many arms? How are they moving?

After testing Veo 3 (via Canva), Sora (v1, via ChatGPT), Vidu (`https://www.vidu.com`), and Firefly, I found Veo 3 most useful, but it's not consistently good, and other options are worth trying too. For me, Firefly produced the least convincing results, with blurry faces and inconsistent characters, and while Sora offers more realistic imagery, its unnatural body movements can be disturbing, and it doesn't always follow your instructions closely enough. Vidu also suffered from unpredictability, sometimes creating characters that disappeared when characters moved in front of one another.

Given the difficulty all these models have had synthesizing complex human movement, we can infer it's a hard problem to solve. I'm sure all these models will evolve, and of course, there are other models (such as Wan and Seedance) available too, but from what I've seen online, they all suffer from similar issues with people and movement. As any conclusions I might draw today would be out of date soon, I won't give any firm advice on which you should try first. Try several, then try another if you can't get good results.

Today, while Veo can produce results that are mostly believable (and Veo 3.1 is an improvement over Veo 3.0), it's not cheap to use. While it seems that a limited version of Veo will become free as part of YouTube, that's not yet available, and it seems that free generations will be capped at 480p. When that goes public, it should be a good place to experiment for free, because 720p and higher generations are expensive.

On a standard Canva AI plan, you can create just five videos per month—barely enough to test it properly. Through Firefly, a Veo 3.1 generation costs 400 credits, so if you used no other premium AI features with a Creative Cloud Pro plan, the 4,000 included generative credits would also allow just 10 videos per month. These costs do change frequently—they were recently twice as high—so check to see the current rates.

Given that Veo 3 can include frames like this in its output, I'm not sure it's worth it:

Figure 8.5 – Veo 3 is better than the others, but it's not good at complex movement

For more extensive experimentation, if you have a ChatGPT Plus account, unlimited access to Sora video generations is included, though there can be delays during busy times. Some services like Runway include unlimited video generation in "relaxed" (i.e., "slow") mode on their top plans, and a service like one of these will be important if you want to explore more fully.

Prompt with precision

It is possible to create relatively clean results from text prompts if you have simple requests, such as a single person, standing still and smiling, or steam rising from a vent, but you still won't always get what you want or need.

To minimize the number of generations required, limit uncertainty by defining your request precisely. For example, if you don't say how many shots or what type of shots you want, you might get a tracking shot, or a static shot, or three shots cut together—ask for a `single static shot with no cuts` if that's what you want.

This isn't always enough, though, because models won't always understand what you want. Asking for a `person standing still while the camera moves` can lead to confusion, and asking for something specific to happen (such as `sharpening a knife`) can lead to unexpected results if the model doesn't know how to do it.

Distinguishing features can be important too. If you don't ask for a person with specific characteristics, you'll get a generic result. Here, I asked Sora for an `adventurer` and received two completely different men. While that could be fine in a brainstorming context, if I had a particular type of person in mind, I should have asked for it.

Yet, even when you do ask, it's not always enough. I requested a camera following an adventurer entering a jungle, but that's not what I got:

Figure 8.6 – The first video started well, but the character then walked backwards; the second character never moves—neither is what I asked for

Though a model may not always understand everything, it's important to provide detailed requests because anything left to chance will fall back to "defaults," and they may not make sense in the greater context. Here's a prompt that doesn't fill in enough blanks:

```
A model stands on a deserted city street, leaning against a lamppost,
swinging a bag slowly
```

Figure 8.7 – Six of the eight attempts with this prompt, and only one (left, middle row) was accurate

I generated eight videos using the same prompt with Sora, and every time it produced:

- A female model wearing a coat, though I hadn't specified gender or clothing
- Night-time, though I hadn't asked for a time of day
- A wide angle, though this seems a sensible choice given the prompt
- A European-style street with vintage lampposts

The bag style did vary from shot to shot, but only two generations showed it swinging slowly, and only four generations actually showed the model leaning against the lamppost as requested. In the others, she stood nearby, hung onto it, merged into it, or stepped around it oddly. The lamppost placement was also pretty random. Of the eight attempts, only one single generation actually showed what I asked for; being detailed isn't always enough.

You may be more successful requesting abstract images, shots without people, because those requests don't fall into the uncanny valley of "human-but-not-human-enough." Still, it's not just human movement we're familiar with; it's all kinds of movement, and in general, AI models don't understand how one thing affects another. If you ask for a blue shoe to fall into a pool of green viscous liquid, the shoe will only sometimes fall consistently, and only sometimes correctly connect with the liquid.

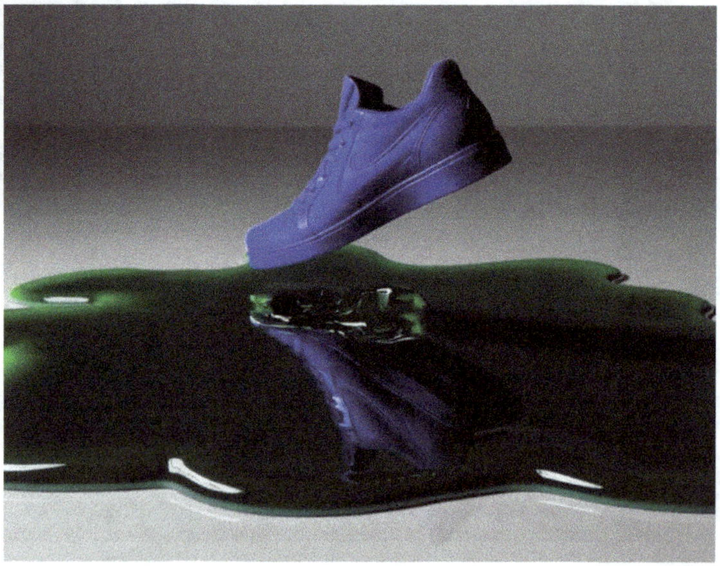

Figure 8.8 – This blue shoe fell, but it bounced against air and created a splash, then fell further

To counter these issues, you can provide longer prompts, specifying with as much detail as possible what you do and do not want. If you're working with Veo 3, this will include dialogue and audio cues and could run to several paragraphs in length. From the Gemini site (`https://gemini.google/overview/video-generation/`), here's an example prompt for Veo 3:

```
A follow shot of a wise old owl high in the air, peeking through the
clouds in a moonlit sky above a forest. The wise old owl carefully circles
a clearing looking around to the forest floor. After a few moments, it
dives down to a moonlit path and sits next to a badger. Audio: wings
flapping, birdsong, loud and pleasant wind rustling and the sound of
intermittent pleasant sounds buzzing, twigs snapping underfoot, croaking.
A light orchestral score with woodwinds throughout with a cheerful,
optimistic rhythm, full of innocent curiosity.
A wise old owl and a nervous badger sit on a moonlit forest path. "They
left behind a…a 'ball' today. It bounced higher than I can jump." the
badger stammered, trying to comprehend it. "What manner of magic is
that?" the owl hooted thoughtfully. Audio: Owl hooting, badger's nervous
chitters, rustling leaves, crickets.
A wise old owl flies away out of the frame and a nervous young badger runs
in a different direction out of the frame. In the background, you can see
a squirrel hurrying past making noise of rustling dried autumn leaves
as it goes. Audio: birdsong, loud and leaves rustling, and the sound of
intermittent pleasant sounds buzzing, twigs snapping underfoot, and the
sounds of squirrels scurrying through the dried autumn leaves. The sound
of an owl hooting in the distance, badger's nervous chitters, rustling
leaves, crickets, sounds that are full of innocent curiosity.
```

Though the output video was technically impressive, using AI to do everything at once doesn't produce professional-grade results: movement is stiff, dialogue expression is not good enough, ambient sound has looping issues, and the overall shot only tells a tiny part of a story.

Worse, because this wasn't created using a traditional animation or audio production pipeline, none of these elements can be tweaked or adjusted in a controllable, predictable way. It doesn't scale to a full production.

As a mockup, it's fine—but honestly, I'd prefer still images in a storyboard. I'd rather imagine what a final shot could be than be distracted by the inevitable issues this approach brings.

If complex, controllable shots can't be achieved—and today, they can't—telling a coherent story of any length is almost impossible with text prompts alone. That doesn't mean this technology is useless in a professional context, though. A montage-style advertisement made of short, simple shots is doable. A short film where a crowd of strange characters say one line each? Sure. A futuristic dream sequence full of special effects? Yep. If your project is able to play to the tools' strengths, you can have success.

With that in mind, most real projects need more control: a specific character wearing a specific outfit, in a particular place. Consistency between shots is also vital: multiple shots often need to show the same characters, dressed in the same clothes, in the same environments. You can't build a real short film with "an owl" in "a forest"—details matter.

We've already used models to generate variations of existing images, and this approach works with some generative video models too. For greater consistency between shots and far greater control over the finished output, I'd recommend using reference images. Let's try it out.

Creating original videos from reference images

A text prompt leaves a lot to chance, but providing an image alongside a text prompt gives an anchor to guide video generation. While multiple generations may still be required for a detailed prompt to be accurately followed, the characters, clothing, and environment should all match the reference image.

Firefly offers this as part of the **Image to Video** feature, and it can currently be used with their own Firefly Video model, or with Veo 2 or Veo 3. Note that with the Firefly model, it's possible to provide a composition reference video, a camera reference video, or a first frame, but only one of these can be used at a time alongside a text prompt. It's also possible to choose a style (such as illustration) by clicking on one of several thumbnails provided.

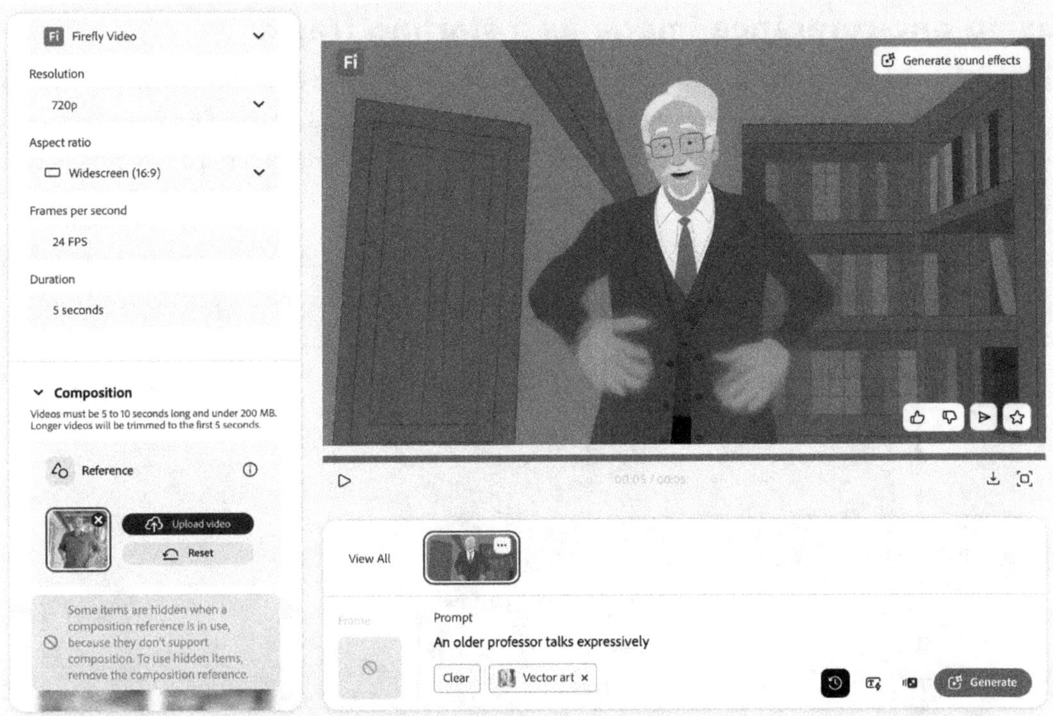

Figure 8.9 – Providing a composition video to Firefly is useful, but without an image alongside, a prompt doesn't give enough control

Unfortunately, because the Firefly model can't accept an image alongside a composition video, you'll spend a video generation's worth of credits each time you roll the dice with a prompt. If you instead switch to the Veo 3 model, only the first frame can be provided—no composition reference—and you'll have to specify styles as part of the prompt.

In an ideal world, I'd like to provide both a starting image and a performance video to follow, but that's not yet possible with this tool. Later in this chapter, we'll cover **Runway's Act-Two**, which can do this, but several services are able to accept an image alongside a prompt to describe what happens.

Using one reference image as a starting frame

Given the speed with which Grok lets you generate images and then transform them into videos, I thought it might be worth trying the earlier `model on a deserted street` prompt. Discussed in the previous chapter, Grok excels at quantity and allows you to simply scroll down to generate more and more images.

Most of the images weren't quite what I wanted: the street wasn't deserted; the pavement and road often didn't make sense. After scrolling down for some time, I found one deserted street, though the system's creative randomness had now changed my original prompt to request an Asian model.

Figure 8.10 – Some of the first images Grok created, and the first deserted street

It's easy to generate a video from an image by pressing the **Play** button visible on the images in the gallery view. While an image is being animated, the play button is replaced with a percentage readout indicating progress, and it took about 10-15 seconds to create the video. If you tap an image to move into single-image view, use the **Make video** button beneath the image instead.

However, either way, the original prompt was only used to create the still images and will be ignored when generating the video. Across several attempts, the model usually walked around rather than swinging her bag.

To adhere to the original prompt more closely, copy the original prompt into your clipboard, tap the image to enter single-image view, press the **Make Video** button, then quickly re-prompt the video generation by pasting the original prompt and pressing **Make video** again. This did produce a swinging bag, but the movement shown had the same unrealistic body movements common to other AI video models:

Figure 8.11 – Technically, this movement is possible, but it's unnatural

As few of the original images adhered to my prompts, achieving specific results might be hard with Grok alone, but it is possible to upload your own image as the starting point for an animation rather than Grok's own generations. I've tested this with several models, with mixed results.

In Firefly, using a starting image with text prompts, I tried to add some subtle motion to this image, expanded to 16:9 from earlier image generations:

Figure 8.12 – Can we turn this still image into a simple animation?

With most of the details provided by the image, I used a simple prompt: `natural subtle movement from a light wind, the camera moves very slowly left to right, and the woman stands still`

Unfortunately, this wasn't enough, and results showed poor *prompt adherence*—that is, the model failed to follow my instructions. Most of the time, the woman started walking, and none of the Firefly generations could maintain her appearance. Why?

AI systems don't understand your request in the way a human would and using a prompt containing "movement" and "moves" is more likely to create just that, despite the additional request that the subject stay still. Using a term such as "pan" rather than "camera moves" might have helped, but I think it's fair to expect imperfectly expressed instructions to be followed.

How did other tools do?

Canva AI also uses Veo 3 and suffered the same issues—walking instead of standing still—as did Grok, across several tests. Runway ML's video generation had the same issue with walking, but with added excessive blinking and bouncy movement. **Higgsfield** (`https://higgsfield.ai`), like the others, gave me a video with my character walking. It offered more natural movement than Runway, and with no extra blinks, but not what I wanted. Image-to-video is a common workflow that's supported by many platforms, so if you have a plan with a provider such as Freepik or Envato already, explore the models available.

In another attempt with a similar prompt, the Firefly **Enhance prompt** option changed "girl" to "young girl," which forced our character to get younger across the length of the clip. Yes, details can help, but incorrect details will ruin your work. Either double-check that an "enhanced" prompt actually matches your request or deactivate it entirely.

Figure 8.13 – First, she walks away, then she gets younger

Using two reference images as the start and end

With either model in Firefly, if you provide a first frame, you can also provide an optional last frame. By transitioning between a logo and a blank frame, this can be used to create interesting transitions, but most filmmakers will want to use this to move the camera with control. If you plan a camera movement by providing a starting and ending frame, the model can move its virtual camera to bridge the gap.

Unfortunately, it's not always easy to create that final frame, because not all image generation models are consistent enough to maintain the same characters and settings with different framing. Sora failed repeatedly to create a closer view of the same person, while the more consistent Gemini Flash 2.5 (AKA Nano Banana) did better.

With this strategy, it's possible to create a second, closer image, then adapt the prompt to reflect the change: `natural subtle movement from a light wind, the camera moves in, and the woman stands still`

Figure 8.14 – A first frame and a last frame, surely this should work?

This failed with Veo 3, producing a video that used a cross dissolve from the first frame to a closer frame—not my frame!—where a similar-looking woman walked away. I'm not sure that a more detailed prompt would help here, since even my simple instructions were often ignored. Other users seem to be experiencing similar issues with prompt adherence, but not all prompts have issues, and not all models are bad at this.

Midjourney (`https://www.midjourney.com/`) can also produce good results and makes the process easy by allowing you to extend a video from its last frame—potentially several times over. While this seems like a simple user interface tweak, it's these little touches that can make difficult things far easier.

Vidu (`https://vidu.com`) is able to take a first and last frame and produce good results with a simple prompt, moving its virtual camera with a slow zoom in, as you might expect.

Figure 8.15 – Vidu did a good job of moving from one image to the next

Using multiple reference images for control

In another useful interface tweak, Vidu allows you to create videos by combining multiple images and referencing them explicitly in a prompt:

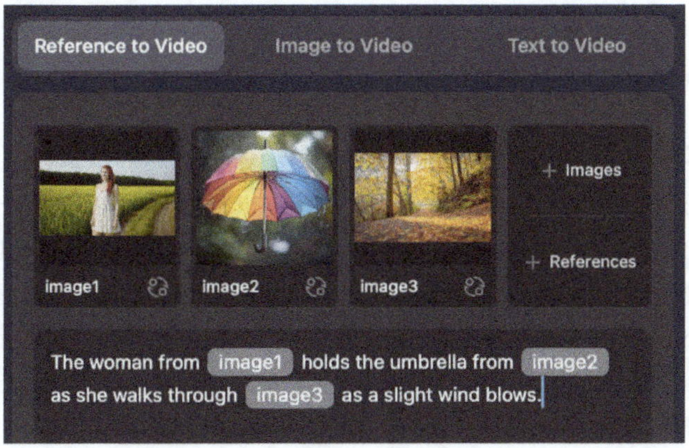

Figure 8.16 – If you want to see how elements could work together, this is a great way to make that happen

This extremely powerful approach lets you mix a character from one image, an object from another, and a location from a third—exactly the kind of control that's useful in the creative process.

Figure 8.17 – Vidu did an excellent job of combining these three elements in a video

Vidu nailed both these requests on the first try, and this would be the platform I'd return to if I needed more control. To be fair, my movement requests were simple—Vidu's characters still can't dance—but given that some other models couldn't make a person reliably stand still, I'll take this as a win. Veo 3.1 also offers this feature, allowing you to provide "ingredients" to be part of a generation, but the precision of the Vidu interface is very helpful indeed.

Simple and complex remixing with Sora

If you don't need quite that much control and can be a little more flexible, **Sora** (`https://sora.chatgpt.com/explore`, through a ChatGPT Plus plan) allows you to upload a reference image for guidance, and then describe what happens in a video in a similar way to Firefly. For a cinemagraph-style effect, turning a still photo into a slowly moving video, this can work well. I tried both of the earlier prompts with the same image, and at least one generation of prompt was acceptable—a much higher success rate:

Figure 8.18 – Multiple remix requests with Sora

More adventurous remix requests are likely to fail in similar ways to the text-only prompts. When I tried `The girl spins around in slow motion as the camera slowly lifts up`, the results included similar body-horror results to the earlier dancing text prompts, and the camera movement instruction was ignored too.

When planning a shot, whether it contains people or not, remember that most of these AI models don't understand how most things affect one another. Food isn't consumed, drinks are not drunk, and if you ask for a meteor to crash into a mountain and for a fireball to destroy everything, it doesn't know how that's supposed to work.

I used Sora to create a still reference image of two dinosaurs and a meteor crashing down, and the illustrative image produced was fine. I then asked Runway to animate it, using this prompt: `A diplodocus and a stegosaurus are eating plants, in an open grassy plain with mountains in the background, as a huge meteor crashes into the mountains and a fireball expands to consume the entire scene.`

Figure 8.19 – In this video, a meteor turned into a flamethrower—it's simply not how these objects would behave

An example like this reveals the flaws that can ruin videos generated from stills. Essentially, generative video models don't understand the situation that would have led to the image, nor what comes after. In this image, the streak behind the meteor is a trail, not the source of the fire, and the mountain was breaking apart from the force of the meteor; it's not an erupting volcano. And if you ask for a video of a chef sharpening a knife, they should be using a tool, not just their hands:

Figure 8.20 – A smiling chef, sharpening a knife by moving his hands near it

Whether you're creating videos featuring people or not, *making things happen* is a challenge. While sometimes you can get lucky, it's too expensive and/or time-consuming to repeatedly prompt and re-prompt with such a low success rate. If you have the patience, consider a site with a plan that allows unlimited generations, even at a slower pace. Runway's top-level plan allows this, as does Sora.

Sora allows unlimited watermarked 720p generations, and for mockups, those limitations are livable. Unfortunately, you need to be on the top-tier US$200/month plan to generate longer 1080p videos without watermarks, but consistency and quality still aren't guaranteed.

If Sora's generations are working well enough, try the **Re-cut** feature, which allows you to define what happens in different parts of a timeline. Given the length limitations, you may prefer to combine separate shots in a video editing application instead.

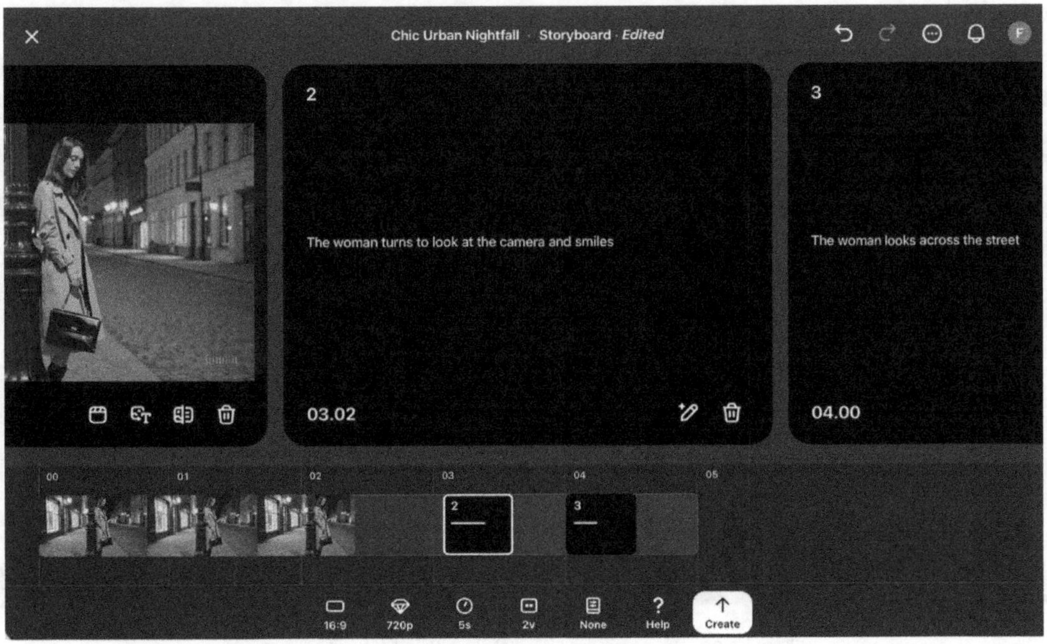

Figure 8.21 – Starting from a previously generated video, I trimmed the end shorter and requested a different action

While I've had mixed results with this feature, being able to control exactly what happens at specific moments is often important, and this feature is worth trying. But not every job needs full manual control. If you're happy to go with a pre-built template, you could consider an entirely different solution.

Using presets to animate reference images

Higgsfield includes some impressive presets called **Higgsfield apps**, each including a simple, eye-catching effect. While writing your own text prompts is obviously more flexible, the trade-off here is the promise of greater prompt adherence. You provide a photo of a person, then choose from options as complex as having that person attacked by a sea monster or as simple as having that person eat a banana. If one of those offers an appealing way to transform an image into a video, and it hasn't already been used widely, it could work well.

Figure 8.22 – Yes, they're presets, but they're cool presets

Of course, you don't have to create from scratch or from a still image. Some tools allow you to work with existing videos, using AI as an effects engine, and this could potentially take a lot of the unpredictability out of the process. Let's take a look.

Creating new videos from reference video and audio

If you have a clean dialogue recording, but need those words to be spoken by an on-screen person, is that possible? Or perhaps you've recorded a piece to camera already, with regular human expressions and gestures, but you want to replace them with someone else, or a cartoon? Both of these things are possible.

Using audio files with digital avatars

HeyGen allows you to upload an audio file (or record one directly on the site), then have a digital avatar say those words. Pre-made avatars are available, or for more control, you can upload a photo of the character you'd like to see talk, or a more extensive video from which a digital twin can be created. Note that if you create your own avatar, you need to have permission to use the images or video involved in the process. There are other providers too—Higgsfield offers the **Lipsync Studio** feature with their own models, alongside Veo 3 and models from Kling.

> Note: both HeyGen and Higgsfield are happy to generate audio from a script, although you'll probably get better results with a real audio recording. We'll return to generative audio in the next chapter.

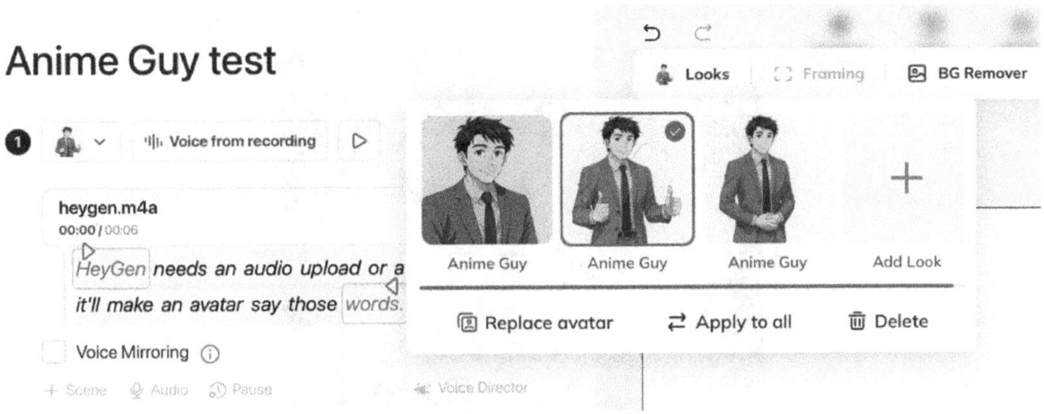

Figure 8.23 – HeyGen can create an avatar speaking your words from your own photos or drawings

The problem I've seen with all avatar-based services is that they're quite robotic. I find that they either over-emphasize gestures or don't use gestures enough, and the results feel inauthentic. While I can appreciate that talking to camera is not a skill everyone has, AI avatars are, so far, a poor replacement for humans.

OK then. What if you record a piece to camera, with audio, gestures, and facial expressions, and then make it look like someone else?

Performance transfer with Runway Act-Two

Runway (`https://runwayml.com`), using their own Gen-4 model, has some unique offerings that can help you transform an existing video into something quite different, and we'll start with **Act-Two**. This tool lets you take a waist-up video of a person talking, then transfer their expressions, mouth movements, and gestures onto an AI-generated character. (Act-One did a similar trick with animated characters, and presumably there will be an Act-Three in the future). In general, this technique is known as **pose transfer** and is also offered by WAN Animate (`https://wan.video/blog/wan2.2-animate`) and some other providers—I expect it to be more widely available soon.

To test Act-Two, I recorded a quick 1080p video of me speaking a few words, then trimmed it and cleaned up the audio in Final Cut Pro—some video editing know-how is still needed. I then generated an image of a professor with Sora, then expanded the image to 16:9 with Photoshop and uploaded both to Runway. Note that it's also possible to upload a character video rather than a still, but Act-Two will only adjust the facial expressions (and not gestures) if you do so.

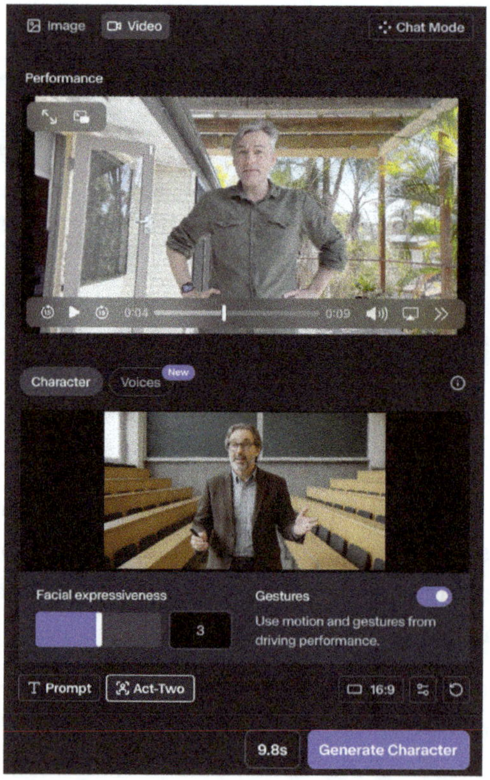

Figure 8.24 – Act-Two requires no prompt, just a performance video and a character image or video

So, did it work? The good news is that the professor did, in fact, exactly copy my movements, and it did an excellent job of matching them. The created video is only 720p at 24fps, which did not quite match up with my original 25fps video, but that's manageable—you can upscale here on Runway and adjust the speed in an editing application if needed.

Figure 8.25 – The pose has transferred correctly, and the result is quite usable—but keep your hands empty

Here are a few tips for better results. First, you should match the pose of your appearance video to the character video as much as possible. If the character is holding a prop, the performer should be holding a matching prop too, but empty hands are more reliable. The "professor" character reference is holding a marker pen in the character image, and as there's no correct way to hold that pen while matching my hand movements, the pen morphs into other objects.

For results that avoid the uncanny valley, try to create obviously unreal characters, such as cartoons or obviously computer-generated characters. We know exactly what humans should look like, but we expect cartoon characters and CGI renders to be a little odd. You can make photo-real humans work, but it's harder.

While pose transfer is useful, **localization** is one area where you want the generated video to be almost identical to the original. Visual dubbing services, including LipDub AI (`https://www.lipdub.ai/`) and Flawless (`https://flawlessai.com/`) are able to convert an existing video in one language into another language with none of the mismatches you'd expect from dubbing alone. While most of the original video remains as it was, all mouth movements are regenerated to match the translated version of the dialogue.

In a Swedish feature film, *Watch The Skies*, the original cast re-recorded their own parts in English, then TrueSync was used to regenerate the video to match. A system is in place to obtain approvals from the original actors, and it's been integrated with Avid Media Composer. With LipDub, the translated voice recording is generated in the voice of the original speaker. We'll return to generative audio in the next chapter, but if translation is your focus, there are services tailored to your needs.

The best aspect of Act-Two is that it enables new kinds of outputs without replacing the performer. Animation is very expensive in traditional production, and if a client is set on an animated avatar, this approach could save money while leaving human artists in charge of the look of the characters and how they move.

While we're looking at Runway, they have another unique feature that promises to retain much more of the original video. Let's dig in.

Transforming existing videos

Runway's **Aleph** allows you to transform an existing video with prompting, retaining most of the original with high-quality results. Examples include style transformations; changing the camera angle completely; changing environments, time of day, or seasons; adding tracked elements; object and reflection removal; relighting; and more.

After uploading a drone video I took for a recent project, I asked for the time of day to be changed to night, and for fireworks to be added. This isn't a shot I could have captured easily—it's not normally allowed to use a drone at night or near fireworks.

Figure 8.26 – My original drone shot, transformed into a night-time fireworks display

Impressively, the positions of all the marquees and people in the foreground were maintained. While some details were skipped, this result was a success. One limitation is that because the output is only 720p, it would need to be upscaled to approach the clarity of the 1080p clip I uploaded, let alone the original 4K clip. Happily, this upscaling is built into the system, and costs just a few credits to perform. It's not magic, but it helps a lot.

One of the advertised Aleph features is to remove a cameraperson from a reflection in an image, and since this can be a tricky VFX task, I gave it a shot. Providing a simple handheld iPhone video at 1080p24 and the prompt shown here, I was hopeful:

Figure 8.27 – Simply asking it to remove the reflected person feels like asking for magic

After about a minute, the result came back, and while it wasn't perfect, the reflected person and their phone had indeed been impressively removed. Resolution was lacking, even after a 4K up-scale; some areas lacked texture compared to the original. The side of the mirror was smoothed out, though it shouldn't have been, and though it's minor, the interior door handle was changed despite a request not to do so.

You may be tempted to composite parts of the new shot over the old one, but because the two shots don't quite match—the processed clip seems to have skipped a frame—this could be slightly trickier than expected. Brightness was also slightly different between the original and downloaded clips, likely due to HDR transformations, but this can be managed.

Figure 8.28 – A few frames of the original clip below and the processed clip above—impressive

While the maximum clip length of five seconds limits what you can do, and considering the preceding issues, this is still a good result. The issues with the replacement areas here are far less problematic than a full re-imagination of the shot would be, and there are many contexts in which the quality limits would be acceptable. Given how complex a tracked object removal task can be, Aleph could work well as a quicker, cheaper alternative.

Tracking comes in many forms, though. As another test, I gave Aleph a new moving drone shot and a logo, then asked it to `Add this logo to a large circular banner on the large blank area of the right side of the building`. While the tracking itself was fine, the logo wasn't placed in the correct spot, and the logo itself was completely reinterpreted and mangled.

Figure 8.29 – That's not the logo I gave it, nor the placement I requested

Another test, to add a whale into the background of a seaside scene, didn't work at all. Instead of augmenting the original, a new, quite different shot was generated.

Figure 8.30 – The created video has little to do with the original

Mixed results for Runway Aleph, then. If you struggle, another approach is to ask Sora for changes to existing videos using the **Remix** feature, but you'll need to turn the Remix strength down to avoid changing the video completely. While Sora can't change day for night like Aleph, it can add a whale:

Figure 8.31 – Yes, that's a whale in the waves with a subtle remix

Sora doesn't have the same level of control as tools such as Runway or Vidu, so you may need to try a few times to get usable results. No matter which systems you end up using, you may need to mix and match still and image outputs with traditional effects techniques such as chromakey and tracking. If you can't make a video generation work, it may be possible to generate a still image and then incorporate that into traditional video using traditional masking and tracking techniques. But there's another solution that might solve this problem.

EbSynth (`https://ebsynth.com`) is currently available on free and paid plans and offers more control than most other solutions we've looked at so far. Here's an overview of the process:

1. Upload a video clip, then scrub through it to find a specific frame.
2. Change that frame somehow, by painting on it, or uploading a replacement for some or all of the image or even selecting part of the frame and then prompting for a replacement.
3. Propagate the changes on that frame throughout the rest of the clip, and the additions will be transformed as if they're painted onto the original image.

The most appealing part of this tool is that it resembles common desktop video editing apps, including a timeline, keyframes, tools, and layers in its user interface. If you've used After Effects, Apple Motion, or a video editing app, you'll understand it pretty quickly.

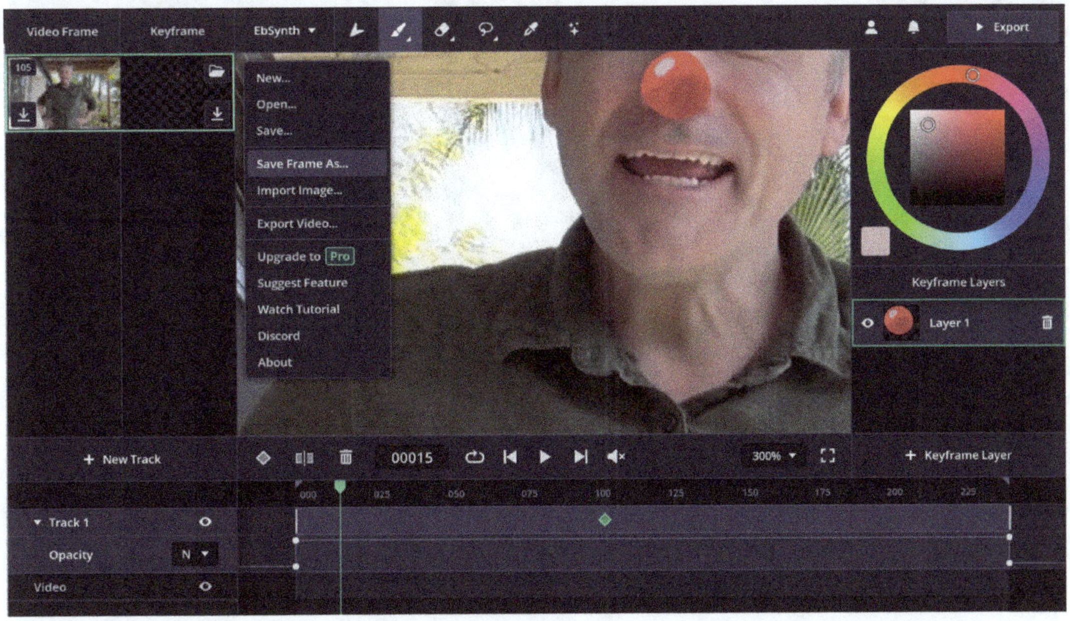

Figure 8.32 – Here, I've painted a red nose onto one frame, then propagated that red nose throughout a clip

Using the built-in painting interface allows you to get started quickly, but the controls are fairly simple and better for experimentation than finished art. To use the more extensive controls available in an app such as Photoshop or Procreate, download the current frame and edit your image locally. Downloading is easy: use the download button at the top left of the interface, or the **Save Frame As...** option in the on-screen menu (both visible in the preceding screenshot).

With the image downloaded, you could apply a filter to the entire image, then upload that newly transformed image. For a more targeted change, you can create a new layer, add something new on that layer, then save the new layer as a PNG and upload that alone. The new image can be repositioned on top of the original image, and changes will automatically propagate throughout the clip.

It's also possible to transform all or part of an existing frame with a generative image model. Optionally, select part of the image, then click the **Generate Image** icon to the right of the other tools. Prompt as you normally would (using Stable Diffusion or Nano Banana) and a new still frame, based on the original, will be generated. You can change an object's color, change a photo into a drawing, or anything else you care to prompt.

Figure 8.33 – This "blue hair" prompt was used in frame 1, then successfully propagated throughout the clip

One limitation is that you're effectively adding paint to the original image, not an actual 3D object. A color change may succeed, but if you were to add an image of sunglasses to a face, when the face turns, those sunglasses will start to look more like body paint than they should. The further the object strays from the original frame, the more likely the illusion will fail, though it is possible to add further keyframes to control the effect more precisely.

Despite the limitations, EbSynth can still allow a performance to puppet a digital double, bring a drawing to life, or add or remove a blemish or tattoo from a real video of a real person. At the time of writing, this tool is quite new, so I don't want to come to any firm conclusions, but I do like the level of control it offers and can see potential applications.

We've now looked at a number of tools and several potentially useful workflows. Let's recap.

Summary

Overall, while some Gen AI video services are too hit-and-miss to recommend, there are some bright spots:

- Vidu was able to pull off some impressive results moving between first and last frames, and it was also able to combine elements in a believable way
- Sora produced mostly good results with simple requests, though these results were less repeatable
- Runway's Act-Two reference videos empower voice and performance artists to use their skills in new ways
- Aleph can sometimes perform genuinely useful transformations on existing videos
- While EbSynth is new, its powerful UI and unique feature set could prove very useful in the right situations

While the other services I've tested here are worth trying, I found them to be less predictable and controllable than I'd prefer, and predictability affects cost. All these solutions are cloud only, and many of them are simply too expensive to prompt repeatedly.

Their unpredictability means you'll often need to perform multiple generations for good results, and even the most expensive plans include serious limitations. Some of those expensive plans do offer unlimited generations at a more relaxed pace, while others just include a higher amount of paid credits, and serious users will churn through those credits quickly.

If you want to use AI generation for video, I'd keep your expectations relatively low, at least for now. Focusing on creating videos for mockup purposes—where perfection is not required—is a lot easier, quicker, and cheaper than creating customer-ready finished pieces.

While testing these services, I experienced repeatable, generation-ruining bugs, and though these issues were eventually solved, I was unable to use some services for days at a time. Video has a long way to go when compared to still images, and it's going to be a tricky problem to solve.

In terms of workflows, while generating video using only text feels like a magic trick, it doesn't scale well to longer pieces. For more predictable results, I'd recommend focusing on image-to-video workflows, using reference video and audio, and transforming existing videos.

There is no magic button to just *make it work*, and the higher your expectations, the more frustrated you're likely to become. While this space will continue to evolve quickly, I don't expect progress to be linear, and I suspect that output will remain unpredictable for some time.

Finally, there are, of course, other generative video models available, and though they're worth trying, most seem to suffer from similar issues to those I found here. In a year, or with a new tool, or with different prompts, you may have very different results. Every run is different, everyone's needs are different, and models are constantly revised. Keep an eye on this space, but don't expect miracles just yet.

In the next chapter, we'll round out the generative section of this book with a look at audio—and there are some pleasant surprises.

9

Generative AI with Audio

In some ways, AI-assisted generative audio suffers from the same imperfection problems as generative video does, especially voice recordings. Though some services can produce completely convincing dialogue, the majority produce stilted, artificial voices. Still, there are a surprising number of solutions in this space, some of which can improve or even revolutionize a video or audio production workflow.

Generative tech today can generate spoken dialogue, music, and other sounds from a variety of text and audio prompts. As is the case with video, humans can still do a better job in most cases, though a human is likely to take longer and cost more than an AI.

If a job is worth doing really well, you should engage a human. Of course, not all jobs are the same, and if you're short on budget or time, or you just want a temporary audio file to replace later, an AI may be just fine. After all, an imperfect AI-made voiceover could fit the bill better than an editor's own voice, making it less distracting to a client reviewing an early draft.

But that's draft audio—can you use GenAI for the final output? While using an AI voice or music for an advertising campaign could carry reputational risk, an internal corporate training video using less-than-perfect audio is far less likely to raise eyebrows.

A hybrid approach is also an option here. A creative using human-made voiceovers can—if the voice talent gives approval—use GenAI to correct mistakes picked up after recording. Not all voice artists will allow this, but if quick changes may be needed, it may be worth seeking permission to use AI to redo short sections of their work.

Finally, what about music? While working with a composer to create a piece would be nice, time and budget constraints mean that's not usually a possibility for most creators. On a budget, sourcing and licensing the right track can be a time-consuming and tricky process.

The idea of conjuring completely original music, at the right length, in the right tempo and key, is enticing, but can it compete with human-made tracks? Increasingly, for shorter tracks and background music used in videos and podcasts, the answer is probably yes. Generated sound effects aren't quite at the same standard yet, but you can retain a good amount of control over the process.

In this chapter, we'll take a look at the state of the art in audio generation:

- Creating synthetic speech
- Synthetic speech with voice cloning
- Replacing part of an existing voice recording
- Creating original music
- Audio translation
- Creating synthetic sound effects

First up, let's see how realistic artificial speech has become.

Creating synthetic speech

Text-to-speech (**TTS**) solutions have existed for decades, but only recently have they actually started to sound human. We've come a long way since the late Stephen Hawking's robotic voice was first heard, and the best AI voices are now nearly indistinguishable from real humans, faking emotion and even sometimes making mistakes.

One service that made waves is Google's NotebookLM (`https://notebooklm.google`), a tool that can generate an entire podcast from any text source. Here's a primer from *The Verge* (`https://www.youtube.com/watch?v=YGtINs3R5EM`). While this is technically impressive, eerie, and potentially quite frightening, it's probably not something of direct use to creative professionals.

Single-shot solutions like this don't offer enough control or variety to be part of most creative workflows, and we'll need to step back a little, focusing on generating speech from text we provide ourselves.

As a baseline, your operating system includes some basic text-to-speech options for reading text aloud, and though they've improved, most of them still sound quite artificial.

On a Mac, you can choose the voice you want to hear in **System Settings**, under **Accessibility > Read and Speak > System voice** (the Siri voices sound the best). With setup complete, select some text in a built-in app such as **Notes** or **Pages**, then right-click and choose **Speech > Start Speaking** to hear it.

Siri and other digital assistants use the best of these voices, but they don't try to sound exactly like a human, and we know they're not. Human-class AI voices are usually too complex to work in real time on a phone, though. These more complex models interpret provided text in a much more comprehensive way, decoding the emphasis and intonation each word should be given, the correct in-context pronunciation, and even how long any pauses should be. As with a human voiceover, there's variation from one recording to the next, and there will be mistakes from time to time.

Though a wildly mispronounced word can sometimes give them away, the best of these voices sound better than a poor or even average human voiceover. The worst of them are little better than system voices, though—don't settle for "OK" when "great" is out there.

Quality isn't always important, though. If you only plan to use a synthetic voice as a temp "scratch" track, giving you something to edit against before you record with a human, a few odd phrases aren't a problem. Of course, timing is still critical, and the better a temp track, the closer your draft edit will be to the final product.

Web-based providers are numerous. As with images and video, some of the models used are available at multiple platforms, while some are unique. Here are the options I've tried:

- ElevenLabs (`https://elevenlabs.io`)
- Artlist (`https://artlist.io/voice-over`)
- Runway (`https://app.runwayml.com/`)
- Uberduck (`https://www.uberduck.ai/app/text-to-speech`)
- Murf.ai (`https://murf.ai`)
- Genny (`https://genny.lovo.ai/`)
- Resemble.ai (`https://app.resemble.ai/hub`)
- Hume (`https://hume.ai`)

In several tests, I was able to produce clear, usable speech with many voices from these providers. **Artlist** and **Runway** both offer a wide selection of professional-sounding choices optimized for video projects, but **ElevenLabs** is the best known, the market leader, and has a huge library of good voices to choose from. If you don't have time to run your own comparisons, start with their most recent voices, currently those built with the "v3" model. We'll return to their agent voices later in the book, too.

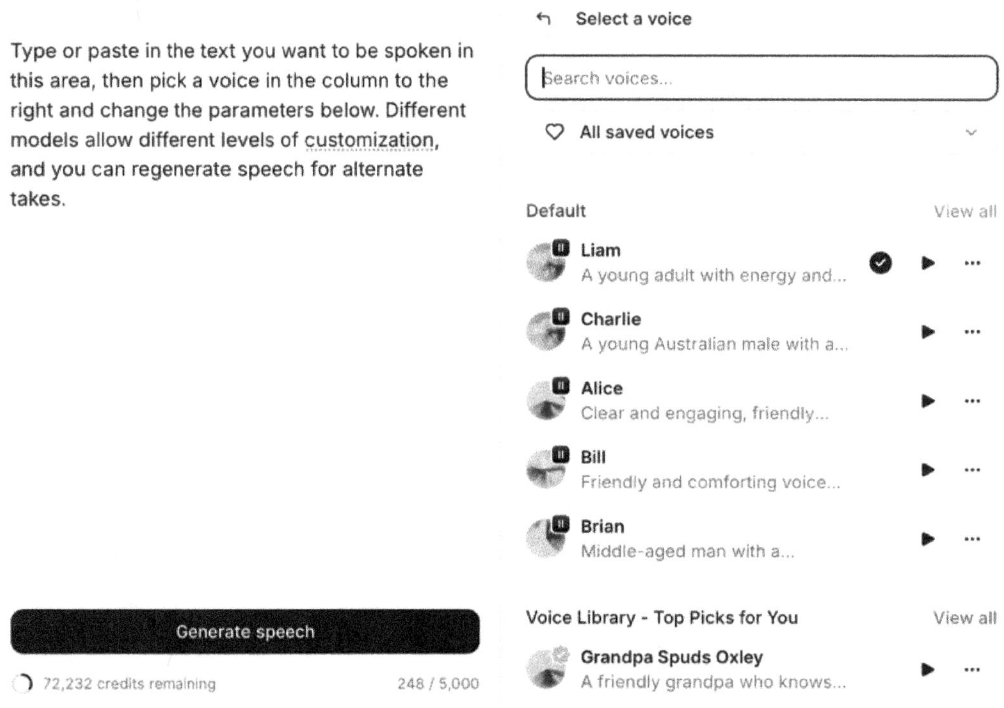

Figure 9.1 – The ElevenLabs TTS interface is similar to other providers in this space; you'll see more controls after choosing a voice

While most of these services aren't expensive, some open-source models can be run entirely offline, on your own device, for free.

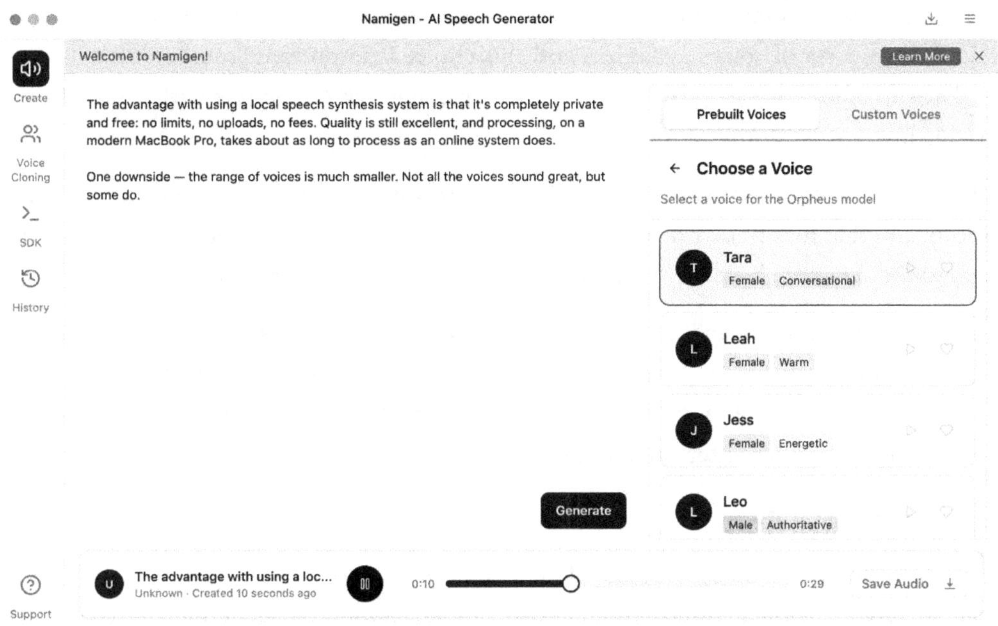

Figure 9.2 – Namigen gives you several options at no cost

Although installing most of these solutions takes some technical know-how, if you have a Mac, you can download **Namigen** (`https://namigen.com`) to get started with the high-quality free models Kokoro, Orpheus, and Dia. **Resemble.ai's** Chatterbox (`https://www.resemble.ai/chatterbox/`) is another popular open source option that can be run locally or online.

> For any jobs for which the budget isn't there, or you need instant turnaround, a digital voice is probably the quickest solution. But remember that real humans offer this service too—with real human performances—and it may not cost as much as you think.
>
> Outsourcing platforms such as Fiverr (`http://fiverr.com`) have many talented humans offering voice-over recording services at low prices. For this to work, you'll need to give your direction in text form and wait a day or two for the job to be completed.
>
> For larger jobs, projects for which performance is important, or with a director who wants to direct, you'll still need to hire a human and record in a studio, in person.
>
> I suspect most people using AI voices wouldn't have hired a human in the first place. Instead, synthetic voices are replacing poor voiceovers or being added where no voiceover would have been considered previously.

To use any of these options is simple: you need a script, and you need to pick a voice. Each service will have its own set of voices available, and this choice is important. You don't want to use a voice that's too familiar, because it'll feel stale—and that's the main risk with premade voices from a big provider.

You'll also want to choose a voice that sounds great to your audience. Most synthetic voices are American, and that may not work in your market. For example, a voiceover for a local Australian company would need to be in an Australian accent, because that's what the local market expects.

However, if I were creating an internationally targeted piece in English, I'd choose an American voice, or perhaps a British voice, or even a different voice in each country. Be sure to ask your client what each local market prefers, because regional accents bring meaning to a local audience that's lost to outsiders. (If you're interested in translation, though, that's covered later in this chapter.)

Style and emotion

It's important to bear in mind the style of generation you're looking for: a narration, a podcast conversation, educational content, or something else. Some services allow you to define this, while others provide specific voices for each purpose.

A dramatic performance is possible with some services, but it's stretching the capabilities of most. If you're planning a radio play or an emotionally engaging audiobook reading, be ready to give up a lot of control, or hire a human.

That's not to say you can't try to step beyond a plain script. More advanced services allow you to specify `[excited]` tags to indicate emotion and `[gasps]` for non-verbal sounds, which can help to guide the generation. The more advanced ElevenLabs v3 model allows this, and also allows for multiple speakers to have a conversation:

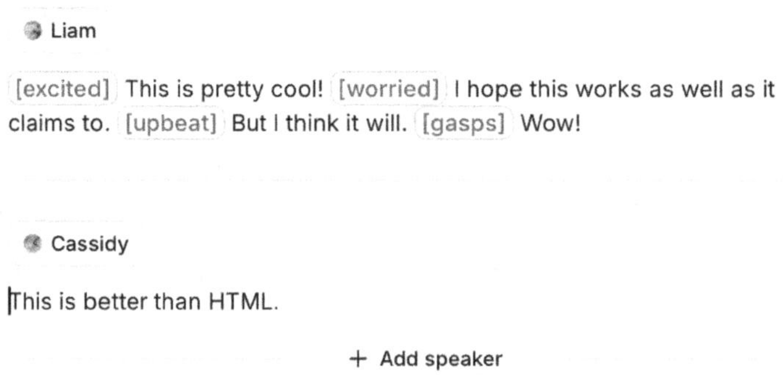

Figure 9.3 – This conversation at ElevenLabs is a good example of what's coming to more platforms

Acronyms will usually be recognised as such, but if they're not, you can try spelling them out letter by letter.

For more control, dig into the settings. Some models allow you to control only one or two parameters (**Stability** is common) while others give you sliders to adjust speed, exaggeration, and more. Here are some controls from Resemble.ai:

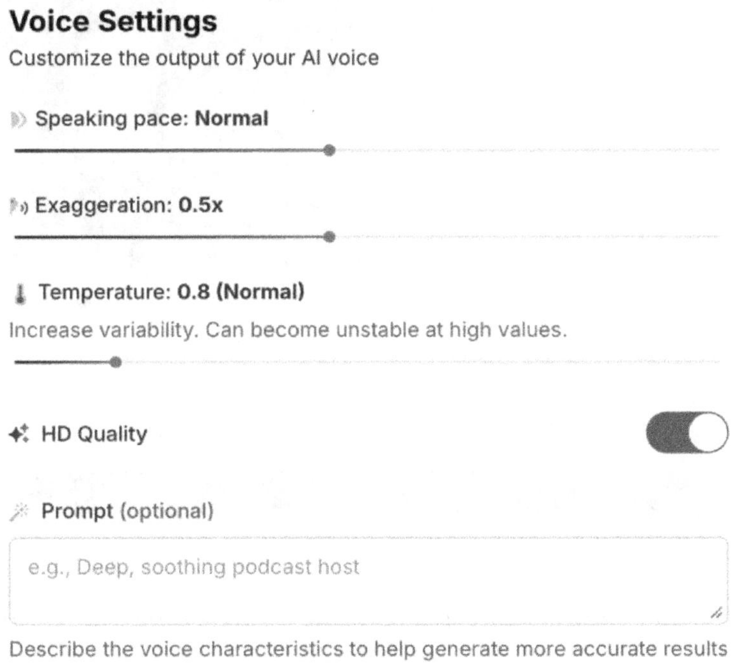

Figure 9.4 – Resemble.ai voices include these controls

If you're struggling to get exactly the right results, try breaking your text up into sections, generating them independently, and reuniting them in an audio or video editing app. That way, you can retry problematic recordings and combine multiple versions—as long as they sound similar enough.

Just as with regular human recordings, each generation will be slightly different, so don't be afraid to just try again if it's not perfect. Conversely, if consistency becomes an issue, and separate generations sound quite different from one another, you may wish to try longer generations, not shorter ones. It may even be worth repeating parts of your script to make sure you get two takes in a single generation.

Note that many AI avatars (discussed in the previous chapter) will offer to generate synthetic speech, though you can record or generate audio independently if you prefer. **Descript** is one service that's happy to animate an image (or a provided AI avatar) to match generated audio, but use with caution, because the visual side of things is not nearly as convincing as the audio side.

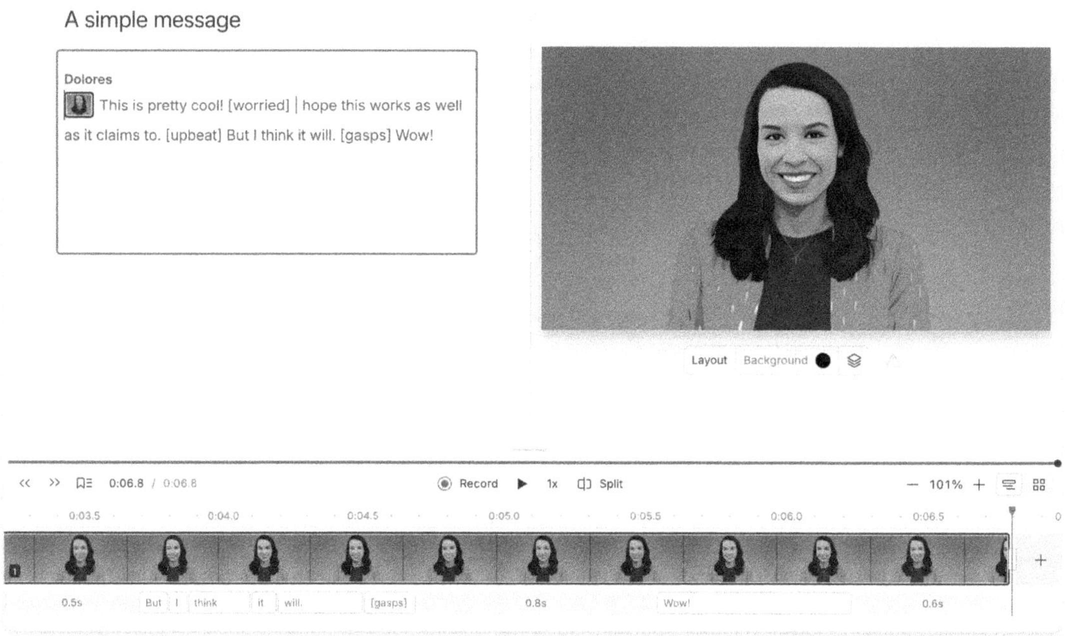

Figure 9.5 - Descript has a desktop app, which makes life a little easier, and avatars are an option, too

While it's possible today to produce human-like output, even the best AI voices have a limited lifespan. The default voices offered in the most popular apps will be used more often and more widely, and as a result, they'll become recognizable and then passé. If you care about design, you don't use default fonts, and if you care about audio, you won't want to use a default AI voice either. Uniqueness matters.

At some providers, such as ElevenLabs and Hume, you can design a custom voice by choosing specific characteristics. This will go a long way toward creating something unique to a particular client, though it could still be imitated.

So... is it possible to create a custom AI voice that nobody else has access to? Indeed, it is.

Synthetic speech with voice cloning

Stephen Hawking knew he was going to lose the ability to speak, and at the time, a robotic replacement voice was the best solution available. Today, if you expect to lose the ability to speak due to ALS or a similar disease, technology can capture your real voice before you lose it, and the next step beyond that tech can clone a voice in an incredibly short span of time.

As an accessibility aid, Apple introduced **Personal Voice** in 2023 (`https://machinelearning.apple.com/research/personal-voice`), and it's still available today. To use it, you must train a model by speaking 10 randomized sentences, and the model can then speak text that you type aloud in a synthetic clone of your own voice. It takes just a few minutes to create, but it's not perfect. A clone of my own voice had some of my characteristics, but it sounds as if I'm speaking in a fake American accent.

Just two years on, voice cloning has advanced to the point where just a few seconds of a voice can be enough to capture its essence. Sometimes, providing longer samples can give better results, but results vary widely. This tech has created the following possibilities:

- A text-to-speech provider can offer many more voices, trained on real people
- Part of a human voiceover can be replaced with a synthetic replacement
- New recordings in the same voice as existing recordings can be generated

There is, of course, an ethical line here—do you have permission to generate audio in a specific person's voice? If an organization has previously engaged a voice artist to narrate their training videos, there are ethical and legal issues stopping you from simply replacing them with a synthetic copy. Most voice cloning services do attempt to verify that permission has been given, so you'll probably need their active participation anyway.

While I wouldn't expect a new public voice to be created from your voice samples without permission, it's always wise to check the privacy conditions of services you use. This is especially true when working with recordings of other people. To test these services out, I've used recordings of my own voice, and I'd recommend you do the same in your own tests. Note that many of the larger names in this space actually require you to read out a verbal permission statement as part of the voice creation process.

While I tested several voice cloning services, not all do an equally good job. You may have more luck than I do, but only some of the services I've tried so far have been able to create a clone of my voice that actually sounds like me. This could be down to my hybrid Australian-with-a-hint-of-UK accent, but I'm surprised at how little success I had:

- **Descript** asked me to read a short script, which took just over 30 seconds, then produced a clone quite quickly. Unfortunately, it sounded like a slightly robotic American version of me—not something I could use.
- **Riverside.fm** includes a feature called VideoDub that lets you retype a word or two that a person has spoken in a video. I didn't get results that sounded like me.
- **Resemble.ai** promises free "rapid" voice clones and asks you to read a short script. Like Descript, it made the voice available quickly, but this time, it sounded nothing like me at all, sounding more English than Australian. Changing the language setting to different English accents gave wildly varying results.
- **Runway** offers a custom voice feature, charging 300 credits (almost half the monthly credits on a Standard plan) to process it. The script provided was far longer, nearly three minutes in length, but the output was a very American version of me, not suitable as a clone.
- **Uberduck** allows you to clone your voice for free, and—surprisingly—it did a very good job of cloning my voice with only 10 seconds of speech. If you want to test the voice cloning waters, this site is quick and effective, and it's not expensive to use, with 1 hour of generations for $10/month.
- **ElevenLabs** offers **Instant Voice Cloning** with just a few seconds of recording, and this is available on all paid plans, including the Starter plan ($5/month). While my instant clone was quick to make and sounded acceptable, it wasn't quite as good as Uberduck's. However, ElevenLabs also offers **Professional Voice Cloning (PVC)** on their Creator, Pro, and Scale plans ($22/$99/$330/month, respectively). This takes significantly more training and has a strict limit of just one high-quality voice per account.

Before you commit, realize that the creation of a professional voice clone is a non-trivial exercise. It requires at least 30 minutes of recorded audio, and preferably up to 3 hours. I'm in the lucky position of having created many, many hours of narrated video training courses, so I uploaded over two hours of high-quality recordings and let it process away. After all those uploads, I also had to record a specific phrase live to verify that it was really me.

Interestingly, if you want to share your voice clone with others, you can. If you choose to add your voice to the **Voice Library**, you'll earn money when your voice is used by others to generate audio. While it remains to be seen whether this is a financial win for participants, there's at least the potential for success.

A few hours later, my voice was ready, and overall, it's pretty amazing to hear words I have only ever typed being said aloud. The realistic voice can be generated using any one of their models, and though the cheaper *Turbo* model is recommended, I heard fewer issues with the higher quality v2 *Multilingual* model. For now, skip the most advanced v3 model, as it's still in alpha; it changed the way my voice sounded substantially.

While most of the audio generated is perfectly acceptable, there's still an occasional pause that feels like it's in the wrong place, or a word pronounced differently from how I would have said it. Just like recording a second take with a real human, a quick regeneration can fix this while introducing other issues elsewhere. Merely clicking **Regenerate speech** is like telling a human, "*Give me another take*" without giving specific guidance. For better results, you could tweak the sliders to control speed, stability, or similarity, or you could add tags to specify emotion, but unwanted pauses can't be totally banished.

You can edit the best parts of each take together, and for many projects, that'll work well enough. This process is similar to how you might work with an outsourced human voiceover artist—providing feedback, and receiving alternate takes of some lines—but it shifts the burden to an editor and isn't as smooth a process as working with a human live in a vocal booth.

All up, these professional voice clones are incredibly technically impressive and very useful. If you want to work with a specific voice-over artist who's willing to train a model with their voice and let you use it, this can work well. If you can record with a real human directly, you'll get better results, but at a higher cost in time and money.

The market is still evolving rapidly and locally run open-source solutions are maturing too. Namigen (discussed earlier) plans to add voice cloning soon, and **IndexTTS2** (`https://indextts2.org`) is available now if you're happy to mess with a command line. You can also test this solution through **Voicv** (`https://voicv.com`).

In the end, though ElevenLabs is leading the market today, competition in this space means that there are several good options to choose from, and some of the base models will be common to several providers. If an AI provider you're already subscribed to offers voice services you can use, try them out.

We've looked at how to generate a narration from an existing voice and also how to imitate an existing voice. Can we use this tech to revise an existing video? As you may have guessed, of course we can.

Replacing part of an existing voice recording

For video and audio creators, a potentially useful trick would be to change the words that someone says in a video to correct their mistakes or rewrite a script after shooting. As mentioned earlier, if you'd like the flexibility to replace part of a human voice recording with a synthetic one, gain permission ahead of time. While a human, given direction from another human, has the potential to record the most accurate, emotive audio, you'll need their approval to put new words in their mouth.

With that approval in hand, if you only need to replace a word or two, the process is easy. Using a provider that can make a good, quick voice clone, you can upload the incorrect section of audio, then type in the correct text and use TTS to make the correct version. Download, splice in the replacement, and you're done: Tyler Stalman has shown this working with Artlist (`https://youtu.be/jCXHOUkeXn4?si=hwRabP5YpnrdyWih&t=806`).

While a simpler TTS model may be able to generate a short section with a bit of coaxing, it's not always easy to match the style of an original delivery well enough to pass as human. Intonation matters, emotion matters, and many models aren't controllable enough to get what you need. Here's one way to make a longer change:

1. Create a synthetic clone of that person's voice.
2. Imitate that person's speech *yourself*, matching their pace and emotion, but saying the right words instead of the wrong ones.
3. Transform your new vocals into their voice, maintaining your emotion and pace.

In the same way that you can create a synthetic video from another video, you can create synthetic speech based on existing speech, potentially allowing greater control over the emotion and pace of the delivery. Artlist offers this (Voice to Voice), as does ElevenLabs (Voice Changer) and Runway (Speech to Speech). It's also possible in DaVinci Resolve, and since the process is less straightforward, I'll take you through it step by step.

> This example is a real-world problem a client of mine experienced. I was filming a speech for professional speaker Daryl Elliott Green (`https://twiceshot.com`) and then delivering a video of the speech to Daryl afterward. Unfortunately, he misspoke at the start of his speech, saying "August" instead of "April" in the first line of his talk. Many clients have made similar mistakes and fixing them used to require rerecording that moment—but no longer.

To use this workflow, you'll need the Studio version of DaVinci Resolve, and you'll need an audio recording of the person to be cloned. About five minutes should be enough, but if you have time, you can provide a longer recording.

1. Select an original clip of the person speaking, then choose **AI Tools > DaVinci AI Voice Training....**

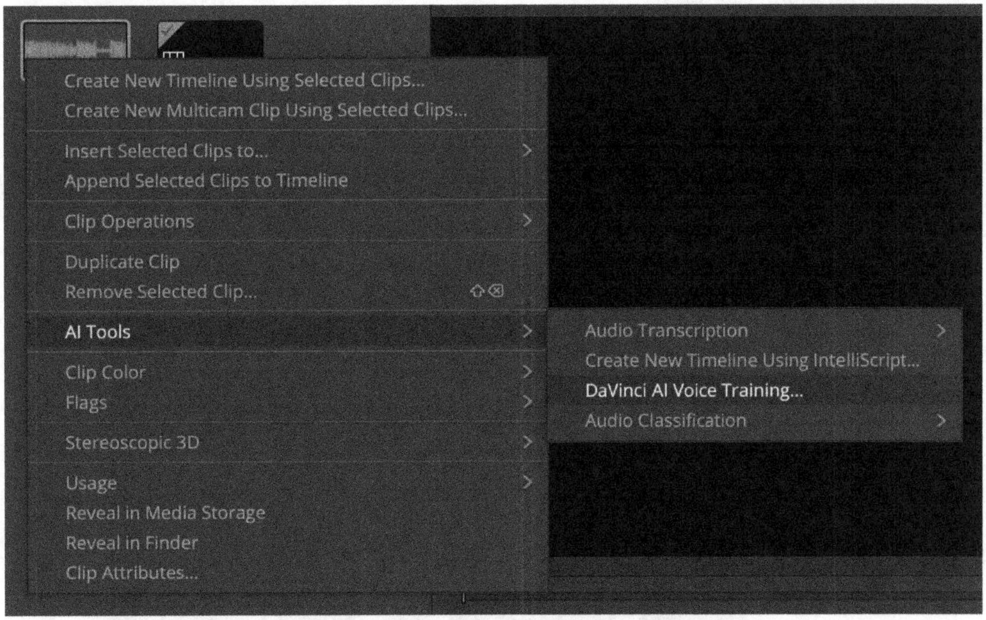

Figure 9.6 – Train a model on a recording of a person's voice, and then you can imitate it

The first time you use this feature, you'll have to download an additional file, or more than one if you're working with languages other than English.

2. After agreeing that you have permission to clone this voice, you can name the voice model and choose the level of accuracy needed—just go with the default **Better** option here.

   Creating the model can take a little while, but it will continue in the background—my MacBook Pro with M3 Max took about an hour to process five minutes of source material.

3. When it's done, record your own voice, speaking the corrected "guide" words with the pace, intonation, and emotion you need. It's easiest to use **Timeline** > **Record Voiceover** to record this to a new track.

   You may find it easier to match the original speech if you listen to it in headphones while you record, and this will also avoid problems with feedback.

4. Select the new track, then choose **Clip** > **AI Tools** > **Voice Convert**. In this dialog box, choose **New Track** from the **Track** menu at the top, and your new voice from the **Voice Model** menu below.
5. Press **Render** to transform the new "guide" clip to that person's voice. If it doesn't sound quite right, undo and try again with a different pitch change value or try rerecording your guide clip.

   The new clip will show up on a new track.

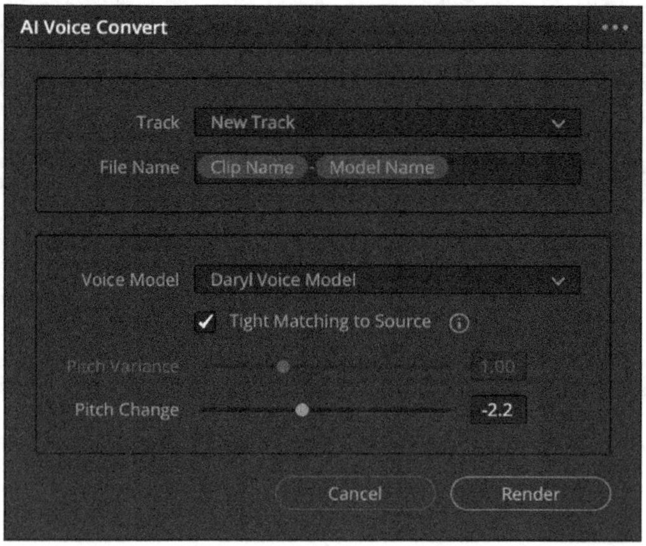

Figure 9.7 – AI Voice Convert can transform a recording into one of a few built-in voices or one you've trained

6. Blade the original clip and the replacement clip, trimming and fading to decide exactly how much of each clip to use.

This workflow enables tricks that would have been impossible just a year or two ago, and the example I've shown here is real—a presenter said one word instead of another, and I've been able to seamlessly replace it by saying it myself.

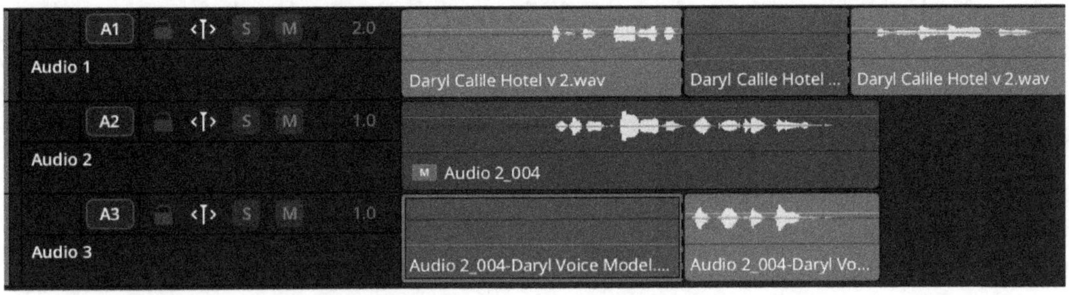

Figure 9.8 – In the timeline, choose what you want to keep from the original and replacement audio

Clearly, the strength of this approach is the control it provides. If you don't have DaVinci Resolve Studio, try one of the voice-to-voice models online, and don't be afraid to rerecord a new guide track (or simply regenerate) if you don't have success the first time.

We've looked at a number of ways to generate voice, but words aren't the only important part of audio. Music is important too, and AI services are happy to help.

Creating original music

Original music is one of the most controlled parts of the modern media landscape. Every video uploaded to every major streaming platform is scanned to identify the music it contains; YouTube's system is called **Content ID**. If you use a track you don't have the rights to, your video can be blocked, or muted, or you could get a copyright strike, or you could lose all monetization for that video.

Finding music for a video can be a little tricky, though. If you search for "corporate uplifting background" on a common stock music site, you'll find several tracks that people have heard before. And even if you make music yourself, programming loops in free software such as **GarageBand**, if you're not original enough, someone else might make a similar track and claim that you're violating their copyright. (Yes, this has happened to me.)

Even musicians playing original pieces have to be careful—if you unknowingly use the same sequence of notes as that of a more famous and litigious artist, they could come after you independently. With copyright issues on one hand and originality issues on the other, it's tempting to look to AI to make music that fits a client's needs.

While some people are using AI to make tracks to be played on streaming services or even sold independently, I'd only recommend using Gen AI to create background tracks for projects where the music plays a minor supporting role. For a project in which music is the focus, hire a human if you can, or use AI-made music as temp music only.

But if you've never heard AI-made music, head to **Suno** (`https://suno.com`) and ask for something you could potentially use as a backing track for a podcast or video. To push the ethical boundaries just a little, I asked for `A song in the style of Daft Punk with lyrics about being on holiday at the beach with friends`, and it understood the brief.

In a short time, I could play four different songs in the right style, based on two different sets of lyrics. Additional partial sample songs were also created with newer models, showing more variation and more complex structure, and most clients would find something here they'd like. If you're a musician yourself, a paid account lets you upload your own music to build on.

When a song has been made, in just a minute or two, be sure to read the lyrics and make sure they're saying what you want. While two songs used lyrics about friends on a beach holiday, two other songs used lyrics written from the perspective of a pool cleaning robot: "*Scrub the algae chase the grime / Perfect pool it's cleaning time.*" Hilarious, still decent music, but not usable.

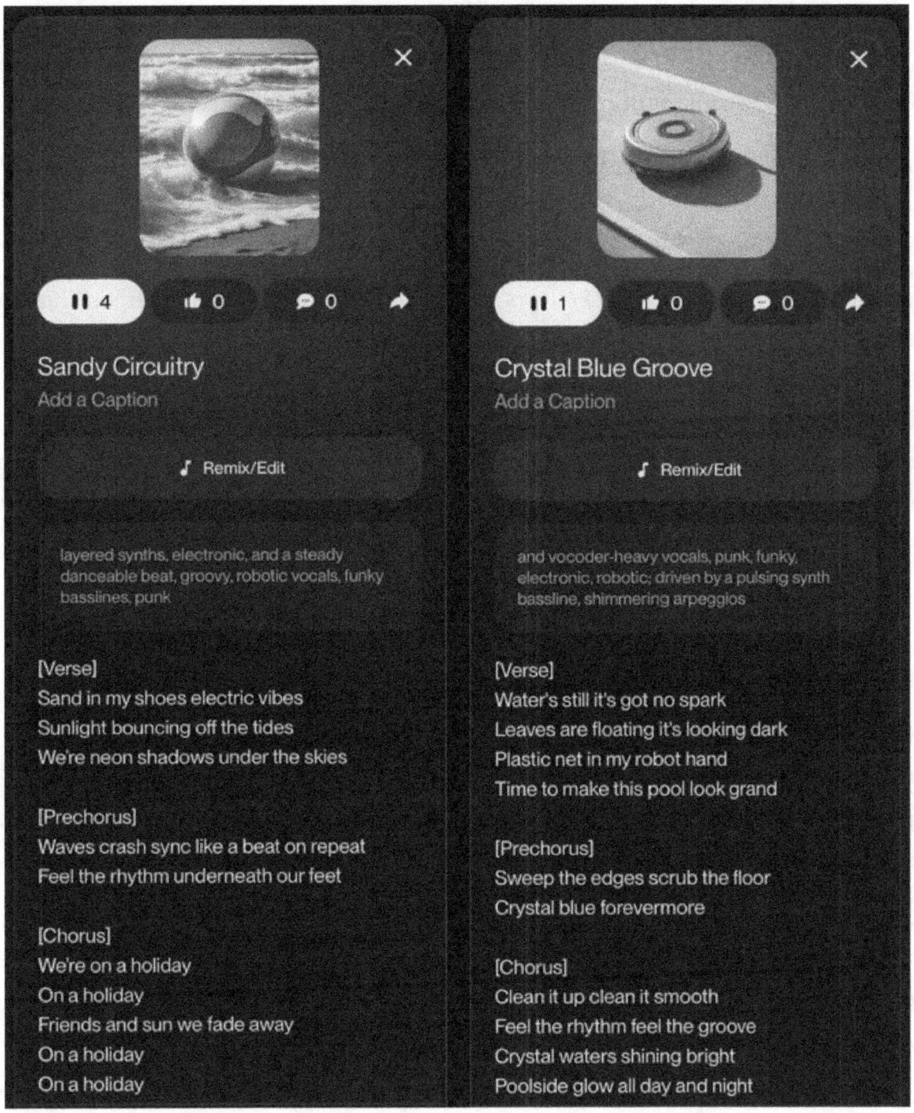

Figure 9.9 – Songs about friends at the beach, sure; songs about a robot cleaning a pool, not so much

The same prompt was rejected at **ElevenMusic** (`https://elevenlabs.io/app/music/`) for including the name *Daft Punk*. After tweaking, the output was more generic, leaning too far into robotic voices instead of the vocoder that Daft Punk are known for, and with more of a generic pop soundtrack behind. Other generations with different prompts suffered from lyrics that weren't sung clearly and an overly simple musical structure.

Udio (`https://www.udio.com`) misunderstood things badly and created a couple of punk guitar tracks. That would have been OK, except these songs included vocals that sounded vaguely like words but weren't, the sonic equivalent of a person with seven fingers on one hand.

Clearly, there are many sites, many styles, and many prompts to try, and you'll need to experiment to find a site that suits your tastes. Mind you, if you know a bit about music, you can step beyond prompting and become an active shaper of AI-made sounds.

Soundraw (`https://soundraw.io/`) allows you to choose a genre, mood, theme, length, tempo, and the instruments to use, then presents you with a selection of tracks that it has just popped together. Scroll down, and you'll see a mixer that you can adjust as the track plays, making parts of the track more or less intense, controlling when the quiet moments hit, when the fills kick in, when the bass drop lands, and even changing the chords used. These tracks may have vocal elements but are mostly instrumental. This is a different kind of music, but it's great if you need more control.

Among people who know music well, opinions vary on these services. Technically, many AI tracks contain artifacts, and it's difficult to separate the musical stems cleanly. If you were hoping to remix these tracks, to remaster them, or to remove some elements, you may struggle.

Still, imperfect AI-made music can function as useful inspiration for professionals, just as imperfect AI-made images can. And again, for a less critical job, imperfect AI music could slot right into a final product, just as imperfect AI images can be "good enough." If you're not a music expert, use these tracks with caution, as you may not hear all the flaws that some of the audience will.

Also, be sure to stay on the right side of licensing; if you plan to use any music you make for any commercial purposes, you'll need to read the fine print carefully. Music made with ElevenLabs can't be used for traditional TV or film purposes, for example. Also, if you use a free or lower-tier account at many of these services, you can't use the music for commercial purposes at all.

As an aside, if you really do know what you're doing and like to create music yourself, can AI help? Indeed, it can, with plugins such as **Output Co-Producer** (`https://output.com/products/co-producer`). This sits inside your DAW and suggests samples that might help based on your prompts and from its analysis of your composition. The samples are human made, so this is not a Gen AI solution, but if you're into making music, you may find it useful.

Before we close this chapter, let's have a quick look at the most useful new solutions for translating spoken dialogue.

Audio translation

In many ways, translating audio is an extension of translating text, with the same issues and limitations discussed in *Chapter 6*. Translations are imperfect, but still useful in many contexts, and the method you should use will vary depending on the task at hand.

Live translation is perfect for a conversation with collaborators who don't speak your language. For this, you can use Apple's Translate app, the cross-platform Google Translate app, or another system. These apps often tie into headphones, letting another person speak in their language while you hear it in yours.

Figure 9.10 – In the Translate app, speaking in one language and having it instantly translated into another still feels like magic

Because speed is critical to a fluid conversation, these systems won't give you perfect results, though they're usually good enough in the moment. In a production context, where accuracy is more critical, we'll look to another solution.

YouTube offers automatic **dubbing** into several languages, turning a video's **captions** into audio using synthetic voices. These voices are relatively robotic, and any emotion or nuance in the original delivery will be lost. Also, since YouTube's automatically generated captions are not usually as accurate as those produced by other transcription services, that can compromise the translated captions and dubs too.

To improve quality, be sure to create your own captions and check them before uploading. If possible, ask a native speaker of a target language to either translate the script themselves or to correct errors in an AI-created translation. At this point, you can use a TTS service to generate new audio, potentially with more expression than a robotic default.

Though different languages are often spoken at different speeds, research has shown that they still deliver information in about the same amount of time (`https://www.cnrs.fr/en/press/similar-information-rates-across-languages-despite-divergent-speech-rates`). Overall, while you can expect a dubbed program to run about as long as the original, the timing of individual sentences is important in the context of a video. While an audio-only podcast has the flexibility for some sentences to take longer than others, the translated audio track on a video has to maintain the original language's timing on every sentence.

As an all-in-one solution for translating audio on videos, ElevenLabs offers a **Dubbing** service (`https://elevenlabs.io/app/dubbing`), which combines transcribed captions, dubbed audio, and offers timing control for each dubbed sentence. To test, I created a French dub of my promotional launch video for my Final Cut Pro Spatial Kit plugin.

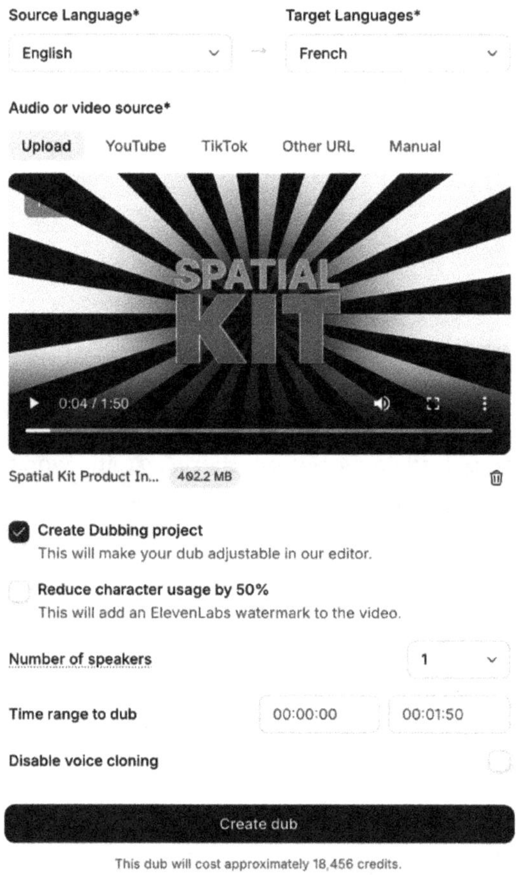

Figure 9.11 – After uploading the video, choose the languages you want to dub to, and wait a short time

Each language is charged separately, and at 10,000 credits per minute, per language, if you don't want watermarked output, it's easy to run through a standard plan's monthly credits. (Note that if you plan to extract the audio from the output, a visual watermark doesn't matter, and costs drop to 5,000 credits per minute, per language.)

The output sounds very impressive, using instant voice cloning to create a foreign translation that sounds more or less like the original speaker(s). As you'd expect, it's not quite as good as a professional voice clone. Importantly, in the Dubbing Studio, you have a chance to correct mistakes in both the original transcription and the translations, and this is a crucial step.

Figure 9.12 – ElevenLabs' Dubbing Studio lets you fix problems and regenerate audio if needed

Firstly, transcription errors happen and should be corrected before translation. For example, though most of the transcription here (*Figure 9.12*) is very good, the very first word, *Cinematic*, simply doesn't exist in the original video. *Cinématique* in the translation is not just superfluous; it also ruins the timing. Happily, the Dubbing Studio lets you adjust the timing of any sentence, so do check for problems, then move or trim audio clips if needed.

Also, remember that translation problems can be subtle, and as there are often multiple potential translations for a particular phrase, the automatic solution may not be the best one. This is especially important with jargon or technical phrases, and you'll want to make sure you speak in a consistent way across all related videos in a language. As already mentioned, you really should ask a native speaker to check any translation.

The transcription and the translated text are both editable, and if you make changes to the translation, you can press the **Generate Audio** button below that section to create a new audio clip. These regenerations are free (within limits), so you can fix problems without worrying that you have to pay significantly more than you'd expected.

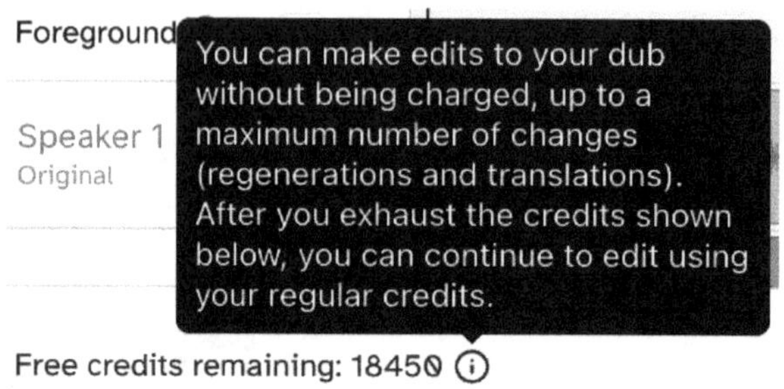

Figure 9.13 – Free changes can be made in the Dubbing Studio if you need to regenerate some sections

ElevenLabs is a powerful solution that I'd recommend, but it's not alone in the market, and it's only a solution for the audio side of translation. Because the video remains untouched when the audio is changed, there's a mismatch between the mouth movements and the words heard. In what seems like a magic solution, AI lip sync, done well, could potentially be a better option.

AI lip sync

Solutions such as **Perso** (`https://perso.ai`), **LipDub** (`https://www.lipdub.ai`), and **Dubly** (`https://dubly.ai`) include not just translation and dubbing but also regeneration of videos to match the newly generated audio. **Flawless** (`https://flawlessai.com/`), mentioned briefly in the previous chapter, offers higher-end features more optimized for feature film workflows.

Some AI lip sync videos can be incredibly impressive, to the point where many viewers won't realize that they have been translated at all. But be careful—the more seamless the end result, the more important it is to make sure the transcription and translation are perfect. Importantly, unless you are fluent in both the source and target languages, you won't be able to assess that yourself.

A viewer watching an auto-dubbed YouTube video using a robotic voice will expect it to make some mistakes, just as the transcribed captions in the original language may contain mistakes. There will also be some level of forgiveness if only the audio has been translated.

However, if you're presenting dialogue in a person's real voice that actually appears to be said by them, that expectation shifts. Translation mistakes are likely to now be seen as a real mistake by a real person. There's also the risk of falling into the *uncanny valley*, with something that looks *nearly human but not quite*. With lip-synced videos, a person's hand movements may not quite match up with the translation, and you can be left with a vague feeling that something's off. This will hopefully be less of a problem as the tech matures.

Whether you choose to use lip sync or not, if you have considerable translation needs, consider a dedicated service. Know that costs can quickly add up, and the more languages you produce, the more content you're creating and the quicker you'll run through your credits. Mind you, traditional translation isn't cheap either, and you'll still need real humans for verification at the very least.

YouTube provides free automatic dubbing available at the low end, and the higher end is well served, though time will tell whether audiences embrace lip-synced translations. While I would personally prefer to hear the original speaker's voice clone rather than a dubbing artist, I'm sure others feel differently. Just as some viewers are happy to read subtitles while others are not, the market will likely embrace a mix of these technologies, just as they have for subtitles and dubbing today.

To end this chapter, let's look at what AI can do for sound effects.

Creating synthetic sound effects

Even if you prefer to use real human voices and real human musicians, sound effects aren't always something you can easily put your hands on. To do this job well by hand requires specialist software such as **Audio Design Desk** (`http://add.app`) and banks of sounds to call on—it's fun if you have the time.

But if you don't think you have time, yes, AI can fill that silence too, either temporarily or perhaps to a standard that's good enough for final output. If you've been using Gen AI to make videos, this could be especially useful; few of these models include audio, and even **Veo 3**, which does include audio, doesn't always get it right.

Firefly is an easy place to start: you've probably got a login and some spare credits, quality is OK, and there are plenty of options to explore. Firstly, you can simply use a text prompt to request audio, and Firefly will give you four variations. I went for something relatively challenging (`Dogs barking at a surf beach`) to test how well it could blend two different kinds of sounds that would actually sometimes be heard together.

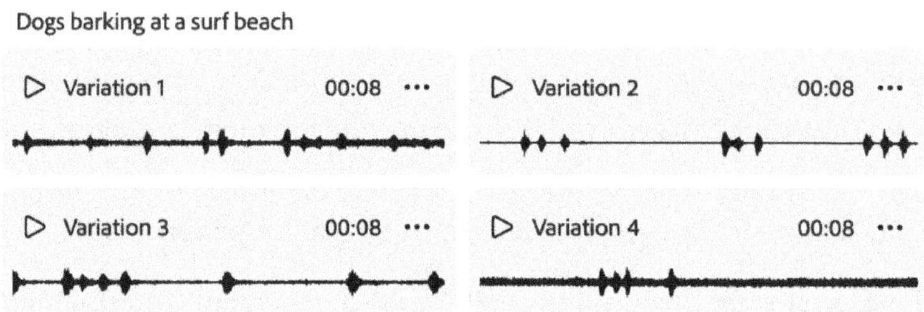

Figure 9.14 – Firefly's four options all sounded good here

A book is not the ideal format for delivering audio, but the waveforms should show you that there is a decent amount of variation in the eight-second files. That's good—there are different beaches and different kinds of dogs, and I wasn't very specific with my prompt. Unfortunately, the quality is not high enough to use for final output; listening on a half-decent pair of headphones reveals muddy audio with compression artifacts.

Asking for the same sound from other providers gave mixed results. ElevenLabs offers sound effects (four variations and duration control), but the quality there wasn't much better. Trying **SFX Engine** (`https://sfxengine.com/app/sound-effects`), which took a little longer, I received files 10 seconds long with a single variation per generation, and the quality was pretty variable.

If you're not confident with audio mixing, asking for a combined sound like this might seem like a good approach, but it may end up compromising the audio quality. When you ask for multiple elements to be combined, the output will only sound good if both source elements work, and you've got no way to swap out just one of the elements.

If you can, it's best to ask for elements separately, then control volume, panning, EQ, reverb, and so on for each sound on its own. It's the classic tale: *the more time you can spend, the better the results*. If you skip all the fun parts with the help of AI, you won't get better at mixing, timing, or positioning sounds in space.

Returning to these sites and asking for elements separately gave better results overall, though quality was still variable. Sounds of dogs barking were OK, while surf waves crashing on a beach tended to sound artificial—something that can happen to sounds (especially of waves) with a data rate that's too low.

This quality issue was evident in many other sounds generated at ElevenLabs. By default, generations are public and sounds that other users have created can be heard and downloaded.

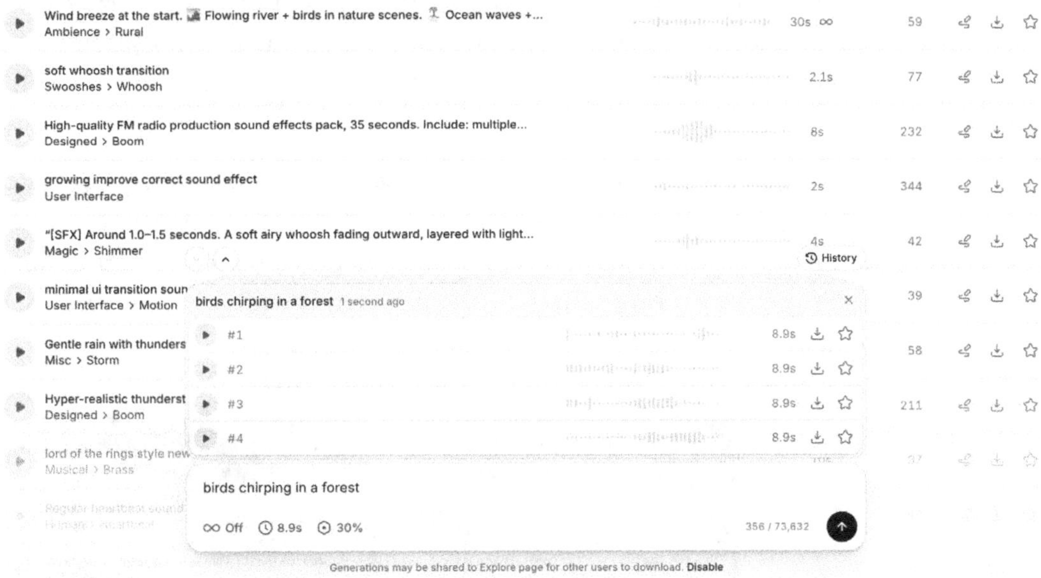

Figure 9.15 – This public feed of sound effects at ElevenLabs gives a good idea of what's possible

Listening to many of these results (from long and short prompts) revealed low-level hums in the background of forest ambience, explosions with clipped peaks, and some unpleasant beeps. It wasn't all bad, but I didn't find many sounds that would compete with a regular sound library. Variety is good, quality is not.

AI does have some tricks that a regular sound library can't quite match, though. On some sites, you can upload a video, and an AI will generate audio to match, with or without a prompt. **KlingAI** (`https://app.klingai.com/global/video-to-audio/`) offers this, and while the video does seem to serve as a prompt enhancement, results were mixed—after all, you're asking for multiple things at once.

A video with nobody walking and no prompt produced audio with scrambled speech or footsteps added, though one or two variations were possibly usable. When I added a simple prompt of `Wind gently rustles the crops in the field`, it got the content right, but all four generations were of poor quality. Another video, of a person walking along a forest track, was paired with the prompt `Wind in the trees with birdsong` and produced artifact-filled audio with bonus (unwanted) running water, thunder, or mistimed footsteps.

I tried Firefly too, and it didn't seem to try to use the source video for inspiration. However, the interface here does encourage you to use short, specific prompts and combine multiple sounds—a good idea. At the time of writing, this feature is still in beta and isn't fully active, but it's worth exploring.

Another potentially useful feature in Firefly is that you can use your voice to imitate the timing of sounds you request in a prompt. I asked for `footsteps crunching into gravel` and provided the timing in a voice recording that I uploaded separately. Four generations all kept the timing spot on, and though the quality wasn't perfect, I could definitely use this as a temp track or a mix with other sounds.

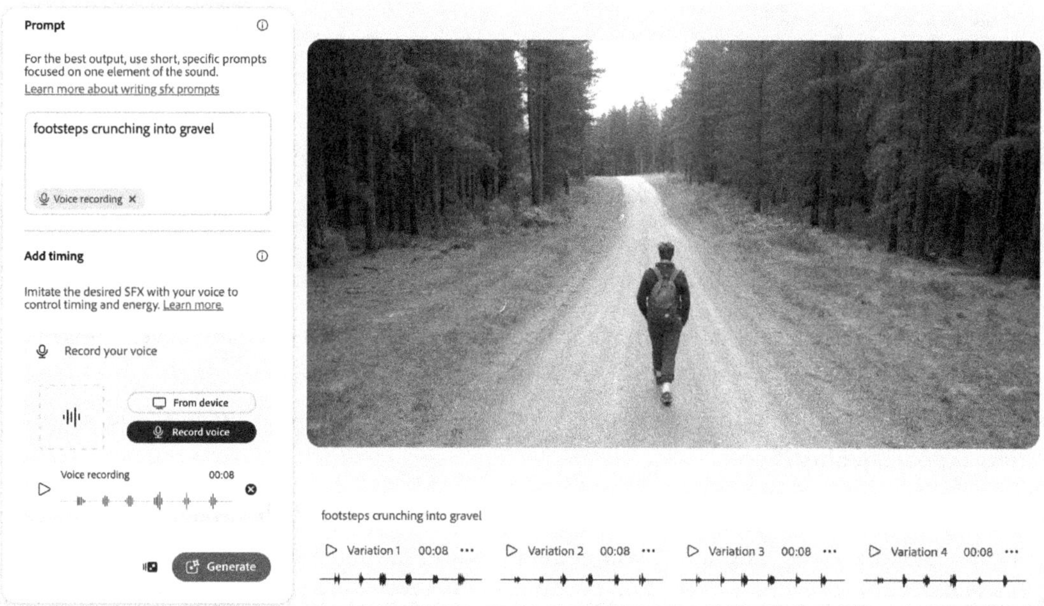

Figure 9.16 – Timing of these footsteps matched the voice recording I provided

For sound effects, quality seems to be a problem with most of these sites. While I can't test all the possible services, I was surprised that the overall quality of sound effects is lower than it was for music. Given that sound effects are easiest to generate one at a time, and they're not always that hard to find, perhaps it's better to mix them the old-fashioned way for now.

Let's step back and sum this up.

Summary

Between speech, music, and sound effects, there are many ways in which AI can help. The speech side of things is perhaps best developed, and whether you choose to use a high-quality premade voice or to train one of your own, I think we're at the point where you could—with the best models—create a synthetic voice that many people would identify as human. Some synthetic music could pass for human-made, especially if it's used at a low volume, but results vary widely in quality. Across the board, sound effects aren't quite there, and though there's huge potential, I'll be mixing by hand for now.

If you're a video or photo expert who dabbles in audio, it's easy to take a quick listen to AI-made audio and potentially be impressed. But if you're a visual expert, and you can spot flaws in visual generations that others might miss, don't let poor audio quality slide by. Audio is critical to a good video, and though AI tools can perform wonders with cleanup, the generative side of things is a mixed bag for now.

Next up, we're stepping into the *Automation AI* part of the book—a brave new world.

Part 4

Automation AI

This concluding part explores the potential of automation tools, including tools designed to accelerate tedious or time-consuming tasks, automatic video-editing solutions, and a discussion of the future of digital assistants and agents, which could upend many more workflows than just creative ones.

This part of the book includes the following chapters:

- *Chapter 10, Automation AI with Images*
- *Chapter 11, Automation AI with Video*
- *Chapter 12, Automation AI with Digital Assistants and Agents*

10

Automation AI with Images

In the first part of the book, we looked at how Utility AI can help you to do your job more quickly: selecting, categorizing, or finding things. If you want more help than that, Automation AI can do parts of your job for you, and there are many image-related tasks to send its way. Automatic image culling, color correction, and retouching are all possible with the right apps.

However, for the best results, I'd recommend using AI to automate only boring, tedious, or time-consuming tasks. No system is perfect, and if you let an automated system make imperfect decisions, you can deliver work that's sub-standard. Some tasks need to be performed with care, and you can't—or, at least, shouldn't—just press a "make it smooth" button to give everyone fresh, plastic skin. There are many different ways an image can be treated—do you trust a computer to make that decision for you?

Of course, we all have to make a judgment about what tasks are worth our time and what tasks can be passed to someone else. In that sense, using an AI-powered app is a lot like outsourcing. Because many of these apps run on your own computer, you may not have to upload thousands of images to a cloud server, which saves time and avoids potential privacy concerns. If you're already willing to outsource some image-related tasks to other humans, outsourcing these tasks to AI instead could help your workflow.

With a focus on images, this chapter will show you how AI can help with the following:

- Automatic image culling
- Automatic retouching
- Automatic image processing
- Writing scripts to speed up design tasks

Let's start by asking an AI to pick out the best images from a large pool.

Automatic image culling

Professional photographers often shoot a lot of photos, and although some clients want to see them all, removing the bad photos is an important part of the job. If a photographer were to share all the original files from a photoshoot, they'd be judged harshly; there may be many more misses than hits, and simple adjustments can make a world of difference in an image's final appearance.

Culling is the first part of the process, in which the best photos are picked out. Obvious duds are removed, groups of shots taken on motor drive are whittled down, and eventually, the best shots are left behind. Different photographers will have different methods, but here's how I cull manually in Adobe Lightroom Classic:

1. Glance quickly at each photo, decide whether it's *good*, and if so, tag it as follows:
    - If good, it gets tagged as 4 stars (good) or optionally 5 stars (great) by tapping that number key on the keyboard.
    - If a photo is better than one I just tagged as 4 or 5 stars, but very similar, I tag the old photo as 3 and the new one as 4 or 5.
2. Repeat until done.
3. View only 4+ star photos.

This is obviously a simplified process, but it works in many apps and leaves you with a pool of *good* and/or *great* photos that you can process further. All these images will be at least color-corrected, while the 5-star images may get more personal attention.

Figure 10.1 - A manual cull in Lightroom Classic doesn't have to take long — can AI do better?

As a test, I timed how long it took me to process a batch of images from a recent shoot. This manual cull of 1,247 of my own images took about 22 minutes and left me with 268 *good* images. Not all of these will make the final cut, but I'm confident I haven't missed anything—I looked at every shot I took, I know what happened, and I can present the shots in the best light. What can AI do?

> Importantly, Lightroom itself will soon include an AI-powered assisted culling feature for portraits only. At the time of writing (October 2025), this feature has not launched, but as it's likely to be public when you read this, be sure to check it out.

Excire Foto (`https://excire.com/en/excire-foto/`) is an option that can automatically analyze your images and group them in several useful ways—we looked at it in the Utility AI section of the book. The locally run app took just over a minute to cull my collection of 1,247 down to 656 with the default profile—pretty quick. This collects images based on similarity, by the person in the photo, and images taken in close succession (e.g., on a motor drive). It also recommended images for deletion, such as blurry shots or those with eyes closed.

Analysis like this will be useful to some photographers, especially those who deal with large quantities of images. However, the danger with this, and with all other automatic culling features, is that a good photo may be rejected. In my testing, while blurry shots were certainly flagged for rejection, not all of the picks were spot on. Some blurry shots ended up being selected, and other shots that looked OK to me were rejected—possibly because they weren't photos of people.

Other photos were rejected seemingly because they were too dark, but sometimes a photographer simply has to work in a dark environment and rescue their shots with extra processing; only a human has the context to make all the correct decisions. If the only shot of a particular subject is less than perfect, you may have to rescue it as best you can.

The good news is that this is OK—it's an assistant, not a judge. There's no need to automatically delete the images Excire suggests, and different culling profiles allow a decent amount of flexibility in how images are recognized and processed. You can create a new profile and choose a selection of characteristics you want to use as the basis for an automatic cull. If you choose photos that have already been analyzed, this will proceed in just a few seconds, so it's easy to experiment with.

Aftershoot (`https://aftershoot.com/`) is another app that includes culling features, and overall, it did a similar job to Excire. Provided with the same images, it took just over six minutes to analyze them and present the rated images. My first pass used the **Customized AI Cull** settings, tagging 552 as **Selected** (5 stars) and 93 as **Highlights** (4 stars), but if that isn't what you want, you can try again without a full re-analysis.

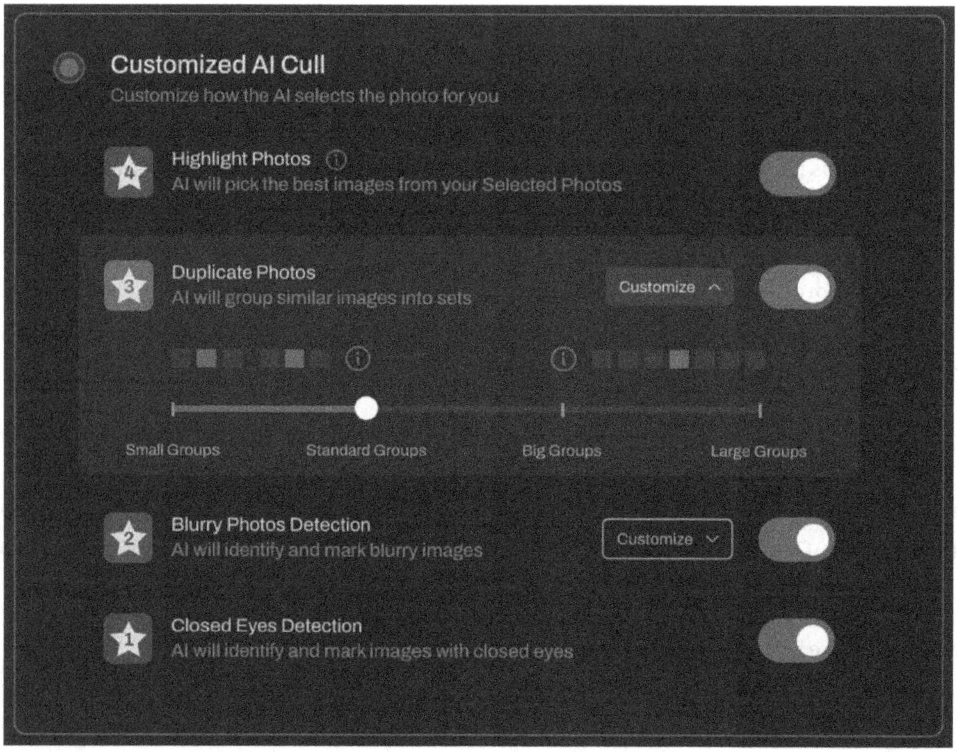

Figure 10.2 – Aftershoot's Customized AI Cull tool gives you a few options

To re-cull, press **Quick Restart**, which takes just a few seconds. The **Automated AI Cull** option removes the more detailed controls, featuring only a simple slider to tell the app how many photos you want:

- **Standard** gives me 503 **Selected** and 84 **Highlights**
- **Few** gives 423 **Selected** and 70 **Highlights**
- The **Extreme** option gives me 161 **Selected** and 430 **Maybe**

That last **Extreme** option is closer to my personal choices, but not close enough to save me time. In the **Selected** group, it chose photos I rejected and omitted photos I chose. The **Loupe** view provides some useful features, automatically grouping similar photos and letting you quickly switch between them, which is helpful when verifying that nothing important has been skipped.

Imagen (`https://imagen-ai.com`) takes a slightly different approach, as it runs in the cloud rather than on your local machine. While this service does have a desktop app and integrates with Lightroom Classic by default, it uploads all images to the cloud for culling, which can make the process take a little longer.

My 1,247 original RAW images take 48 GB of space in their native format—RAW files aren't small. Imagen compressed them with the Adobe DNG Converter before upload, and though I have an upload connection speed of 100 Mbps, it still took 7.5 minutes to upload the images, and it was over 19 minutes before I could review its work.

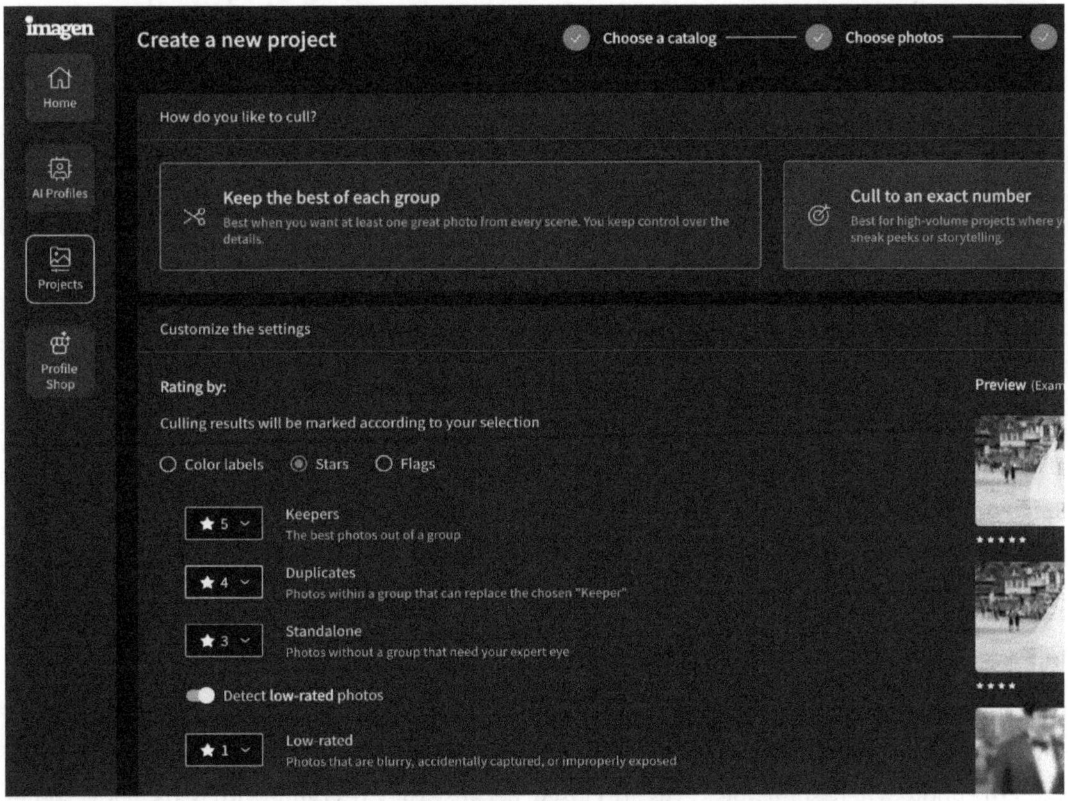

Figure 10.3 – Imagen lets you keep the best shots, or produce a specific number of images

The main focus of culling here is to identify the best photos within each group; it identifies **Keepers**, **Duplicates**, **Standalone**, and **Low-rated** images. Usefully, you can identify the best photo of each group or cull to an exact target number of images, but there's no slider to let you be more or less fussy. With the default settings, it chose 336 **Keepers**, and while it did mostly OK, a couple of my favorite shots were somehow tagged as 1-star duds.

Because the photos are now online, moving between images isn't as fast as it is in the local apps, and some information, such as an image's filename, isn't available in the main interface. You'll need to set up an "AI Profile" before you begin a culling operation, defining a preferred look that Imagen will use to preprocess all your images. It's not a final look, but it's a lot closer to final than looking at the raw images and imagining what you'll do with them.

Narrative (`https://narrative.so`) offers similar culling features to both Excire Foto and Aftershoot. When you drop a folder full of photos into the app, it'll quickly start recognizing faces in your photos, then mark which are in focus and any eyes that are closed. After about three minutes, the first pass was done, and a minute or so later, all the images had been flagged with an initial rating: 860 **potential picks**, 200 **unlikely picks**, and 187 **undesirable picks**.

Figure 10.4 – Narrative did a quick first pass, but it didn't cut the pool down too much

Related images were grouped, making it easier to choose between similar shots, and it's also possible to filter based on how well a shot was focused. For a first-pass edit, this is useful, but I'd have preferred a deeper cut.

Working with imperfect results

Unfortunately, across all these apps, some good photos were listed as "undesirable" because the very best photos don't always tick the right boxes in the eyes of an algorithm. Sometimes, you want the photo where someone's eyes are closed, because they're crying with tears of joy. Sometimes, an out-of-focus moment is still perfect. Sometimes, the only photo you have of a person smiling has issues, but you have to use it anyway.

Software also can't know about the particular requirements for each photoshoot. For example, the photoshoot I used to test all these products featured panels of five people talking on a topic, sharing a microphone between them. I wanted to deliver at least one or two photos of each speaker holding the microphone and speaking, as that's a photo they'll each want to share. But an automated cull doesn't understand that subtlety—how can it? Therefore, the trickiest culling tasks will probably involve some manual work, and that's certainly possible.

If any AI-based culling solution has hidden a shot, you'll have to take things into your own hands. After the first pass, I would recommend taking a very quick look through the collections of "worst" photos to make sure that nothing important has been lost. If you see anything worth saving, reclassify that shot as *good* or *great* and move on.

Whether these tools are useful to you or not depends on how many photos you need to process and how quickly that needs to happen. If you find it difficult to cull quickly, these tools might be extremely valuable, but if you're already fast at this process, perhaps not so much. Professional photographers shooting several events each month have the most to gain here, though occasional photographers could still save time.

If you're considering adopting one of these solutions for your work, you'll want to download all of them and test them out yourself. Culling is a personal process, and I don't think there's a clear winner in terms of culling performance. Each one is available as a free trial but be aware that if one of these apps makes `.xmp` sidecar files, the metadata (including photo ratings) will show up in another of these apps if you pass it the same images. For a clean test, be sure to pass a fresh copy of your test images and make sure it can export to a format you're happy with.

Pricing is quite variable between these apps, and while Excire Foto is available as a one-time purchase, Aftershoot and Narrative require a subscription between US$10 and US$60 a month. Culling is available on the cheapest plans, but if you need to adjust images too, you may need to move up to a more expensive plan. Culling on Imagen costs US$18 per month or US$12 per month on an annual basis, but the next step, automated image adjustment, is on a per-image basis. (It's also worth noting that **Evoto**, a solution for automated retouching discussed in the next section, will soon offer culling too.)

Next, let's look at another common task you may want to automate straight after culling: image processing.

Automatic image processing

While this process means different things to different artists, most professional photographers will adjust exposure, sharpness, white balance, skin texture, and more before sending a final image to a client. A batch of images from an event might include basic exposure, white balance, and sharpness corrections, while the hero images from a wedding might include more extensive, focused adjustments made in a tool like Photoshop.

Many of the more basic adjustments can be automated to some degree, and indeed, most image-editing applications include some kind of automatic enhancement option—some of which make use of AI to make their decisions.

Apple's **Photos** app has an **Auto Enhance** button, **Luminar Neo** has several AI-powered adjustment tools, **ON1 Photo RAW** includes AI-powered raw processing, and **Pixelmator Pro** has an **ML Enhance** button. Even Photoshop's **Auto Levels** has an **Enhance Brightness and Contrast** feature that uses machine learning to make its decisions.

Many photographic features do make use of AI, but the magic largely happens behind the scenes, leading to a better version of an older algorithm. Here, we'll look at more overt uses of AI that can help you do your job more quickly.

First up, we'll focus on solutions that process images in bulk, turning a potentially time-consuming process into a quicker one. With all these solutions, you can tweak as you wish after the initial automatic pass, and there's no need to live with the defaults if they don't work on a particular image.

How does this work if you do it by hand? To perform the basic process manually in Lightroom, I'd filter to show only the selected images, and then do the following:

1. Use the sliders to correct an image typical of each separate location.
2. Copy that correction.
3. Paste that correction to all other photos in that same location.
4. Tweak the exposure on each image as needed for consistent exposure.

If specific images need extra work, control lighting or perform retouching.

While I usually tackle each job on its own, some photographers would prefer to start from a premade preset instead. Making images look consistent can take some time, especially with photos taken within a space with variable lighting, but if you're using Lightroom, the masks that select people will adapt automatically to each image when you paste a correction. This goes a long way to giving you a consistent look across many images, so... do you need anything else?

A good, modern AI-based image-processing system will be able to blend the best of the one-shot "enhance" tools with an understanding of their own preferred style and potentially perform more complex operations too. Automatic retouching is an option with some of these services, but you'll want to find a balance between automation and preserving the character of each image. Not every client wants a skin-smoothing filter applied.

While Excire Foto focuses mostly on organization, the other culling apps discussed here can also perform automatic processing, if you want it.

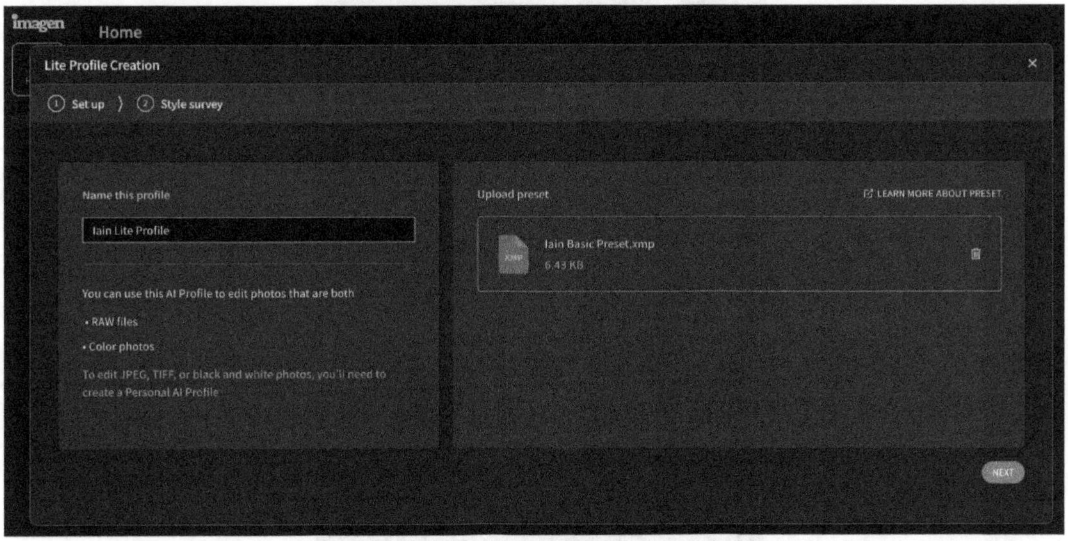

Figure 10.5 – An AI profile can start from a simple preset, but uploading thousands of images is preferred

Aftershoot, Imagen, and Narrative all offer to build a customized professional AI profile from a large collection of your own processed images. Aftershoot and Imagen are also happy to create a quick profile from a preset you provide and give you a quick quiz to confirm your exposure, temperature, and tint preferences. All three sites also offer a selection of predefined styles, including some free defaults and some styles from other photographers, available as an additional purchase.

Your profile, from any source, can now be used to process all your images. In some ways, this is just like choosing a custom **Look-Up Table (LUT)** in a video-editing application, although presets offer more flexibility than LUTs do. In my testing, the results weren't bad, but they weren't bespoke either. These apps do claim to improve their results over time, as you add more images to the training set, so if you want to make one of these solutions work for you, don't give up too quickly.

Imagen does offer some basic retouching (including teeth whitening), but with far fewer controls over skin smoothing than Aftershoot. While both include automated cropping, straightening, and subject masking, Aftershoot adds more extensive control over spots, wrinkles, flyaway hair, and overall skin smoothing. It also allows different effects to be applied to different kinds of faces (masculine, feminine, elderly, and child). These presets are perhaps a little too strong, and though the controls here aren't extensive, they are tweakable.

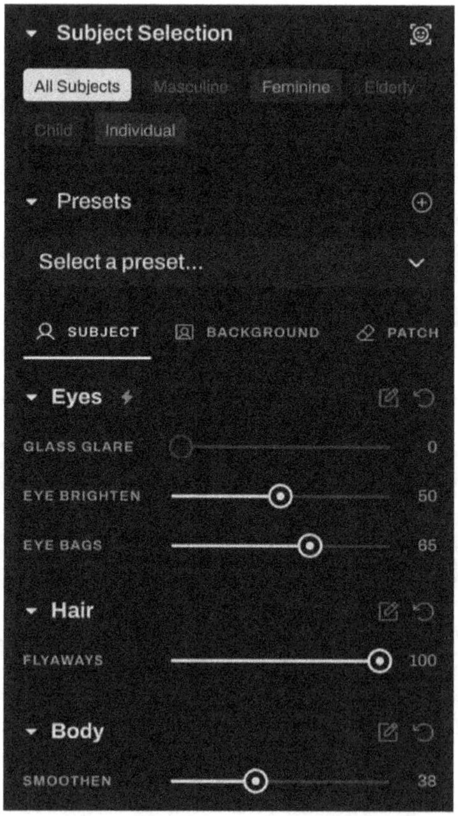

Figure 10.6 – Aftershoot's retouching options

Pricing is where the services diverge wildly; some are all-inclusive, while others charge a per-image fee. Aftershoot and Narrative offer a monthly plan with a fixed price, with editing included on the more expensive plans. Imagen's monthly plans only include culling, and there's a per-image charge for editing. If you need to process a lot of images, this can cost significantly more.

As with culling, try out the free trials available, see which solutions work best for you, and remember that local, partly manual processing is also an option. There's some clever AI in the selections in apps such as Lightroom and ON1 Photo RAW too, but presets will only take you so far.

Let's refocus on retouching, though. In Lightroom, this is a limited, largely manual process, making Aftershoot perhaps worth considering if you'd like to automate this process a little more. While Aftershoot's options are a little deeper than the other tools discussed so far, there's a lot more that can be done. If bulk retouching is especially important for your workflow, it may be worth considering some more specialized options.

Automatic image retouching

Prompting is one way to deal with some retouching issues, and it's probably the best approach when you have a specific problem that can't be dealt with by hand. Still, prompting isn't designed for batch processing, has resolution limitations, and can be unpredictable. More complex retouching tasks, including color matching, glare removal, tattoo removal, clothing smoothing, and background cleaning, are better dealt with using dedicated tools like **Evoto** and **Retouch4me**.

These tools use AI algorithms to perform not just exposure and color correction but many more subtle corrections that would have once required human attention. As the feature sets of many culling, sorting, and processing tools are often updated, check to see whether any tools you currently use have introduced any new features recently.

Evoto includes a desktop app and provides a full suite of portrait-retouching tools, as well as background replacement, clothing adjustments, and color matching. If you're doing a lot of portrait work, and especially if your tasks include adjusting makeup and body reshaping, this could be a good choice. Tethering support is also included, allowing you to retouch your images as you shoot them for instant client approval.

While the options here are comprehensive (only a few are visible in the upcoming figures), sliders can't always offer enough flexibility. Another danger is that you'll be tempted to over-use the controls here, potentially leading to overprocessed, samey results. While I wouldn't recommend just turning everything up to its maximum settings, restraint is up to you.

Figure 10.7 – Here's our earlier image in Evoto, with several portrait-retouching options and makeup applied

While portrait-retouching apps are popular on mobile phones, these features are still rare in desktop workflows, despite their potential value to professionals. Many of the controls here give results that rival what a professional could produce in a tool such as Photoshop—except much more quickly. Of course, a full-featured image-processing tool like Photoshop is still the best place to make unusual, specific changes with full manual control, but not every job needs bespoke treatment.

If you'd like to stay within Photoshop and potentially retain full control, Retouch4me (`https://retouch4.me/products/retouch-plugins`) offers retouching tools through a panel in Photoshop, producing layered corrections that can be turned down or masked out selectively. If you're using another image-editing tool, you can also use Retouch4me's desktop app called **Arams** to access the same plugins, then download layered TIFF files for further adjustment.

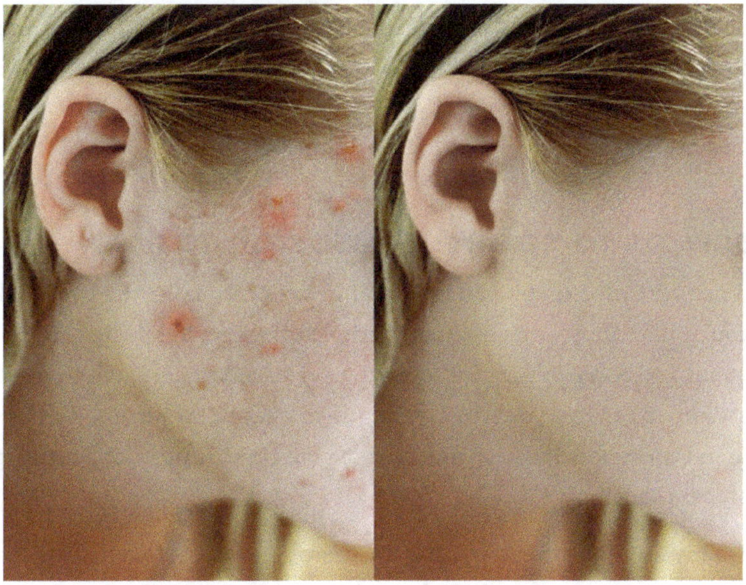

Figure 10.8 – Before and after: the results are a huge improvement, though not quite perfect

The pricing model here is flexible. Plugins can be purchased outright, with a perpetual license and free updates, or images can be processed online for a per-image cost. You can buy credits as a single purchase, or as a monthly subscription at a cheaper rate. If you do choose to process images online, Retouch4me has a third tool on offer, **Apex**, which can work as a plugin or standalone app.

Comparing the results between Evoto and Retouch4me, both did a good job, though individual preferences may guide your choice. While Evoto produces an overall smoother result more quickly, it's easy to overdo the corrections with hyper-plastic results. For me, the layered results I can finesse after processing make Retouch4me the winner, and if you need just a couple of modules (**Heal** and **Dodge & Burn**, for example), you can buy those plugins outright and use them forever. The online options do allow you to use all retouching modules at once for the same one-credit-per-image cost, and purchasing all the modules outright isn't cheap—so weigh up your options carefully.

While any of these tools can provide a serious workflow boost, you'll still face an issue common to all outsourced work—you haven't gained any skills. No tool is perfect, and no approach works every time; a retouching expert needs to know their tools well and know the best approach to tackle a particular task.

To enjoy a long career, you'll need to learn how to deliver *consistently* good results, and no one tool does that on its own. Try some of today's tools out yourself and see which ones, if any, work with your photo style and budget.

Lastly, what about the image-adjacent graphic design world? Is there anything AI can do to make that quicker or easier? Yes, but not directly.

Writing scripts to speed up design tasks

Obviously, the ease with which you can create AI images can make the overall design process easier, even if you replace these images after the mockup stage. But designs themselves? Generative image systems today are optimized toward pixel-based images, with only the occasional vector-based systems. In general, you'll be creating an image of a layout, not the layout itself—and those systems aren't very good. If you spend most of your time using Adobe InDesign, can AI help you with that process somehow?

While there are many ways to automate software, there's no one system that works on every platform and across every app. Some apps do include built-in automation features, such as Photoshop, which offers recordable **actions** to help users repeat tedious tasks. This system has worked well for many years, but AI has the potential to make it better, quite soon.

In late 2025, Adobe previewed an upcoming release of Photoshop that's set to include a prompt-based AI Assistant, though at the time of writing, it's still in beta (and web only). When released, the Photoshop AI Assistant should be able to rename your layers and control many Photoshop features, but it's not quite ready yet.

On the web, Firefly has launched **Creative Production** (`https://firefly.adobe.com/inspire/creative-production`), which allows users to "process thousands of images with bulk actions," though the list of preset workflows is currently quite small. I'm sure the feature set will grow, but I'm not sure if this will be able to process local files or just online ones.

Taking another approach, in *Chapter 12*, we'll look at upcoming techniques that might let third-party LLMs control your computer for you. Continuing the theme, that's not ready yet either.

However, a lower-level option that works *today* is **scripting**.

On the Mac, there's AppleScript, a scripting solution that can talk to many, but not all, third-party apps, and that includes many Adobe apps. Within each Adobe app, there are usually one or more scripting solutions, and in InDesign, you can use AppleScript on the Mac, VBScript on Windows, or JavaScript on either.

Unfortunately, since most designers are not also programmers, the pool of people who understand both InDesign and scripting well enough to produce advanced scripts is pretty small. Although I can both design and code, I'm not a great programmer, so I hadn't set my sights too high—until AI came along.

One of the things that LLMs are good at is writing code. Both ChatGPT and Claude will actively integrate into more serious development environments or provide code that you can copy and paste into a simple text file. While I don't expect that most readers of this book to be advanced coders, even a free ChatGPT account should be enough to help you get started.

What's the goal? To write a free script to make a tedious job simple. This is essentially very simple *vibe coding*, and while this approach does not scale well to a serious app, it's perfect for simple scripting.

> Before we begin, a quick note. If scripting is too daunting, maybe you can use a tool to write scripts for you? **MATE** (`https://www.omata.io/mate`) is an AI assistant for creatives that supports workflows in InDesign, Illustrator, and Figma. Right now, this tool is still experimental, so I can't recommend it for production workflows, but keep an eye on its progress and try it yourself.

Still, simple code is nothing to be afraid of. Let's dive in!

Scripting in Adobe InDesign

InDesign includes several example scripts, and they're a good place to get started:

1. Open the **Scripts** panel by choosing **Window** > **Utilities** > **Scripts**.
2. Try some example scripts by opening **Application** > **Samples** > **JavaScript**, then double-click on the examples to run them. Here are a few of the most useful ones:
    - **FindChangeByList** will remove multiple spaces after periods, multiple paragraph returns, and many other things too—it's a great cleanup tool for messy text

- **PlaceMultipagePDF** is invaluable if you need to place all the pages of a PDF onto separate pages within an InDesign document
- **Sort Paragraphs** is a great way to alphabetize a list

3. Right-click the **User** folder and choose **Reveal in Finder** (Mac) or **Reveal in Explorer** (Windows).

To make your own InDesign scripts, I'd suggest trying one of two approaches: starting from scratch or starting from existing work.

Starting an InDesign script from scratch

First, you can try simply explaining the problem to your LLM of choice (I'd recommend ChatGPT) and see what it produces. You'll then download the script, place it into your `User` script folder, then find it in the **Scripts** panel and double-click it to run it in InDesign. See whether it works as claimed!

If it fails, InDesign will usually present an error, listing the line of code that had an issue—but the script might simply not do quite what you expected. Either way, tell the LLM what went wrong, telling it any errors that occur, or describing what didn't work as expected. The LLM will revise its script, so copy, paste, and repeat the process until you succeed.

This can work, but it doesn't always, no matter how confident the LLM may be. Sometimes you'll be met with refusal, sometimes you'll be given a script that does nothing, and at other times, if you're on a free plan, you'll hit the limits of what's possible. This is where some coding know-how will come in handy—you *may* be able to fix the problem yourself.

Adapting an existing InDesign script

The second approach is to find a script—perhaps one written by a human—that does something similar to what you want. (Most public scripts are intended to be shared freely but do check the license before proceeding.) You can then upload this script to ChatGPT and ask it to change the script to do what you want. Vibe coding works best if you ask for one improvement at a time.

For example, when working on board games, I frequently had to export high-resolution print-ready PDFs as well as lower-resolution interactive PDFs for web use, and I had to perform these steps for several documents at once. I couldn't find a script to export all these at once, so I found a script that did something similar, and provided it along with this request:

```
This is a JavaScript script for InDesign. Currently it selects a folder
full of files to export. I'd like it to export all open files instead. Can
you please change the code and give it back to me?
```

ChatGPT was able to figure out how to do this and returned a script that exported all currently open documents at once. I then asked:

```
Currently the script outputs just one file, but I want it to output an
interactive PDF and a print PDF. The interactive PDF needs a suffix of
"WEB" before the ".pdf" and the print PDF needs a suffix of "PRESS" before
the ".pdf". Can you help?
```

...and it worked. I didn't need to lift a finger or redo anything; ChatGPT just got it right. Now, every time I need to export all currently open files to two differently named PDFs, the experience is consistent and quick. I wouldn't have been able to write this script on my own, and I've never seen this script anywhere online before.

Not every vibe coding script will proceed as smoothly as this one did; sometimes an LLM will get stuck on the wrong path, either referring to imaginary functions or approaching a task in entirely the wrong way. If a script request becomes an exercise in frustration, abandon the chat and start fresh.

Scripting in Adobe Illustrator

The same approaches that worked in InDesign should also work in Illustrator. To get started, you'll find scripts in two places *next to the Adobe Illustrator application*:

- In the `Presets` > `en_US` > `Scripts` folder, you'll find the options shown in the **File** > **Scripts** menu
- In the `Scripting` > `Sample Scripts` > `JavaScript` folder, you'll find several examples that can be run from **File** > **Scripts** > **Other Script**

For something less practical, but more fun, I started an Illustrator script request like this with ChatGPT:

```
Please create a script for Adobe Illustrator that draws several new
straight lines, connecting two points along a curve that a user has
selected, in the style of Barbara Hepworth's string sculptures.
```

Note: While I did reference the famous artist Barbara Hepworth here, I wasn't trying to "steal her style" as these patterns aren't unique. When I was about 10, I wrote my own computer programs in BASIC on an Apple II to make patterns like this before I discovered Barbara Hepworth had done the same thing with string in real life, and I've made many animated interactive versions since.

The script that ChatGPT wrote, in a short time, was over 200 lines long. I copied it, opened TextEdit, selected **Plain Text**, pasted, and then saved it with a `.jsx` file extension. (It's a good idea to use a text-editing program such as BBEdit, which displays line numbers even in its free mode, but any plain text editor is fine to get started.) Back in Illustrator, I created a new file, drew a circle, and ran the script with **File > Scripts > Other Script**. The script presented several dialog boxes for me to provide parameters for the effect, and I clicked **OK** through the defaults, to find... an error.

After telling ChatGPT the error, it was able to suggest a quick fix. I replaced the problematic line of code and ran the script again. After clicking through the default options once more, Illustrator successfully connected multiple lines on the circle.

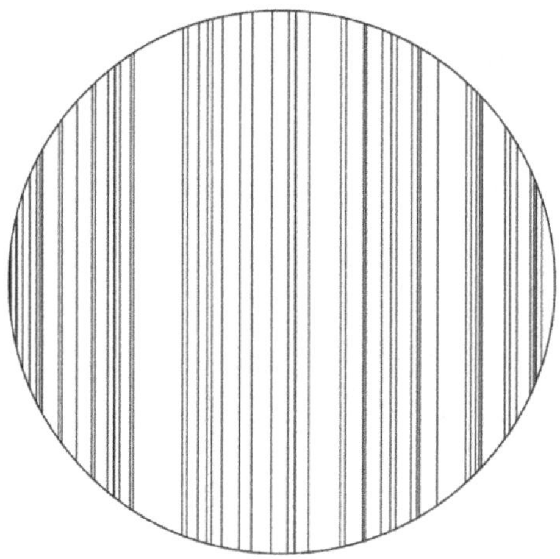

Figure 10.9 – Not like Barbara Hepworth's work at all, but I'm impressed it worked

While the output was not, in fact, anything like Barbara Hepworth's sculptures, the script did manage to draw several new lines connecting opposing points on a circle. This wasn't quite what I wanted, so I asked again:

```
That's a great start. Ideally, I'd like to see the new lines placed at
equal intervals from one another, and typically the lines will cross over
one another, so if position 1 meets with position 10, position 2 meets
with position 11, and position 3 meets with position 12, and so on. Please
make a script that makes designs like that?
```

ChatGPT took a minute or so and came back with a script that did exactly what I wanted. I drew a quick S-shaped curve, ran the script, and was given this:

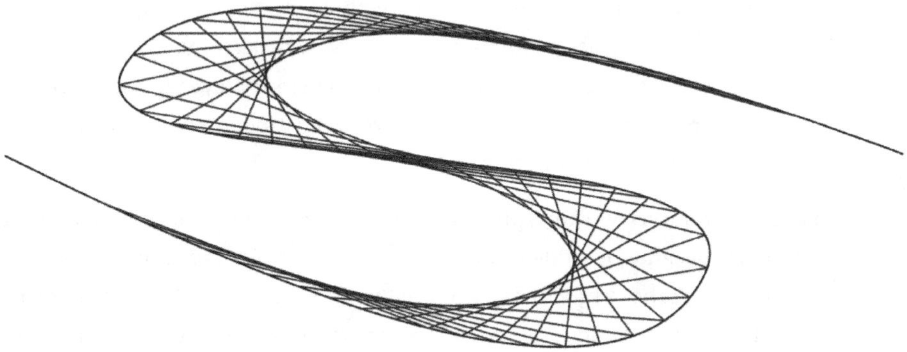

Figure 10.10 – This is a lot more like a Barbara Hepworth string sculpture

It's pretty amazing that I can have an idea for an automated design process and have a working script of any standard, let alone success, within a couple of minutes, with just a couple of requests. If you've ever wanted to make geometric vector art but weren't sure how to start, it's never been easier.

But hang on — is that still art?

If an artist manually drew many lines connecting two points on another line, they could probably sell that as art. But if that same artist gave the task to an apprentice and sold it under their own name, is that fair? It's certainly the kind of thing Andy Warhol did in *The Factory* (`https://en.wikipedia.org/wiki/The_Factory`).

Taking that to the next level, if I were to write a computer program to make this kind of art, which is exactly what I've done over many decades, is that art? It's hard to sell intangibles, but my code-driven animations have been shown in public art installations, so let's assume it does qualify as art.

AI automation is clearly taking this a step further, because I no longer need to know how code works to create a program—I can now just ask for it. While I'm sure that this makes the art produced even less legitimate in the eyes of many, seen from another perspective, it's simply another level of abstraction between an artist and their vision. Abstraction is nothing new.

In early computers with graphics capabilities, you could place a pixel by hand, and then it became possible to draw a line (`https://en.wikipedia.org/wiki/Bresenham's_line_algorithm`). Eventually, anti-aliasing made those lines smoother, and though you could implement Bresenham's line drawing algorithm today (as I did, back at university), there's simply no need.

Today's tech has abstracted away the details of implementing 2D and 3D graphics, game mechanics, windowing systems, text entry, writing files to storage devices, and everything else we expect. APIs and libraries mean we generally work at a much higher level now, and few people want to engage directly with the hardware. If you want to make a game, why re-invent the wheel when Unreal Engine, Unity, and Godot are available?

While some people will want to dig a little deeper, more of us will want to make more things more quickly, or make them of higher quality, because we no longer need to get stuck on implementation details. If more people are able to express themselves through digital art, that's welcome.

Of course, making art is only a tiny part of the power of scripting. Scripting can open up more efficient workflows across many apps, but each designer has a unique way of working and a unique set of favorite apps and will need to discover the most appropriate tasks to automate.

To get started, pay attention to how you work, trying to identify common tasks that are time-consuming, tedious, or error-prone. Saving to multiple formats and saving files with specific suffixes are easy wins, but Adobe apps aren't the only candidates for automation. Finally, if you're short on inspiration, find existing scripts for the apps you use, then think of ways those scripts could be changed.

Time to wrap this up.

Summary

Reading this, you may worry about the future of design and image processing, but we're safe for a while. Not everything can be automated, and the interesting parts, the creative parts, and the interactions with other humans are still something that human designers are best at. Each image still needs manual attention to look its best, and in a wholly automated process, applying the same heavy settings to every image will produce poor results.

Working efficiently is important, but good design still takes time, and a client needs to realize that they're paying for all the discarded ideas, false starts, and manual reprocessing that lead to the final work. As automation eliminates boring tasks, you can either produce more work in the same amount of time or produce better work by spending more time on the creative aspects in the same amount of time. It's not always wise to optimize purely for quantity—choose well.

Next, it remains to be seen whether video production has the same potential for automation as some image production tasks do. Let's take a deeper dive into moving images.

11

Automation AI with Video

Video editing can sometimes be a time-consuming task, but modern AI tools are ready to assist, making some parts of the process significantly easier. Earlier in the book, we looked at how a text-based editing workflow can help to streamline the editing process, and now, we'll look at solutions that try to automate the editing process more completely.

Some of these systems are entirely online, some are entirely offline, and others use a hybrid model. Some are aimed at editors, some are aimed at a more general audience, and capabilities vary quite a bit. Some systems try to do everything, including generating a new background (and even an AI avatar) as part of the edit, while others aim to give you a rough cut you can finesse further in your editing application of choice.

When you assess some of these video services yourself, keep an open mind to how they could help your workflow, even if you want to tweak (or entirely manage) the final edit yourself.

Some of the features discussed here do cross over into Utility AI, and it would certainly be possible to use these features (such as transcribing, logging, and organizing) without automating the actual editing. For more on text-based editing and adjacent transcript-based workflows, head back to *Chapter 4* in the *Utility AI* section of the book. Text-based editing is at the heart of many automatic editing solutions.

But how far do you want that automation to go? While non-editors may want a service to completely edit a piece for them, experienced creatives will probably want to retain final control. AI is rarely perfect, and as you'll see, it's not great at placing all the edits in exactly the right places. But *imperfect* doesn't mean *bad*, and automation can still give you *something* instead of a blank timeline.

In this chapter, we'll look at the following main topics:

- Automatic editing with DaVinci Resolve
- Simple automatic editing
- Prompt-based automatic editing

Let's find out whether editors (like me!) can be replaced with AI, starting in the desktop app that has the most AI smarts: DaVinci Resolve.

Automatic editing in DaVinci Resolve

DaVinci Resolve (`https://blackmagicdesign.com`) is a professional **non-linear editing (NLE)** app that we've discussed already, and it includes some features for automatic editing. In both the free and Studio versions of the app, you can automatically remove silences, and in the Studio version, you can also use **IntelliScript** to cut automatically based on a script, or **IntelliCut** to help separate different speakers in a single audio track.

Technically, removing silences isn't actually classed as an "AI" feature in Resolve, but it automates the process and won't take long to mention. In the **Edit** page, select a clip, then choose **Clip** > **Audio Operations** > **Ripple Delete Silence**. This feature isn't terribly smart, and if your source audio is on the quiet side, you can expect some of your words to be deleted. Happily, you can adjust the threshold by which silence is detected, so dial it in.

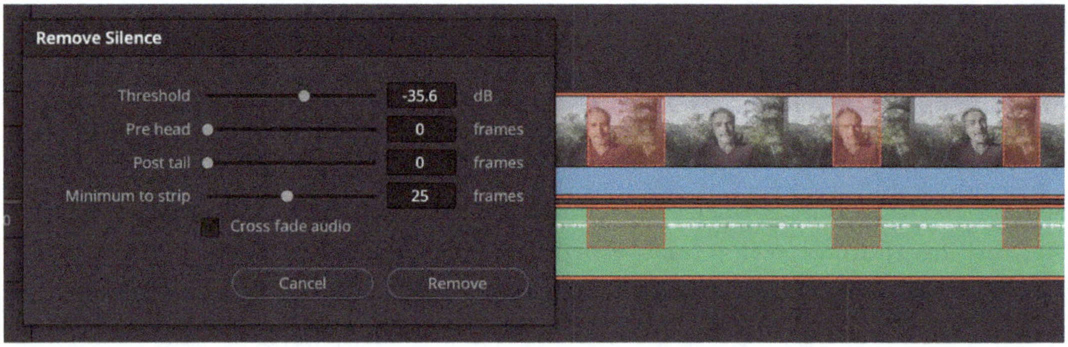

Figure 11.1 – It's not AI, but it does a similar job

Without AI smarts, this feature only gets half the job done; as we'll see soon, AI really can help to detect duplicate sentences, coughs, and retakes.

IntelliScript is a feature that could save a great deal of effort, and it's remarkably easy to use. You start with a transcript of a clip, which you can generate in Resolve itself, or with MacWhisper or another tool. Next, edit that transcript in any text editor, removing any text you don't want and only leaving the parts you want to keep.

Finally, right-click on your source clip and choose **AI Tools > Create New Timeline Using IntelliScript...**:

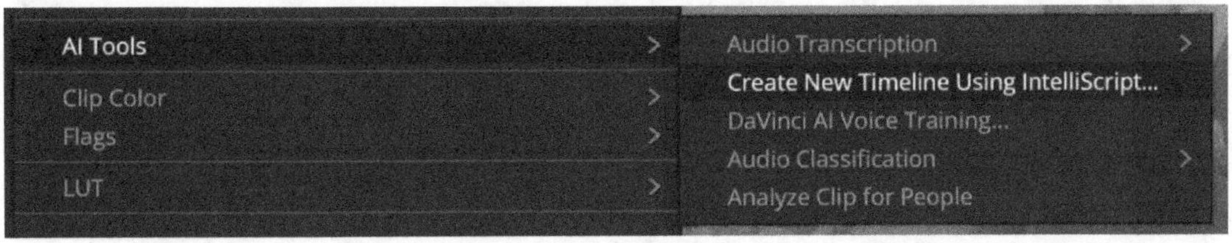

Figure 11.2 – Just right-click on your clip, then choose a text file, and you're done

In a short period of time, Resolve will find all the segments of video that you've asked for and put them back-to-back in a timeline. Not every edit is perfect, but it's remarkably good.

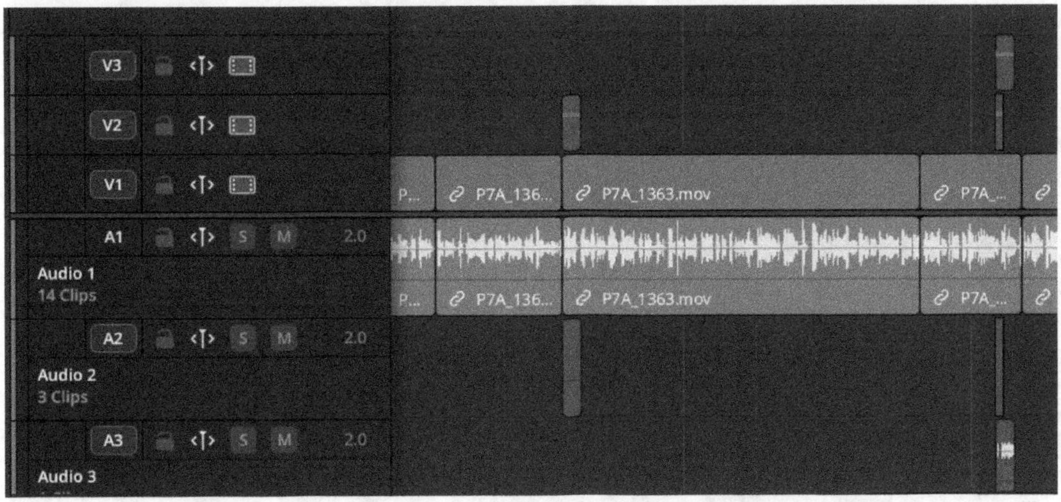

Figure 11.3 – The quickest way to a rough cut is to follow the script

If multiple segments of the original recording match up with the chosen lines in the script, they're added on tracks alongside the main match, as shown in the preceding figure. To evaluate them, press *D* to disable the main clip and again to enable the alternate clip to find the best take. Note that if you're working with multicam clips, be sure to make your multicam first, then apply the IntelliScript feature.

Lastly, on the **Fairlight** page, there's a feature that can help with audio tasks. When multiple speakers have been recorded into a single microphone, it's sometimes necessary to treat their voices independently. Though blading the clips around every speaker is tedious, Resolve can help make the process a little easier.

To start, add a clip to a timeline, then head to the **Fairlight** page, right-click the clip, then choose **AI Tools > Checkerboard to New Tracks**, like this:

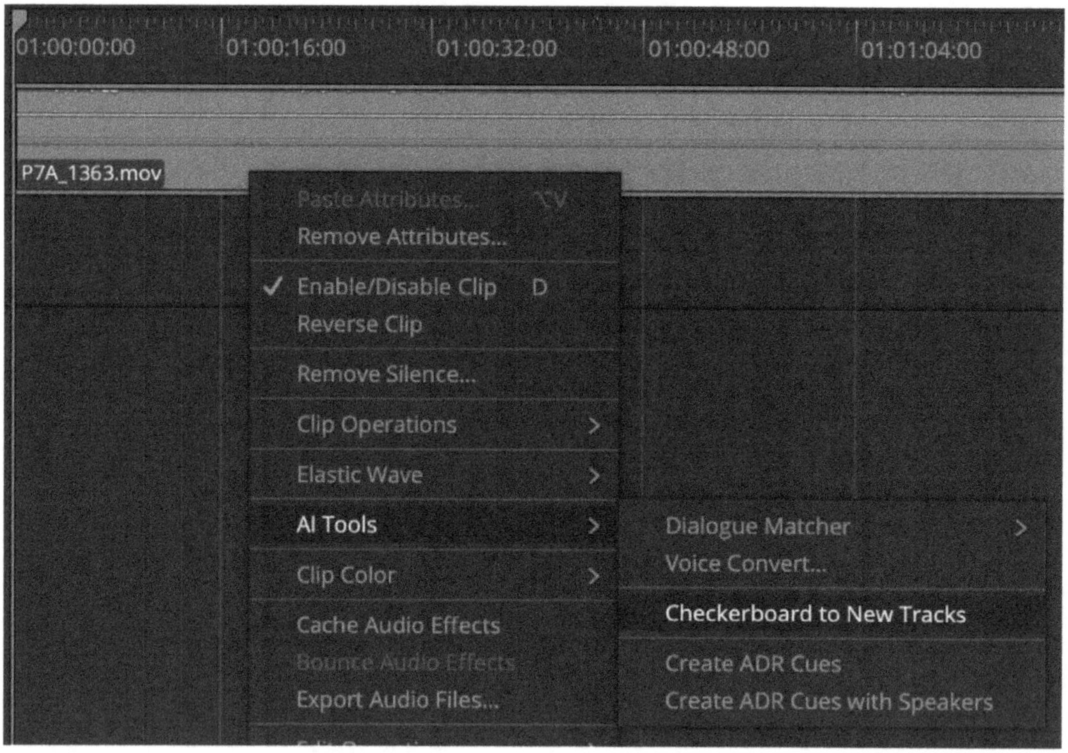

Figure 11.4 – This command makes it a little easier to separate multiple speakers

Transcription commences if it hasn't happened already, and processing follows. While the results aren't perfect, especially if speakers talk at the same time, in general, this feature does a good job.

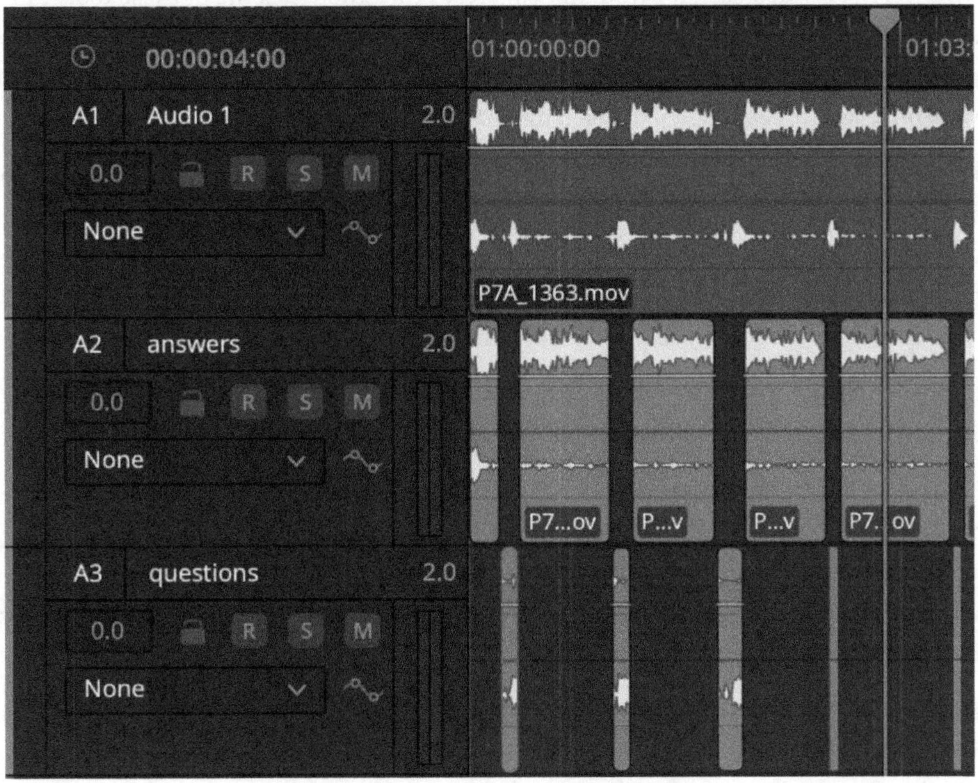

Figure 11.5 – The output, after renaming the tracks

It's a good idea to rename the tracks, either using the speakers' names or simply `questions` and `answers`. The cuts might not be perfect, but they're still useful, which makes applying track-based effects much easier. Resolve has many other AI-based features—we discussed a few in *Chapter 4*—and new ones are frequently added. It's a great app, and can be used alone, or alongside other NLEs, such as Final Cut Pro or Premiere Pro.

But while Resolve is a fully-featured NLE, smaller specialist apps and websites can also help to automate your edits. Let's start with some basic options.

Simple automatic editing

Even if I weren't a video editor, I wouldn't sugarcoat this: though some of these tools can produce a time-saving rough cut, none of these AI tools can put together a complex final cut worth watching. So much of what goes into a finished edit is the result of intuition, of knowledge picked up while on location, of scribbled notes in the margins of a printed script.

If your needs are very simple, and you've never edited anything before, you might be tempted to think that you can record yourself talking, get the AI to pick the best bits, and then generate some B-roll to illustrate some points. In fact, some solutions we've already looked at emphasize the generative side of things, including HeyGen, which will generate AI speakers and AI B-roll to create a video from the script you provide (or which another AI wrote).

That's not our focus here; we're trying to edit real footage of real people into a good edit. But alas: prepare for disappointment. Editing has just too many variables for an AI to get it all right the first time, and the delivery methods available mean that it may not be easy to correct the issues created.

Every cough, "um", or silence that an editor removes requires thought and careful timing. Are you trying to mask the edit completely, planning to cover it up with B-roll, or is this an especially emotive moment, and you need to leave it all in? How long should the pause around an edit be to best serve the narrative that this edit delivers?

What if you notice that the point made about 30 seconds in is similar to a point made about a minute later, and one of them should be removed, but you don't think you can cleanly remove the one the client wanted? There's no one perfect answer to all these questions, and every video needs somewhat unique treatment, even if you're cutting to a "house style." Even though most humans aren't video editors, we've all seen a lot of video content, and we know a bad edit when we hear and see one.

However, AI can help you to remove obvious mistakes or repeated lines to build a rough cut. If you've got a longer interview piece, you may find value in asking an AI to cut out the bad stuff (coughs, interviewer questions, and so on) so you can get to the good part of the job more quickly.

To create a sample clip, I recorded myself talking to the camera for 1 minute 41 seconds, including long pauses, short pauses, coughs, dead-end thoughts, and repeated deliveries of the same lines. To challenge audio processing capabilities, I didn't use an external microphone, and a small amount of wind added just the right level of difficulty. This became the main test clip I sent to all the automatic editing services I tested.

To provide a baseline for comparison, I also did the edit myself, trimming out the bad, zooming in to mask jump cuts, and finessing every edit, to produce a 50-second finished piece. In Final Cut Pro, this took me about five minutes, and I'd expect an experienced editor to be able to perform this task in any modern NLE in a similar amount of time.

To test the capabilities of these apps further, I also uploaded a longer real-world interview, but it's important to realize that editing tasks don't usually scale in a linear fashion. Rather, the more interviews you have to work with, the less of each one is likely to make the final cut. Editing workflows change significantly as the total input duration goes up, and you may not want to just "cut out the bad bits" on longer projects. Real-world editing requires you to connect a thought from one person to a thought from another, and that's a more subtle process.

The ideal situation for a simpler automatic edit is, therefore, a longer, continuous piece to camera with plenty of mistakes, coughs, and pauses. Can an AI figure out what's good and what's not?

Veed.io (`https://veed.io`) is a web-based video editing platform that enables text-based editing. I uploaded my main *1:41* test clip to the system, where it was transcribed, and chose the **Magic Cut** option:

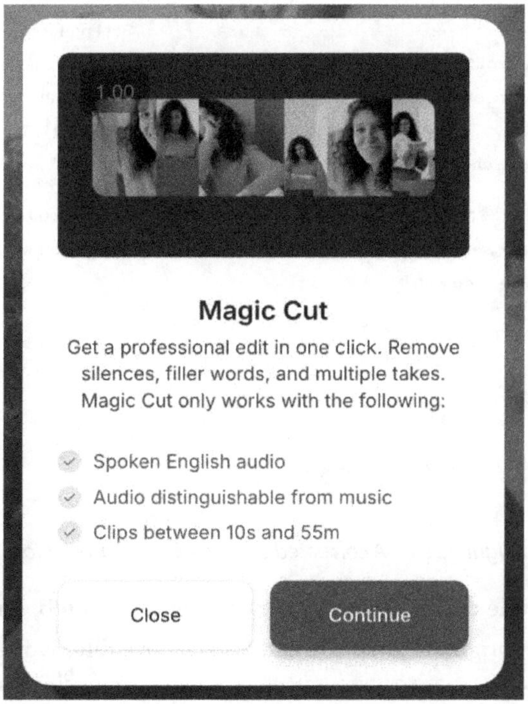

Figure 11.6 – Magic Cut enables basic automatic editing

The initial cut did spot some of the repetitions and intentional mistakes in the original piece, but as you might expect, it didn't do a perfect job. Some of the pauses that I wanted left in were removed, some of my words were trimmed too tightly, and some of the mistakes remained in the cut. Magic Cut wasn't quite what I needed, but it got partway there.

Correcting the edit was straightforward, as the text-based editing interface makes it clear which parts of the transcript have made it into the final edit. Unfortunately, this display doesn't visually differentiate between pauses and other noises such as coughs, making it a little harder to decipher, but it's still easy to work with. Cutting in this way provides a way for a non-editor to get close to a finished edit, and it didn't take long to get up to speed.

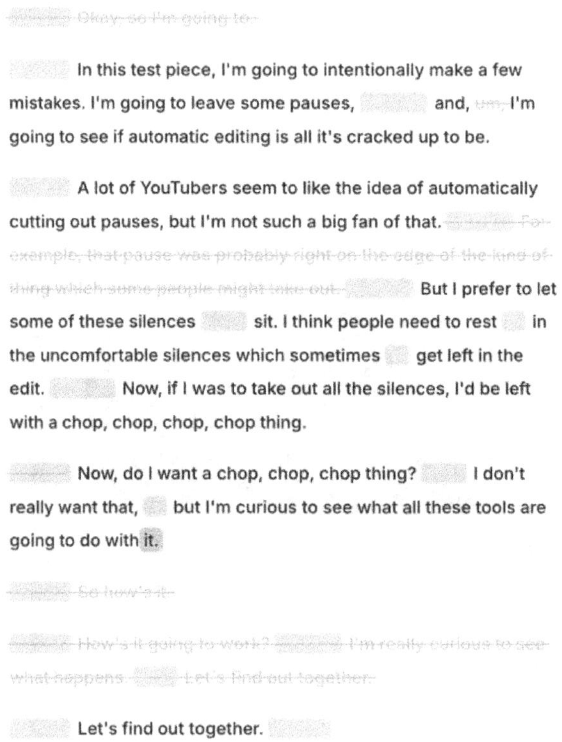

Figure 11.7 – A corrected text-based edit in Veed.io

Other features here include audio cleaning, which does a good job, striking a decent balance between *processed* and *the original audio*. You can also remove filler words, trim silences, convert between aspect ratios, remove backgrounds, and some more advanced options. A feature to make your speaker always look at the camera didn't work well for me; it made my eyes look odd.

Though there are useful features here, the absence of one makes the site significantly less useful. Veed.io unfortunately doesn't export to an NLE-friendly format, so you have to get the edit perfect within the web-based interface. Therefore, this app aims to replace video editing apps rather than augment them, and that's not what I want. If I can't get the output back on a timeline in my NLE of choice, it's not useful to me as a video professional.

I need to be able to color-correct, or at the very least, work with Log footage. I need to be able to add my own titles or transitions. Above all else, I need to be able to finesse the edits. Text-based editing is useful for a rough cut, but it's too hard to move an edit by a few frames to make the pauses just right. As a few frames can be the difference between an OK edit and a great one, I think many professional editors want timeline exporting so they can add the final finishing touches themselves.

If you have simpler needs, Veed.io might be fine. The Lite plan starts at US$24/month (or US$144/year), but you'll need the Pro plan for 4K export and some additional AI features such as avatars and voice dubbing.

Gling (`https://www.gling.ai/`) is a solution that runs locally and starts by asking you to choose between an AI edit or extracting shorts before transcribing your clips. At this stage, it's possible to connect multiple clips into multicams and even to upload a script. With one or more clips ready for transcription, you'll choose your default options:

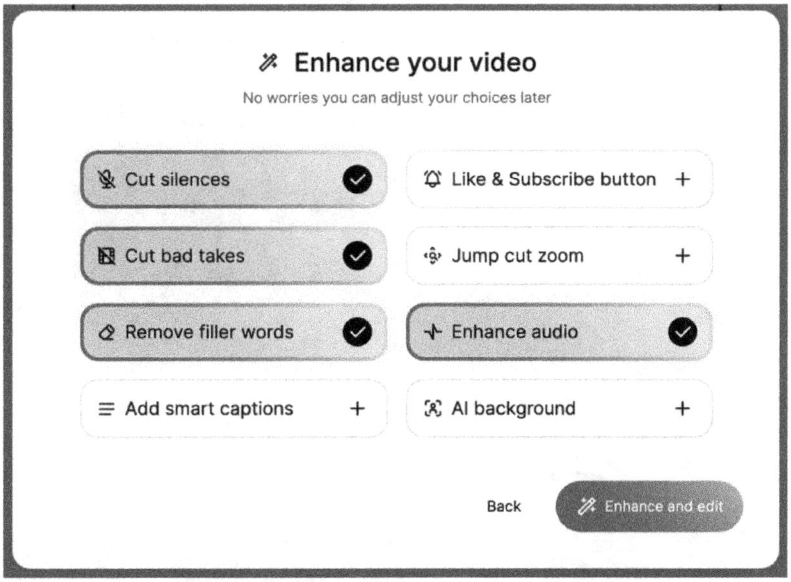

Figure 11.8 – Gling includes several options for processing

When processing is complete, which has taken less than the running time in my tests, the video is presented in a timeline at the bottom of the screen and with a text-based interface to the left. The automatic edit took out more pauses than I would ideally remove, but repeated phrases were correctly removed, as was a false start at the beginning.

Gling isn't designed to perform more complex edits for you, or to make judgements about which take is best—that's your job. Unfortunately, pauses and coughs aren't shown in the text-based editing interface, but it's still quite easy to make edits.

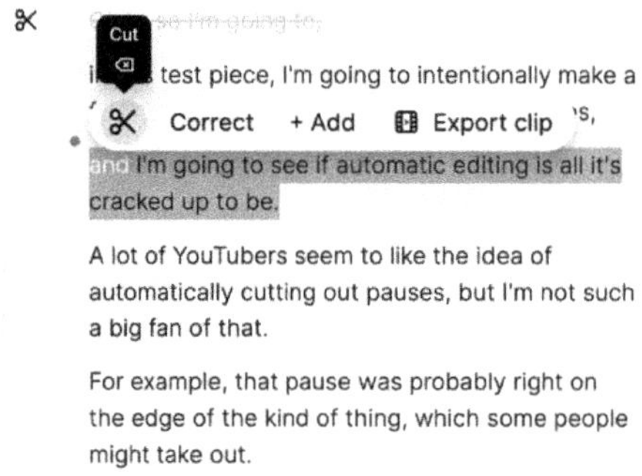

Figure 11.9 – Select a line, then cut it out or restore it if you wish

Each section of video that's been included can have effects applied or removed using the "magic wand" icon that appears on each clip in the timeline at the bottom of the window, or you can use the **Enhance** menu at the top to apply these effects to all the clips in your timeline.

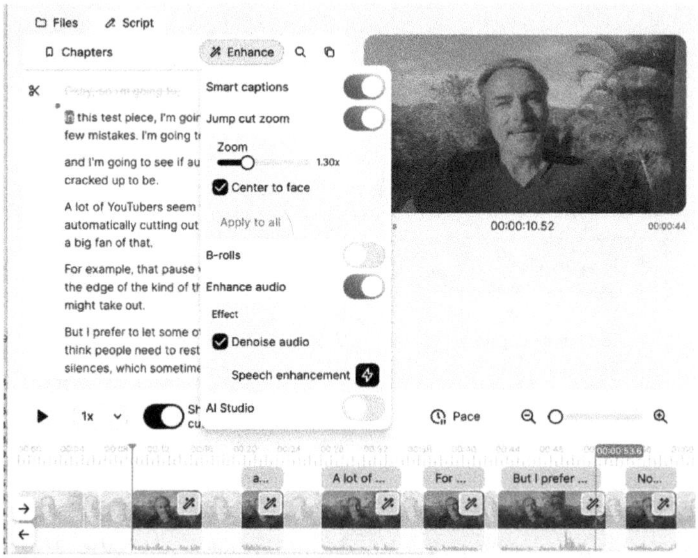

Figure 11.10 – Controls in Gling are quite simple, but work well

As well as text-based editing, it's possible to zoom right in on the timeline and make frame-by-frame edits—necessary if a word fragment has been omitted.

Crucially, after this processing, you can export to one of several NLE-friendly formats: FCP, Resolve, and Premiere are all supported. Both closed captions and open captions, jump zooms, and all your edits will survive this journey, but audio cleanup won't—you'll have to fix that yourself.

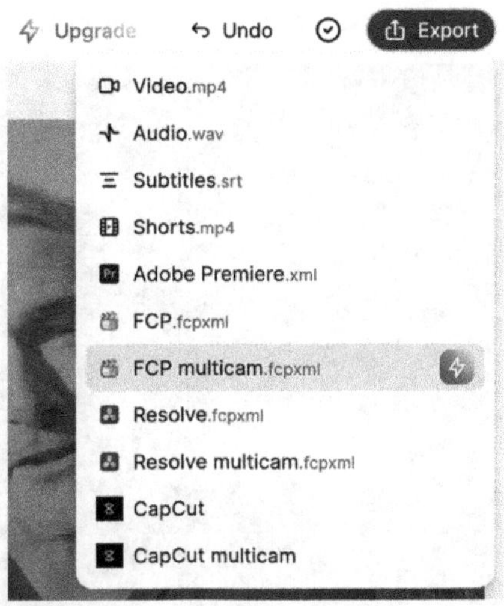

Figure 11.11 - Several different options for exporting are included

Note that if you've shot with multiple cameras, you'll want to be using Final Cut Pro or Resolve for best results, because multicam export to Premiere is not supported. The easiest workflow is to upload only the angle with the best audio, let Gling do its thing, then download in multicam format.

Back in your FCP or Resolve, you can open the multicam container (which you may need to "reveal" from your timeline), then add and sync the other angles. Return to your main timeline, and you can now switch between angles manually.

Gling isn't expensive, but you will need a paid plan to regularly export to an NLE-friendly format. The first timeline export you make on the free plan is free, but after that, you'll have to pay at least US$20/month (or US$120/year) for this feature. As you can test it for free, send it some of your clips and see whether Gling's edits will save you time.

If these solutions don't provide enough flexibility, some other tools can be given much more specific instructions. Let's prompt a couple of them.

Prompt-based automatic editing

Riverside (`https://riverside.fm`) is a well-known editing platform with several features to support web-based editing workflows. Through the prompt-based **Co-Creator** feature, I asked for an output of about 50 seconds in length, and it intelligently figured out what to include, doing a pretty good job but trimming some phrases a little too tightly, clipping off part of a word. My further prompts were sometimes successful and sometimes not.

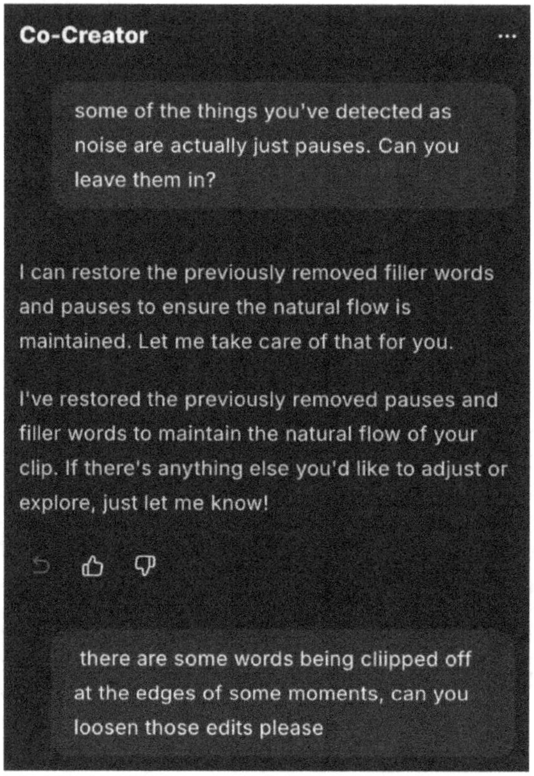

Figure 11.12 – Prompting with Co-Creator is a little unpredictable

In my first request in the preceding figure, the AI wasn't able to adjust the tolerance by which pauses were being detected as noise and re-added obvious coughs to the edit. In the second request, the specific words that had been cut off in the edit were not restored. Still, being able to ask for a specific duration did work well as a first step, making prompting a mixed bag. Happily, the text-based editing interface is comprehensive and makes it easy to add or remove parts of a transcript from the finished piece.

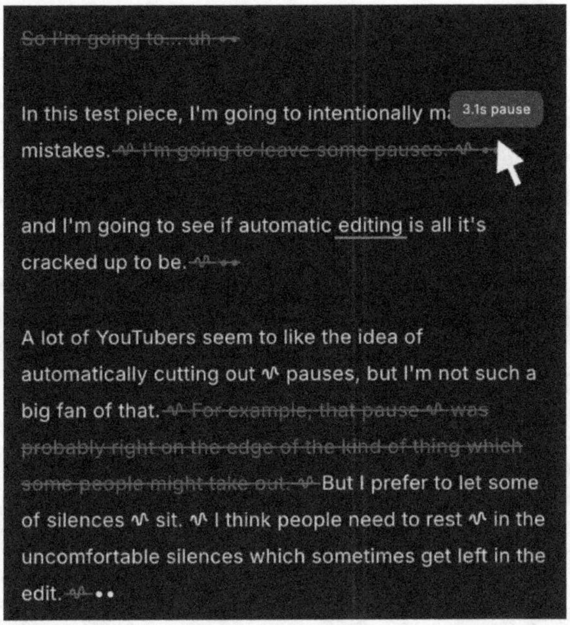

Figure 11.13 – As you hover over a pause (...), Riverside will tell you how long it is, and noises are shown by a squiggle

The text-based editing here is a step up in complexity from both Veed.io and Gling, as it can differentiate between a cough and a pause, and will even tell you how long a pause is—just hover over it. Note that background noise can cause silences and pauses to be confused with one another; as ever, better quality inputs give better results.

A Riverside feature called **VideoDub** was mentioned briefly in an earlier chapter on Gen AI with audio, and if you want to give it a try, select a word, then choose **VideoDub** above it. You can type in a replacement word, and a new generation will take the place of the original audio. Sadly, this didn't work well for me, as the synthetic speech that was generated didn't match my own voice.

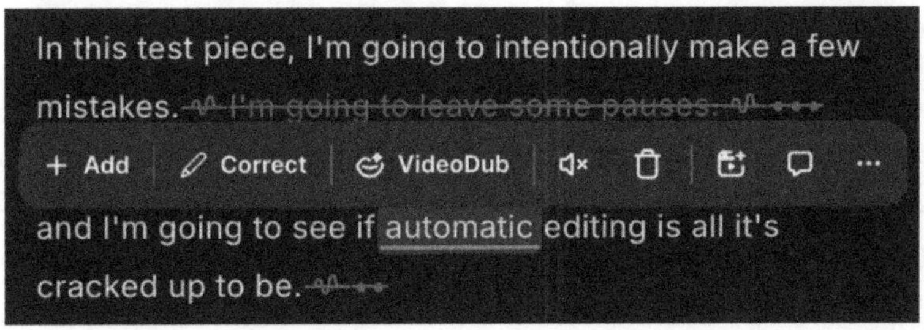

Figure 11.14 – VideoDub may work well for you, but the audio didn't sound like my original speech

As well as the prompt-based Co-Creator, you'll find additional AI tools to remove pauses, filler words (or "fluff"), improve audio quality, force eye contact, and more. Unfortunately, the quality of the audio cleanup features wasn't great, and to me, it sounded quite processed.

On the plus side, the timeline interface at the bottom of the window is quite flexible, allowing fine control over exactly where each edit is placed. If you're comfortable with a web-only interface and want to do most of your editing here, Riverside might work for you.

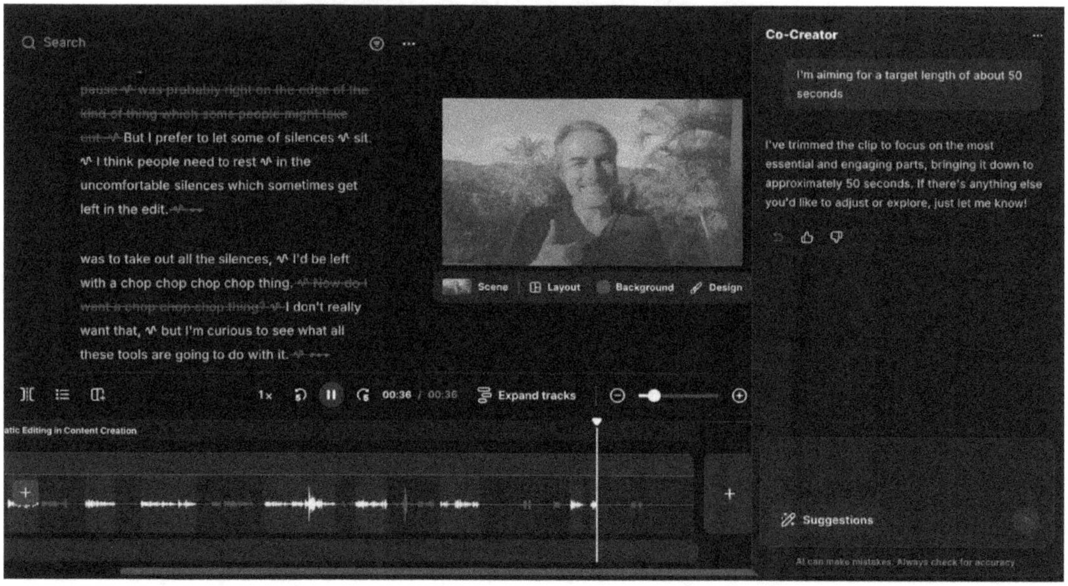

Figure 11.15 – The editing workflow in Riverside is well thought out

Unfortunately, if you're a video professional, this tool doesn't offer the same flexibility that Gling does with its timeline exports. Only timeline exports to Final Cut Pro and Premiere Pro are supported (not Resolve), and neither includes multicam support. Worse, though, this feature is only supported on a Business plan, for which a fixed price is not shown. Without timeline exports, Riverside can't easily slot into an existing video editing workflow like Gling can. Costs start at US$29/month (or US$288/year) for the Pro plan.

Descript (`https://www.descript.com/`) is an app we looked at in the context of generative audio, but there's a full promptable video editing system hiding in there, too. Much like the other systems, after you've uploaded your source clips, they'll be transcribed and then shown in a text-based editing interface.

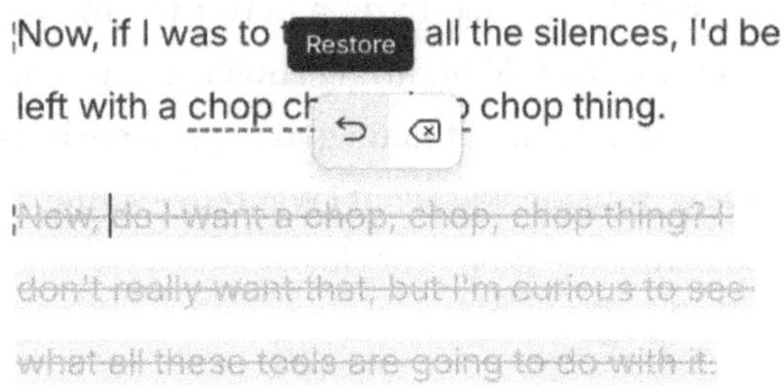

Figure 11.16 – Pauses are shown with a vertical bar (|), but coughs aren't shown

One strength here is that the words are also shown in the timeline at the bottom of the window, which makes it easy to find specific words in a video. Waveforms are initially hidden but can be revealed with a quick click on one of the words.

Figure 11.17 – The words on the timeline are a useful addition

Several preset AI tools are presented, including **Edit for clarity**, **Studio Sound**, and tools to remove filler words or retakes. I found these preset options to not be as effective as I would have liked; not all duplicates were found, not all coughs were removed, and audio quality was pretty crunchy after **Studio Sound** was applied—it was too strong for my tastes.

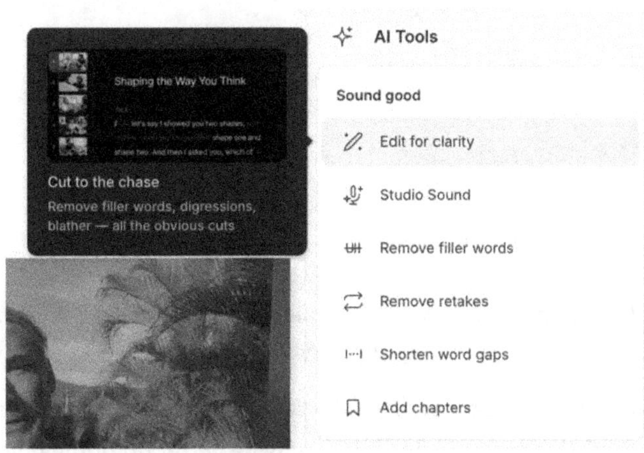

Figure 11.18 – Presets to get you started

However, the prompt-based system seemed to do a better job in my testing. The assistant is called **Underlord**, which seems like an odd branding choice, but it works pretty well. I asked for the total length to be cut to 50 seconds, and it managed to preserve most of the right parts of the video and cut the rest. Not every decision was what I wanted—sometimes a cough was removed without the partial sentence before it—but it got close.

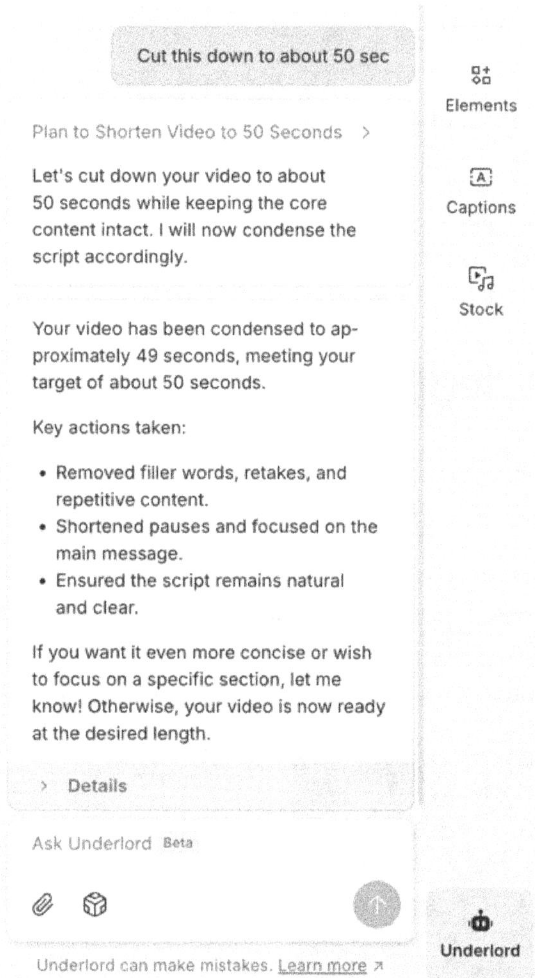

Figure 11.19 – Underlord responds to English language requests and is more flexible than the preset options

Although I tried to correct some of these errors by talking to Underlord, it didn't do quite what I wanted. If you want something simple done, you may be better off doing it yourself.

While Descript did manage to place the edits well, not trimming off the edges of any words, I did find that some segments that should have been trimmed out were left in. Editing via the transcript is easy enough, allowing you to restore cut words or remove additional ones using the mouse alone, or with keyboard shortcuts.

When you're done, you'll probably want to export this to a timeline-friendly format and make the final cut in your NLE, but this requires a paid plan at the Creator tier or higher, for US$35/month (or US$288/year). Multicam isn't supported, so it won't be suitable for multi-camera shoots. If you're using Descript for other purposes, then Underlord could be useful, but I suspect that serious editing jobs may be better handled with Eddie.

Eddie AI (`https://heyeddie.ai`) is a service with a local app, ChatGPT mode to support prompt-based interactions, and AI-driven rough cuts. Further, it not only allows *exporting* to timelines across all common NLEs but *importing* from them too. You can choose from several options right now, but I'd expect them to change soon. Upcoming options allow a URL to be provided, from which Eddie can learn more about a video's subject, but you can just chat if you wish.

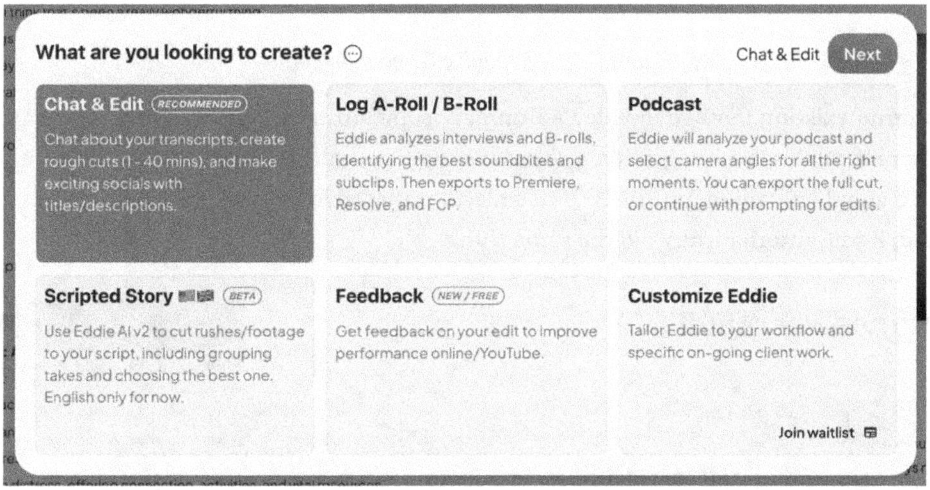

Figure 11.20 – Several ways to start an edit in Eddie

Eddie requires at least 5 minutes of footage to get started, making it a little trickier to run basic tests, so I pushed it a little harder by giving it my longer test interview. While it's possible to upload a timeline with a shorter clip repeated, Eddie's strengths are not in simply removing coughs and pauses. It won't add a punch-in zoom to mask jump cuts, and there's no traditional timeline to adjust yourself.

Eddie aims to be more of an assistant at arm's length, and it's able to tackle more complex tasks.

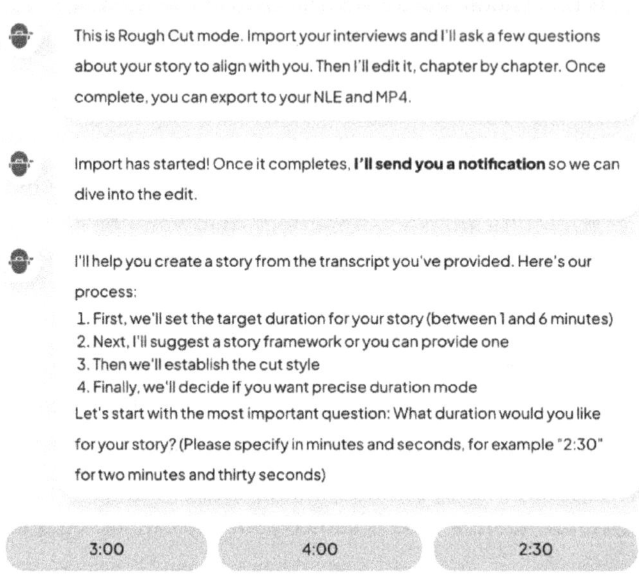

Figure 11.21 – A rough cut begins in Eddie

By accepting existing footage in video editing apps, including single clips and multicam clips direct from Final Cut Pro, integration into an existing video editing workflow becomes quite a bit easier. To avoid uploading multi-GB source files, I transcoded my clips first, but I needn't have bothered; Eddie automatically did the same thing.

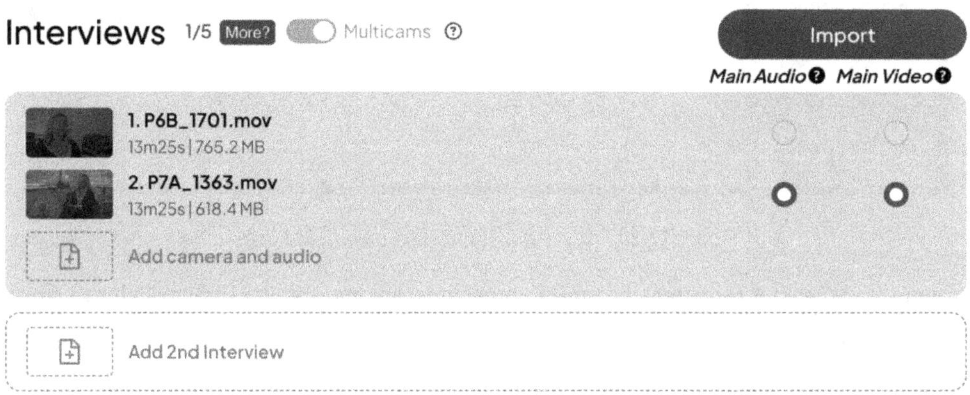

Figure 11.22 – Two source clips being combined into a single multicam before transcoding

AI-based rough cuts will do well with some kinds of interviews and presentations to camera, but not so well with others. Although it's possible to upload many interviews together, an AI can't know exactly which sentences are most important and is likely to pick answers that are less than ideal.

After all, a human editor may not pick the best answers for a particular video piece on the first go; this process requires deep knowledge of the subject matter and can often require that a client look through transcripts themselves. Telling a story is a job for humans, and the AI doesn't understand what's valuable.

Eddie does all the right things, though; not just guessing but asking for more information before proceeding. It asked about the target length, whether we wanted to exclude the interviewer or not—the right questions to ask. Still, while it started with one of the best interviews I've had the pleasure of shooting, it didn't assemble the best parts of it into a story on its first attempt—how could it? It's not human. It can't read emotion from a transcript. It missed the magic, though it honestly didn't do too badly.

Of all these tools, the options in Eddie provide the most flexibility, but a human still needs to craft the story. A human needs to listen, not just to the words, but to how they are said. Eddie might come up with a nice edit quickly, but equally, it might not. Complex jobs require a lot more planning and thought, and it's not easy to join together disparate threads of distinct conversations to create a greater narrative.

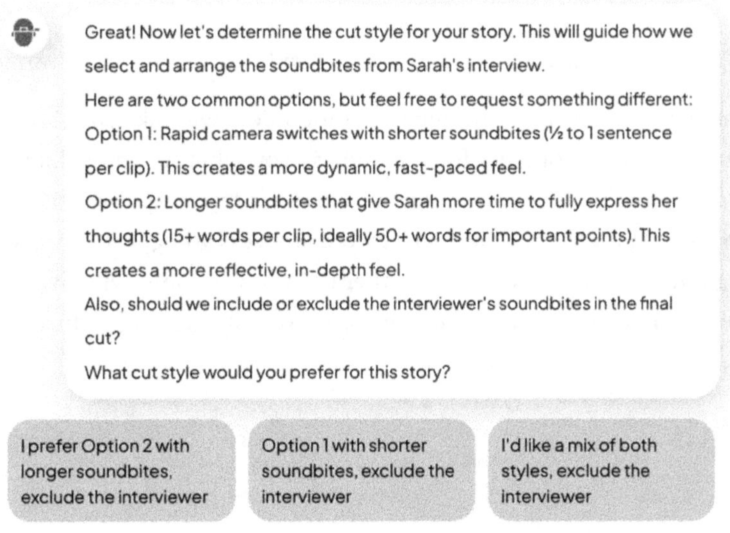

Figure 11.23 – Pick from the preset buttons, or type your own response if you prefer

The great news is that because Eddie leans into prompts and encourages conversations, you can ask it to make substantial, detailed changes. You're not left out; the more you know about the original source material, the more likely you are to get to a great result. For example, if there is a line you know you want to include, you can just ask for it, and Eddie will find it and add it for you. Treat Eddie like a collaborator, and it'll revise its edits along with your requests. Preset buttons allow you to ask for basic options, or you can just type something else in the text entry field.

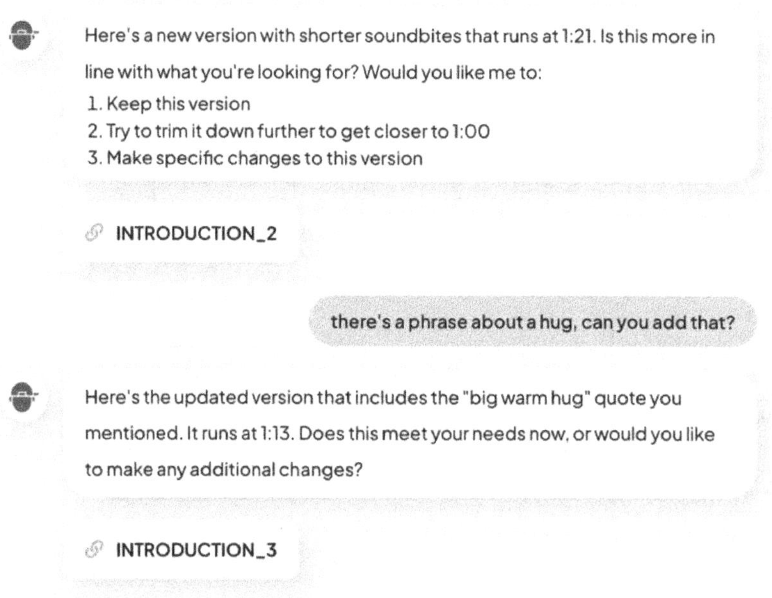

Figure 11.24 – Eddie asks a lot of questions, and you can ask it your own, too

When you're talking to the system through a prompt, Eddie will take you through the different parts of the edit that it's put together for you and ask you whether you're happy with what it's done. There's no timeline to fuss with, and though you see a transcript from time to time, changes are made by you asking for them directly, or by the answers you give to its questions. If you're not sure, asking Eddie to cut longer pieces rather than shorter ones will give you the flexibility to make the final cut later, but you'll be acting more like a director or producer than an editor.

Interestingly, this system refused to take out "ums" to preserve authenticity. I respect that and can take them out myself if I need to—that's one reason I shot multiple angles, after all.

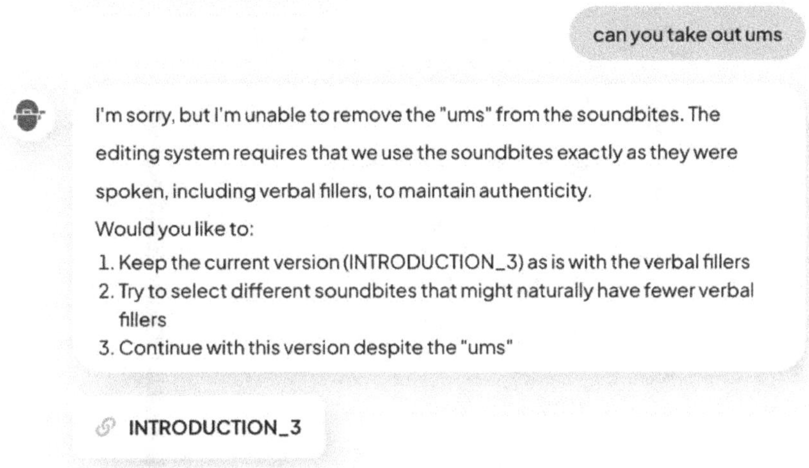

Figure 11.25 – I respect that Eddie refused to take out the ums

While I'd still like to finesse a final cut into shape in an editing app myself, I can definitely see a place for this in longer interviews or moderately complex edits. If a client asks for a specific answer to be included, I don't need to find exactly where those words are. If Eddie can find them by searching the transcripts, it'll find them and add them for me. That sentence it chose to omit? Just ask for it.

You can ask for longer cuts, shorter cuts, more cuts, fewer cuts—whatever this version of the story needs. Use it as a pre-editing tool if you like or try to tell the whole story. Work with multiple clips at once, or take them one at a time, as you wish.

After all the interactive edits, Eddie was able to assemble a decent rough cut—a little long, but a great starting point for further cuts, or as source material for integration with other edited interviews.

The cut is shown as a video you can watch in the app, read as a transcript, or simply drag an icon and drop it into your editing app.

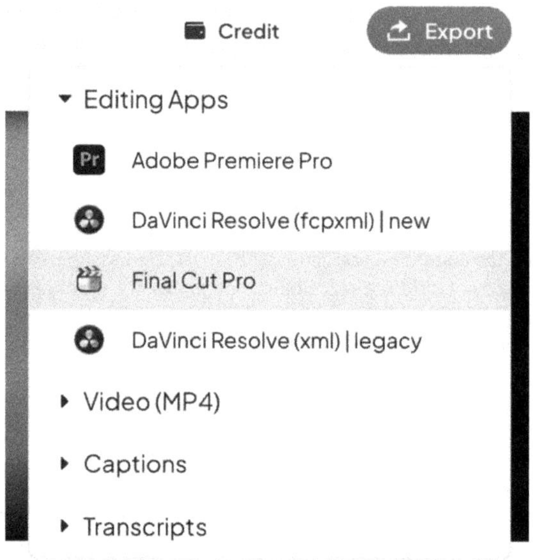

Figure 11.26 – Pick from a variety of different formats, then drag away

That XML file can be delivered as a multicam clip with a single angle, or even a multicam clip set up with multiple clips, synced (by audio) for you, and the files it references can be linked back to your original full-size media. You're now free to choose angles and make fine adjustments. Yes, there's a reference MP4 as well, but you'll probably want to make the final export from your own NLE.

Integration with FCP, Resolve, and Premiere is present, and it's easy to both drag clips to Eddie or finished edits back the other way. Helpfully, you can also drag a completed timeline *into* Eddie, then ask it to chop out some social media-friendly moments. This might not be the hardest task in editing, but I'm sure many editors will appreciate it.

Honestly, Eddie surprised me. Although the approach is really quite different from the other apps here, its capabilities will probably be more useful to serious editors than the other apps I've looked at. While Gling could be handy for rough-cutting more predictable pieces, Eddie is the only solution to marry a prompt with an NLE timeline export, and it's very welcome.

Costs start low but can become expensive. The Plus plan starts at US$25/month (or US$252/year) and allows multiple exports from 4 separate projects each month. If you need more than that, Pro starts at US$125/month (or $996/year) and allows multiple exports from 10 projects per month.

Using AI to manipulate XML

Automatic video editing isn't the only way to assist the video editing process with AI, but it's the most accessible. While it's possible to use an LLM to mess around with the text files that describe an edited timeline, this process ends up being quite technical and somewhat error-prone. While there's potential here, I think the process is a little too tricky for most editors to follow.

Still, if you're curious to explore, start with this video by Peter Wiggins (`https://youtu.be/ixoJdNL4RpM?si=VMgoydkvIVbL-pkB`) and then continue with his other videos.

Summary

This space is more complex than I expected, with a wide variety of tools and capabilities on show. Simpler editing tasks can be dealt with by several tools here, but if you have more complex tasks in mind, you'll have fewer options:

- If you only need a finished video from a piece to camera, then Veed.io or Riverside could work for you, but if you need a timeline, they're either not capable or charge a lot for the privilege.
- Gling provides a good solution for a specific YouTuber-talking-to-camera problem, and if you deal with longer projects often, its text-based editing combined with XML export could save you a good chunk of time.
- Descript allows for more complex requests, though, as it doesn't export in multicam format, it's not really suitable for jobs that require it.
- While Eddie isn't the best fit for shorter jobs, it could save a lot of time on larger ones and on more complex editing tasks. I was surprised at how well it was able to make sense of my requests and pleased with the results.

These products are aimed at different audiences, and I'd recommend trying a few to see which one(s) suit you best. It's a more complex space than I expected and given the depth and variety of the video editing workflows out there, you'll want to test a few of these solutions for yourself.

Finally, we've come to the last chapter in the book. It's time to see how agents and digital assistants can help us today and in the coming years.

12

Automation AI with Digital Assistants and Agents

Modern voice-driven digital assistants such as Siri and Google Assistant seemed like magic when they were first introduced, but the limits of their capabilities soon became clear. Though digital assistants are still remarkably useful to create appointments and reminders, to launch apps, and to dictate our messages, modern LLMs like ChatGPT can do a lot more than that—with voice, even. Why haven't our digital assistants simply been replaced with LLMs?

The answer to this is complex and is a mix of privacy, reliability, and cost concerns. Regardless, the process has already begun. It seems inevitable that Google Assistant will eventually be completely replaced by Gemini, and that Siri will become smarter.

The unreliability of today's basic assistants is a key reason why they aren't used more already, while privacy is a key flashpoint with LLMs. Cost is also a concern, and using general-purpose LLMs to answer every current request to digital assistants would need a significant boost in power.

Yet, even though the challenges are huge, so are the potential impacts. In this forward-looking chapter, we'll look at how digital assistants are likely to evolve over the next few years, how creative professionals may find them useful, and why many previous attempts to integrate AI-powered tools into our daily lives have failed.

Modern operating systems are currently adapting to a future where LLMs have a more tightly integrated place in our computing lives, and the potential for automation is huge. While not every application you use today can be automated, either because they're not set up for it or because the process is too cumbersome for most people to manage, this is set to change.

In this chapter, I'll draw a distinction between *digital assistants*, which follow simple instructions, and *agents*, which perform a chain of tasks for you, sometimes including concrete actions. There's some fuzziness in the middle—you might ask a digital assistant to perform agentic tasks—but it's a good place to draw the line for now.

You've probably already interacted in some way with AI-powered agents, likely through an automated telephone system. Once only found at larger companies, today, it's possible for individuals to create agents for their own use or perhaps to talk to clients on their behalf. Agents could help you with creative tasks such as marketing, perform and summarize research, provide someone to talk to, or act as a virtual call center.

While today's LLMs are happy to do research for you, agents perform more complex tasks such as planning your schedule and booking your holidays or buying your lunch and having it delivered. Some humans won't ever trust an AI with their credit card details, but I'm sure many will, and the further humans are removed from decision-making, the greater the risks.

Agentic tools aren't just useful to creative professionals, but they're likely to be an important part of the public AI narrative and worth a look. Today, tools branded as "agents" are available from major AI providers. Also, building an LLM directly into a browser (as Atlas now builds ChatGPT into its browser) can bring additional agentic abilities, filling out forms or completing purchases while you watch.

Through much of this book, I've tried to keep a focus on practical, testable solutions, but as the agentic story is still being built, this chapter looks a little further into the future. Agents and our future digital assistants are both important, but parts of this story are still in beta.

In this chapter, we'll look at the following:

- Digital assistants, today and into the future
- AI-powered wearables
- AI-powered browsers
- Agents: doing complex tasks for you

It's a multi-pronged story, across mobile, desktop, and voice interaction models. Let's start with digital assistants.

Digital assistants, today and into the future

When you ask today's digital assistants to do something for you, it's typically a simple operation in a single application: setting a timer, taking a photo, or reminding you of a task when you get home. Voice is a transformational part of the package here, as it allows you to perform tasks on a screen that's too small to be convenient, or while you're otherwise engaged.

LLMs such as ChatGPT and Claude are smarter than Siri or Google Assistant, so why can't they do everything that today's digital assistants can? Firstly, because they don't have access to all the same data, and secondly, because a new LLM-based system has to handle nearly everything that the current system can, or some users will refuse to use it.

This "partial replacement problem" has played out already with some Google phones that have transitioned from Google Assistant to Gemini as the built-in voice assistant. If a quick, simple task (such as setting an alarm) that was once handled explicitly by Google Assistant is handled less well by Gemini, that's a failure in the eyes of many. Replacing existing systems is hard, and replacing the digital assistants used by billions of users is very hard indeed.

Still, it seems inevitable that digital assistants will be upgraded to the point where they can do many things that agents do. It's happening for Gemini, it's expected for Siri, and even Microsoft's Copilot now has an optional friendly blob-like face named Mico (`https://arstechnica.com/gadgets/2025/10/microsoft-makes-copilot-human-centered-with-a-90s-style-animated-assistant/`).

> This isn't Microsoft's first tilt at digital assistants. Here are a few past attempts:
>
> - The animated paperclip **Clippy** (`https://en.wikipedia.org/wiki/Office_Assistant`) lived in Microsoft Word in the 1990s, famous for "*It looks like you're writing a letter.*"
> - **Microsoft Bob** (`https://en.wikipedia.org/wiki/Microsoft_Bob`) was a short-lived attempt to provide a more friendly user interface to Windows 3.1, introducing a cartoon dog called Rover and the Comic Sans font. Unsuccessful, the product was introduced in March 1995 but discontinued in August of the same year.
> - **Cortana** (`https://en.wikipedia.org/wiki/Cortana_(virtual_assistant)`) was Microsoft's most recent attempt, first demonstrated in 2014, but it was replaced by the AI-powered Copilot in 2023.

While traditional digital assistants have access to your local data, such as contacts and emails, cloud-based LLMs don't have the same privileges. Each of us stores a great deal of personal data on our phones, and we don't want that made public. In contrast, chats with LLMs (on free accounts at least) are often used to train those LLMs further.

In a world where most large tech companies (with the exception of Apple) make money selling your personal data to advertisers, many people are wary of trusting third parties with their calendars, files, and emails. They're also right to be wary of data loss if the wrong files were to be deleted by a malfunctioning AI.

Apple's response to this has been to move slowly and carefully, but the features in Apple Intelligence were designed with privacy in mind. The simplest tasks are run on-device, while more complex tasks are run in Apple's own Private Cloud Compute environment, to which Apple itself does not have access (`https://security.apple.com/blog/private-cloud-compute/`).

Even if an LLM provides all the features of today's digital assistants, and the privacy issues are overcome, there's a third problem: how to talk to all your apps. Siri or Google Assistant can handle basic tasks that tie into common operating system features, such as email or messaging, but third-party apps must explicitly tell the system what they can do and how those features can be used. An LLM needs not just this knowledge, but an easy way to tell those apps to do things.

Today, this process is somewhat manual and involves building custom automations. For example, if you want to get more out of Siri, you could create a *shortcut* (in the system-wide automation engine called **Shortcuts**) that performs actions in one or more apps, then trigger it with your voice. Alternatively, on desktop platforms, you might rely on scripting support, or even on simulating clicks or button presses. Not all apps support shortcuts or scripting, and simulating button presses is error-prone and unreliable.

In short, most automation systems today are rigid and brittle; they break easily. A universal way for an LLM to understand and control any app could mean that an AI could (finally) start doing more of our work for us. Since 2016, apps on Apple platforms have been able to declare *App Intents*, which describe the functions they can perform, the data they expect as input, and what they'll provide as output. These aren't human-facing; they're to help apps talk to one another.

Apple has also integrated *foundation models* (basic LLMs) into the system-wide automation system, Shortcuts. In the latest operating systems, Apple Intelligence lets you generate output from an on-device model, a private model on Apple's servers, or even ChatGPT, and then do something with that output. While many LLM outputs are plain English, text formats such as JSON enable flexible inter-app communication strategies.

Here are some examples of uses you could put this to: `https://appleinsider.com/inside/ios-26/tips/how-to-use-apple-intelligence-in-shortcuts-to-save-time-every-day?utm_medium=social&utm_source=threads`. Foundation models are a useful bridge between LLMs and today's automation solutions, but they don't necessarily open the floodgates to full system control.

Some upcoming systems might be more comprehensive. Let's take a quick tour through some ways in which existing computer systems could be controlled by AI tools.

MCP: a cross-platform future automation system

If digital assistants are going to take on more agentic properties, LLMs will need to be able to interact more directly with apps, and that's where Anthropic's **Model Context Protocol (MCP)** (`https://modelcontextprotocol.io/docs/getting-started/intro`) comes in. While *App Intents* and *foundation models* are Apple-only, MCP is a cross-platform solution that connects most LLMs to permitted data sources and apps, providing a new, secure connective layer.

In theory, if an operating system enables support for MCP, and the apps on that system support MCP, an LLM could control your apps for you, performing many more tasks than today's digital assistants or automation techniques can. Indeed, this gets very much into the territory of agents, and that's probably where we're heading eventually, but this level of control would also allow LLMs to perform a wider variety of simple tasks directly for you.

How far away is this? We can't be sure, but initial MCP support is expected to arrive in macOS and iOS soon (`https://appleinsider.com/articles/25/09/22/ios-26-could-get-a-major-ai-boost-with-the-model-context-protocol`) and it's coming to Windows, too (`https://developer.microsoft.com/en-us/windows/agentic/`). Details are yet to be finalized, but there's movement behind the scenes.

Interestingly, an unreleased Mac-based AI-powered automation tool called **Sky** was recently acquired by OpenAI (`https://openai.com/index/openai-acquires-software-applications-incorporated/`), so we can expect further progress in this area.

Since it's going to take some time before all our apps, operating systems, and LLMs are MCP-ready, an intermediate step could be for AI tools to drive our computers for us, using standard human user interfaces. That work is happening, but if an AI can understand how our software works, could we ask it to look at our screens and teach us how to use new apps? Surely, if a computer knows how our software works, this should be easy... right?

AI assistance with desktop apps

Gemini Live (`https://gemini.google/overview/gemini-live/`) can watch you use your computer, then answer your questions informed by what it sees you doing. Other systems can perform this trick too, but Gemini Live is publicly available and easy to access—try it if you like.

While this sounds great, it's far from perfect and quickly becomes frustrating. Essentially, the AI system has the understanding of someone who's read a manual about a program but is not an expert themselves.

I tested this by asking Gemini to watch me use Adobe InDesign, omitting important details from my questions, and seeing whether it could still guide me to the best answer available. I've taught design and video apps to students many times, in-person and over a screen share and video call, so I know what to expect and what the answers should be, but a novice won't.

Figure 12.1 – Here's the opening splash screen in InDesign, with my basic question and a response

When I dropped a hint about being in Australia, Gemini did correctly suggest A4 as a common page size. This is just the kind of thing I was hoping for, but I'd have preferred Gemini to recognize where I was and realize this on its own. More troubling, even though I'd said I was making a flyer, it didn't think to mention including a 3-mm bleed until I explicitly said I was printing it 2,000 times.

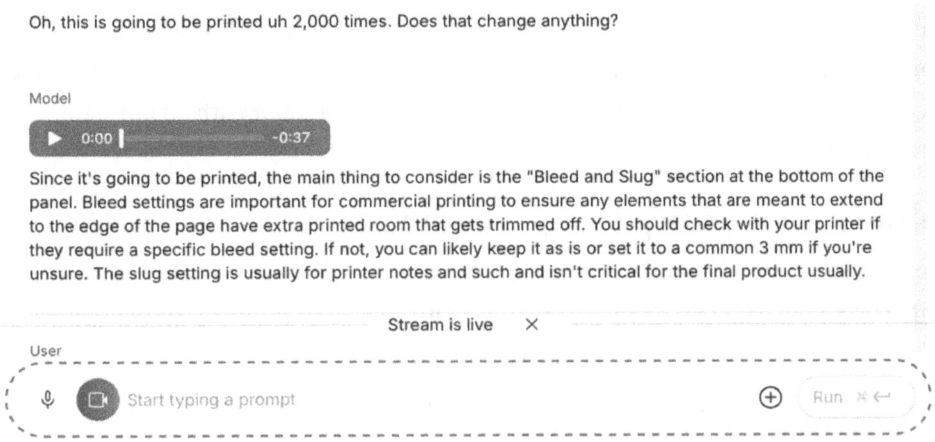

Figure 12.2 – Bleed is important for most professionally printed documents, and should have been mentioned without my prompting

Judging from how some of the advice was expressed, it felt like I was being guided by someone who had just learned the app rather than someone who knows the app well. A novice user could easily follow these instructions and be led into disaster—the AI didn't really understand best practice and simply answered the question asked rather than providing the information really needed.

In a similar experiment run by Mark Spencer of Ripple Training (`https://youtu.be/dCj7-Bgjl0I?si=0VJDPYEvW8j29hIU`), he tried to get an AI to teach him Final Cut Pro, and I think it's fair to say his experience was worse than mine.

While it got some things right, it got plenty wrong, referring to non-existent buttons and shortcut keys. Mark's an expert and knew the answers to all the questions he asked, but a novice would have tried, failed, and given up.

When learning, reading a manual isn't enough; you need *informed experience*. There's a huge gap between a reference manual and a teaching manual, and humans need to be taught in a more organic way. Software companies will often teach the "official" way to perform a feature, but trainers who know that a feature doesn't work properly are smart enough to tell you so.

Today, I can't recommend asking a computer to teach you how to use software, and this is *easy mode* compared to asking a computer to do something for us. How can I expect a computer to do tasks *for me* when it can't even tell me how to do it reliably? To do it for me, an AI needs to get every tiny step correct along the way, and a basic mistake early can cause huge problems later on.

Continuing unreliability is a huge reason why AI is not yet (and possibly not ever) ready to take over from humans at all these tasks. Yes, MCP would make this faster and easier, but if that speed doesn't also come with reliability, we won't be able to trust an LLM with all our data. Let's step into statistics to understand why.

Reliability: how many 9s do you need?

A term often used as a high standard for the availability of a computer system is known as **five 9s**, meaning that it's available 99.999% of the time, or just over 5 minutes a year of downtime. Let's apply that metric to the reliability of an AI system instead.

If a system makes 1 mistake in 100 decisions, it's 99% reliable—two 9s. A system that's wrong 1 time in 100,000 decisions would be 99.999% reliable—five 9s. So, how reliable does a system need to be when giving advice?

When taking advice, I simply expect that advice to be *mostly* reliable, and I probably don't even need to get to two 9s (99%) in terms of reliability. But screen-watching AIs are nowhere near two 9s yet; if you compare a screen-watching system's claimed knowledge to what an expert would tell you, they're probably around 80% correct, and that's just not enough. Bluntly, if 20% of what a human told me was wrong, I wouldn't trust them, and I'd stop listening to them entirely.

But advice has a lower threshold for success than performing tasks, and LLMs are known to hallucinate, to panic when pushed, to ignore directions. When you ask someone to do your job for you, they've got to do it to your standard.

So, if you're passing a small office job to a junior human colleague, you may be able to tolerate a few mistakes. If you can check the results yourself, then an imperfect result can be corrected, either on your own or by asking your colleague to fix the problem.

The same is true for a job you pass onto an AI but remember that each sub-task carries a risk of failure. The less confidence you have, the more frequently you'll need to check on progress.

A 20% failure rate in someone's work output would be a huge problem, and right now, AI models trained to operate regular computers often sit below 80% on their benchmarks. Simply, we're not there yet, and according to Sayash Kapoor, we'll need new techniques to get there (`https://youtu.be/d5EltXhbcfA?si=hoajlz1CVJg351bp`).

Benchmark Performance

Benchmark	Source/Harness	Gemini 2.5 Computer Use 10-2025	Claude Sonnet 4.5	Claude Sonnet 4	OpenAI Computer-Using Agent model
Online-Mind2Web	Official leaderboard	69.0%	—	—	61.3% (Operator)
	Measured by Browserbase	65.7%	55.0%	61.0%	44.3%
WebVoyager	Self-reported	88.9%	—	—	87.0%
	Measured by Browserbase	79.9%	71.4%	69.4%	61.0%
AndroidWorld	Measured by Google DeepMind	69.7%	56.0%	62.1%	Could not measure - No model access
OSWorld	Self-reported	OS control not yet supported	61.4%	42.2%	38.1%

Figure 12.3 – Gemini 2.5 Computer Use's performance on common benchmarks, from https://blog.google/technology/google-deepmind/gemini-computer-use-model/

As tasks get more critical and as there's less time to verify that output, reliability becomes even more important. Reliability is already one reason why people stop using digital assistants; they either don't hear correctly, or they can't perform the actions requested, or they simply fail to do it.

In some AI-assisted situations like a self-driving car, there's no room for error. On the road, there's often very little time to react to a steering mistake a car has made, and a flaw in this software can be quickly fatal.

Uncertain reliability is a fundamental issue facing self-driving software being added to regular cars: it's very difficult to transition from a system that's "pretty good" to "perfect." How can you safely transition from not trusting the car to completely trusting the car? At what point can you relax?

If the software is merely "assistive," it isn't expected to be perfect—let's say it's 99% there. A human driver is intended to remain attentive and ready to take control should the software make a mistake—and I do regularly have to take control of my own car when it suddenly slows down for shadows. However, as the software gets better, humans will inevitably grow to trust it. At 99.999% correct behavior, with fewer interventions needed, a human is likely to relax and stop paying attention. When, finally, there is a problem, something the car should avoid but doesn't, a human can't react in time.

To be fair, humans aren't perfect either, and in the grand scheme of things, the average future AI driver may end up being safer than the average human driver. The difference is that when an AI makes a mistake, it's likely to be one that a human would not, such as driving into the side of an overturned truck. The AI had never seen it, or its sensors couldn't detect it properly, but a human simply wouldn't make the same mistake.

Digital assistants face far lower stakes, but a similar problem of trust, and the more steps there are in a process, the higher the chances that one of them fails. Today, if Siri fails to do something, you'll sigh, fire up the right app, and do it yourself. But what if a "smarter" system confidently says it's done it—how do you know?

How can you be sure they're going to do a job correctly and completely when they've failed so often in the past? If ChatGPT couldn't tell you how many "r"s there are in "strawberry" last year, how can you transition to asking a future version of ChatGPT to book a holiday with your credit card? This might be a task that works most of the time, but one time out of a thousand, it buys the wrong plane ticket or sends you to a city's alternate (but less convenient) airport.

As more of us trust more of our data to more powerful systems, we'll hear of more disasters. Today, you can hook your credit card into an LLM and ask it to order and deliver a product to you—say, a bottle of water. And though that might work most of the time, given the stakes, there will be scammers ready to take advantage of newly empowered bots. The more levels of automation we put between ourselves and the products and services we purchase, the higher the chance of a scam.

For now, I think it's likely that firm barriers will remain between digital assistants and all the apps and data on our computers. We'll be a little more explicit about the data we provide to AI-powered systems, and digital assistants will gradually become more capable.

While I expect digital assistants from the major players in phones (Apple and Google) to continue to dominate here, there have been several attempts to sidestep these behemoths. Is it likely that an AI-powered hardware device could come from another player? Let's see.

AI-powered wearables

One area of exploration in the AI field has been a new kind of device that's not a phone, a watch, a tablet, or a personal computer. The **Humane AI Pin** was an unsuccessful attempt to create an AI-powered wearable device that listened to your voice and performed tasks for you. While the agentic potential of this device was part of the appeal, I think it's fair to say that appeal wasn't realized, and the AI Pin was discontinued within a year. The **Rabbit R1** was another unsuccessful attempt to break into this market, and though this wasn't a wearable, it made similar claims of being able to perform more complex tasks on your behalf.

In the real world, these devices haven't been able to integrate well enough into our existing device ecosystems to crack the market. Most of our devices have screens, and as this is a far more efficient way to transmit information than voice alone, it seems inevitable that screen-less devices will struggle to handle tasks that require complex human input.

Some devices available today set their sights a little lower, focusing on transcription. They aim to listen to everything you hear, transcribe it, then let you interact with it, summarizing meetings and helping you find forgotten details of conversations. In practice, these screenless wearables (such as the **Limitless AI Pendant**) don't seem to have caught on yet.

It's hard to fit additional wearable devices into our lives. If you already have a digital watch and a phone, you'd probably prefer to use one of those devices to tackle transcription than add a third device. While an AI service built around transcription only works when you activate it, this can be a plus, as regular humans may not be keen to be constantly recorded.

To try this yourself, you can use one of the transcription apps mentioned in an earlier chapter, such as MacWhisper, but a few services that can offer smart AI analysis of transcripts include the following:

- Granola.ai (`https://granola.ai`)
- Otter.ai (`https://otter.ai`)
- ChatGPT (using *Record* mode in the macOS app)

Returning to wearables, smart glasses seem like the next commonly worn item to be tech-ed up, though the video recording aspects of today's more limited devices have caused issues, too. Can you trust a massage therapist (who needs her smart glasses to see) to not be recording her sessions? While Meta's **Ray-Ban Smart Glasses** include a flashing LED to indicate that the camera is in use, this LED can be blocked, creating a new privacy problem.

In the future, when glasses become much more capable, will a user be able to wear smart glasses while watching a movie in a theater? Back in 2014, the **Motion Picture Association of America (MPAA)** banned wearable recording devices (including Google Glass at the time) from movie theaters (`https://www.androidcentral.com/piracy-concerns-spur-google-glass-wearables-ban-movie-theaters`), but can that stand when people need those same devices to see at all?

Time will tell whether these devices replace phones for many or most people, but I suspect that we'll have a mix of devices in use for some time yet. Many in tech promote a narrative of "killer" devices that completely destroy others, but outside the near-total annihilation of traditional dumb phones by the iPhone (and subsequent clones), replacing old devices takes time.

For a user to replace one device with another, a new device needs to do everything their current device does *well enough*. Watches didn't replace phones; they augmented them. Because we share information by showing each other our phones, I don't see smart glasses completely replacing phones for a while yet.

The AI-powered wearable market is set for a shakeup with an expected new OpenAI device designed by Jony Ive, well-known for his work at Apple. But unless this new device does something amazing, much better than existing options and without omitting any important features, it'll augment rather than replace.

After all, a key reason for the Humane AI Pin's failure was the lack of a screen and the lack of integration. While the integrated green laser projector was innovative, the information density and image quality were far too low to compete with a phone. Photo quality was similarly lacking and wasn't well integrated.

Still, the new OpenAI device could succeed where the AI Pin failed, simply because there's more money behind it, and ChatGPT is widely known and used. Time will tell.

AI-powered browsers

The World Wide Web has seen a massive influence from AI recently. Web publishers have seen marked drops in traffic as Google's AI summaries mean that fewer visitors click through to original sources. It seems that AI's influence will grow further due to a confluence of factors.

First, Google itself is de-emphasizing search results almost completely with its new **AI Mode**. As of late October 2025, any Google search I make now has the option of AI Mode, which essentially sends the phrase to Gemini. I tried this:

```
what's the best way to edit a video quickly in final cut pro?
```

Before we get into the response, the main issue is that it's not a well-crafted question. If a student asked me this, I'd ask more questions to figure out their problem(s) before offering a solution. Google's response, as you may have expected, gives fairly generic advice that's a little uneven, and sometimes dated.

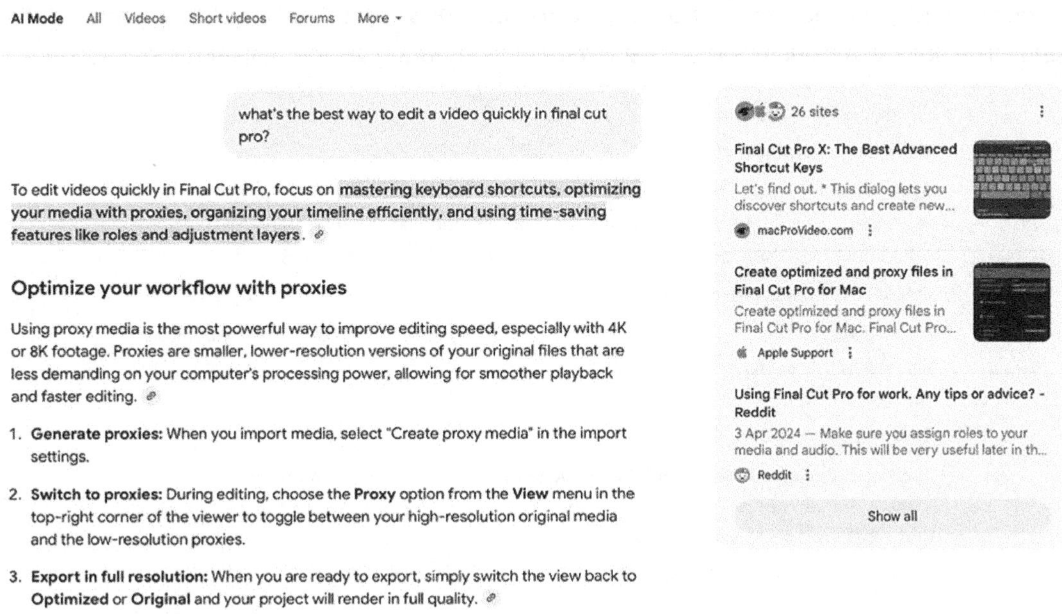

Figure 12.4 – Google's AI Mode gives an imperfect response to an imperfect question

While I appreciate that an article I wrote called *Final Cut Pro X: The Best Advanced Shortcut Keys* is the top-linked article in the short block of external links shown, I wrote this article about 10 years ago. Other advice refers to unofficial *adjustment layers*, while an update in the last year introduced official *adjustment clips*, and proxies won't always help you work more quickly.

You'll get similar results asking the same questions in any web-connected LLM, and I've found that AI-powered answers can often give better results for detailed questions. There's obvious utility in having an AI sitting alongside a search engine when that's what you're looking for, but I think traditional search still has value.

As Google search becomes more AI-driven, you may wish to explore alternate search engines such as DuckDuckGo (`https://duckduckgo.com`) and Kagi (`https://kagi.com`) if AI can't find a good result quickly.

Comet is an AI-powered browser from Perplexity that takes over search, and the response to the same question I asked about Final Cut Pro felt like a random grab-bag of generic advice.

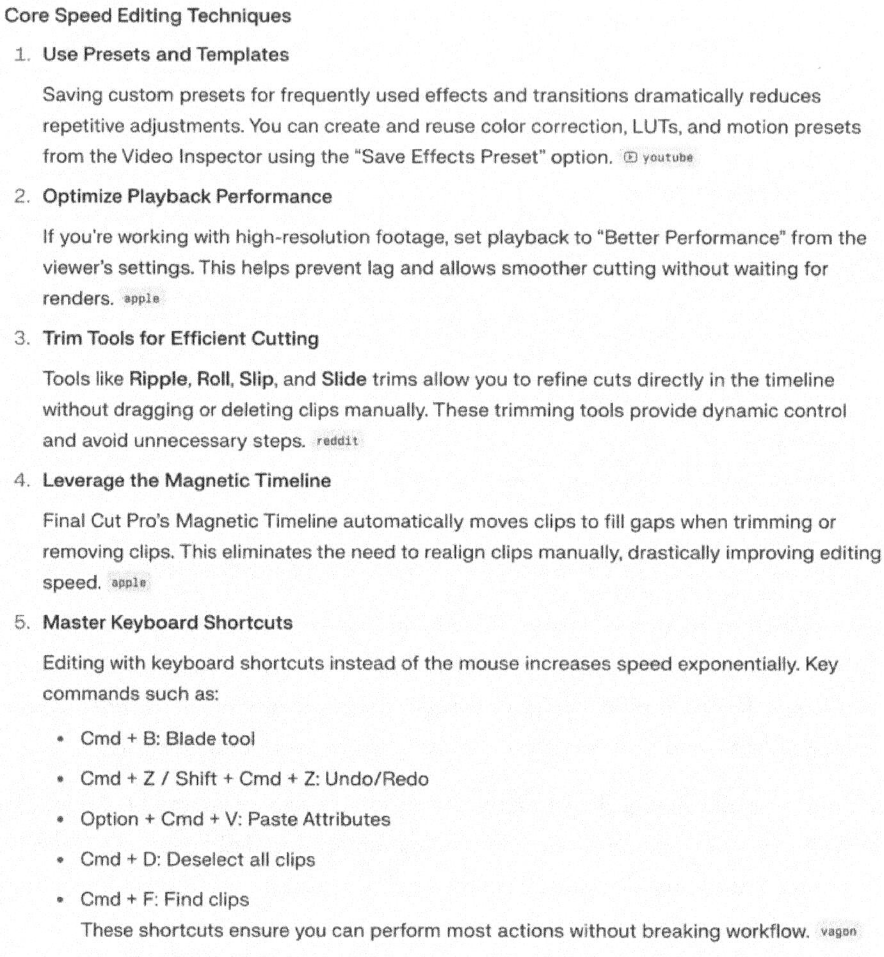

Core Speed Editing Techniques

1. **Use Presets and Templates**

   Saving custom presets for frequently used effects and transitions dramatically reduces repetitive adjustments. You can create and reuse color correction, LUTs, and motion presets from the Video Inspector using the "Save Effects Preset" option. youtube

2. **Optimize Playback Performance**

   If you're working with high-resolution footage, set playback to "Better Performance" from the viewer's settings. This helps prevent lag and allows smoother cutting without waiting for renders. apple

3. **Trim Tools for Efficient Cutting**

   Tools like **Ripple, Roll, Slip**, and **Slide** trims allow you to refine cuts directly in the timeline without dragging or deleting clips manually. These trimming tools provide dynamic control and avoid unnecessary steps. reddit

4. **Leverage the Magnetic Timeline**

   Final Cut Pro's Magnetic Timeline automatically moves clips to fill gaps when trimming or removing clips. This eliminates the need to realign clips manually, drastically improving editing speed. apple

5. **Master Keyboard Shortcuts**

   Editing with keyboard shortcuts instead of the mouse increases speed exponentially. Key commands such as:

   - Cmd + B: Blade tool
   - Cmd + Z / Shift + Cmd + Z: Undo/Redo
   - Option + Cmd + V: Paste Attributes
   - Cmd + D: Deselect all clips
   - Cmd + F: Find clips

   These shortcuts ensure you can perform most actions without breaking workflow. vagon

Figure 12.5 – Perplexity offering a poorly expressed grab-bag response to my imperfect question

However, the real power of an AI browser is to perform functions on the web page you're looking at, not just for better search. I went to the home page of Reddit, brought up the Assistant from the top right of the window, and asked it to summarize the page. In general, this was accurate, and hilariously, it includes a headline about Reddit suing Perplexity in these headlines (on 23 October 2025):

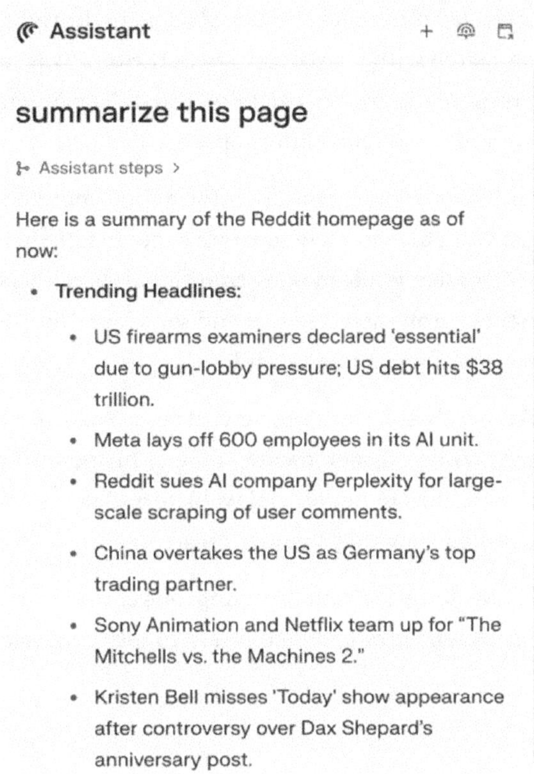

Figure 12.6 – This Perplexity summary of Reddit includes a story about Reddit suing Perplexity

While summarizing a page is an obvious use, the key reason I suspect most of the LLM makers are getting into browsers is that they'll drive more traffic to their own LLMs. If you start on a Wikipedia page about World War II and ask the on-board AI for a summary of pivotal moments, that's convenient. If you then want that information shown in a timeline diagram, that's LLM territory, and in this case, Perplexity ends up being the one you're using. Microsoft Edge includes Copilot, and we can expect further integration there. I would expect Google Chrome to include Gemini at some point, too.

Firing up the just-launched (at time of writing) **ChatGPT Atlas** browser (Mac only, paid accounts only for now), it's a little different from Comet. You'll start on the **Home** page, where typing a query in the top bar simply sends it to ChatGPT, which is happy to reference past chats in its answer. Compared to Google and Comet, it gave a slightly better answer, possibly informed by the context of my past enquiries.

For a more traditional search, you must click the **Search** icon, to the right of **Home**, and from that page, you can see a Google search with its AI overview at the top. This may suit you, but I'm not sure that ChatGPT's own response is always what I'm initially looking for—it's an extra layer of interpretation between me and the original information.

Yes, a good AI summary is likely to present more information more quickly than a traditional search, but sometimes I just want to read a few separate pages in full, then make up my own mind. Atlas makes asking ChatGPT easier, while making traditional search less accessible. On the plus side, it's possible to right-click on any selected text and send it to ChatGPT for more information, clarification, or a summary, and that can be helpful.

For a far more negative take, here's Anil Dash's review: `https://www.anildash.com/2025/10/22/atlas-anti-web-browser/`. While I disagree with some of his points (as he did, I searched for `Taylor Swift` and was shown links to her official website and other web sources in the results, while he was not), it's a detailed view that's worth a read.

Even if you don't need an LLM alongside your browsing, one of the key reasons you might choose to use Atlas is that it offers **Agent mode**, which offers to *take over your browsing* and perform complex tasks for you.

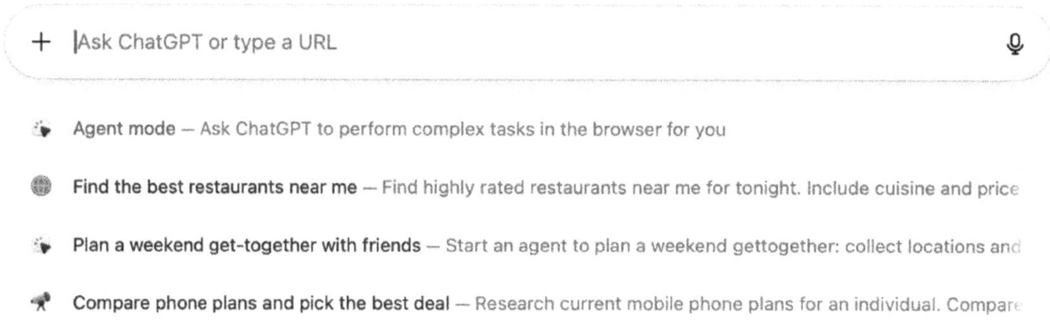

Figure 12.7 – Agent mode in ChatGPT Atlas

So, is this the promised future where AIs start doing things for us? With the history of our past ChatGPT interactions to guide it, can we offload some tasks to an AI safely? Let's take a deeper look in the next section.

Agents: doing complex tasks for you

The terminology here has gotten messy, so let's clarify a few terms:

- **ChatGPT Atlas's Agent mode** is running within a browser on your computer, with ChatGPT able to step in and take control.
- **ChatGPT Agent** is a browser in a box that runs on OpenAI's servers. You can input your own personal information if you wish, but you're not performing tasks on your own computer.
- **ChatGPT's custom GPTs** are specially trained versions of ChatGPT tailored to fix a specific problem, and you may give them agentic tasks.

Starting with Atlas, I tried to use it to research external SSD prices, a task familiar to video editors, and asked it to build a spreadsheet of the top 10 4 TB external SSDs in Australia. On my behalf, it interrogated many sites, asked me to log in to my Google account, created a Google Sheet, populated it with useful data, and then revised that sheet on request.

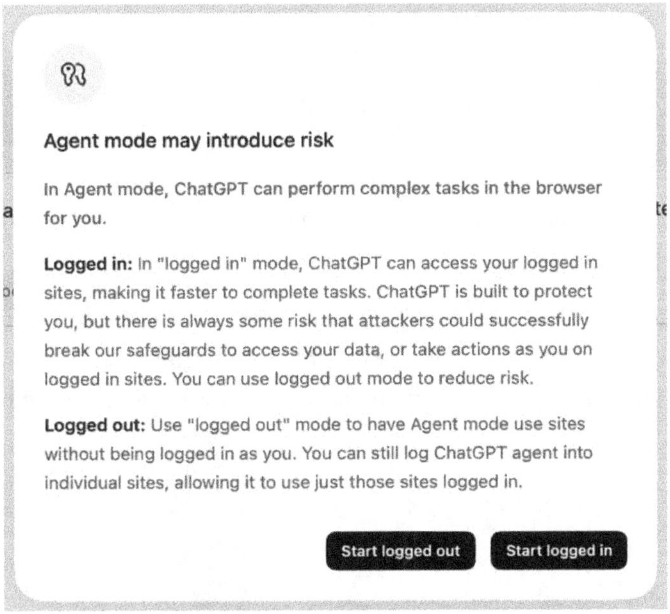

Figure 12.8 – Atlas can start logged out or logged in, but if you want a spreadsheet, it'll ask you to log in to Google Docs

In some ways, it's fascinating to watch ChatGPT "thinking" out loud as it completes this task. Because it controls the regular Google Docs user interface, deleting rows and moving data around as I watch, it's less efficient than normal ChatGPT, making odd mistakes while typing in the prices. I would have expected it to maintain an internal version of the data and then simply repopulate the whole spreadsheet, but it did get there eventually.

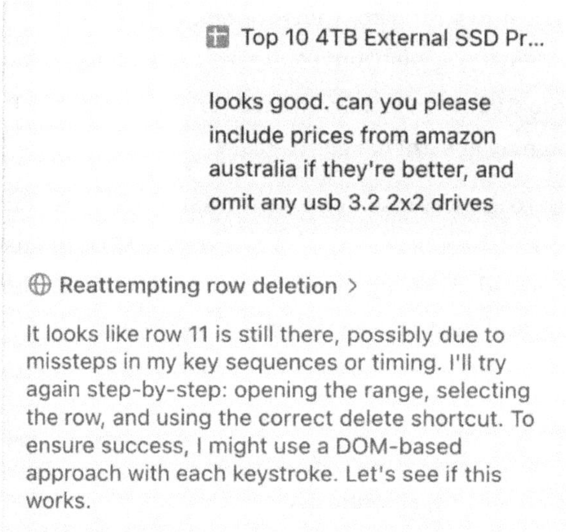

Figure 12.9 – Asking for revisions to my original request took longer than expected

In another test, I asked my family what they wanted to eat for dinner, with several specific dietary requests, and then asked Atlas to order it. There were four items in the full request, and Atlas did manage to correctly add each of them to the order before stopping, as requested. Here's part of the process, showing Atlas thinking, trying to figure out how to select **No Egg**:

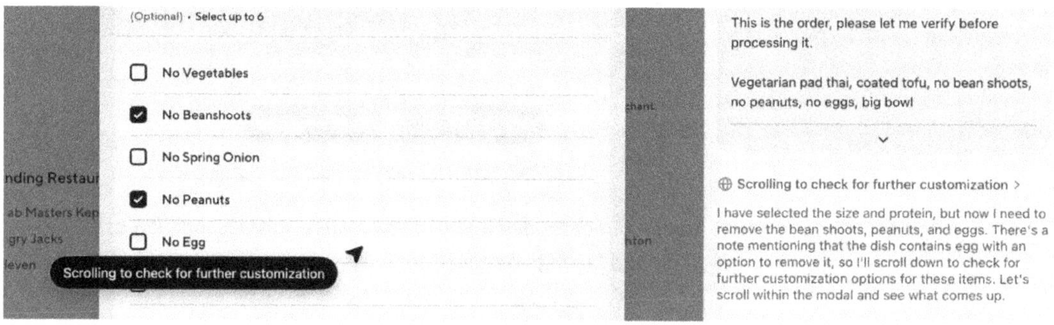

Figure 12.10 – Atlas's public thinking process when selecting dietary requirements

While it's compelling to watch this in real time, I don't think it's something I'd regularly want an AI to do, simply because it's not fast enough. The process took more than six minutes, with misclicks adding significant time, and it would have been much quicker to do it myself.

ChatGPT Agent performs similar jobs in a similar way, but in its own browser in the cloud, not yours. In this context, if you need to give it access to your own personal accounts, it'll ask you to log in manually. The two approaches are similar, but Atlas has less friction.

AI is most useful when given a tedious task that would have been difficult to do on my own, and ordering food is easier for a human than an AI at this point in time. This is especially true if you already know what you want, and I'm not really interested in letting an AI decide my diet.

So, what about a task where the outcome isn't as fixed? As previously mentioned, some caution is warranted when trusting an AI with important tasks or expensive purchases. Anil Dash (in the article linked previously) tried to book a flight with Atlas, and while it was able to navigate to the purchase page, the flight dates requested had changed from his original request. Traditional pre-AI search did better here.

As a counterpoint, Ars Technica gave Atlas a number of low-consequence tasks (`https://arstechnica.com/features/2025/10/we-let-openais-agent-mode-surf-the-web-for-us-heres-what-happened/`) with mostly good results. If you want to start using this yourself, beware of security concerns. If humans can be fooled into clicking malicious links, an LLM certainly can too—and it may not recognize red flags like a human would.

AI browsers do have a place, and whether you just want to integrate an LLM's core services with traditional web browsing or embrace agentic functionality, they're worth a look. Equally, if you prefer using traditional web search (while that's still an option!), then perhaps using a regular browser is just fine.

While I can see that there's potential for automation with more predictable workflows built around formal text and fixed processes, most creative workflows are a little fluffy. Several agent-related tools sit adjacent to creative workflows and might be valuable to you. While I won't be exploring them here, they include the following:

- **Motion** (`https://usemotion.com`) is a popular AI-powered scheduling system that offers to manage your time for you, including project tracking. On its higher-tier plans, it offers to create AI employees to manage sales, marketing, and other tasks (not to be confused with Apple Motion, an underrated animation program that's well-integrated with Final Cut Pro).

- **Notion** (`https://www.notion.com`) is an AI-powered workspace including wikis, project tracking, notes, and documents. It includes AI agents that can perform tasks on the data created within its systems, and scales to teams.
- **ElevenLabs Agents** (`https://elevenlabs.io/app/agents`) is a feature of ElevenLabs that aims to replace a traditional telephone answering system. Workflows here allow you to connect synthetic voices (examined in an earlier chapter) with LLMs to let you guide user interactions using English language instructions connected in a graph. A testing platform is also included.

These tools are far from the only agent-focused tools in the market, but we're straying a long way from "creative" territory, so I'll leave it there.

> While we're off-topic, one tool which isn't an agent, but which *is* a fascinating example of what we might be using in the future is **Sesame** (`https://www.sesame.com`). Right now, they offer a preview of a chatbot, with two voices, Maya and Miles. (Mobile apps with the same "Sesame" name appear to be unconnected scams.)
>
> Sesame doesn't perform tasks; it's a voice-only chatbot that's happy to talk, acting as a sounding board or helping you work through a decision. Intriguingly, it has ethics, and I'll leave you to chat with it yourself to discover the details. It's fast to respond, sounds quite human-like, and is the closest system I've heard to the synthetic companion from the movie *Her*.
>
> Rather than AI-powered text summaries, this is perhaps closer to the AI future many of us imagined. It seems that many humans use LLMs simply as someone to talk to, and if risks are appropriately mitigated, it could be very popular.

To close this section, let's take a closer look at one more kind of agent, potentially as a useful way to answer questions and perform tasks specific to a company or a domain of expertise.

Building a custom GPT

First up, know that this process is on the edge of the scope of the book, so I'll approach this only at a high level. Doing this well is a technical process, but if you're that way inclined, feel free to dive deeper.

Building a custom GPT is a different beast entirely from using an agentic browser. Essentially, this process lets you build a specialized version of ChatGPT, one that can answer questions with additional knowledge and context, and a clear focus on a particular subject area. Many already exist and clicking **Explore** in the ChatGPT sidebar is a great place to get started.

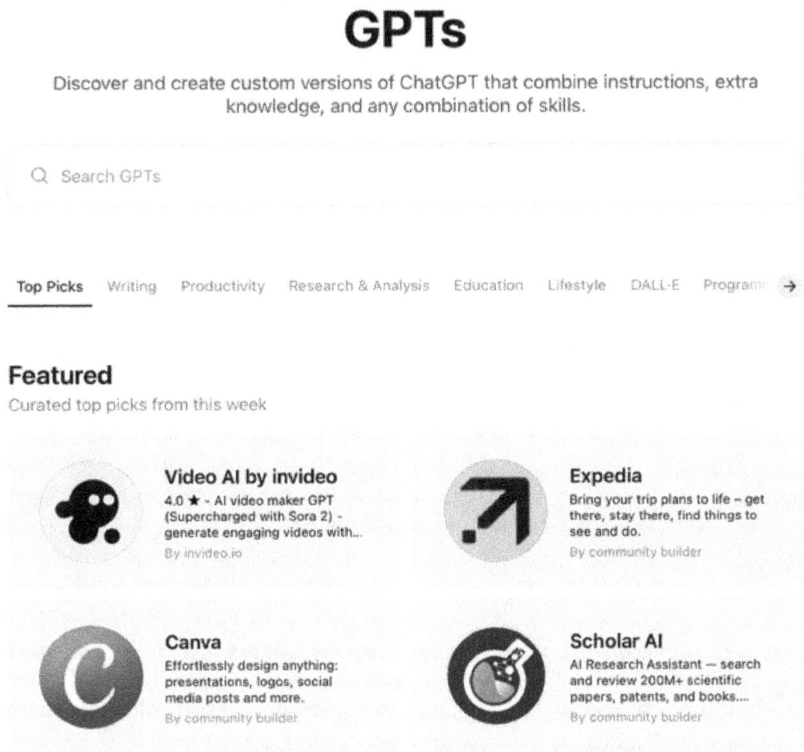

Figure 12.11 – Looking for ideas? Many custom GPTs are publicly accessible

If you're a creative in a company with a written cache of codified, domain-specific knowledge, you might be able to use this to build an agent to help your junior staff. Perhaps a client might want your help creating an agent to advise their own staff?

Alternatively, you might want a custom GPT to answer questions in a domain of expertise adjacent to your own. However, since that's knowledge you don't already have, it's likely to be a product you purchase from someone else, not a custom GPT you make yourself.

Creating a custom GPT isn't a trivial process, and you may need to go through the process a few times to get it right. The order in which you add knowledge to a custom GPT matters, and if you do it in the wrong way, you can end up with a bot that simply doesn't work properly.

If you fail at your first attempt, try building again with slightly different content, or even the same content in a different order. Developers can use backend API tools, but the more user-friendly frontend approach can work just as well or even better.

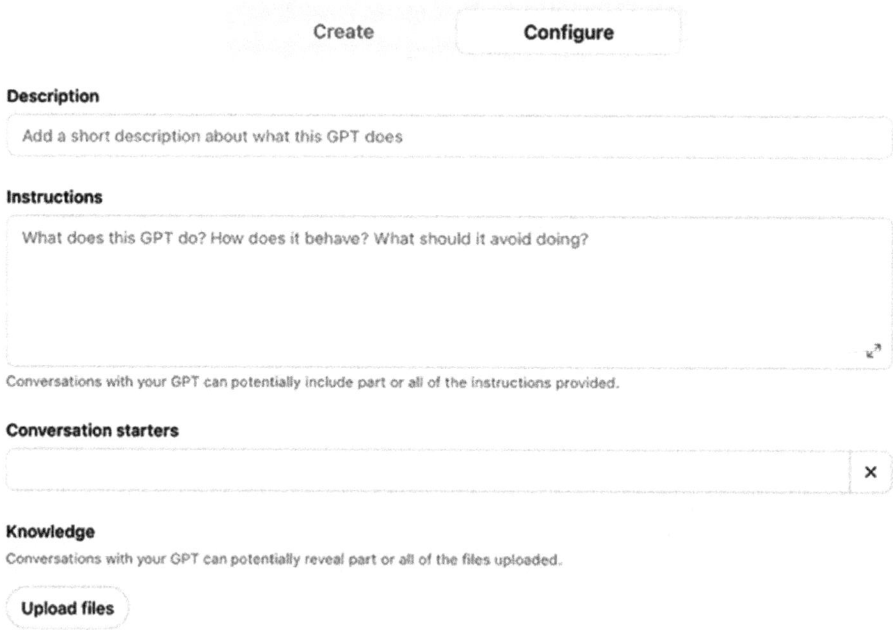

Figure 12.12 – Some of the frontend configuration fields in the custom GPT creation UI

Your goal here should be to narrow the scope of what an LLM tries to do. The *vanilla* ChatGPT tries to be all things to all people, but a custom GPT needs focus.

Give it instructions on how to behave: effectively, a custom system prompt. This should constrain it to a specific set of tasks, guiding how it should interact and how it should speak to its target audience. Of course, you'll also need to upload documents containing any domain-specific knowledge your bot needs. This could be a set of guidelines, processes, or a user guide for custom software programs.

Definitely keep an eye on privacy. Though custom GPTs are tied to paid accounts (and not used to train ChatGPT itself), it's still possible to make a custom GPT *public*. If you're including top-secret company data, you'll obviously need to make sure that it remains *private*.

On the other hand, you might want to create a custom GPT that is available to the public. This could share some of your knowledge for the price of an email address, to help you build your own audience. It's up to you.

Still, if you've created a custom GPT, as users may not know the best questions to ask, they may struggle to get the best from it. By providing guidance as to the best ways to use your custom GPT and even providing examples of prompts that work well with it, you'll give your users a better chance of success.

For some ideas on how this can work best, I spoke to Anna Harrison of **RAMMP** (`https://www.rammp.com`), a company that develops custom GPTs to help small business clients with marketing.

> RAMMP builds a custom GPT for each of its clients, training it with information about that client's business, their current social media output, and their goals. After the training, each client has a custom agent, a personal marketing advisor, and an assistant with a unique personality. This could mirror the client themselves or someone else. To help users get the most from their agent, RAMMP also includes two other components:
>
> - **Diagnostic**, a tool to audit current marketing efforts and find out where conversion isn't working.
> - **Helpers**, a library of workflow prompts you can ask the custom GPT to solve specific problems. These prompts might include a quarterly SEO audit, creating a marketing strategy, or setting out a social media calendar.

Throughout this book, I've recommended trying to use AI tools in a field close to your existing knowledge, and this approach gels with that. A business owner or freelancer knows their products and their customers but may not know the best way to market themselves.

By giving clients an extra nudge, telling them what's going wrong and how to best prompt their agent, knowledge gaps are neatly filled. If you're considering creating a custom GPT, think about how its users will communicate with it, and guide them if you can.

Custom GPT functionality allows regular humans to explore the potential agentic future on their own, without having to know all the details of APIs or explore code. It's a next step that not all will want to explore, but which could solve problems that the regular ChatGPT (and other LLMs) cannot.

Other AI providers have similar, but not identical, functionality. If custom GPTs don't work for you, perhaps explore Claude Projects (`https://support.claude.com/en/articles/9517075-what-are-projects`), which let you upload additional private documents and collaborate with other users. You might also want to explore one of the more specific agent-focused tools, such as Motion, Notion, or **Zapier** (`https://zapier.com/agents`), though all these services have slightly different capabilities.

The future is going to be fascinating. Let's wrap up this chapter, and then the whole book.

Summary

Speaking to digital assistants on phones was a big innovation, but like any new technology, we got used to it, found its limits, and it didn't end up changing the world. I suspect LLMs will, over the next few years, seamlessly take over from less powerful digital assistants.

With increased capability, more of us will start to offload more of our working tasks to agents of one kind or another—but not everyone, not every job, and not all of the time. If LLM-powered digital assistants do change the world, it'll be in small steps.

We might start by manually automating what we're already doing, but if AI tools can become reliable enough, the tasks we trust them with will grow larger. They might be slower than us today, but once they start talking directly to the data structures behind the apps we use, they'll be faster than we ever were.

Browsers are a useful stepping stone, but many creatives work in regular desktop apps, not just on the web. Soon enough, though, automation engines will get better at controlling our regular computers, and things that are hard for experts will become easier for everyone. Hopefully, we'll have more time to produce better work, not just make more work in the same amount of time.

Will these agents be better than humans? Not on every metric, and they won't be used in every task. Many agents and custom GPTs will find their niches, and some will be a perfect fit. But many creative jobs will remain manual, and many existing creative people will never use AI.

That's just fine. There's room for many different approaches, and AI will bring new ways to express creativity, too.

Final thoughts

If you're a creative professional interested in the potential of AI-powered tools, I hope this book has helped you understand not just what's possible but also what's worth pursuing. Anyone who sees the creation process as a worthwhile task rather than a chore to be outsourced probably has mixed views on AI right now.

In the **Utility AI** space, there are many ways to optimize workflows while leaving you entirely in control of the process. There are few downsides to being able to find a photo or video more quickly, or to asking an AI for feedback on your thoughts. Many of these tools run offline, with no ongoing costs—a win all round.

In the **Generative AI** space, there's huge potential for seeing how new ideas could work, for collaborative brainstorming, and some tools make otherwise cost-prohibitive VFX or retouching tasks attainable within normal budgets. But GenAI is best used as part of a greater whole, and clients who've been sold the lie "just do it with AI" will discover that this works about as well as "just fix it in post."

In the **Automation AI** space, there's the potential to take away the tedium from some tasks, but don't expect perfect results. When we recognize the limitations of today's tools and embrace the best aspects of them, they can really help, even if they can't do the whole job. There's huge potential here, but it's just over the horizon.

However you use AI, never lose sight of what you enjoy about what you do. If you're a designer, an editor, a retoucher, or a photographer, you probably enjoy getting your hands a little dirty with the tools, making many small changes toward a final vision. Those details matter, and they're the ones most at risk for those who adopt AI for every task.

AI systems often encourage us to think of tasks at a high level, like a CEO. If a CEO wants a task completed, they ask their staff to do it, and the CEO doesn't worry about the details. But somewhere down the line, those staff do make a whole lot of tiny, informed decisions on the CEO's behalf, and those decisions matter. If nobody sweats the details, such as when an AI falls back to a default setting, the overall product can suffer.

We saw this happen with template-based design systems before AI, and that's not going to stop. Not all clients care that their designs look unique, but if they want to stand out, they should. Templated systems and AI-driven content tend toward homogeneity, but great design brings something extra.

Often, the job of a creative is to dive deep into the details, interrogating each decision and analyzing its consequences. What if that pause is held a little longer, or that title made a little larger, or that word just a shade more grandiloquent? These changes matter, maybe not in ways that are immediately obvious at the highest level, but they sum to a greater whole.

Another issue is that if you can suddenly make anything (at a lower quality setting), then you're entirely free from constraints... but *constraints inspire creativity*. A blank page is easier to fill if you have a 300-word limit; a one-page flyer is easier to complete with a style guide in hand. An endless supply of low-grade imagery doesn't help focus a vision.

It's also valuable to be a novice sometimes. When you learn a new skill, somewhat adjacent to your existing skills, you'll try to map your existing knowledge onto the new area. Sometimes that fails, but sometimes it inspires new techniques. The same magic can happen when you work with other professionals, and if we rely on AI to fill in human-shaped gaps, we'll see less of it.

In the creative industries especially, insights are often found when you work across different media or collaborate with other specialists, and the best of these are when you compare notes and discover unexpected synchronicities. These are not insights discovered in committees.

If we're not careful, extensive use of AI could bring a generation of people who create without enjoying creating. If you only prompt rather than make, chasing ROI instead of beauty, your work will be lacking. It's not a bad thing to bring the power of creation to those who have great ideas, but AI *alone* isn't the way to make the best work.

In more sinister ways, AI could shrink the pool of expert creatives, as fewer people grow their skills by using them. Creative muscles must be exercised, and prompting for results is like taking a taxi rather than walking.

With or without AI, implementation details matter, and if we all start taking the details for granted, we'll be worse off for it. Avoiding tedium is fine, but don't let your skills atrophy by passing every job to AI tools. AI is fantastic as an assistant and an idea factory, or to help with specific elements of a task, but replacing humans will lead to worse creative output.

Yet, I do think there's plenty of scope to use AI well. If you can perform a task, and there's any chance you might learn new skills by doing it, then do it. But if it's a boring job that you've done before, you're short on time, and Automation AI is a net win, why not? Beyond saving time, if inspiration runs dry, Gen AI can give you more new ideas than you can use, and Utility AI can help you work more efficiently.

What's next? AI isn't going away, but I would expect the current landscape to change hugely over the next few years. Here are a few predictions:

- Superintelligence? Unlikely.
- AI bubble bursting, and some AI companies going under? Likely.
- Pricing chaos? Probably.
- GenAI images and videos getting better? Of course.
- Hallucinations and imperfections? Continuing.
- Social issues from AI overuse? Yep.
- Privacy problems from lax security? Already a problem without AI.
- AI addiction? It's already happened.

There's nothing more certain than change, and it'll be a wild ride from here. We've never been able to *wish* for things before, and a whole new world awaits.

Thank you so much for taking these first few steps with me.

13

Unlock Your Exclusive Benefits

Your copy of this book includes the following exclusive benefits:

- Next-gen Packt Reader
- DRM-free PDF/ePub downloads

Follow the guide below to unlock them. The process takes only a few minutes and needs to be completed once.

Unlock this Book's Free Benefits in 3 Easy Steps

Step 1

Keep your purchase invoice ready for *Step 3*. If you have a physical copy, scan it using your phone and save it as a PDF, JPG, or PNG.

For more help on finding your invoice, visit `https://www.packtpub.com/unlock-benefits/help`.

> **Note:** If you bought this book directly from Packt, no invoice is required. After *Step 2*, you can access your exclusive content right away.

Step 2

Scan the QR code or go to `packtpub.com/unlock`.

On the page that opens (similar to *Figure 13.1* on desktop), search for this book by name and select the correct edition.

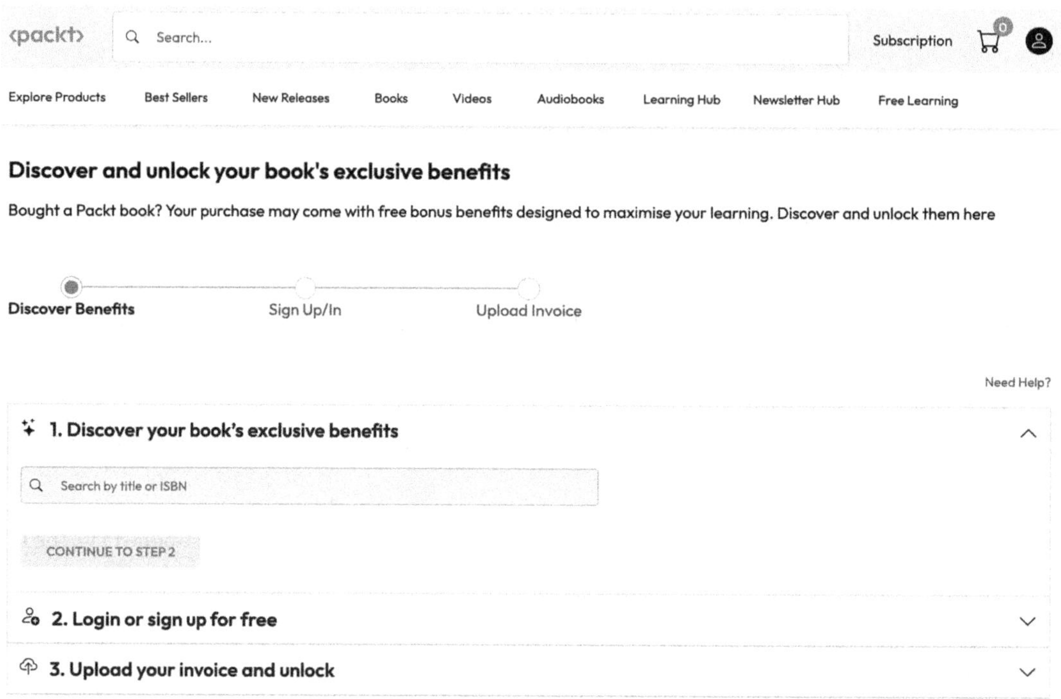

Figure 13.1: Packt unlock landing page on desktop

Step 3

After selecting your book, sign in to your Packt account or create one for free. Then upload your invoice (PDF, PNG, or JPG, up to 10 MB). Follow the on-screen instructions to finish the process.

Need help?

If you get stuck and need help, visit `https://www.packtpub.com/unlock-benefits/help` for a detailed FAQ on how to find your invoices and more. This QR code will take you to the help page.

Note: If you are still facing issues, reach out to `customercare@packt.com`.

Other Books You May Enjoy

If you enjoyed this book, you may be interested in these other books by Packt:

Mastering Adobe Photoshop 2026 - Second Edition

Gary Bradley

ISBN: 978-1-80602-171-0

- Create advanced mock-ups using smart objects and branding workflows
- Master retouching, recoloring, and content-aware edits non-destructively
- Use AI-enhanced tools for image generation, background edits, and retouching
- Design and automate high-volume social media content for multiple platforms
- Animate titles, GIFs, and videos using Photoshop's timeline and frame tools
- Develop immersive visuals using brushes, textures, gradients, and effects
- Blend, collage, and compose surrealist artworks with professional finesse

Final Cut Pro Efficient Editing - Second Edition

Iain Anderson

ISBN: 978-1-83763-167-4

- Organize and manage media from multiple sources with ease
- Edit video using an intuitive interface and powerful tools
- Streamline workflows with customizable workspaces and shortcuts
- Sync multicam interviews and master advanced trimming
- Enhance edits with AI color tools and audio workflows
- Collaborate smoothly with built-in editing tools
- Create visual effects and motion graphics titles
- Export projects in multiple formats for any platform

Packt is searching for authors like you

If you're interested in becoming an author for Packt, please visit `authors.packt.com` and apply today. We have worked with thousands of developers and tech professionals, just like you, to help them share their insight with the global tech community. You can make a general application, apply for a specific hot topic that we are recruiting an author for, or submit your own idea.

Share your thoughts

Now you've finished *AI for Creative Production*, we'd love to hear your thoughts! Scan the QR code below to go straight to the Amazon review page for this book and share your feedback or leave a review on the site that you purchased it from.

`https://packt.link/r/1806025817`

Your review is important to us and the tech community and will help us make sure we're delivering excellent quality content.

Index

Symbols

A

B

C

F

G

H

I

J

K

L

www.ingramcontent.com/pod-product-compliance
Lightning Source LLC
LaVergne TN
LVHW060022210926
848481LV00013B/3772
9781806025817